THE ROUTLEDGE COMPANION TO CRITICAL THEORY

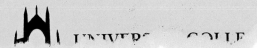

'An excellent introduction to the field.'

Robert Eaglestone, *Royal Holloway, University of London*

'Comprehensive and wide-ranging, this volume combines accessibility with scholarly soundness to offer an up-dated and engaging coverage of all the essential schools in modern critical theory.'

Professor Galin Tihanov, *Lancaster University*

The Routledge Companion to Critical Theory is an indispensable aid for anyone approaching this exciting field of study for the first time.

By exploring ideas from a diverse range of disciplines, 'theory' encourages us to develop a deeper understanding of how we approach the written word. This book defines what is generically referred to as 'critical theory', and guides readers through some of the most complex and fundamental concepts in the field, ranging from historicism to postmodernism, and from psychoanalytic criticism to race and postcoloniality.

Fully cross-referenced throughout, the book encompasses manageable introductions to important ideas followed by a dictionary of the names and terms that students are likely to encounter. Further reading is offered to guide students to crucial primary essays and introductory chapters on each concept.

Simon Malpas is Lecturer in English Literature at Edinburgh University. He is author of *The Postmodern* (2005) and *Jean-François Lyotard* (2003), editor of *Postmodern Debates* (2001) and, with John Joughin, *The New Aestheticism* (2003).

Paul Wake is a lecturer in English Literature at Manchester Metropolitan University. He has published articles on narrative theory and postmodernism. His monograph, *Conrad's Marlow: Narrative and Death in Youth, Heart of Darkness, Lord Jim and Chance* will be published in 2007.

Also available from Routledge

Poetry: The basics
Jeffrey Wainwright
0–415–28764–2

Shakespeare: The basics
Sean McEvoy
0–415–36246–6

Literary Theory: The basics
Hans Bertens
0–415–35112–X

Contemporary British Novelists
Nick Rennison
0–415–21709–1

The Routledge Companion to Postmodernism (second edition)
Edited by Stuart Sim
0–415–33359–8

The Routledge Companion to Russian Literature
Edited by Neil Cornwell
0–415–23366–6

Who's Who in Contemporary Women's Writing
Edited by Jane Eldridge Miller
0–415–15981–4

Who's Who in Dickens
Donald Hawes
0–415–26029–9

Who's Who in Shakespeare
Peter Quennell and Hamish Johnson
0–415–26035–3

Who's Who in Twentieth-Century World Poetry
Edited by Mark Willhardt and Alan Michael Parker
0–415–16356–0

THE ROUTLEDGE COMPANION TO CRITICAL THEORY

Edited by
Simon Malpas and Paul Wake

Routledge
Taylor & Francis Group

LONDON AND NEW YORK

First published 2006
by Routledge
2 Park Square, Milton Park, Abingdon, Oxon OX14 4RN

Simultaneously published in the USA and Canada
by Routledge
270 Madison Ave, New York, NY 10016

Routledge is an imprint of the Taylor & Francis Group, an informa business

© 2006 Simon Malpas and Paul Wake for selection and editorial matter;
individual contributors their contributions

Typeset in Times New Roman by
Book Now Ltd
Printed and bound in Great Britain by
MPG Books Ltd, Bodmin

British Library Cataloguing in Publication Data
A catalogue record for this book is available from the British Library

Library of Congress Cataloging in Publication Data
The Routledge companion to critical theory/[edited by] Paul Wake and Simon Malpas
p. cm.
Includes bibliographical references and index.
1. Criticism. 2. Criticism (Philosophy) I. Wake, Paul. II. Malpas, Simon.
PN81.R68 2006
801'.95–dc22   2005033937

ISBN10: 0–415–33295–8 (hbk)
ISBN10: 0–415–33296–6 (pbk)
ISBN10: 0–203–41268–0 (ebk)

ISBN13: 978–0–415–32295–8 (hbk)
ISBN13: 978–0–415–32296–5 (pbk)
ISBN13: 978–0–203–41268–8 (ebk)

CONTENTS

ACKNOWLEDGEMENTS

We would like to thank our colleagues in the Departments of English at Manchester Metropolitan University and English Literature at Edinburgh University for their support during the writing of this book. We would also like to acknowledge the invaluable support of MMU's Research Institute who created a research post in the early stages of the project, without which it may never have got going. The editors and readers at Routledge have offered invaluable advice and assistance throughout the project, and, but for their enthusiasm, professionalism and encouragement, it is unlikely that this book would ever have been completed. Thanks too must also go to all of the contributors who have made working on this book a real pleasure and to whom its overall quality must be attributed and to Mary Garland for her help with the proofreading.

We should also like to offer our thanks and gratitude for their patience to our long-suffering partners, Erikka Askeland and Christine Kessler.

Simon Malpas and Paul Wake

EDITORS' INTRODUCTION

STUDYING CRITICAL THEORY

To some students approaching it for the first time, critical theory can appear obscure, arcane, obfuscatory and even a distraction from what should be the real focus of one's interest – the literary texts, works of art, films or television programmes, historical periods or forms of behaviour and experience that one expected to discuss on courses in literary criticism, history of art, media studies, history or psychology. Theory is, however, none of these things.

Although theoretical writing can often appear to be very complex and to employ vocabularies and ways of thinking that are different from those with which most of us might be familiar, it engages with questions, ideas and issues that are crucial to our experiences of identity, culture and society, and focuses precisely on the ways in which literature, art, the media, history and individuals communicate and interact in the world in which we live. Critical theory allows us to explore the cultural production and communication of meanings in precise and nuanced ways, and from a range of different perspectives. It questions the ways in which we might be used to making sense of artistic, historical or cultural artefacts and prompts us to reconsider our beliefs and expectations about the ways individuals interact with material things and with each other. Put very simply, critical theory aims to promote self-reflexive explorations of the experiences we have and the ways in which we make sense of ourselves, our cultures and the world.

Critical theory has become a necessary element of advanced study in the arts, the humanities and the social sciences because of the now widely shared recognition that meaning is neither natural nor immediate. Language is not a transparent medium through which ideas can pass between minds without alteration. Rather, as almost all of the essays and entries in this book acknowledge, it is a set of conventions that influence or even determine the sorts of ideas and experiences people are able to have. Language is cultural (some thinkers even claim it is the essence of culture), and therefore open to criticism and change. If linguistic meaning were naturally given, for example, why would there be more than one language? A word does not mean what it does 'naturally'; rather meanings arise on the basis of complex linguistic and cultural structures that differentiate between truth and falsity, reality and fantasy, and good and evil, and are inextricably tied up with value judgements and political questions, as well as with identity, experience, knowledge and desire. By exploring the processes by which texts, objects and even people come to be associated with particular sets of meanings, critical theory sets out to question the legitimacy of common sense or traditional claims made about experience, knowledge and truth. On this basis, different critical theories set out to explore our fundamental beliefs about existence and question the guiding structures and suppositions that organize our interactions.

A similar thing goes for ideas about the meaning of a work of art, a literary text or a film. Since *Hamlet* was first performed, there have been hundreds, even thousands, of different analyses and discussions of the play, each approaching it from a different perspective to generate a variety of arguments about its impact upon a reader or audience. If there were a single 'correct' or 'true' reading shouldn't somebody have found it by now? The fact that there is not a single correct reading of the play, that it cannot be solved like a mathematical formula, is crucial to its continuing interest. *Hamlet*, like any other artistic work or cultural artefact, can be read in many ways, from a range of perspectives, in order to present different ideas and images about the ways in which we live. The practice of literary study, like the practices of analysis in similar disciplines, is necessarily open to rereading, reworking and continuing argument.

And this is why theory is so important for students of the arts, humanities and social sciences. All of the multiple readings to which a work, text, artefact or event are open will be based on a theory: a set of beliefs about what it means, what meaning itself is, how communication takes place and how the world works. Each of us in our day-to-day interactions with others and the world carries such, often implicit, beliefs around in our heads. The point of studying theory is to make them explicit, and to question them. This, of course, has had, and continues to have, a significant effect on the subject areas themselves. In each disciplinary area, theory draws on ideas from other disciplines (so, for example, literary theory imports ideas from philosophy, history, linguistics, psychology and sociology, to name but a few) in order to think about the ways in which text and reading interact with the world. The result of such borrowings and interactions has often been a fundamental questioning of what is at stake in a particular area of study, a reorganization of syllabi and canons of texts to be studied, as well as significant redrawings of disciplinary boundaries as imported ideas are reworked to develop new possibilities and modes of enquiry.

In recent years critical theory has become firmly established in many arts, humanities and social science disciplines as an object of study in its own right. Often referred to simply as 'theory', it has transformed study in each of these areas in myriad ways. And, if it has become less controversial as the practice of asking theoretical questions about disciplinary methodologies has become more widespread, it has lost none of its excitement and potential to challenge. However, theory itself is neither a homogeneous discipline nor a unified movement. Although it has broken down many of the traditional boundaries between different disciplines, this does not mean that a new meta-discipline of critical theory has emerged. Nor has theory simply provided a set of clearly defined rules and concepts which can simply be learned like arithmetical formulae and then applied at will to grasp the truth about a text, object or culture. The diverse schools, thinkers, ideas and concepts that fall under the umbrella of critical theory have to be read and discussed in their own right, and judged in terms of their similarities and differences, at least as often as they are applied as critiques of anything outside the field. This is unsurprising if one considers even for a moment the complexity of the ideas developed by critical theorists and the strong tendency of theory to reflect on its own authenticity and utility.

In whatever discipline it appears, however, critical theory provides a multi-faceted and wide-ranging critique of many of the most important issues and problems that one might encounter in the contemporary world. Anyone with an interest in the culture that they inhabit will gain important insights from engaging with the arguments and positions taken up by theorists and responding to what they have to say. *The Routledge Companion to Critical Theory* is designed to help make these arguments and issues more accessible, and to trace the relations that obtain between the different movements and thinkers. It will help readers to orientate themselves in what is often a difficult and always a fascinating field of study by providing outlines of many of the main trends, analyses of the key thinkers, and clear definitions of the cardinal terms and concepts.

THE STRUCTURE AND SCOPE OF THIS VOLUME

The Routledge Companion to Critical Theory offers help both to specialist students and also to those who come across theories and theorists in books, articles and lectures and want to understand the ideas underpinning the arguments that they encounter. It thus offers both detailed analyses of particular ideas and broad surveys that contextualize what sometimes appear to be obscure assertions about contemporary culture, thought and politics.

Because critical theory is such a large and complex area of study, *The Routledge Companion to Critical Theory* is designed to fulfil this purpose in two ways. First, it will help you to find your bearings in broad general area, such as narratology or postcolonialism. Second, it will provide you with specific information about key figures like Jacques Derrida or Edward Said, as well as critical terms such as differend or rhizome. In this way, the *Companion* goes beyond the scope of an ordinary dictionary by placing the individual definitions in an explanatory context that elaborates on their meaning and importance.

The first half of this book is given over to a series of essays that, read together, present a picture of the range and scope of contemporary critical theory, as well as charting its development in the humanities. These essays outline key movements and approaches to culture, and explore some of the main areas of theoretical analysis by introducing their key tenets and their most influential proponents, and assessing the different ways in which they have had an impact on critical practice. Each essay is accompanied by suggestions for further reading that include both significant primary texts and accessible introductory volumes.

Taken together, these essays provide the reader with a firm grounding in critical theory and a good sense of where to go next to explore particular ideas, issues and thinkers in more detail.

The second half of the volume is a critical dictionary, which comprises almost 200 short essays on terms and thinkers that students are likely to encounter during their studies. The aim throughout is to provide straightforward definitions that give the sort of information that will be useful for both the general reader who wants to get to grips with a new name or term and the specialist reader of critical theory who wishes to find out where to go next. Most of the more extended entries also contain brief details of further reading for those who wish to explore ideas or theorists in more detail.

HOW TO USE THIS VOLUME

The essays in the first half are designed to work alongside the definitions in the second. To facilitate cross-referencing and help build up a comprehensive picture of critical theory, names and terms that have separate entries in the second section are picked out in bold type when they first appear. Also, at the end of many of the entries are indications of the chapters in the first half of the book that discuss the areas of theory that relate most closely to the name or term. For example, in the essay on psychoanalysis in Part I the first use of the name Jacques **Lacan** will be picked out in bold (as will the cognates of the word – such as **Lacanian**), which indicates that there is a description of his work in Part II. This, in turn, will pick out terms such as **imaginary**, **symbolic** and **real**, which are key ideas developed by Lacan, and each of which has an entry of its own. Equally, each of these terms will refer the reader back to the chapters in which it is used or alluded to. By following these cross-references, the reader will be able to build up a comprehensive idea about the central tenets of Lacanian psychoanalysis and its relationships with other theoretical movements and ideas. To this end, the index will point out yet more references to consult for information about any of the names and terms included in the book. The two parts of this book are thus designed to interact with each other in order to allow access to more or less detailed information depending on what is required, and make links between the many different areas of critical theory to build up a clear and detailed picture of this important field of study.

CONTRIBUTORS

The contributors to this volume are drawn from a wide range of academic disciplines and are all experts in their particular fields. They are, in alphabetical order:

Apollo Amoko
Neil Badmington [NB]
Catherine Belsey

Andrew Benjamin
Mark Bolsover [MB]
Ginette Carpenter [GC]
Claire Chambers [CC]
Christelle Charbonnier [CHC]
Christopher Robert Clark [CRC]
Laurence Coupe [LC]
Glyn Daly
David Deamer [DD]
Rachel Farebrother [RF]
Daniel Haines [DH]
Donald E. Hall
Susan Hekman
Keith Hughes [KH]
Linda Hutcheon
Huw Jones [HJ]
Dominick LaCapra [DL]
Rob Lapsley
Kate McGowan [KMc]
Simon Malpas [SM]
Christopher Marlow [CMa]
Chris Michael [CM]
Angelica Michelis [AM]
Kaye Mitchell [KM]
Jessica Mordsley [JM]
Judith Pryor [JP]
Sean Purchase [SP]
Theresa Saxon [TES]
James Scott [JS]
Akiko Shimizu [AS]
Robin Sims [RLS]
Tamsin Spargo [TS]
Ralph Strehle [RS]
Ailbhe Thunder [AT]
Paul Wake [PW]
Paul Walton [PSW]
Ross Wignall [RW]
Andrew Williams [AW]

Authors of entries in the 'Names and terms' section are identified by their initials.

Part I
CRITICAL THEORY:
INTRODUCTORY ESSAYS

1

STRUCTURALISM AND SEMIOTICS

KATE MCGOWAN

MEANINGS 101: WHAT IS A SPINSTER?

Perhaps this is not a very challenging question since a spinster is, quite obviously, simply an unmarried woman. Yet we already seem to know that a spinster is so much more besides. I'm sure if I asked you to describe a spinster, you would do so easily. A whole stock of images, I'm prepared to bet, would spring readily to mind. Think about it, briefly. Is Cameron Diaz a spinster? Why not, she's an unmarried woman? Why, when you hear or see the word 'spinster', do you so readily think of someone who is more like the Queen of England (even though she is, in fact, a married woman) than, say, Naomi Campbell? Why do we seem to share a conceptual notion of a spinster as someone who is boring, conservative, shy and retiring, rather than someone who is enchanting, adventurous and daring? And how do we come to know these meanings even when we don't, if you're like me, regularly use the word 'spinster' in our vocabulary?

One way of answering these questions may lie in the fields of knowledge we call structuralism and **semiotics**. If you have ever wondered about cultural meanings generally – why some lies are white and bad actions always draw black marks – then you have already begun to consider how the culture you inhabit generates the meanings it does, as well as what might be at stake in those meanings for culture generally. If this is the case, then structuralism and semiotics will interest you because they can help you to pursue those questions with a great deal more rigour than basic common sense. In the course of this chapter, I shall introduce some fundamental principles of these interrelated terms, and try to show exactly what they can offer us as cultural critics of varying kinds. In addition to the two terms themselves, we shall look at the ways in which each has been taken up in the fields of literary and visual studies, as well as within cultural studies as a whole. Let's start with structuralism.

STRUCTURALISM

As an academic discipline, structuralism is primarily concerned with the study of structures – that is, how things get organized into meaningful entities – as well as the structural relationships between things. Its premise is that whatever things mean, they will always come to mean by virtue of a set of underlying principles which can be determined by close analysis.

Structuralism's understanding of the world, then, is that everything that constitutes it – us and the meanings, texts and rituals within which we participate – is not the work of God, or of the mysteries of nature, but rather an effect of the principles that structure us, the meanings we inhabit and so on. The idea is that the world without structures is meaningless – a random and chaotic continuum of possibilities. What structures do is to order that continuum, to organize it according to a certain set of principles, which enable us to make sense of it. In this way, structures make the world tangible to us, conceptually real, and hence meaningful. Once discovered, so the theory goes, structures show us how meanings come about, why things seem to be just the way they are and, by implication, what might lead us to contest them.

One of the central principles of the structuralist project, at least through the twentieth century, arises from the work of a Swiss linguist by the name of Ferdinand de **Saussure**. In a series of lectures given at the University of Geneva between 1907 and 1911 Saussure argued that language provides a foundational structure for the world around us by organizing it into tangible entities that we can, as an effect of that language, then describe and discuss. Without language, Saussure argued:

> thought is a vague, uncharted nebula. There are no pre-existing ideas, and nothing is distinct before the appearance of language.
>
> Against this floating realm of thought, would sounds by themselves yield predelimited entities? No more so than ideas ... The characteristic role of language with respect to thought is not to create a material phonic means for expressing ideas but to serve as a link between thought and sound, under conditions that of necessity bring about the reciprocal delimitations of units ... language works out its units while taking shape between two shapeless masses.
>
> (Saussure 1974: 112)

So nothing is distinct before the appearance of language. While as humans we have the capacity for generating thought and sound, it is not until we enter language that we are able to organize that capacity and to make the necessary cultural associations between thought and sound. Although this account of language may seem mildly tame to us now, it nonetheless provided a highly significant assertion about language, the implications of which were to revolutionize the way we think about how we think.

Prior to Saussure, language had been thought of simply as a system for naming an objective reality which was presumed to exist before, and outside of, language itself. Within this way of thinking, the real world is clearly already there, while language simply comes along to label it in all its specificities. If we return for a moment to the example with which this chapter began, we might be able to observe the workings of this assumption about language more closely. In the pre-Saussurean understanding of language, then, unmarried women would be understood simply as a natural and inevitable phenomenon of human life, and therefore readily intelligible as such. The function of language in this understanding would simply be to provide the vocabulary – the word 'spinster' – in order to label that existence. Language, in other words, would play no role in the formation of the entity, or the idea, of 'spinster' as we know it. But, stated like this, the process already seems questionable.

In order for the idea 'spinster' to become meaningful in language, the concept of 'women', as the other of 'men' in the duality 'women and men', would have to come first. The idea 'spinster' could not, in other words, exist without a corresponding idea of gender as male and female. But any meaning for 'spinster' is of course also dependent on the prior establishment of the concept of marriage, as well as a differential understanding of the status of 'women' and 'men' in relation to marriage. Indeed, in this example, meaning begins to seem to have a great deal more to do with value, and specifically cultural value, than the model of language as a naming system might suggest. The meaning of spinster is, after all, surely not inevitable, natural or true, but rather the product of a system of cultural values which are open to debate. If this is the case, then far from simply naming an objective reality, language would seem to play an important role in realizing reality, as well as its meaning for us within the linguistic communities we inhabit. If we did not have the linguistic term 'spinster', would we think of female existence in the ways that we do? It is certainly relatively easy to imagine a social community in which the concept of a spinster might have no meaning whatsoever – not necessarily because unmarried women do not exist, but rather because women are not simply valued, or thought of as meaningful, in relation to whether or not they are married to men.

While this example is not too difficult to follow – it does not really challenge our assumptions about the world at this time in history – it does nonetheless illustrate a principle which can be disturbing to the way we see things generally. What if, for example, we lived in a linguistic community which did not differentiate between 'women' and 'men' in the ways that we do so readily, and apparently so naturally? What if the language we spoke did not have gender as such? Would we still be able to think it? Say there were three terms for gender, or six, or twelve. Imagine what that would do to the ways in which we think about human existence and take for granted the apparent naturalness by which we experience it? Of course, there are cultures other than English-speaking ones within which gender is more than the two terms 'woman' and 'man'. Hindi, for example, has the term 'hijra', meaning something it is difficult, in English, to comprehend fully since it is not translatable as either man or woman, nor as something neutral or in between. Gender as three categories literally shifts what is, or at least can be, thought of as gender as we in English believe we know it. If you speak more than one language, you will already be familiar with the impossibilities of translating conceptually from one language to another, and so have plenty of examples of this yourself.

While the problems of translation can be interesting and amusing, however, they also have wide-ranging implications. In the examples I have given it should be apparent that different cultures, that is different linguistic groups, think about the world in different ways. One way of responding to this observation, and the history of imperialism attests to this, would be to conclude that some cultures think about the world in better ways than others, or with a greater degree of sophistication and authenticity. Another way might be to think more carefully about, and with more attention to, just exactly how these meanings come about. In order to do this, we would have to start again with our thinking, this time with a different model of what language is and what it does. And, that is where Saussure is useful to us.

As I have already suggested, for Saussure language is not simply a system for naming a reality which pre-exists it. Turning that notion on its head, Saussure argued instead that language is in fact a primary structure – one that orders, and therefore is responsible for, everything that follows. If this is so, then it seems fairly straightforward that different languages will divide, shape and organize the **phenomenal** world in different ways. While this understanding of language allows us to see cultures other than 'our' own as relatively different, by implication it must also show us that the culture we claim as 'ours' is in turn neither natural nor inevitable. That is, it demands that we recognize as *structurally produced* the culture which seems to us most obvious, most natural and most true.

What Saussure's work gave to structuralism, then, was an account of language as a primary structure, a system of **signs** whose meanings are not obvious, but rather produced as an effect of the logic internal to the structural system that language is. In addition, perhaps Saussure's most radical claim was that within that structure meaning is generated through the logic of **difference**. He writes, for example, that:

> Everything that has been said up to this point boils down to this: in language there are only differences. Even more important: a difference generally implies positive terms between which the difference is set up; but in language there are only differences *without positive terms*.
>
> (Saussure 1974: 120)

In this model, it is language which enables the world to be constituted to us as intelligible. The exact constitution of that intelligibility will depend on the language we speak and, as a result, will be different depending on the language we speak. It might be important at this stage to point out that this does not presume a disappearance of reality as such. The real world is still understood to exist in these terms. However, it does insist that we can only come to know the real within the terms which language provides for us, in which case, it might be said that rather than using language to describe the real as we find it, language structures that real so that we are able to find it in the first place.

The implications of this are huge, and I shall come back to them in detail when we get to semiotics. For the purposes of our discussion of structuralism, however, it is enough at this point to say that the significance of Saussure's theory is threefold: (i) it gives us the notion that language is not natural but systematic; (ii) that language is the primary system of cultural existence and that it works to structure what we think we know; and (iii) it shifts the emphasis of cultural study firmly in the direction of attention to texts and the evidence they can be said to provide of the linguistic construction of meaning.

One result of this shift has been the development of the importance of structuralist textual analysis within the fields of literary, anthropological, visual and popular cultural study. This is important, since it moves critical attention away from concern with the **author**, together with themes, characters and plots in texts, and begins to focus instead on the structural principles by which texts themselves are able to operate meaningfully.

In 1928, a Russian critic by the name of Vladimir **Propp** undertook what is generally considered the first structuralist analysis of literary texts. Drawing on the work of Saussure on language, Propp analysed 100 Russian folktales and showed that a single set of structural principles was at work in them all. Just as sentences in everyday language are determined by the internal rules of language as a system – grammar, syntax and so on – so Propp proposed that stories can be seen as the result of an analogous grammar of storytelling. In order to tell a story, narrative structures must be in place to shape language into story form. If this is the case, then the meanings which arise from the narrativization of language can be seen to depend to a very large extent on the structures of narrative form, in which case, form itself is far from incidental to the creation of meaning. One result of Propp's work, then, was to establish the intrinsic structural relation of form in literary work to its content.

Concerned as it was with the identification of deep structures of narrative, Propp's work does not really pay very much attention to meaning in the cultural sense that we are more familiar with now. It remained, in these terms, rather formalistic. However, it did provide us with an important basis from which to begin to discuss the ways in which *what* texts mean can be derived from an initial analysis of *how* they mean.

Interestingly, this concern with the ways in which structures can be said to give rise to meaning was by no means limited in its early manifestations to the analysis of written texts, as the work of the structural anthropologist Claude **Lévi-Strauss** can be used to demonstrate. Borrowing specifically from Saussure's work on language, Lévi-Strauss was able to show that structural analysis is as relevant to the study of what he identified as the 'customs, institutions and accepted patterns of behaviour' of specifically cultural groups as it is to the written texts those groups may produce. Indeed, in his foundational work *Structural Anthropology*, he argued that by isolating and analysing the structures through which social communities constitute themselves, anthropology could:

> be in a position to understand basic similarities between forms of social life, such as language, art, law and religion, that on the surface seem to differ greatly. At the same time, we shall have the hope of overcoming the opposition between the collective nature of culture and its manifestations in the individual, since the so-called 'collective consciousness' would, in the final analysis, be no more than an

expression, on the level of individual thought and behaviour, of certain time and space modalities of the universal laws which make up the unconscious activity of the mind.

(Lévi-Strauss 1963: 65)

The question of the structural meanings of more conventionally understood texts was taken up again in Europe in the 1960s by a number of cultural critics at work in fields such as art, film and literary studies. A broader discussion of these works can be found in Chapter 2 of this book which focuses more specifically on narrative. However, in order to illustrate the significance of structuralist method to analyses of cultural meaning within these academic fields, it is worth briefly summarizing two of them here.

Writing in 1957, in a work entitled *Mythologies*, the French cultural critic Roland **Barthes** stated that 'a little formalism turns one away from History, but ... a lot brings one back' (Barthes 1993: 112). What this implies is that if structuralist analysis of narrative is to be useful to the critic of culture and its meanings, then it must start but not end with a detailed reading of the formal properties that make meanings possible. Barthes gave an example of this in his own rather painstaking analysis of a nineteenth-century short story by the French writer Honoré de Balzac, entitled 'Sarrasine'. Here, Barthes identifies five codes of narrative structure which enable the novel to work as such. However, what those codes are is less important to Barthes' analysis than the fact that they seem to play a double role in producing cultural meaning for the text. While the codes enable the story to be told – without them its telling would not be possible – they also seem to mark its limits. In Barthes' account, the story of 'Sarrasine' revolves around the figure of a castrato whose gendered identity the structures of the story itself cannot contain. The central figure of Sarrasine (the name implies the feminization of a masculine **referent**) remains ambiguous throughout. It cannot be male and it cannot be female, though the structural principles of narrative try to make it each in turn in order to make it intelligible. In this case, a structural analysis of storytelling is seen not simply to confirm the structures of meaning to which narrative gives rise, but rather to challenge them. Ironically, it is a structural analysis of the form of the story that makes possible a certain kind of escape from the confines of the structures upon which that story itself has to be built. By starting with the structural principles of textual form, Barthes is able to show what he calls the 'footprints marking the escape of the text; for if the text is subject to some form, this form is not unitary' (Barthes 1990b: 20).

This gesture of identifying the structures of a text in order to show the impossibility of the terms upon which it attempts to make its meaning is important because it opens up a discussion of the relationship of narrative to cultural value. It also fosters the possibility of resisting the apparently obvious meanings of cultural texts which it might otherwise be tempting to understand as simply confirming the status quo of cultural convention.

Drawing on the work of Barthes, the French literary critic Pierre **Macherey** went on to apply the principles discerned by him to a concerted theory of literary production as well as reading practice. For Macherey, the structural properties of literary works are interesting in as much as they can be seen to fail to contain the multiplicity of cultural meanings upon which they are necessarily built. In the light of this, Macherey advocated a reading practice which would focus not on the coherence of the text, but rather on its contradictions, its strangenesses and inconsistencies: 'it can be shown that it is a juxtaposition and conflict of several meanings which produces the radical otherness which shapes the work: this conflict is not resolved or absorbed, but simply *displayed*' (Macherey 1978: 84).

He argued that if the work of the literary critic was ever to be more than parasitic on the literary text – simply reprising its meaning as though it were determined once and for all by the sense of the text – then it must be read 'symptomatically' for instances of non-sense. In other words, he urged that we attend to the structural laws of the text only in order to show the instances in which they are broken – the symptoms, that is, of the text's own resistance to those laws. Again, the argument advanced by Macherey is most compelling in its full complexity. However, for the purposes of illustrating its importance to structuralism, I shall explore just one aspect of it here with an example of my own.

In Deuteronomy, Chapter 22, verse 5, it is written that: 'The woman shall not wear that which pertaineth unto a man, neither shall a man put on a woman's garment: for all that do so are an abomination unto the Lord thy God.' Now the obvious reading of this fragment of text would be something like: it is wrong for women and men to dress the same. But to read it in this way would simply be to reprise the text, to reinforce its obvious meaning by putting it into other words which are simply substitutable for the original without attending to its cultural implications. Those implications, however, are ambiguous if we follow Macherey's line of analysis. By isolating just a few oddities of the linguistic construction of the verse, it is possible to produce an entirely different reading. Take the term 'shall not'. This implies, in a kind of legalistic way, that something is strictly forbidden. It is a bit odd, it seems to me, that God (via Moses) feels so strongly about clothes as to issue an edict demanding women and men to observe strict codes of dress that 'pertain' only unto them. Is gender so precarious that women wearing clothes which 'pertaineth unto' men (and, of course, vice versa) threatens its undoing? If so, what is gender? Does it really boil down to 'garments', and if it does, is that not social rather than natural? 'Abomination' seems to suggest a huge transgression and one has to wonder what is at stake here. What, symptomatically, is this text so afraid of and why? Also, what on earth were people up to that meant God was forced to issue a statement forbidding them to wear each other's clothes? Perhaps, rather than being simply a testament to the word of God, this verse can be made to show that the word of God is, in this instance, symptomatic of a failure of meanings to stay where they are put.

Of course playing with meanings, showing the terms upon which they are constructed in order to show the ways in which they may also be contested, places a very different emphasis on the function and effect of the sign itself. Indeed, we seem to be moving from general principles towards the specificities of the individual signs which work within those principles to make cultural meanings possible. In order to address this issue, it is useful now to turn our attention more clearly to what the 'semiotics' part of this chapter's title may imply.

SEMIOTICS

Semiotics is concerned with signs. As an academic discipline, semiotics is primarily concerned with the life of signs – from their production as an effect of signifying systems, right through to the particular implications of the significations they can be said to carry within the cultural systems in which they operate. If language works, in Saussurean terms, to structure the **real** as we know it, then the signs of which any language is composed may be said to constitute the minutiae of that real in all its specificities. If this is the case, then signs deserve special attention when it comes to any kind of analysis of cultural texts.

One advantage of thinking of signs as systematic – that is, as an effect of signifying systems – is to open up the possibilities of thinking about systems as more than just language as we understand it commonsensically to simply mean speech. If you have ever looked critically at an advertisement, you will already be aware of systems of signification which are not wholly verbal. Indeed, there are whole regimes of signifying systems that are primarily visual. Art, for example, is one such system of signification, as are film and advertising, all forms of writing, and sign language, which itself clearly signifies without recourse to any form of sound. What connects these different systems of signification, however, is their function as systems of signs and, for Saussure, this makes each of them comparable to language as he has described it. Indeed, for semiotics, the sign system of language is still primary and continues to provide the fundamental basis from which meaning can be said to arise. Where sign systems are acknowledged as visual, gestural or marks on a page, they are understood to work *like* language in that they are analogously effective only when understood as part of an underlying system of logic. In each case, it is still the structural rules and regulations of the system from which they arise that makes visual, gestural and written signs intelligible as such.

Let us take film as one particular example. What is film? Well, technically, it is a series of marks made by the play of light on a photosensitive surface. But it is also a particular combination of those individual marks into sequences which can then be projected at speed to produce an apparently continuous stream of images. In turn, these images themselves can be understood to provide a particular set of suggested meanings. Take, for example, a single image of a deserted and dusty outcrop of rocks. If I cut that image between an image of a mother and child and one of an unshaven man with a rifle, my single image comes to signify something like danger. On its own, that single image has the capacity to signify a whole range of things – it could mean peace or desolation – but that range is limited by its place in a system of signification we can call the shot sequences of film. The meaning of the single shot, then – the deserted and dusty outcrop of rocks – is not intrinsic either to the shot itself or, rather more remarkably, to the rocks themselves, but is rather determined by the association of the shot with what comes before and after it in the sequence. And it is in this sense that the signifying system which is film can be said to operate just like language.

No language I know operates without the presumption of relationships between the elements which compose it. Verbal language may well be composed of individual words, but these words in themselves are not entirely meaningful until they are associated with other words in a highly structured sequence. If I were to write the words 'horse' 'pigs' and 'busted', for example, I would be writing words which have meaning within the English language, but I would not be making sense since English presumes a set of structural laws for the combination of words in order for meaning to be generated. Of course, even the words themselves are ambiguous since their meaning can vary in English usage – 'horse' can mean a four-legged equestrian animal, but is also potentially food (at least in France), and in slang terms, so I'm told, heroin. Each of these potential meanings would seem to have nothing necessarily to do with the marks h-o-r-s-e as I construct them on the page, but rather a whole lot to do with the cultural associations drawn between those marks (in this case the written sign 'horse') and a conceptual notion. Both the marks and the conceptual notion, then, are an effect of the cultural value of a sign as it operates socially. However, as can be seen from the example of 'horse', even that cultural value is not entirely fixed. Indeed, the meaning of the sign 'horse' is implicitly not present in the sign itself. 'Horse', as a sign, depends to a large extent for its meaning not on what it is (since that is overdetermined) but rather on its relative position within a sequence of signs that we can say, in language, roughly equates to a sentence.

I could, after all, write 'I love horse' and so narrow its potential for meaning to food or heroin. I could write 'I love horse, but hate pigs', but that might remain equally, if differently, ambiguous. It could mean that I love eating horse but don't like bacon sandwiches, in which case the meaning of 'horse' is temporarily delayed onto, and determined by, the pigs which follow. But, it does not end there since 'pigs', in the colloquial use of British English, can also mean 'police', in which case the individual sign 'horse' could still mean heroin. The best I can say is that I have ruled out the four-legged equestrian animal. If I wrote 'I love horse, but hate pigs. Last week I got busted', then my sentence structure could narrow the meaning of 'horse' a little further to mean, most obviously, heroin. That meaning, however, is still far from fixed, since it would always be vulnerable to a shift in meaning by whatever I might write next.

I could go on. It may be sufficient, however, to draw the following three conclusions from this example: (i) signs function to constitute meaning only within the terms of the system of which they are a part; (ii) while all sign systems function according to their own structural principles, they all function nonetheless *like* language; (iii) all forms of cultural text can therefore be understood as signifying systems, the meanings of which are not fixed for all time but, rather, are open to change.

Film is, as I have suggested, one such example. When understood in the terms of systems of signification as I have just described them, film becomes meaningful as cultural text precisely because of the terms of the system which constitutes it as such.

Any story film tells, any meanings it provides, will not be natural in its obviousness, but rather the effect of the signification of a whole series of signs and their relative positions within the rules of combination for the system which is film. Films in this sense do not simply reflect a pre-ordained reality, but rather work extremely hard to manufacture one. If this is the case, then films become important sites not only for the constitution of cultural meanings, but also for the contestation of cultural values. Of course, this is not simply the province of film, but might just as easily apply to any system of signs participating in the constitution of cultural meaning and value in any society and at any given moment in time. As such, as well as film this would include the visual regimes of advertising as easily as literary text.

Just as structuralism could be said to have changed the ways in which we engage with texts like literature or the bible, so semiotics (hand in hand with structuralism) can be said to have changed the ways in which we are able to engage with the specificities of meanings comprising texts. Again, it can change what it means to read, as well as the practice of reading itself. This obviously has implications for cultural study in that it implies all forms of cultural text are equally rich in meaning and, potentially, sites at which meaning can be contested. In this sense, a pop video is as replete with significance as, say, a poem by John Donne. And presumably each can be analysed critically just as easily as the other. All that separates them, if anything does, is a notion of value.

This should not necessarily mean, however, that the only implication of structuralism and semiotics as forms of cultural analysis would be to do away with the study of literature in favour of more populist forms of signification. Indeed, there is an important argument to be made for retaining the study of literature alongside more populist forms in order to show that the meanings it produces are as entirely cultural as anything else. There might even be an argument for suggesting that it is even more important to apply the reading practice to which semiotics gives rise than to any other kind of text. That would of course lead us to a whole new reading practice in relation to literature, but that might be no bad thing.

Indeed, to read literature as a system of signs would be to open literary texts themselves to a process of decoding capable of revealing not just its structures and forms but also the ideological implications of the very syntax and grammar from which it is composed. As an act of cultural critique, this seems to me to be well worth exploring.

FURTHER READING

Barthes, Roland (1990b) *S/Z*, trans. Richard Miller, Oxford: Blackwell.

This book is, as its preface states, the trace of work done during a two-year seminar (1968–9) at the École pratique des Hautes Études. While it provides some interesting principles of structuralist analysis, it is nonetheless an extremely close reading of Balzac's novella line by line. It is, perhaps, the implications of Barthes' painstaking reading which remain of interest to students today.

Barthes, Roland (1993) *Mythologies*, trans. Annette Lavers, London: Vintage.

This is a highly readable and engaging text which outlines Barthes' theory of the structure of '**myth**' as well as offering a series of short essays on aspects of French bourgeois culture as examples of how the theory may be used to engage with the everyday. These essays range from readings of advertisements for soap powder, through wrestling matches, to an exhibition of photographs entitled 'The Great Family of Man'.

Lévi-Strauss, Claude (1963) *Structural Anthropology*, trans. Claire Jacobson and Brooker Grundfast Schoepf, New York: Basic Books.

This is now a classic structuralist text and shows the ways in which structural analysis informed a great deal of our understandings of culture.

Macherey, Pierre (1978) *A Theory of Literary Production,* trans. Geoffrey Wall, London: Routledge and Kegan Paul.

For anyone interested in reading against the grain of conventional meanings, Pierre Macherey's account of the process of production of literary texts is an important starting-point.

Propp, Vladimir (1958) *Morphology of the Folktale*, trans. Laurence Scott, Austin and London: University of Texas Press.

This study asserts that the fairytale is an important prototype for all narrative structures. It also examines the ways in which the narrative patterns of fairytales work to establish 'norms' through which their content is, subsequently, stated as obvious. Propp's point was to de-familiarize the 'obviousness' of the content of the tales he studied, and to locate it instead in the realms of cultural value.

Saussure, Ferdinand de (1974) *Course in General Linguistics*, trans. Wade Baskin, London: Fontana.

This is an interesting publication since it is derived from the transcription of notes made by students who attended Saussure's lectures on linguistics at the University of Geneva between 1907 and 1911. It is a key text in structural linguistics and remained central to the tradition of poststructuralist thinking in Europe through the twentieth century. It is, of course, primarily concerned with aspects of linguistics as a quasi-scientific study and can be rather dry if read in its entirety if this is not your main interest. However, key passages from it have been widely anthologized.

2

NARRATIVE AND NARRATOLOGY

PAUL WAKE

Narratology, which has roots in structuralism and which draws much of its terminology from linguistic theory, is the study of the ways in which narratives function. Rather than being the study of any one particular narrative, an individual novel for example, narratology begins from a consideration of the ways in which narrative itself operates. This said, the value of narratology lies in its application, and the narratologist Shlomith Rimmon-Kenan makes a valuable point when she suggests that narratology should have a 'double orientation' that allows it to 'present a description of the system governing all fictional narratives' and, at the same time, 'to indicate a way in which individual narratives can be studied as unique realizations of the general system' (Rimmon-Kenan 1983: 4). This 'double orientation', which marks out much of the best of narrative theory, can be seen in works such as Roland **Barthes**' *S/Z* (1990b), which presents both his narratological theory and a remarkably close reading of Honoré de Balzac's short story 'Sarrasine' (1830); Gérard **Genette**'s *Narrative Discourse* (1972; trans. 1980) which sets out its rigorous methodology alongside a reading of Marcel Proust's novel *A la recherche du temps perdu* [*Remembrance of Things Past*] (1913–27); and Peter Brooks' *Reading for the Plot* (1984), a discussion of intention in narrative that is combined with what have become influential readings of several texts, notably Joseph Conrad's *Heart of Darkness* (1902) and William Faulkner's *Absalom, Absalom!* (1936).

Before moving on to consider the specifics of narratological theory, it is important to understand a little more about its object, narrative. To many the term 'narrative' will immediately suggest the kind of stories found in novels, but whilst the aim of the narratology of early structuralist theorists such as the **Russian formalists** was to identify what might be called 'literariness', narrative is not confined to the novel. On the contrary, narrative can be found in numerous aspects of life: not only in other forms of art (drama, poetry, film) but in the ways in which we construct notions of history, politics, race, religion, identity and time. All of these things, regardless of their respective claims to truth, might be understood as stories that both explain and construct the ways in which the world is experienced. As Barthes famously said, 'narrative is international, trans-historical, transcultural: it is simply there, like life itself' (Barthes 1977a: 78). It is this all-permeating, and in some senses constituting, aspect of narrative that makes its study central to so much of contemporary critical theory.

The idea that narrative can be found in so many contexts might begin to account for the wide array of terminology that is employed in its discussion.

Accordingly, the familiar literary terms 'story' and 'plot' might variously be designated, with subtle variation in meaning, *fabula* and *sjuzet* (Russian formalism) or *histoire* and *récit* (Genette, French structuralism). Whilst this varied terminology makes it clear that there are several versions of narratology, it also suggests a level of abstraction in narrative theory that allows its translation across diverse media. The suggestion of an almost universal application notwithstanding, it is fair to say that contemporary narratology emerged from literary study, and what follows here mirrors this trajectory, focusing on narratology in its literary aspect before suggesting ways in which narratology interacts with other theoretical disciplines such as postmodernism, historiography and postcolonial theory.

STORY AND PLOT

At the heart of narratology lies the assumption of a dualism within every text: that there is, on the one hand, story and, on the other, plot. Before considering the implications of this division it is necessary briefly to define its two elements.

Story is, put simply, 'what happens'. It is the sequence of events that lie somehow 'behind' the text, or rather it is the sequence of events that can be abstracted, or constructed, *from* the text. In this context an event can be defined as 'something that happens' (Rimmon-Kenan 1983: 2): for example, 'the dog was taken out for a walk'. In most cases it would be usual to speak of a succession of events: 'after the walk the dog went to sleep'. Plot is the particular presentation of the story in the narrative, a sequence that need not parallel the temporal sequence of the story events, but that supplies information about the causal relations between them. Accordingly, plot introduces causality to what become a chain of events. In the above example the implications are (i) that it is the same dog and (ii) that it is tired as a result of the walk.

One clear way of distinguishing between story and plot is the distinction that narrative grammatologists, working at the level of the sentence, make between 'deep' and 'surface' structures (see, for example, Algirdas Julien **Greimas**' *On Meaning*, 1987). Deep structures correspond to stories, whilst surface structures – the literal arrangement of the words that make up a sentence – are comparable to plots. The sentence 'Walking dogs should be encouraged' has a single surface structure (plot) and two deep structures (stories). Accordingly, this single sentence can be read as an invocation to encourage dog owners to exercise their pets (story 1) or as a suggestion that perambulating dogs should be cheered on and applauded (story 2). Conversely, the sentences: 'The dog ate my homework' and 'My homework was eaten by the dog' have different surface structures (plots), i.e. they differ in their word order, but have the same deep structure (story). The meaning of both sentences is the same, despite the variation in its presentation.

Whilst the distinction between story and plot is both persuasive and well established, it does demand close attention. This dualistic approach is a useful working hypothesis, but there is disagreement about whether such a division is actually viable. According to the story–plot distinction, the reader is allowed no direct access to story, which can only ever be reconstructed from the plot, the narrative. The suggestion that the reader cannot access story is, perhaps, somewhat counterintuitive and appears to challenge the well-established dualism that exists between story and plot. Barbara Herrnstein Smith pursues this challenge in 'Narrative Versions, Narrative Theories', criticizing the tendency for isolating 'pure' story from the particular form, the individual text, as 'naïve Platonism' (Mitchell 1981: 209), arguing that for any particular narrative there are potentially multiple stories. There is clearly a need to maintain an awareness that both story and plot are derived from the text, something that is accomplished by Genette's *'récit'* (narrative), the 'oral or written discourse that undertakes to tell of an event or a series of events' (Genette 1980: 25), which makes clear the necessary relation between plot and text.

Despite these legitimate calls for caution, the distinction between story and plot provides a useful way of approaching narratives. One of the implications of the split is the suggestion that story, which is only ever available as a paraphrase, is translatable from medium to medium, whilst plot appears to be text-specific. This is to say that an individual story can appear in numerous distinct texts and across a wide range of media: for example, J. R. R. Tolkien's *The Lord of the Rings* has appeared as a trilogy of novels (1954, 1954, 1955), an animated film (Ralph Bakshi dir. 1978), numerous computer games (1985–2004), a radio play (Brian Sibley, 1981) and, most recently, as Peter Jackson's highly successful trilogy of films (2001, 2002, 2003). Despite this variety of media and 'authors' there is a general consensus that the story of *The Lord of the Rings* is recognizable in each instance.

This view of the translatable nature of story was advanced by the work of Russian formalist Vladimir **Propp**. In *Morphology of the Folktale* (1928) Propp studies the formal aspects – what he terms their 'morphology' – of 100 folktales. Plot is considered in terms of its use of 31 functional units: for example, 'The hero leaves home' or 'The villain is defeated'. Propp argues that whilst no single folktale features all 31 functions, all tales can be summarized in terms of the functions that they contain and which, he claims, always appear in the same order. Similarly, character, which is regarded as secondary to plot, is discussed in terms of 'roles', such as 'the villain' or 'the helper'. Propp concludes that all folktales share certain formal features and consequently that they can, in fact, all be reduced to one of only four classes of folktale. Propp's work was largely neglected until the late 1960s when it was taken up by structuralist critics, in particular French structural anthropologist Claude **Lévi-Strauss** whose discussion of myth in *Structural Anthropology* (1963) develops and refines Propp's ideas. Lévi-Strauss identifies what he terms 'mythemes', the smallest units of myth from which all myth is created. Other theorists who have advanced comparable ideas include Claude Bremond, Joseph Campbell, Greimas and Gerald Prince. Aspects of structuralist narratology have been adopted, and adapted, by film theory, where it is usefully employed alongside discussions of **genre**.

The type of structuralist theory exemplified here by Propp would later be criticized by Fredric **Jameson** in *The Political Unconscious: Narrative as a Socially Symbolic Act* (1981), where he suggests that the way in which Propp organizes his material is itself an overriding narrative. According to this view, narrative is about **power**, property and domination rather than universal archetypes. To consider plot in this way is to recognize its dual status as both a noun, 'a/the plot', and a verb, 'to plot'. Reading plot as a verb insists on the presence of a plotting agent, or agents. For example, the plot in 'Gunpowder Plot' refers to the intention of the conspirators, or plotters, to blow up the House of Lords in 1605. In this version of narrative theory, questions of who has the authority to speak and of who controls narrative become central, and so the 'official' narrative of the events of 1605 was controlled by the state and legitimated the persecution of Catholics under James I.

Time

The most obvious way in which story and plot relate is in terms of time. If a story is a sequence of events then its temporal aspect must be presented in the narrative. What might be termed 'text-time' is a spatial pseudo-time that is limited by both reading and writing practices; in other words, usual reading practices dictate that a text is read from beginning to end and that only one passage is read at any one time. This ensures, in the majority of cases, that text-time will appear in a linear form and that, as a result of this, it is unable to correspond exactly to the often multilinear strands of story-time. To clarify: whilst several events might occur simultaneously in story-time they can only be presented sequentially, one after the other, in text-time. The discrepancy that thus arises between story-time and text-time is at the heart of many arguments that would separate story from plot, and accordingly it is given a great deal of attention in narratological works.

Narrative techniques include analepsis (also referred to as flashback or retrospection) in which the time-line of the main narrative is interrupted by an earlier scene; so, for example, whilst recovering from illness Lockwood hears the events of *Wuthering Heights* from his housekeeper Mrs Dean: 'These things happened last winter, sir' (Brontë 1992: 315). Conversely, prolepsis (known variously as flash-forward, foreshadowing and anticipation) is a technique by which a narrative interrupts the main story-time with an event, or events, that properly belong to its future. Whilst prolepsis may occur with less frequency than analepsis it can be used to great effect. For example, the opening lines of Chuck Palahniuk's *Fight Club* (1997) start a narrative that will move circuitously back to its own beginning:

> Tyler gets me a job as a waiter, after that Tyler's pushing a gun in my mouth and saying, the first step to eternal life is you have to die. For a long time though, Tyler and I were best friends. People are always asking, did I know about Tyler Durden.
>
> (Palahniuk 1997: 11)

The possibility of prolepsis provides a useful insight into narrative structure, laying bare the assumption that an end will be reached and that the sequence of events moves towards an end point. This is an idea explored by Frank **Kermode** in *The Sense of an Ending* (1967) in which he argues that narrative is impelled by the expectation of a concordant, i.e. a necessary and complete structure. A further related technique is the use of ellipsis, the omission of events from the narrative. The 1990s action film *Demolition Man* (Marco Brambilla dir. 1993) provides a dramatic example of ellipsis, its narrative jumping 40 years from the crime-ridden Los Angeles of 1996 to the serene San Angeles of 2036 where arch-criminal Simon Phoenix (Wesley Snipes) unexpectedly awakens from a 35-year stint in the Cryopenitentiary. Unable to cope with the violent twentieth-century criminal, the authorities revive old-fashioned cop John Spartan (Sylvester Stallone), himself sentenced to life in the Cryopenitentiary, pitting him against his old adversary. Missing 40 years from the centre of a story is an extreme example of a narrative ellipsis; commonly the technique is used to avoid narrating inconsequential events. The analysis of ellipses can reveal much about social taboos, which can themselves be regarded as part of the narrative about the way society views itself. *Demolition Man* plays on this notion by including the commonly elided fact that characters must sooner or later use the toilet, whilst emphasizing society's preference for omitting such scatological detail by refusing to specify the purpose of the 'shells' that are, presumably, intended to facilitate Stallone's character's ablutions. Identifying ellipses, which are often sites of textual **aporia**, is a reading practice that is central to deconstruction.

This ordering appears not only in what is included in a narrative but also in the number of times that events are presented in the narrative. In Genette's terms, in 'singulative' narrative a single event in the story is narrated once; in 'repeating' narrative a single event is presented more than once; and in 'iterative' narrative an event that is repeated in the story, such as the weekly winding of a clock, might be narrated just once – so we read that Tristram Shandy's father 'one of the most regular men in every thing he did . . . made it a rule for many years of his life, – on the first Sunday night of every month throughout the whole year, – as certain as ever the Sunday night came, – to wind up a large house-clock which we had standing on the back-stairs head, with his own hands' (Sterne 1949: 45–6).

In providing a terminology with which the temporal construction of texts can be discussed, narratology makes clear, by dint of its very methodical nature, the *constructed* nature of all texts. Plotting is an act of selection and organization, and the implication of this is that every text is constructed from a certain position.

NARRATING AND FOCALIZATION

Every text has a narrator, however subtly they might be presented. As Mieke Bal says, 'As soon as there is language, there is a speaker who utters it; as soon as those linguistic utterances constitute a narrative text, there is a narrator, a narrating subject' (Bal 1985: 121–2). The relation between this 'narrating subject' and the story, effectively what he or she says, can be usefully discussed in terms of **mimesis** and diegesis. Plato (*c*.428–347 BC) uses the terms in the third book of *The Republic* in order to distinguish between types of speaking: diegesis refers to the points at which the poet speaks with her or his own voice, whilst mimetic speech occurs when the poet tries to create the illusion that the characters themselves are speaking. According to this understanding drama becomes the clearest instance of mimetic art. Plato's distinction, filtered through Aristotle's (*c*. 384–322 BC) more general use of the terms in his *Poetics*, approximates the way in which they are used in contemporary literary studies and they can be equated to the more familiar terms 'showing' and 'telling' (see Lodge, 1992). The following passage from Jack Kerouac's novel *On the Road* (1957) is mimetic; it 'shows' what happens by presenting its dialogue without any evidence, excepting the quotation marks, of the narrator:

> 'Sallie, I want to go to New York with you.'
> 'But how?'
> 'I don't know, honey. I'll miss you. I love you.'
> 'But I have to leave.'
> 'Yes, yes. We lay down one more time, then you leave.'
>
> (Kerouac 1991: 100)

By way of contrast, the following passage, whilst still presenting speech, contains diegetic, telling, elements:

> 'We'll all watch over each other,' I said. Stan and his mother strolled on ahead, and I walked in back with crazy Dean; he was telling me about the inscriptions carved on toilet walls in the East and in the West.
>
> (Kerouac 1991: 267)

In the first sentence the diegetic nature of the passage is marked by the narrator's 'I said', whilst in the second sentence crazy Dean's words are paraphrased, presented as summary. However useful this distinction might be it is worth recalling that, as Genette points out, 'no story can "show" or "imitate" the story it tells' (Genette 1980: 164), because, whether oral or textual, narrative uses language – a system of **signs** that signifies without imitating. Mimesis can only ever be an illusion, a consensual acceptance of what is, and what is not, representative of the **real**.

If narrating is thus connected to speaking, focalization has to do with seeing. Focalization has similar optical-photographic allusions to the more familiar 'point of view' but, by dint of its technical nature, avoids the possible suggestion that the person 'seeing' (perspective) should be the same as the person 'speaking' (narrating) which might be inferred from the term 'point of view'. However, the apparent neutrality implied by this terminology masks, to a certain extent at least, the notion that focalization *is* supplied from a certain perspective. In other words, focalization, like narration, is never neutral.

Film theory, which must contend directly with the medium's apparent lack of a conventional narrator, provides useful comment on the positioned nature of focalization in its formulations 'monstration' and 'auteur theory'. Monstration refers to the way in which early films were 'shown' to the audience with little or no interpretative narratorial 'telling'. By contrast, auteur theory (from the French for 'author') emphasizes the creative role and influence of the director, suggesting that films combine elements of both showing and telling. Although monstration and auteur theory, in terms of narration, occupy opposite ends of the scale, both reveal the focalizing presence as positioned, however unobtrusive that positioning may be.

Focalization can be either external or internal. An external focalizer operates 'outside' the story. Such a narrator, often described as 'omniscient', has complete comprehension of the story, which will necessarily be written in the third person ('she said'). Jane Austen's *Northanger Abbey* (1818) is a third-person narrative with an omniscient narrator, beginning 'No one who had ever seen Catherine Morland in her infancy, would have supposed her born to be a heroine' (Austen 2003: 15). External focalizers can be 'impersonal', apparently neutral, or 'intrusive' such as the narrator of Henry Fielding's *Joseph Andrews* (1742) who repeatedly interrupts the story: 'The disconsolate *Joseph*, would not have had an Understanding sufficient for the principal Subject of such a Book as this' (Fielding 1999: 39). Internal focalizers appear, usually as characters, within the story itself. These narrators display partial knowledge of the story, which can be written in either the third or the first person ('I said'). For example, Ian McEwan's novel *The Cement Garden* (1997) is a first-person narrative, 'I did not kill my father, but I sometimes felt that I helped him on his way' (McEwan 1997: 9). Internal focalization can be 'fixed' (derived from a single character), variable (from a succession of characters), or 'multiple' (from numerous characters at the same time).

So far the focalizer has been equated with the narrator; however, this is not necessarily the case. The distinction between focalizer and narrator is well illustrated in Charles Dickens' novel *Great Expectations* (1860–1) which is narrated in the first person by Pip (fixed-internal focalization). In this instance it would seem reasonable to expect that Pip will be both focalizer and narrator; however, it becomes clear that the events are focalized by Pip as a child and recounted, or rather narrated, by an older, adult Pip.

NARRATIVE COMMUNICATION

D. H. Lawrence famously stated 'Never trust the artist. Trust the tale' (Lawrence 1990: 8). Whilst these words encapsulate the ideas of text-centred literary studies, and **New Criticism** in particular, they also, unintentionally perhaps, indicate the beginnings of what might be called the 'communication model' of narrative. The sentence contains three elements, placing them in a specific relation to one another: 'trust(er)', 'tale' and 'artist'. Numerous critics have considered the ways in which these three elements interact in what Seymour Chatman calls the 'narrative transaction' (Chatman 1980: 147), a phrase that usefully acknowledges the complicity of both addresser and addressee in the process of communication.

Russian formalist and member of the Prague Linguistic Circle, Roman **Jakobson,** sets out his highly influential model of oral communication in 'Linguistics and Poetics' (lecture 1958, pub: 1960; 1987). Arguing for the linguistic analysis of poetics, Jakobson proposes a model of verbal communication in which an 'ADDRESSER sends a MESSAGE to the ADDRESSEE' (Jakobson 1987: 66). In his subsequent discussion of the 'poetic' function (the emphasis of the message itself which is dominant in artistic/literary artefacts) Jakobson hints towards the more detailed models of communication that would be developed to discuss narrative:

> Ambiguity is an intrinsic, inalienable character of any self-focused [poetic] message ... Not only the message itself but also its addresser and addressee become ambiguous. Beside the author and the reader, there is the 'I' of the lyrical hero or of the fictitious storyteller and the 'you' or 'thou' of the alleged addressee.
>
> (Jakobson 1987: 85)

Jakobson's linguistic model of communication and particularly this recognition of the multiple origins, and recipients, of a poetic text have been, as will become clear below, highly influential on narrative theory.

The application of this kind of communication model to narrative was popularized by Wayne C. Booth in *The Rhetoric of Fiction* (1961), which is notable for the introduction of the 'implied reader', a reformulation of Jakobson's 'alleged addressee'. The culmination of the various attempts to account for narrative communication can be seen in Chatman's diagram:

Narrative text

Real author → | Implied → (Narrator) → (Narratee) → Implied | → Real reader
author   reader

(Chatman 1980: 151)

This diagram illustrates six constituents of narrative communication. Within the boxed section the 'Implied author' and 'Implied reader' are unbracketed to signal that they are immanent in narrative, whilst Narrator and Narratee are bracketed to illustrate that, in Chatman's view, they are non-essential. These four elements are the real concern of literary or text-focused narratology.

The implied author is, distinct from the real author, constructed by the reader from the text. This 'author', unlike the narrator, has no voice; he or she tells us nothing. The implied author is best viewed as a constructed set of norms or standards against which a narrative can be judged, and not in some vaguely personified form. The necessity of the implied author can be seen, for example, in Jonathan Swift's satire 'A Modest Proposal' (1729) in which the narrator proposes the sale of infants' flesh as a solution to Ireland's poverty: 'a young healthy child, well nursed, is at a year old a most delicious, nourishing, and wholesome food' (Swift 1984: 493). As the real author of 'A Modest Proposal' Swift can only be recognized as a satirist, and not as an advocate of cannibalism, if the reader acknowledges a distinction between him as real author and the implied author (and the class to which he or she belongs) whose selfishness is the subject of the satire. The implied reader is a similar construction; this is a reader who is **interpellated**, assumed and constructed by the text. To continue with the example of Swift's satire, it can be inferred that the implied reader of 'A Modest Proposal' is not of the classes that will give up their infants for food, and that he or she might be inclined, through a lack of sympathy, to consider the idea in earnest. Accordingly, the satire succeeds when the real reader reacts against the implied reader, disassociating her or himself from this textually generated counterpart.

Chatman's view that the narrator is non-essential is hard to sustain. Whilst the presence of a narrator may not always be obvious, as is the case in third-person narratives, a narrator is necessary if narrative is to be produced. Bal makes the astute, if curiously phrased, point that '"I" and "He" Are Both "I"', arguing that in a narrative in which 'the speaking agent [the narrator] does not mention itself . . . it may as well have done so' (Bal 1985: 120). In other words, every narrative utterance could be prefaced by 'I narrate'. According to this view the narrator's presence or absence is always a question of degree. By way of contrast, the narratee, who is the recipient of the narrative communication, is non-essential, replaceable by the implied and real readers.

Beyond the confines of the boxed section are the 'Real Author' and the 'Real Reader', both of whom are outside of the narrative instance, essential in real terms and yet considered to be beyond the reach of narrative theory which is concerned with the internal textual evidence. Accordingly author criticism becomes part of biography and psychoanalytic criticism. Narratology, in its early attempts to explain meaning as a result of narrative structures, might be seen as a contributing factor to the eventual proclamation of the 'death' of the author. This position is persuasively argued by Barthes in 'The Death of the Author' (1968; trans. 1977) in which he famously suggests that there is no access to the author of a text, and consequently that there is no access to a final, correct, reading of any text. Barthes writes: 'a text is not a line of words releasing a single "theological" meaning (the "message" of the Author-God) but a multi-dimensional space in which a variety of writings, none of them original, blend and clash' (Barthes 1977a: 146). Barthes' suggestion, which can be regarded as a challenge to a version of narratology which sees narrative structures as generating meaning, has become a widely accepted aspect of literary criticism. What Barthes makes very clear is the fact that, as a site of communication, narrative demands participation from the reader, and the more complex suggestion that narratives function in relation to one another. See also Michel **Foucault**'s 'What is an Author' (1977) and Maurice **Blanchot**'s 'Literature and the Right to Death' (1981) for further consideration of the author.

Critical attention has also been focused on the other extreme of this communication model in what is known as reader theory. Reader theory can be characterized as having two movements or phases. The first is **reception theory**, advanced by a predominantly German group of theorists whose members included Hans Robert **Jauss**, Karl-Heinz Stierle and Wolfgang **Iser**. Iser's *The Act of Reading* (1978) and Jauss's *Towards an Aesthetic of Reception* (1982) might be seen as its core works. Reception theory draws heavily on **phenomenology**, and is concerned with the ways in which texts are apprehended in the reader's consciousness. According to this approach, texts are partially open, containing 'textual indeterminacies' which the reader interprets/completes through the process of 'actualization'. Reader-response theory, and particularly that of Stanley **Fish** (see *Is There a Text in This Class?*, 1980), both develops and responds to reception theory, placing more emphasis on what the text does *to* the reader, thereby opening the text up to apparently limitless interpretations. As with biographical criticism, placing the origins of meaning outside the text can be seen as a challenge to narratology's text-centred approach.

This challenge becomes greater still when narratology encounters modern technologies such as the internet (see, for example, Janet Murray, *Hamlet on the Holodeck: The Future of Narrative in Cyberspace*, 1997) and computer games (see Barry Atkins' *More Than A Game: The Computer Game as Fictional Form*, 2003). When narratives are stored as **hypertext**, in which readers have a degree of control of what is read and in what order and in what detail, or as games in which the reader/player has an active role in shaping a narrative's quality and success, the boundary between author and reader becomes increasingly problematic. A further implication of both hypertext and game fictions is that the predominant Aristotelian concept of plot as linear and necessarily complete is challenged by a refigured notion of plot that brings into question the status of beginnings and endings, as well as the idea that these new 'texts' can in any way be considered fixed or complete. Formulating a response to the questions posed by these technologically advanced, and advancing, texts is just one of the challenges facing narrative theory today.

NARRATIVE LEVELS, METAFICTION AND POSTMODERNISM

Diagrams like Chatman's fail to account for the ways in which texts can relate to themselves (and to other texts), relationships that can be discussed in terms of narrative levels. Accordingly, discussions of narrative time, or the relation between narrator and story, can readily be mapped in terms of level, a tendency that leads, not always entirely productively, to the possibility of representing textual structure in diagrammatic form.

For example, a text may have more than one 'level' of story. A character in one level may appear as the narrator of another. In other words, texts can contain stories within stories. These two narrative levels are typically referred to as 'narrative' and '**metanarrative**': 'the *metanarrative* is a narrative within the narrative' (Genette 1980: 228). Once these narrative levels have been identified it becomes possible to locate the narrators and characters within the text. For example, Joseph Conrad's novella *Heart of Darkness* (1902) contains two readily identifiable levels of narrative. In the first narrative level a group of old friends are gathered together aboard a ship on the Thames listening to Marlow tell a story about a journey he made as a youth. That story, in which the young Marlow sails his steamer up the Congo in search of Mr Kurtz, is the metanarrative. By identifying these two levels it becomes possible to locate Marlow as a character of the first narrative (who does little but narrate), as the narrator of the metanarrative *and* as a character of that metanarrative.

Commonly, the co-existence of different narrative levels manifests itself in the appearance of the narrating voice, so, to continue to use the example of *Heart of Darkness*, the older narrating Marlow is able to remark on his own storytelling technique: 'it seems to me that I am trying to tell you a dream – making a vain attempt because no relation of a dream can convey the dream-sensation' (Conrad 1983: 57).

The kind of self-awareness exhibited by Marlow in relation to the story in which he is simultaneously a character and a narrator is described as metafiction, 'writing which self-consciously and systematically draws attention to its status as an artefact in order to pose questions about the relationship between fiction and reality' (Waugh 1984: 2). Metafictional narratives, which have a tendency to take their own fictionality and the problems of representation as the subject of story, are often associated with the postmodern and are evident in the works of authors such as Angela Carter, Salman Rushdie and Kurt Vonnegut. However, meta-fiction is not the sole purview of twentieth-century writers. Laurence Sterne's *The Life and Opinions of Tristram Shandy* (1760–7) is a prime example of a meta-fictional text – as is Miguel de Cervantes' *Don Quixote* [*Don Quijote de la Mancha*] (1605–15). The connection between metafiction and postmodernism is readily apparent in, for example, Jean François **Lyotard**'s *The Postmodern Condition* (1984), where postmodernism is identified as being characterized by an 'incredulity towards metanarratives' (Lyotard 1984: xxiv). Whilst Lyotard's use of 'metanarrative' differs from, say, Genette's, the central questions of narratology are asked repeatedly, in differing forms, by postmodern theory.

NARRATIVE THEORY AS CRITICAL THEORY

As the relation between metafiction and postmodernism might indicate, narra-tive theory plays an important part in a great many areas of contemporary cultural and critical theory. Narrative is, as was suggested in the introduction to this chapter, a central part of the way in which we live our lives and so it is to be expected that narrative theory finds application in many areas of critical theory.

Psychoanalytic criticism is one area in which aspects of narrative theory are readily apparent. Psychoanalysis, the 'talking cure', concerns itself with the telling and interpretation of stories. The possible application of aspects of narrative theory should be evident: for example, **Freud**'s notion that dreams have both manifest (surface) and latent (underlying) meanings lends itself to the type of theory that concerns itself with the relation between plot and story. French psychoanalyst Jacques **Lacan** (1901–81) pursues the idea of the subject as being inscribed in a pre-existing system of signs, and his suggestion that the **unconscious** is structured in a similar way to language shares many of the concerns of narratology, in particular in its deployment of linguistic theory. The relationship between psychoanalytic theory and narratology is not, as this might imply, one-way. For example, Freud's **death-drive**, or *Thanatos*, which he describes in 'The Ego and the Id' (1923) as a desire to 're-establish a state of things that was disturbed by the emergence of life' (Freud 1991b: 381), has been used to good effect by Peter Brooks to investigate the dynamics of plot in terms of the drive towards ending in *Reading for the Plot* (1984).

The writing of history is another such instance. Distinguishing between the poet and the historian, Aristotle writes: 'Where the historian really differs from the poet is in his describing what has happened, while the other describes the kind of thing that might happen' (Aristotle 1963: 17). It is not, according to Aristotle, a question of the form this description takes, but of its object. However, this conception of the historian's task conceals the level of invention that it entails. A much quoted passage from German philosopher G. W. F. Hegel makes this clear: 'The term *History*, unites the objective with the subjective side, and denotes . . . not less what has *happened*, than the *narration* of what has happened' (Hegel 1991: 60). History is not discovered but constructed; in other words, facts do not speak for themselves – the historian selects and interprets facts. Accordingly, histories are always composed, created and situated narratives, and it follows that they should be approached as such. This understanding of history as narrative informs the work of American historian and theorist Hayden **White** whose *Metahistory: The Historical Imagination in Nineteenth-Century Europe* (1973) has been highly influential. White's work, which is self-consciously formalist in approach, identifies the structural components of historical accounts, distinguishing between what he calls 'different levels of conceptualization in the historical work: (1) chronicle; (2) story; (3) mode of emplotment; (4) mode of argument; and (5) mode of ideological implication' (White 1973: 5). White's historiography is, then, a historical narratology and his wide frame of reference includes writers associated with literary/narratological study such as Erich Auerbach, Roland Barthes, Northrop **Frye** and Roman Jakobson.

Attempts to bring narratology into inherently political and ideological theories, such as feminism, gender and race, have met with mixed success. The difficulties of such a move are exemplified by the challenges suggested by Susan S. Lanser in 'Towards a Feminist Narratology' (1986), which is anthologized alongside Nilli Diengott's response, 'Narratology and Feminism' (1988) in Martin McQuillan's *The Narrative Reader*. Lanser identifies 'three crucial issues about which feminism and narratology might differ: the role of gender in the construction of narrative theory, the status of narrative as mimesis or semiosis, and the importance of context for determining meaning in narrative' (McQuillan 2000: 198). To summarize: the first implies that narratology has been based on a masculinist **canon**; the second that narrative, being largely concerned with linguistic signs, has little to say about the relation between the text and reality; and Lanser's third suggestion is that narratology, unlike feminism, is unconcerned with contexts, focusing its attention on the text in isolation. Lanser goes on to suggest the need for a feminist narratology to emerge. Diengott refutes this claim, suggesting that whilst Lanser is correct in identifying the divergences between feminism and narrative theory the notion of an interpretative feminist narratology is a misunderstanding of the nature of narratology, which she regards as a purely theoretical poetics. This suggestion that narratology is, and must remain, a sterile theoretical tool is misleading, and whilst narratology may be largely neutral in political terms it can be, and has been, readily applied to a wide range of critical positions. Overtly political questions such as 'Who speaks?', 'How is it possible to speak?', 'How does what is said reflect and construct what is?' are all posed by narrative theory.

Postcolonial theory asks exactly these questions. For example, Edward W. **Said**'s *Orientalism* offers a consideration of the version of North Africa and the Middle East, 'the Orient', that was constructed by the Western colonial powers (Britain and France) in the late nineteenth and early twentieth centuries. According to Said, the Orient is a fabrication of the West, an image that may or may not have any basis in reality but which has, regardless of this fact, real effects in the real world. In other words, orientalism is a narrative written from a particular perspective. Orientalism, in common with other forms of narrative, comments on its subject, its writers and its readers. The question of who controls, or is controlled by, language is explored by Kenyan novelist and playwright **Ngũgĩ** wa Thiong'o (1938–) in *Decolonising the Mind: The Politics of Language in African Culture* (1986) where he writes, 'Language, any language, has a dual character: it is both a means of communication and a carrier of culture' (Ngũgĩ 1986: 13). Bengali cultural and literary critic Gayatri Chakravorty **Spivak** (1942–) takes up the question of who is permitted to speak in her challenging and thought-provoking essay, 'Can the Subaltern Speak?' (1988). In the context of subaltern studies, subaltern designates non-elite, subordinated social groups such as the colonized illiterate peasantry, tribals and the lower strata of the urban sub-proletariat: groups that are the subjects of discourse and whose identities are constructed from positions that they themselves do not control. Spivak's question comes to address both the space inhabited by the female subaltern and the historiographical practices of the Subaltern Studies group itself.

Whilst few contemporary critics call themselves narratologists, or perhaps even think of their critical practice in terms of narratology, narrative theory plays a significant role in critical theory. Narrative theory has found useful application to the examples of psychoanalysis, historiography and postcolonial theory in various theoretical areas including, among others, postmodernism, Marxism, deconstruction, feminism, gender, phenomenology and film theory. As Lyotard remarks, 'Narration is the quintessential form of customary knowledge' (Lyotard 1984: 19), and, as such, understanding the ways in which it functions is a crucial part of critical theory.

FURTHER READING

Brooks, Peter (1984) *Reading for the Plot: Design and Intention in Narrative*, Cambridge, MA: Harvard University Press.

This extremely lucid work engages with the dynamics of narrative plotting through a series of close readings of literary texts.

Chatman, Seymour (1980) *Story and Discourse: Narrative Structure in Fiction and Film*, Ithaca, NY: Cornell University Press.

Chatman's book offers a very clear description of narrative theory, and is particularly strong on the relations between author, text and reader.

Genette, Gérard (1980) *Narrative Discourse: An Essay in Method*, trans. Jane. E. Lewin, Ithaca, NY: Cornell University Press.

One of narratology's central texts. Very thorough on the interaction between narrative, story and narrating, and particularly clear on the function of time in narrative.

McQuillan, Martin, ed. (2000) *The Narrative Reader*, London: Routledge.

An extremely useful collection of extracts from key narratological texts.

Prince, Gerald (2004) *A Dictionary of Narratology*, Lincoln: University of Nebraska Press.

An accessible dictionary with clear and straightforward definitions of key narratological terms.

Rimmon-Kenan, Shlomith (1983) *Narrative Fiction: Contemporary Poetics*, London: Routledge.

A valuable introduction to narratology that maintains a focus on literary fiction.

3

MARXISM

GLYN DALY

The history of the relationship between critical theory and Marxism has been an ambiguous one. On the one hand, there have been those who have affirmed an axiomatic connection: i.e. Marxism as *the* critical theory of capitalist society. In this regard Marxism has tended to be viewed as a totalizing **discourse** under which all possible forms of social critique can be subsumed (e.g. the problems of class, race and gender all boil down to capitalist exploitation). On the other hand, there are those who argue that critical theory represents an evolving (postmodern) intellectual tradition that, in rejecting all forms of naturalism and necessity, cannot be reconciled with Marxist thought and, moreover, renders the latter redundant.

Both positions are equally entrenched. For Jacques **Derrida** – regarded by many as the philosophical architect of contemporary critical theory – the boundary between Marxism and critical theory is considerably overdrawn. Indeed he maintains that his own highly influential theory of deconstruction is something that already names a deep connection with Marxist openings: 'Deconstruction has never had any sense or interest, in my view at least, except as a radicalization . . . in a certain *spirit of Marxism*' (Derrida 1994: 92).

Despite orthodox interpretation, Marxism has never comprised a unified position that simply needs to be explained in order to grasp its universal veracity and import. Marxism is as much a part of history as any other discourse, and as such continues to undergo processes of innovation and change in order to deal with the limitations and inconsistencies that would be inevitable with any historical enterprise.

This chapter begins with an appraisal of some of the central innovations of Karl **Marx**'s thought, and in particular the radical new emphasis he gave to the themes of context and **power**. From here it moves to a consideration of the **Frankfurt School** and their attempts to develop a context-based critical theory as a way of engaging with modern capitalism and its socio-cultural forms. It then addresses the type of discourse theory that has evolved precisely as a way of advancing a more integrated analysis of social reality. While this type of analysis is commonly associated with the poststructuralist perspectives of thinkers such as Michel **Foucault** and Derrida, it has also taken on an increasing importance in the Marxist and post-Marxist traditions through such theorists as Antonio **Gramsci**, Stuart **Hall**, Ernesto Laclau and Chantal Mouffe. Finally it explores certain aspects of the thought of Slavoj **Žižek** that, in some sense at least, marks a return to Marx.

MARX

In the language of the French philosopher Jacques Rancière (1999), we might say that the fundamental and enduring legacy of Marx consists in the fact that he told the truth about the lie of liberal capitalism. That is to say, the dominant view of the capitalist economy as a 'free market' – where individuals are deemed to be at liberty to make their own contracts and to sell their services to the highest bidder – was shown by Marx to be the great liberal **myth** of the **modern** age. Originating with the thought of the Scottish political economist Adam Smith – which is very much alive today in neo-liberal discourse concerning **globalization** – this myth affirms that the free market is the universal formula for achieving a rational, innovative and harmonious social order (indeed a new world order).

What Marx demonstrated was that far from comprising an open and neutral environment the capitalist economy is first and foremost a *power structure*. The basis of this power structure is class oppression. For Marx, capitalism is a mode of production that revolves around a basic antagonism between two fundamental classes: the bourgeoisie and the workers (or proletariat). As the minority ruling class, the bourgeoisie are defined by their monopolization of the means of production and subsistence (i.e. all that is necessary to make a living: land, raw materials, technology and so on). The proletariat, by contrast, comprise the vast majority and are defined precisely in terms of their lack of access to the means of production. This is a condition that was created through a power process. By buying up the old feudal estates, the emergent (industrial) bourgeois class proceeded to expel the people that lived there and to redirect them to the new factories in the cities. In this way the latter were transformed from peasants – with at least some access to productive means (land, livestock and so on) – into workers without any such access and who were consequently *forced* to sell their services (their labour power) in exchange for a wage.

This wage, moreover, is only a fraction of the revenue generated by the workers' end product. Workers create 'surplus value' (by transforming raw materials into saleable commodities) for which they are not remunerated and which in turn becomes the very source of profit for capitalists. Workers are paid far less than what they are truly owed. Capitalism is characterized by this systematic 'theft' of surplus value from the workers. Wage slavery becomes the new form of servitude.

Capitalism represents the highest stage of development and civilization – 'it [capitalism] has accomplished wonders surpassing Egyptian pyramids, Roman aqueducts and Gothic cathedrals' (Marx and Engels 1977: 111) – and yet its dynamic of change and progress is ultimately a restricted one. There are two main aspects here. The first is the tendency towards overproduction. As emerging enterprises create more advanced, diverse and cheaper products, then not only does this steadily reduce profit margins, it also begins to undermine the entire capitalist structure of property relations. An example of this would be the internet, where all kinds of copyright material and products (texts, music, pharmaceuticals, software and so on) can be obtained freely or at much reduced prices. Faced with this type of threat, the typical response of transnational corporations is to increase monopolization by buying up the smaller enterprises and actively stifle competition, innovation and development in order to protect markets and profits. So there is an inherent tension between the revolutionizing drives within capitalism (technological advances, etc.) and capitalism itself (a productive mode based on profit). Indeed the 'old world' problem of scarce resources and excessive demands is virtually reversed. Capitalism is a system that constantly overproduces and which seeks to manage its demand for profit by artificially inducing (market) scarcity in order to maintain and inflate demand.

The second aspect concerns social organization. As Marx emphasizes, the modern age is marked by an increasing tendency towards cosmopolitanism, where everyone is in principle entitled to participate in the markets of production and consumption regardless of social background. In this regard capitalism is something that repudiates all previous social relations of tradition and hierarchy ('all that is holy is profaned, all that is solid melts into air' – Marx and Engels 1977: 111) but only insofar as it reinforces the basic relation of class exploitation itself. This social relation is what might be called the *necessary exception* and remains an inherent and unsurpassable limit for capitalism and its cosmo-politanizing influences.

The thematic contribution of Marx to critical theory can hardly be exaggerated. Against the classical models of economic abstraction derived from liberal thought, Marx sought to analyse socio-economic relations in terms of *social context*. And this perspective extends to the entire experience of identity itself. As he puts it, 'the human essence . . . is the ensemble of social relations' (Marx, in Marx and Engels, 1977: 14). In other words, human identity is itself a product of history. It is not a pre-given entity – as in such terms as 'human nature', 'rational actor' and so forth – that accords naturalistically with capitalism. This is simply a convenient fiction of liberal thought.

Marx's central point is that the modern economy is a thoroughly human construction: the result of a concrete set of historical conditions. In contrast to the liberal promise of a social harmony produced by a free market, Marx shows that capitalism cannot resolve the fundamental social antagonism (class exploita-tion) on which it is based. Without this antagonism there would be no capitalism as such. This means that capitalism does not have a rational or objective ground (as liberal orthodoxy maintains). Rather, the *grounding* of capitalism – its consistency and stability – is something that is artificially generated and sustained through specific power relations. And this idea of grounding – without ever reaching a final ground – has become a keystone of contemporary philosophical thought. This is the main intuition that lies behind Derrida's theory of deconstruction.

At the same time there is also a tendency in Marx to fall back on a rather mechanistic account of human development which renders some of his theo-retical openings ambiguous and inconsistent. For example, despite stressing the importance of context in his social analysis, Marx nevertheless maintains that there is an underlying and deterministic logic to history that can be conceptually grasped and which foretells a final outcome. In this theory of historical materialism Marx argues that history itself will reach an ultimate resolution with the revolutionary overthrow of capitalism and the inauguration of a truly harmonious communism. Communism represents the supreme epoch of human existence where no further social transformation will take place (precisely because there are no antagonisms under communism to drive social change). Thus while his critique of *liberal* capitalist utopia is a compelling one, he does not manage to get beyond utopianism as such. In this regard Marx remains very much within the grip of idealist **Enlightenment** philosophy and the myth of a reachable ground.

Similarly, Marx maintains in various texts that workers have *objective interests* in communism, which means that they will inevitably rise up against their capitalist overlords. But if the orientation of the human being depends upon the 'ensemble of social relations' then is there any guarantee that this will happen? The Czech Marxist Kautsky, for example, was to observe that by the early twentieth-century workers were far more interested in trade unionism and social democratic (party) politics than revolutionary communism. This has led writers such as Lichtheim (1974) to argue that Marx's view of inevitable revolution really only held credibility under the conditions of nineteenth-century capitalism. As these conditions have been transformed through social reform/welfarism (not least as a result of trade union activity and social democratic politics) this view is neither relevant nor likely.

Yet such tensions in Marx's thought have not led to stagnation or obsolescence. Rather they have been the source of an ongoing history of creative intellectual development in which, in general terms, Marxism has come to be viewed less as an objectivist science and more as a mobilizing force and/or ideology within the social imagination. As well as opening up alternative avenues of enquiry, new perspectives have been developed that have attempted to incorporate a far greater sense of context and historicity in theoretical endeavour and application. It is to these perspectives that we shall now turn.

THE FRANKFURT SCHOOL: CAPITALISM AND ALL THAT JAZZ

The term critical theory was first coined by the Frankfurt School. Founded in 1923, the School – organized formally as the Institute for Social Research at the University of Frankfurt – was essentially a Marxist think-tank that comprised some of the most influential thinkers of the time: Max **Horkheimer** (who took up the directorship of the Institute in 1930), Walter **Benjamin**, Theodor **Adorno**, Herbert **Marcuse** and Erich Fromm, among others. Having moved to Geneva during the Second World War, the School returned to Frankfurt in 1950 with a view to analysing systematically the central features of contemporary capitalist society.

The Frankfurt School can be seen as a reaction to the type of classical, or 'scientific', Marxism that had been developed by the Second International under the leadership of Friedrich **Engels**. For the latter, Marxist theory had already determined what the underlying laws of historical development were, and hence it was essentially a question of waiting for these laws to manifest their full revolutionary effects – the collapse of capitalism was simply a matter of time. This led to a passive conception of politics and a tragic policy of political inaction in the face of early European fascism.

Against this type of intellectual aloofness, the Frankfurt School affirmed that theory should be grounded in social reality. The Left could not afford to wait for the world to conform to an abstract model of development (i.e. historical **materialism**) but had to begin to think on its feet and to develop the theoretical tools and concepts for practical and contemporaneous forms of political intervention.

In his seminal work, *Critical Theory*, Horkheimer argued that critical theory should not be thought of as a detached rationalistic appraisal of the 'concrete historical situation', but as something that acts as a 'force within [that situation] to stimulate change' (Horkheimer 1998: 206). What gives this type of theoretical endeavour its critical edge is precisely this aspect of reflexive engagement with the world in such a way that the latter might be transformed progressively.

Against this background the School was concerned to initiate a new type of approach along three main lines of intellectual development: (i) a fundamental emphasis on historical context rather than abstract theory; (ii) a systematic engagement with the cultural forms that contemporary capitalism was giving rise to; (iii) an analysis of the new types of social **subjectivity** that were being engendered as a result of these cultural forms.

A central assertion was that capitalist society was moving to a new level of ideological sophistication through what Horkheimer called the '**culture industry**'. Culture had replaced religion as the new 'opium of the masses' in framing a subtle order of conformism. According to Benjamin the emerging context was one in which the possibility of independent art forms was becoming more and more compromised by an ever expanding mass culture whose basic tendency is towards the banal and mediocre. And this tendency is insidiously political. Not only are cultural enterprises and artefacts increasingly managed and produced on a mass scale for consumption purposes but, at a deeper level, they feed into a self-perpetuating milieu of docility. Mainstream theatre, radio, television, internet and so on can be seen to be already in the service of a certain pacifying bourgeois culture. Indeed all such media may be said to be at its *most ideological* precisely when it aspires to this idea of neutral entertainment: that is to say, when it implicitly accepts, and consequently *naturalizes*, the power configuration of the capitalist status quo – thereby displacing and eviscerating all sense of critique and critical energy.

This is reflected further in Adorno's famous statement that 'to write poetry after Auschwitz is barbaric' (Adorno, 1983: 34). Thus what is truly barbaric is the kind of cultural practice that leads to an active forgetting and/or ignoring of human atrocities and the very socio-economic system that underpins such atrocities. It is a critique that in today's world would point to the way in which people tend to be more exercised about the outcome of the various versions of *Big Brother*, *The X-Factor* and so on than appalling suffering and abjection on a global scale.

The School especially targeted the cultural reflexivity of contemporary capitalism. In this context, the musical mode of jazz was seen as a paradigmatic expression of the latter. On the surface jazz appears to be the very embodiment of spontaneity, innovation and improvisation. In reality, however, all such improvisation is ultimately fake: it is always structured around certain musical motifs that govern its rhythms and repetitions and which, in turn, are circumscribed by harmonious resolution; it is always so many *variations* on a theme.

In a similar way, capitalism is a system that seemingly allows for all kinds of individual expression and innovation but only to the extent that it creates a kind of monotheistic attachment to the system itself. It creates a conformism through diversity (an *e pluribus unum*) in which more and more forms of individualistic 'improvisation' are accommodated on the basis of an underlying collectivist consumer culture. The apparent freedom that is won under late capitalism is finally 'freedom to be the same' (Horkheimer and Adorno 2002: 136). While 'we' (as in the West) seek to personalize our computers/mobile phones through a thousand different styles, ringtones and screensavers, this only serves to underline the fact that we are all 'wired': plugged into a basic profit-making matrix. This affects the very forms of 'individuality':

> Existence in late capitalism is a permanent rite of initiation ... Individuals are tolerated only as far as their wholehearted identity with the universal is beyond question. From the standardized improvisation in jazz to the original film personality who must have a lock of hair straying over her eyes so that she can be recognised as such, pseudoindividuality reigns.
>
> (Horkheimer and Adorno 2002: 124–5)

Reflected in today's rather comical image of middle-class youth adopting the language and gestures of the gangsta rap and hip-hop movements, the modes of individuality are increasingly managed and packaged through the culture industry. In this sense, the modern conjuncture is even more tragic than Marx anticipated. Whereas Marx identified the essential condition of capitalism as one of enforced servitude (wage slavery), the Frankfurt School alluded to something even more insidious: a willingness in people to inscribe themselves within the very system that oppresses them; to defer to the widespread mythology of those who have 'made it': the rags-to-riches millionaire, the lottery winner, the pop/sports idols and so on. Contemporary subjectivity is thus one of perverse *collaboration*. As in the phenomenon of the Stockholm syndrome – where hostages identify with their terrorist captors as a desperate survival strategy ('if I am accepted within the group then I won't be victimized/eliminated') – late capitalism is a kind of Stockholm syndrome writ large: a skewed and rather desperate faith in our own socio-economic betrayal.

POLITICAL CULTURE AND RESISTANCE

A central objective of the Frankfurt School was to find ways of resisting, and indeed breaking out of, the cultural manipulations of late capitalism. On these grounds what Benjamin admired about the German poet and playwright Brecht was not only his development of political critique through art but his demonstration that art itself is a political venture: an enterprise whose ultimate responsibility is to something **Other** – to critique itself.

For Brecht, bourgeois culture attempts to dissipate our creative potential for critique and contestation and, more widely, to repress any awareness that reality is a political, not a given, construction. It is a culture that reduces its audience to the status of mere spectator and which presents the existing power structure as a naturalistic backdrop of reality against which various sentimentalist dramas are played out. Brecht, by contrast, is someone who avoids any easy dramatic solutions or reconciliations. His task is to destabilize the audience/auteur relationship and to show that our capacity for achieving freedom is something that (in an almost Rousseauian sense) has to be won through active participation.

Adorno developed a similar argument in respect of the musical styles of Stravinsky and Schoenberg. For Adorno, Stravinsky's compositions may be characterized as the mood music for contemporary capitalism: homophonic string-based melodies; a kind of early muzak that stupefies. Schoenberg's music, by contrast, refuses the conventional harmonious resolution in favour of an 'atonal' kind of musical expression. Yet Schoenberg's approach is far from random. In his development of the twelve-tone serial (one that prohibits any repetition of notes until the eleventh note has been played) Schoenberg develops a system of musical expression that is uncompromising in its organization.

Implicit in Schoenberg is a displacement of the traditional music/noise distinction. Music is not a naturalistic construction or a pre-given form (the 'music of the spheres', etc.) that can be simply counterposed to 'noise'. Rather it comprises an undecidable terrain of diverse conventions and ordering principles that allows for phonic developments along incommensurably different lines. What we have with Schoenberg is not only the music but a representation of the contingency of the ordering of musicality as such – a kind of anti-muzak that cuts against the musical grain.

Thus the importance of such figures as Brecht and Schoenberg was seen to derive from their ability to act as exemplars of resistance against the dominant forms of bourgeois culture. In this way new possibilities for *politicizing* culture can be opened up with a view to developing radical and innovative opposition to the bourgeois paradigm. Through higher and more autonomous forms of artistic endeavour the idea was that people would be shaken from the culturally induced stupor that reinforces the view that capitalism comprises the naturalistic horizon of reality itself. On this reading, the School can be seen as reconceptualizing culture as an undecidable terrain of contestation in which different types of (passive/active) consciousness and subjectivity can be constructed and which, in principle, allows for the mobilization of political resistance. Culture – and more especially 'high culture' (as opposed to mass/popular culture) – can become a fulcrum for effecting progressive transformation.

The legacy of the Frankfurt School has developed in two main and divergent ways. The first of these reflects an optimistic belief in the power of high culture to oppose and transcend the superficial materialism of the bourgeois ethos. Echoes of this approach can be found in the thought of Jürgen **Habermas** who exhibits a kind of Enlightenment-based faith in the civilizing influence of what he calls 'communicative rationality' and its perceived capacity for overcoming ideological distortion and social conflict. In general this type of approach has been criticized for being elitist in its views concerning a 'higher' culture and rationality and, at the same time, somewhat patronizing and naïve.

The second is more sceptical and pessimistic. Here the very strength of the School's interventions has arguably become a major weakness. In stressing the extent of interconnectedness between culture and the economy in an overall configuration there has been a strong tendency in Marxist thought – and especially Marxist structuralism – to endow that configuration with an absolute centre: the functionalist logic of capital. With thinkers such as Louis **Althusser** and Fredric **Jameson**, for example, capitalism is generally affirmed as a totalizing structure that draws all the elements of socio-cultural life ('high' and 'low') together under its instrumentalist rationality. In consequence the popular classes become thoroughly incorporated into the capitalist system. Yet if social identity is subject to such a degree of structuralist closure then how can any form of political resistance ever arise? In effect we would seem to be presented with a simple inversion of Marx's position: instead of being pre-programmed to overthrow capitalism, the masses are doomed to conformist subordination within it. The Castor of determinism has been substituted for the Pollux of fatalism. This is precisely the world of Marcuse's 'one-dimensional man' (Marcuse 2002) where human life is reduced to a kind of consumerist puppetry. It is a world eerily encapsulated in Georg Romero's masterpiece, *Dawn of the Dead*, in which the zombies – obsessively patrolling a shopping mall – are constantly drawn towards a promise of life through the empty gestures of retail therapy.

POST-MARXISM AND DISCOURSE THEORY

Although pre-dating the Frankfurt School, the thought of the Italian Marxist Antonio Gramsci may be said to mark a crucial break with the former. For Gramsci modern society is not a closed totality organized around a fixed centre of capitalist rationality. He does not reduce socio-cultural practices to the economic (or vice versa). Society is viewed rather as a field of contestation in which different elements are combined to form a specific construction: what he calls an historical bloc. In a highly radical move, Gramsci extends this type of analysis to the question of objectivity itself:

> It might seem that there can exist an extra-historical and extra-human objectivity. But who is the judge of such objectivity? Who is able to put himself in this kind of 'standpoint of the cosmos itself' and what could such a standpoint mean? It can indeed be maintained that here we are dealing with a hangover of the concept of God ... Objective always means 'humanly objective' which can be held to correspond exactly to 'historically subjective': in other words, objective would mean 'universal subjective'. Man knows objectively in so far as knowledge is real for the whole human race *historically* unified in a single unitary cultural system.
>
> (Gramsci 2003: 445)

The objective world, and our subjective inscription within it, is something that is *made* and not given to us in **metaphysical** terms. Similarly there exists no identity – either as a positive essence or as a closed structural form – beyond the historical processes of identification themselves. The orientation of the worker, for example, is not pre-ordained but depends upon social configuration within a given social context. While the view of the proletarian masses as avenging agents of social revolution is excessively optimistic, the pessimistic Frankfurt School view of the masses as docile Stepford workers is equally extreme. Gramsci rejects *both* determinism and fatalism and shows identification to be a historico-political matter without any final resolution.

In the development of an alternative post-Marxist tradition writers such as Hall and Laclau and Mouffe have sought to combine the insights of Gramsci with a range of 'continental' philosophical currents: Foucault's **genealogical** method, Jacques **Lacan's** analysis of the **signifier**, Wittgenstein's development of the notion of language games, as well as Derridean deconstruction. This emerging tradition is one that gives a new centrality to an expanded conception of discourse.

Discourse theory adopts a realist position in that it affirms the existence of a material world external to thought – this is its starting point. What it rejects, however, is the traditional idealist notion that that world can be described in an unmediated and direct sense – as if from a 'God's eye' point of view. On the contrary, we always have to interpret the world through discourses, i.e. specific configurations, or systems, of meaning. Discourse is not limited to the purely linguistic but applies equally to action and our physical engagement with the world in general. For example, the physical act of dining in a restaurant is one that simultaneously involves the interpretation of signs, the use of speech/gestures, the observation of social protocol and so on, as part of an entire meaningful process. Such a process – the structured integration of linguistic and non-linguistic practices – is an instance of discourse.

For discourse theory there exists a fundamental and irresolvable gap between the external world of objects and the way we interpret that world. This means that, in contrast to Enlightenment philosophy and today's followers of Habermas, it is impossible to transcend all discursive contexts and stand in the cold light of Reason; it is impossible to penetrate through to any 'extra-discursive' realm of positivistic Truth. Put simply, nothing can be interpreted beyond interpretation itself – there is no final description of the world as it 'actually is'. Objects, practices and events can only be apprehended through the assignment of meaning, and this assignment is neither fixed nor neutral but always takes place within a historical framework. As Derrida puts it, 'there are only contexts without any absolute centre or anchorage' (Derrida 1988: 12).

In this sense we might say that discourse designates an ongoing series of historical attempts to give form to what is essentially formless. While discourses seek to (relatively) stabilize meaning, no discourse can establish a total closure or fully determine the nature of an object. A specific wooden structure, for example, can be a 'table', a 'desk', an 'altar', a 'public platform' and so on, without being *essentially* any one of these: its meaning depends on how it is *articulated* with other objects, rituals, social practices and so on, in a discursive context. There are two central points here. First, there is nothing in the object itself that can stabilize its meaning in an absolute ('extra-discursive') sense. Second, and consequently, the meaning of any object can always be subverted and articulated in a radically different way. We are confronted, in other words, with an eternal politics of meaning and identity.

If we take the idea of 'womanhood', we can see how its construction within the terms of Victorian discourse is radically different to what it is today. What allows for feminist subversion is not any positive feminine essence but precisely the lack of any essence: the persistence of a basic negativity. In this sense we can say that feminist subversion not only reflects the failure of Victorian discourse to naturalize the meaning of gender but effectively the failure of *all* attempts to naturalize such meaning . . . including that of feminism. Feminism does not come any closer to what womanhood *really* is. Feminism too is an artificial construction – something that has to be reproduced and defended through institutional arrangements – and can lead in a variety of different discursive directions: conservative feminism, left feminism, post-feminism and so on. This type of approach has been developed extensively by Hall (and others) in respect of **ethnicity**, nationhood and a whole range of cultural identities.

Does this mean that everything is in a constant state of liquidity where meanings change from one moment to the next? Evidently not. People can and do identify with all kinds of positions – the biblical account of the universe, political conspiracies, for and against genetic manipulation, pro-/anti-globalization, etc. – and produce all kinds of material to support their claims. But whether these achieve wider *credibility* is entirely another matter. And credibility is not the result of any naturalism or imperial measure but is always a human-contextual matter where interpretive collectives – scientists, academics, judges, journalists, policy-makers – broadly establish the nature of 'evidence', 'coherence', 'best practice' and so on. Such categories depend for their constitution on the specific discursive formation in question and the success of the latter depends, in turn, on its ability to exclude/repress other possible formations. What 'grounds' a formation is not any supra-historical ground but precisely the dimensions of repression and exclusion that structure its intelligibility.

This is the meaning of Laclau and Mouffe's assertion that 'antagonism constitutes the limits of every objectivity' (Laclau and Mouffe 1987: 125). That is to say, objectivity is something that has to be circumscribed – as a field of (relatively) stable meanings – against that which would overwhelm/negate it. In other words, objectivity depends upon frontiers of exclusion that in providing the sense of limits are simultaneously constitutive and affirming of a specific discursive formation of objectivity. Objectivity is a (historical) power construction that is always partial and provisional and which is essentially prone to further subversion and reconfiguration – just as the gendered objectivity of Victorian socio-sexual life has been subverted and reconfigured.

Foundationalism is consequently turned on its head. Objectivity cannot be identified in positivistic terms but is shown to grow out of negativity and antagonistic repression. The question is no longer the idealist one of *what* objectivity is (what is its intrinsic nature, etc.) but rather *how* it is constituted. For discourse theorists the answer lies with the historical positioning of the frontiers of exclusion. In this sense all objectivity may be said to reflect the eternal attempt to ground historically what is epistemologically ungroundable.

It is on this basis that Laclau and Mouffe advance their impossibility-of-Society thesis. A fully integrated Society is impossible precisely because it too is founded on frontiers of exclusion. The consistency of any (historical) society relies upon some kind of boundary that is established between belonging and non-belonging; between the registers of 'us' and 'them'. While the nature and positioning of such a boundary is historical, its presence is a transhistorical and constitutive necessity for social organization as such. All social formations are *essentially* unstable because their positive consistency depends upon the exclusion of a 'surplus' negativity (Otherness) which can never be fully mastered or resolved.

ŽIŽEK: RETURN TO MARX

Insofar as all ideology presents some kind of achievable utopianist dream, then, by definition, it may be said to exist in a state of denial as regards the impossibility of Society. But if this is the case, how does ideology deal with the fact that it cannot deliver the utopian object? It is in this context that the influential Slovenian philosopher, Slavoj Žižek, has developed a compelling perspective that, in a certain sense, represents a return to Marx. For Žižek, ideology does not simply deny impossibility but restages our encounter with it in such a way that it appears resolvable. That is to say, ideology attempts to disguise impossibility and to reinterpret it as if it were a potentially removable obstacle. Žižek takes as an example of this the ideological role played by 'the Jew' in Nazi discourse:

> Society is not prevented from achieving its full identity because of Jews: it is prevented by its own antagonistic nature, by its own immanent blockage, and it 'projects' this internal negativity into the figure of the 'Jew'.
>
> (Žižek 1989: 127)

Through ideological fantasy impossibility is restaged as a crime of theft/sabotage that must be prosecuted. The 'Jew' functions as an embodiment of negativity (the negation of Society) and, in so doing, serves to support the very fantasy of an achievable (Aryan) utopia. By equating impossibility with a historical Other ('Jews', 'Palestinians', 'Gypsies', 'Muslims') ideology seeks to create precisely this type of illusion of an ultimate resolution.

It is this notion of embodied negativity that is at the heart of Laclau and Žižek's dispute over the notion of class (see Butler, Laclau and Žižek 2000). Laclau makes two compelling points: (i) the industrial working class, which in the days of the early Marxists exhibited a certain socio-cultural homogeneity, has become increasingly fragmented due to socio-economic transformations; (ii) the political orientation of class is not pre-given (it can be progressive and/or reactionary) and, in consequence, cannot function as the natural leader or sovereign coordinator for all social struggle.

Žižek, by contrast, wants to keep the notion of class but not in straightforward terms. His perspective is concerned less with the analytical status of class (that Laclau rightly criticizes) than with the *locus* of class: that is, with the position of the radically excluded – the world's destitute, displaced and outcast. These excluded and radically impoverished groups function as today's symptoms, i.e. as constitutive of, and yet debarred from, the development of global (i.e. Western) capitalism. In this broader sense, class is not a positive identity but rather the opposite: a signifier of embodied negativity. Class becomes the name (or one of the names) for the basic failure/impossibility of capitalism to constitute itself as a universal cosmopolitan system (see Žižek and Daly 2004). On these rather different grounds, Žižek nonetheless affirms Marx's fundamental insight that capitalism cannot function without the type of systematic exclusion that is embodied in this way.

Here Žižek develops a different slant on the question of impossibility. For Žižek the key issue is not so much the impossibility of Society but the social-ization of impossibility: that is to say, how is impossibility situated in defining the limits of the possible in concrete terms? Impossibility should not be regarded as merely a neutral category but as something that social ideology engages with reflexively. Contemporary political culture, for example, tends to be dominated by an ethos of irony where demands for radical transformation are treated with cynical suspicion. To this effect, political engagement is already limited by its own sense of limitation and impossibility as such.

When Western leaders speak of a new world order, for example, this is always in terms of an expansion *within* the terms of existing liberal capitalist principles, i.e. a development in which the latter remain firmly in place. However, a truly alternative global order – one that would involve a radical reorganization of power relations in egalitarian terms – is consigned to the sphere of the whimsical (e.g. a noble idea but human nature dictates that this is impossible). The limits of the liberal capitalist conjuncture thus delineate a naturalistic horizon that defines the realm of the possible against what is deemed impossible.

In connection with the Frankfurt School, and more lately the work of Jameson (1992), Žižek is concerned to analyse today's capitalist reality as a socio-cultural whole. In this regard he detects a certain complicity between the type of contemporary postmodern culture that is frequently endorsed in discourse theory and the logic of capital. There are two main aspects here. First the ongoing pluralization of identities is one that provides more and more opportunities for commodification and consumption. Even so-called ethical consumption provides market opportunities for organic food, green products and so on. Second, and perhaps more insidiously, the postmodern emphasis on difference is one that tends to assume a kind of level playing-field – all identities must be respected and considered equally without prioritizing one type of identity or social struggle over another. The effect of this, however, is to render real poverty, global hunger and social exclusion virtually invisible and/or abstract (such things happen 'else-where'). Thus what is overlooked is precisely this dimension of the necessary exception vis-à-vis the culture, or economy, of differences. Just as slavery showed the symptomatic truth (the embodied negativity) of Athenian democracy as a tyranny of citizens, so too today's abject multitude discloses the truth of post-modern capitalism as a tyranny of differences: a global differential inclusiveness that in order to function relies upon even deeper trenches of exclusion. The (negativized) truth of our cosmopolitan world is the figure of the displaced migrant whose minimal demands are viewed as somehow costing the earth: threatening social cohesion ('our way of life'), draining national resources and spreading disease, crime, prostitution and so on.

What Žižek affirms, by contrast, is a politics of the act. The act (which is derived from Lacan) refers to a radical break with an existing pattern of social existence in such a way that it opens up new possibilities for reconfiguring that social existence. This type of politics is one that engages directly with impossibility, as it is historically situated in circumscribing the realm of the possible. In other words, it takes on the impossible not in terms of 'the impossible *to* happen' but rather 'the impossible *that* happened' (Žižek, in Butler, 2005: 145). The revolutionaries of eighteenth-century France, for example, may be said to have achieved the impossible by breaking out of the politico-cultural matrix of the enduring pre-modern world and reconfiguring social existence along radically new and secular lines. In seeking to break out of the matrix of the possible (what is considered 'natural', 'common-sense', the 'way it is', etc.) a politics of the act may also be considered as a politics of impossibility.

In order to break out of the global–liberal–capitalist matrix of possibility, Žižek argues that we need to stand with today's symptoms – the negated classes – against the type of postmodernism that puts its faith in more and more forms of differential absorption. And this implies a rejection of the postmodern prohibition regarding political prioritization (that we should not elevate certain social struggles over others). For Žižek it is vital that we prioritize systemic abjection precisely in its status as necessary exception: as something that, as Marx knew well, holds up the mirror to contemporary globalization and its fake cosmopolitanism.

In traditional Marxist discourse critical theory was generally seen in terms of establishing an objective fulcrum that would enable rational and emancipatory social change. The history of Marxist intellectual development, however, has seen a gradual abandonment of this type of ambition. From the Frankfurt School through to Gramsci and contemporary post-Marxism, the idea of theoretically determining an *external* principle for social transformation has steadily given way to a basic emphasis on context and historicity.

Does this mean consequently that critical theory no longer has a critical edge or any sort of purchase on an alternative normative vision? The postmodernist liberal philosopher Richard **Rorty** would answer this in the affirmative. For him the ultimate achievement of contemporary critical theory is, in a way, its own dissolution. That is to say, what critical theory serves to demonstrate is that there is no theoretical basis for radical collective emancipation. Indeed the very emphasis on the differential contingency of all Being is something that, according to Rorty, gives implicit endorsement to a liberal ideal: one in which individuals qua individuals are free to pursue their personal goals and ideals about how to live (Rorty 1989, 1991).

Yet post-Marxists would reject the idea of any kind of naturalistic fit here (such an idea would itself be regarded as somewhat metaphysical). Rather the emphasis on contingency and discursivity is viewed precisely as a *stimulus* for imagining social possibilities beyond what currently exists. In this way figures such as Hall, Laclau and Mouffe have tended to stress the importance of alliances between disaffected groups with a view to advancing progressive forms of subversion along the lines of a deeper and more expansive democratic culture.

Žižek, however, argues that democratic subversion is not enough, as it already defers too much to the 'grammar' of contemporary political encounter. We should not play by the conventional postmodernist rules of emphasizing difference and pluralization within the existing social horizon. For Žižek there needs to be a more elementary break with the today's matrix of identitarian politics. Insofar as the developing new world order is a human power construction, then we are all implicated in both its functioning and the way it produces poverty, hunger and abjection as an inherent set of symptoms. On these grounds, our ethical responsibility to the excluded classes becomes the source of a new type of resistance – a mobilizing identification with the negated outcast –

and a politics of action that seeks to break out of the very circumscribed order of possibility that relies on and reproduces such symptoms.

This brings us full circle to the analysis of Marx and his vision of an International (a political movement without regional boundaries) that is capable of taking on the capitalist system. Yet, in contrast to Marx, the content of such an International would not be fixed or pre-given. For Žižek, as indeed for Derrida, such an International would be defined by its constituencies of exclusion and by an unplacatable spirit of politico-ethical involvement and responsibility. It would be an International that constantly strives to remind us that we cannot hide behind terms such as 'globalization', 'market reality', 'regional stability', 'national interest' and so on, as if they described a neutral order of social existence. And it is surely in this sense that a characteristically Marxist critical theory will continue to find its critical edge: in the radical indictment that we have no alibis.

FURTHER READING

Butler, Judith, Laclau, Ernesto and Žižek, Slavoj (2000) *Contingency, Hegemony, Universality*, London: Verso.
This is a collection of intriguing polemical exchanges between three major philosophical figures – Judith Butler, Ernesto Laclau and Slavoj Žižek – who represent important, and contrasting, intellectual traditions.

Derrida, Jacques (1994) *Specters of Marx: The State of the Debt, the Work of Mourning, and the New International*, trans. Peggy Kamuf, London: Routledge.
A crucial text by Derrida that revivifies the work of Marx and which, through a series of encounters with Shakespeare's *Hamlet*, develops an inspired deconstructive critique of the modern condition.

Horkheimer, Max and Adorno, Theodor W. (2002) *Dialectic of Enlightenment*, Stanford, CA: Stanford University Press.
This is a major text by two key figures of the Frankfurt School. Among its highlights it introduces the reader to their highly influential 'culture industry thesis'.

Laclau, Ernesto and Mouffe, Chantal (1987) *Hegemony and Socialist Strategy: Towards a Radical Democratic Politics*, London: Verso.
A difficult but rewarding work that reformulates the Marxist problematic in the context of a new emphasis on discourse and a thoroughgoing critique of essentialism. The recent edition also boasts a new preface that helps to clarify the authors' political perspective.

Žižek, Slavoj and Daly, Glyn (2004) *Conversations with Žižek*, Cambridge: Polity Press.
A wide-ranging text that introduces the reader to some of the main arguments and ideas from one of the most influential thinkers of our age.

4

POSTSTRUCTURALISM

CATHERINE BELSEY

A WAY OF READING

From the point of view of a critical theorist, the main interest of poststructuralism is its invitation to read differently. Although it is often presented in the form of a set of prescriptions and precepts, poststructuralism developed in a series of practical encounters with texts: the critic Roland **Barthes** (1915–80) read Balzac and instances of French popular culture; psychoanalyst Jacques **Lacan** (1901–81) read **Freud** – and *Hamlet* and Sophocles; while the philosopher Jacques **Derrida** (1930–2004) also reads *Hamlet*, as well as Rousseau, **Marx** and a succession of other works, many of them philosophical. At the same time, poststructuralism is not reducible to a methodology. Instead, it offers a distinctive relationship between readers (or viewers) and texts.

Poststructuralism proposes that the meanings of words, images, stories or other texts are not to be found elsewhere, in the mind of the **author** or in the world depicted. Since they have no external, extratextual guarantees, meanings are unfixed, discontinuous and unstable. Does it follow, then, that poststructuralism locates them in the mind of the reader, holding that we make them up, or that interpretation is purely 'subjective'? Not at all. The poststructuralist account of the reading process is more challenging than that, but more interesting too, since it allows texts to give us back more than our own reflection. How, then, does it work?

MAKING SENSE

We need to go back to the beginning, to reflect on the way children, for example, learn to make sense of what they see and hear. When their fond carers point to a cat and ask them to repeat the word, it looks as if the children are learning to recognize and name cats. And so in a way they are. But cats come in very different sizes and colours: there are variously Siamese, Persian, and tabby cats, not to mention cheetahs. In these circumstances, it cannot be that an image of a cat imprints itself on the retina as the standard by which this recognition and naming takes place. Instead, language begins to come into being for the child as it learns to distinguish confidently between cats on the one hand and, on the other, say, dogs, which also come in very different sizes and colours, and arguably offer even less in the way of visual resemblance to one another.

The primary property of language is that it differentiates. We can confirm that vocabulary is not acquired simply by pointing to **referents** (things in the world) when we remember that later the child will go on to learn to use words such as 'justice' and 'honesty'. Sadly, we do not always learn the meanings of those terms from actual examples. On the contrary, in fact: we often construe them by differentiating a positive ideal from instances of injustice and dishonesty.

If abstract values are not learnt from referents in the world, what about words that name nothing material, but are crucial, even so, to the process of reasoning, such as 'because', 'although', and 'if'? There is nothing for them to correspond to.

Does language name ideas, then? Poststructuralism would say not. On the contrary, ideas come into sharp relief for us when we learn the meanings of the terms. Of course, there are exceptions – coinages often compounded from existing terms: 'poststructuralism' came 'after' 'structuralism'. Similarly, poststructuralism itself notes the conventional tendency of Western philosophy to assume that meanings exist before language names them, and calls this assumption '**logocentrism**', inventing a new term by putting together the Greek *logos* (meaning, sense, idea) with the familiar suffix 'centrism' (propensity to centre on). But mostly individuals do not in practice come up with an idea and then look around for a word for it. On the contrary, we are much more likely to come across a term and wonder in the first instance what it means. While dictionaries can give the impression that words are full of meaning, like containers with a content, experience shows that confidence in using a new vocabulary has more to do with the ability to *distinguish* when a specific term is appropriate. And an expanded vocabulary offers access to ever finer distinctions. To know how to use '**power**', 'mastery', 'sovereignty' and 'autonomy' is to be in a position to analyse some subtle political differences.

The Swiss linguist Ferdinand de **Saussure** (1857–1913) gave a preliminary impetus to poststructuralism without knowing it when he put the case that ideas do not exist in some psychic realm independent of language. If they did, all languages would name the same concepts (Saussure 1974: 116–20). But anyone who has ever struggled with the process of translation from one language to another knows that different languages make distinctive differences. How, for example, would you distinguish in English between the French *science* (knowledge) and *connaissance* (knowledge), not to mention *tu* (you) and *vous* (you)? But they are not interchangeable, and the French know the difference.

THE SIGNIFIER

Meanings are not confined to words. Images, maps, traffic lights, gestures all signify. Saussure preferred to discuss the **signifier**: the spoken, written, drawn or otherwise material indicator that does the signifying we learn to interpret. Moreover, signifiers are not always equivalent to individual words or images. 'How are you?' is a single signifier, and what it signifies is a polite interest in the well-being of your interlocutor. Is Picasso's *Guernica* best seen as an assembly of signifiers, or one? It is possible to break the painting down into its individual components or, alternatively, to read it as a single condemnation of the horrors of war.

Saussure called meaning the **signified**. The signified is distinct from the referent; indeed, as I have suggested, many words we use constantly have no referents. Meaning resides in signifying practice, in the material *text*, where the signifier 'text' is understood in the broadest possible sense to include, for instance, images, maps, traffic lights and gestures.

(How revealing that conventional English has no single word to embrace the range of signifying practices Saussure's theory enables us to bring together for the purposes of interpretation. What poststructuralism's detractors condemn as jargon is often an attempt to stretch the existing distinctions to accommodate a new way of relating them to one another. And how awkward that English has no single word for the range of addressees of these texts. Here I uneasily refer to them all as 'readers', with occasional references to 'viewers', in order to remind myself that 'reading' is also to be understood figuratively.)

Signification is a matter of social convention. It is hard to see how green lights have any natural connection with safety, but we are so accustomed to this convention that it has entered into the English language: schemes and projects are metaphorically 'given the green light'. But the fact that meaning is conventional removes it from the realm of individual **subjectivity**. If I choose to read red lights as meaning it is safe to proceed, I might not last long. If I consistently interpret 'How are you?' as an invitation to punch my interlocutor, I can expect to be locked up. Language – or signifying practice – does not belong to individuals. Instead, it already exists before we are born into a world where people reproduce it all round us. Though it constantly changes, these modifications prevail only to the degree that they are shared. In that sense, meanings belong to other people. Lacan calls language 'the **Other**'. If I opt to hijack it for purely private purposes, I must expect to be seen as psychotic.

DIFFERANCE (WITH AN A)

Is interpretation a matter, then, of laying hands on the signified? Sadly, no. We cannot confront meaning itself, the pure concept, as a free-standing idea. On the contrary, what we encounter is always the signifier in its materiality. And the signifier, Derrida (1973) argues, 'defers' the meaning. In other words, the red light, or the greeting, or the painting always stands between us and the danger, or the warmth, or the condemnation it represents, so that we never meet these meanings as pure ideas. Representation implies an absence: your representative stands in for you when you are not there in person. The idea represented in language is not there *in itself* either. Instead, the signifier takes its place, relegates any supposed pure concept to an inaccessible background, supplants it. (This does not mean that events do not happen in the world, or that they have no implications for us when they do. You cannot encounter the idea of danger as pure concept independent of the signifier, but you can still crash your car, and take the material consequences of that. Those consequences can be *named*, discussed and analysed, however, only in a language that may not quite match them.)

When it comes to interpretation, then, all we can be sure of is the signifier or signifiers that constitute the text. And that is what we interpret: a materiality (sounds, images, words on a page or computer screen, contrasting colours) that signifies as a result of social convention, where meaning is not guaranteed by anything outside the text, whether as idea or thing, and is not available for direct inspection either.

GOOD NEWS EVEN SO?

No wonder, then, that poststructuralist writing often seems so elegiac in its mode of address. And no wonder it has so many detractors. Poststructuralism takes away the comfortable certainty of traditional criticism that meaning could be definitively settled – by reading the author's biography, perhaps, knowing the cultural history of the time, or just pointing to the way things are.

But how comfortable and how certain was that belief? Not very, in practice. Meaning seemed to be just as hotly contested then as now. After all, the biography, the context and the state of the world were themselves subject to interpretation. For all the reams of paper produced to denounce poststructuralism, its account of language does not ultimately change all that much, we might think.

And yet poststructuralists would probably argue that this new way of looking at textuality changes everything, and in the end, paradoxically, for the better. The debates about the meaning of a given text continue, but they are located where they belong: in the process of interpreting the text itself, and not in appeals to external authority. There can be no one single correct reading of a text, but there can still be misreadings, as a result of inattention, unfamiliarity with the signifiers, or failure to recognize resemblances or allusions to other texts. If texts lose what once passed for 'depth' (access to the psychological state of the author) or 'truth' (fidelity to the world we seem to know), they gain in complexity and density. And rather than needing a cultural context in order to make sense of them, we learn about the culture that produced them from the texts themselves. Texts (in the broad sense) are, indeed, the only available instances of that culture. And the texts that tend to form the material of cultural criticism (more interesting, usually, and more enigmatic than traffic lights) cannot be closed down by the one final definitive reading that would surpass all others. Instead, they can be shown to reveal more than their authors knew, and more than previous critics have identified.

INTERPRETATION

How is this done? Take fiction. Instead of looking for the author behind the text, poststructuralism begins by attributing meaning to difference. Even the simplest story differs from the other stories that it also resembles. While both are fairytales, 'Beauty and the Beast' differs from 'Cinderella' to the degree that its heroine is more active: she domesticates the Beast, and loves it in spite of appearances, with the effect of transforming it into a handsome prince. And what happens when Disney retells the story as a twentieth-century movie? Beauty becomes a reader, and she is drawn to the Beast in the first instance by the huge library in his palace. Each instance is intelligible in its resemblance to and difference from other parallel texts, or **intertextually**. Whether their authors intended it or not, the stories themselves allude to other stories belonging to the same **genre**. Epics invoke and differ from other epics; individual instances of science fiction take their differential place within a tradition of science fiction.

This emphasis on difference, incidentally, is what distinguishes poststructuralism from structuralism. Structuralism focused on the resemblances between stories, reducing them, in effect, to variants of a single, endlessly repeated narrative. Roland Barthes marked a turning-point in 1970, when he opened *S/Z* by repudiating his own earlier flirtation with structuralist analysis as 'undesirable, for the text thereby loses its difference'. How ironic, he reflects, that Saussure's attribution of meaning to difference should lead to the flattening out of texts 'under the scrutiny of an in-different science' (Barthes 1990b: 3).

Poststructuralism acknowledges the resemblances and then goes on to attend to the differences both between and within texts. First, the relations between them. Genres set up distinct expectations: romantic comedies, like the fairytales they draw on, generally have happy endings; tragedy ends in death. But what happens when *King Lear* rewrites the folktale of the king whose youngest daughter is the only one to tell the truth, and then breaks with the genre to end in catastrophe? It feels, if the critical tradition is to be believed, like the bleakest of all Shakespeare's tragedies. And arguably this is because it *does not* fulfil the expectations its intertextual fairytale allusions have set up. The founder of psychoanalysis Sigmund Freud (1856–1939) locates the '**uncanny**' in a clash of genres. What looks like realism turns out to include an unexpected supernatural component that causes a frisson by unsettling our comfortable relations with a familiar genre.

Indeed, form and content cannot be read separately. Style in general, itself a form of signification, is necessarily a place where meaning resides. If ideas never exist as free-standing entities, it makes no sense to isolate an imagined content independent of the specific genre, vocabulary, sequence of images or lighting effects which compose *this* individual work.

ADDRESSING THE READER

By drawing on – or breaking with – the conventional assumptions shared to varying degrees between author and reader, or artist and viewer, texts offer their addressees a certain relationship to the world they depict. They invite us to take up a position in response to the account of things they construct, to feel reassured, saddened, mystified or challenged. Traditional detective stories, for instance, seem to invite the reader to share a confidence that, whatever criminal events may take place in the course of the story, a knowing figure will emerge to reveal the truth, and justice will eventually prevail. In the process, they offer the reader the reassurance of a certain knowledge. The classic **realist** text begins in enigma, but it promises to deliver that form of closure which is also a disclosure: in the final chapter or reel, if not before, the sequence of events will be made clear and the motives of the characters laid bare. We shall be able to look back through the story, reinterpreting retrospectively where necessary, to see that the narrative made sense all along, though not always the sense it seemed to make at the time.

By contrast, some of the irritation, hostility or 'boredom' readers feel in response to modernist and postmodernist works amounts to an irritation with their difference, a frustration that such closure is withheld. But a more sceptical age than the Victorian epoch, which specialized in classic realism, tends to see narrative closure as delivering a false certainty and an illusory transparency. In life, it might be argued, we never see motive so clearly or uncover the truth so unequivocally. The initial project of much modernism, it is worth remembering, was a deeper verisimilitude. Alternatively, texts may set out to lay bare their own intertextual composition, knowingly alluding to existing works, or breaking the illusion that they give transparent access to a fictional world, by self-referentially naming their own textuality and inviting the ironic complicity of their readers. Conceptual art asks us to be shocked by the unconventionality of each work, but also to place that shock in a respected line of descent from Marcel Duchamp, who in 1917 offered a readymade urinal for exhibition as a work of art.

THE READER'S ACTIVE ROLE

Are we, then, always at the mercy of the text, alternately reassured, dismayed, challenged, gleeful or shocked, according to genre? Not necessarily. No text can ensure a specific reaction, and the vocabulary of conventional criticism does less than justice to the complexity of the reading process when it affirms that a work can 'force' us to respond in a specific way. On the contrary, poststructuralist readers have taken an active role in identifying the strategies of the texts they analyse. They thus read other-wise, refusing simply to succumb to the blandishments of the text – at least on a second, more analytical reading.

Psychoanalysis has been influential here. The main interest of psychoanalysis for poststructuralism has not been as a guide to content, explaining the state of mind of the characters, and still less of the author. Instead, it offers a model of *attention* to the text. Freud's innovation was a concentration on the utterances of the analysand. Psychoanalysts listen closely to what is said, but they do not take it at face value. Instead, they treat the thematic content of the utterances as **unconsciously** designed to mislead, to distract both speaker and analyst from unconscious issues, commonly **desires** that cannot or must not be fulfilled. They therefore look for the moments of *in*coherence or *un*certainty, which betray another concern, unspoken because, perhaps, unspeakable. They understand that consciousness seeks a specific relationship with the analyst which obscures unconscious wishes, and they adopt a distance that prevents them from fully subscribing to the relationship the analysand proposes. If we apply this procedure to the practice of cultural criticism, we can see that the text may reveal more to a reader who does not simply accept at face value the reassurances or challenges it offers, but looks instead for the differences *within* the work.

In *S/Z* Roland Barthes brought such a reading to bear on Balzac's classic realist short story 'Sarrasine' (Barthes 1990b). On the face of it, the narrative uncovers the solution to the enigma it sets up. But certain hesitations and concealments betray another agenda, which gives us a new kind of access to the forbidden desires of nineteenth-century French culture. In a meticulous, phrase-by-phrase analysis Barthes identifies sequences of vocabulary and imagery not explicitly connected by the text itself, but linked by the critic, to expose the impossibility of sustaining the gender differences taken consciously for granted in the work.

DECONSTRUCTION

Deconstruction also finds both more and less in the text than its author might have 'had in mind', but it approaches the issue from the perspective of language rather than psychoanalysis. If meaning depends on difference, the meaning of the self-same always bears a **trace** of the differentiating other. In other words, the signifier necessarily alludes to the terms from which it differs. We understand a signifier by reference not to the world, or ideas, but to another signifier that defines it *as* different. For example, if 'good' is not accessible as a pure, free-standing concept, but is brought to mean in and by its difference from evil, the definition of 'good' always retains a trace of the repudiated evil. We apprehend each by reference to the other; and in consequence a trace of the other is always capable of incursion into the self-same.

No wonder, then, that Milton's *Paradise Lost* has such difficulty in holding apart its mighty opposites, God and Satan. Since William Blake, criticism has suspected that Milton was of the devil's party without knowing it. But perhaps the logic of Milton's epic depends on the way language works, as much as on the revolutionary sympathies of its author. The story requires its villain to be created good by a loving God, but susceptible to evil, turning in the process to hate, and capable of undergoing punishment for this disobedience. It is thus the devil who is shown as subject to temptation, capable of inner debate, able to suffer intensely. In order for the God of love to be everything that the devil is not, the poem makes God aloof, remote and inflexible and therefore, in certain respects at least, unloving. The differentiating other reappears where we should least expect it. Meanwhile, Satan paradoxically loves and therefore envies the Eden he destroys. But these doublings and reversals by no means constitute a weakness in Milton's poem. On the contrary, they turn the story he tells from a moral fable to a tragedy.

Can the epic's final stance be settled by an appeal to Milton's known radical sympathies? If we could date it with certainty, would we know how to read it in the light of a specific political context? Poststructuralism would say not. The only way to tease out the position it offers on authority and revolt would be by a meticulous attention to the textual details of the poem, and even then, since the signified is always deferred, not accessible, an element of undecidability would remain.

Paradise Lost is more widely admired than read these days, and in any case it might be argued that we hardly needed poststructuralism to identify its ambiguity. What, then, can be said about the classic detective stories that are in many respects its popular and secular descendants? Surely the works of, say, Agatha Christie offer the most straightforward, least ambiguous account we could hope to find of the opposition between good and evil? Crime is always brought to justice.

If Derrida's account of **differance** holds, however, we should expect to find an element of undecidability there too. In my view – and only a minute textual analysis would show for sure – while traditional crime fiction condemns murder as cruel and inhumane, it is often the inhumanity of the detective that it also puts on display. Justice's delegate is permitted no allegiances and, in the capacity of detective, no human sympathies. Like Milton's God, he or she must remain inflexible, capable of cruelty. Chillingly, even the fluttery Miss Marple has 'a mind like a bacon-slicer'. The virtue that binds the social fabric here is not compassion, but the relentless authority of an inhuman abstraction.

DESIRE

What draws us to works of art, or literature, or fiction? All known human societies seem to tell stories. Cave paintings are among the earliest extant instances of human culture, and since then people have widely chosen to decorate their walls, or surround themselves with images. Why?

Jacques Lacan consistently returned to the appeal of art, giving the question a central place in his *Seminars 7* and *11* (Lacan 1992, 1994). Cultural objects, he argued, allude to loss; they name or indicate the lack which also characterizes the human condition; and in the process they enlist desire.

According to Lacan's account, the accession to language entails both a gain and a loss. The little human animal, if we can imagine a child that is not already surrounded by signifying practices at birth, would be continuous with the organic world it inhabits, an undifferentiated part of it. But language, Lacan proposes, drawing on Saussure and, to a degree at least, anticipating Derrida, cuts off that direct relation to the world, in so far as the signifier interposes itself between us and our relation to things. The signifier, which differentiates and divides, offers a way to specify our wishes, but at the same time its advent divorces us from a direct apprehension of what Lacan calls 'the **real**'. The real is unnamed, unnameable, concealed in the shadows cast by the light language throws on the entities it denominates. The signifier names the referent in its absence; it thus relegates the real, obscures it, renders it missing from consciousness by taking its place. (Derrida would go on to deconstruct the opposition between presence and absence in his account of differance.)

At the same time, as human organisms we continue to inhabit this inaccessible real. In the speaking being, Lacan argues, unconscious desire emerges in the place of its loss. We long to fill the gap made by the lack of access to the real with something that would reunite us directly with the world, seeking a succession of objects of desire. It is easy to see how sex plays its part here, enlisting the human organism and the speaking subject inextricably in a love story, where the physiological activities of sex are also intelligible as signifiers. But Lacan insists that sex is not the *origin* of desire. Nor does it allay desire. None of our conscious objects of desire, including the sexual objects, will fully deliver the complete satisfaction they promise, since they cannot by definition replace what has been lost.

Art, Lacan argues, does not offer to replace it either. Art is thus not a substitute for love, as it tends to be in the work of his predecessor, Freud. Instead, it enables us to acknowledge the loss at the level of the signifier. Lacan understands the term 'art' in the broadest sense. (Again we encounter an inadequacy in a conventional vocabulary that distinguishes between high and popular culture, and between visual, aural and written texts.) As an example, he offers the work of the potter. A vase, for instance, he argues, operates on the real in exactly the same way as the signifier. It carves out of the continuity of the real a substance that surrounds a lack. Where there was previously an organic continuity, there is now a material object with nothing at its centre. The vase *makes* emptiness. Architecture works in a similar way: palaces and temples are a way of enclosing vacancy, their decorative surfaces fencing off the absence they both produce and surround. Perspective painting introduces the illusion of space into a continuous and two-dimensional canvas.

Art thus 'pacifies' desire by bringing its cause into the light of day. It puts on display not what is lost, which remains unnameable, but the fact of the loss itself, an analogy for the hollow at the heart of the speaking being. Ironically, then, the positive seduction of art for the viewer is the negativity it inscribes.

This is not necessarily a thematic negativity, though Lacan takes a special interest in tragedy, as well as the poetry of the troubadours, addressed to an absent, unattainable mistress. The lack at the heart of the work comes into existence whenever a signifying surface is shaped or decorated. Fiction, for instance, presupposes an absence. Even the most illusionist forms, the Victorian novels and narrative paintings, Hollywood movies and television soap operas that present themselves as a window onto a world we can believe we recognize, are no more, in the end, than signifiers surrounding vacancy. That is what fiction means. There is nothing beyond the signifiers themselves, the words on the page, paint on a canvas, the set, or the actors' impersonation of fictitious characters.

ENIGMA

Adapting this account, we might see the elusiveness of a substantial conclusion, a definitive reading or a final meaning as integral to art's appeal. What draws us to cultural texts in the first instance is the promise of closure, their offer to deliver an answer to the questions they raise, in conjunction with a reluctance to arrive at that moment, and a readiness to withhold the complete disclosure that would cause us to lose interest. Isn't the resolution of the plot always just slightly disappointing? To the degree that they sustain their mystery, texts also retain their fascination. Research indicates that very few people reread the last popular romance; instead, they prefer to start another. By contrast, the texts we return to again and again are more likely to be those that keep us guessing in some particular respect, or seem to conceal a secret we cannot finally master.

At the same time, if Derrida is right about differance, closure is never finally achieved. Even popular romances keep their options open to some extent, as I discovered when I noticed that, in accordance with the conventions of the genre, moments of passionate ecstasy are consistently defined in images of disaster: earthquakes, floods, tempests, fires (Belsey 1994: 21–41). Perhaps Lacan's insight is confirmed in this apparently most unlikely of quarters: pleasure entails naming a loss.

WHY READ?

If we go along with the poststructuralist view that closure is always ultimately withheld, is there any point in reading at all? If in due course we shall encounter undecidability everywhere, why bother?

It is a reasonable question. There are, in my view, two related answers to it: in the first place, reading can reveal the pleasures of the text; and in the second, while the world itself becomes increasingly undecidable, we make decisions none the less, and reading can expose the role of representation in the construction of choices.

First, then, if we allow that closure is not possible, one of the projects of interpretation becomes the attempt to resolve not the question the text itself raises, but the broader issue of the work's appeal to readers and viewers. Why have particular cultures or cultural moments been drawn to specific works more than others? What is it in *this* text that gives pleasure? What specific position does a particular text offer a reader? What knowledge does it withhold? What desire is indicated and pacified there?

The question of pleasure is one traditional criticism has preferred to evade, or to mystify by reference to 'great art'. That phrase has rightly become suspect, since it obscures a good deal more than it reveals, or dignifies a personal preference by an appeal to a supposed generality. The difference of 'art' becomes a value. Moreover, the term too readily turns prescriptive: a list of the criteria of great art carries the implication that we *ought* to like any work which fulfils them.

Poststructuralism offers the possibility of a more culturally relative account of the pleasure of the text, and permits us to differentiate between forms of pleasure without recourse to prior value judgements.

In the second place, society itself requires us to make decisions in a world that increasingly acknowledges undecidability in the areas that matter. Gender studies, for instance, pays more and more attention to the way the binary oppositions between two sexes do not hold in practice: the supposition of an antithesis between masculinity and femininity is giving way to the recognition of a range of differences. Postcolonial studies juxtapose the alternatives of assimilation, separatism and multiculturalism in the context of **globalization**: what are the differences we want to hold on to in an increasingly homogenized world? Justice is desirable but it includes an element that is inhuman: where do we stand? Dictatorship is out of the question, and yet we increasingly perceive the contradictions of democracy, where opinion is so easily constructed and antagonisms incited. The idea of opting out of all these undecidable questions is more and more attractive, until it becomes apparent that our actions inevitably align us one way or another, whether or not we have consciously decided to take a position. Even opting out represents a choice: to leave thing as they are.

There is no escape, then, even in a world of undecidability, from choosing, and the possibilities, which have material implications, are understood at the level of the signifier. In the poststructuralist account, fiction foregrounds this, makes it explicit. Poststructuralism repudiates the view that fiction *reflects* the world: the signifier constructs an illusion of reality not its **simulacrum**. At the same time, however, fiction repeatedly confronts its readers with choices. Which suitor would *you* marry? Which suspect would you blame? Which account would you rely on? The fictional characters decide – and readers decide whether they are right or wrong. These decisions are not always straightforward. King Lear makes the wrong choice; so does Othello. But what about Hamlet?

Cultural criticism offers a 'safe' environment to practise making choices. But more than this, in the process of posing alternatives, fiction, and perhaps all art, draws attention to the seductive and ambiguous capabilities of the signifier. We understand the world in relation to the way it is represented to us. We are not necessarily at the mercy of any one representation: although there is no understanding independent of the signifier, there is always more than one account of reality in circulation, and we are thus able to place ourselves outside what society presents as obvious.

Poststructuralism offers the reader an overt awareness of the complex and unstable positions offered by specific modes of address, and a recognition that all texts – including advertisements, news stories, religious exhortations and internet chat, as well as fiction – may be enlisting us in both more and less than we bargained for.

If so, poststructuralism, often presented by its detractors as an arcane, jargon-ridden mumbo-jumbo that has no purchase on the world, turns out to have a good deal more to say about life than might have seemed likely at first glance.

FURTHER READING

Barthes, Roland (1993) *Mythologies*, trans. Annette Lavers, London: Vintage.
First published in French in 1957, this book has now become part of what we take for granted, but without losing any of its wit and charm.

Barthes, Roland (1990a) *A Lover's Discourse: Fragments*, London: Penguin.
Demonstrates the intertextual derivation of our most intimate experiences.

Belsey, Catherine (2002a) *Critical Practice*, London: Routledge.
Makes the case for reading literary texts in the light of French theory, specifically the work of Louis Althusser, Pierre Macherey, Roland Barthes, Jacques Lacan and Jacques Derrida.

Belsey, Catherine (2002b) *Poststructuralism: A Very Short Introduction*, Oxford: Oxford University Press.
Does exactly what it says on the cover. It does not confine itself to the implications of poststructuralism for critical theory, but attends to its radical political implications, with particular reference to Michel Foucault and Jean-François Lyotard.

Belsey, Catherine (2005) *Culture and the Real: Theorizing Cultural Criticism*, London: Routledge.
Considers the implications of Lacan's account of culture for the process of interpreting texts, including film, visual art and fiction.

Derrida, Jacques (1998) *Monolingualism of the Other; or, The Prosthesis of Origin*, Stanford, CA; Stanford University Press.
As approachable as any Derrida, this short book foregrounds the concern with language that first made Derrida famous.

5

HISTORICISM

SIMON MALPAS

Defined in the most straightforward terms, one might say that historicist criticism of literature and culture explores how the meaning of a text, idea or artefact is produced by way of its relation to the wider historical context in which it is created or experienced. For historicism, all meaning is therefore historically determined. In other words, nothing means 'naturally', eternally or universally; rather, meaning emerges from the languages, beliefs, practices, institutions and desires of particular historically located cultures.

To students who have had much experience of critical, literary or cultural theory, this will probably appear to be a pretty straightforward and even commonsense claim. Nowadays, the critical approaches that lie at the basis of historicism have become some of the most prevalent techniques of reading in the humanities: they are frequently taken for granted in contemporary books and articles, are often introduced at the very beginning of degree programmes, and students tend to be expected to take notice of them (albeit usually implicitly) when they write essays. This was not always the case, however, but is rather, to a large extent, the outcome of the success of two key historicist movements in literary and cultural studies that began in the late 1970s and early 1980s and have come to dominate the humanities in the years since then: the predominantly American 'new historicism' and the mainly British '**cultural materialism**'. The aim of this chapter is to explore these two forms of contemporary historicist theory, to introduce the key theoretical tenets upon which they are based, to outline their shared premises and the points at which they differ, and to illustrate the ways in which they might be put to work in the processes of writing criticism. Before this, though, it will be useful to develop the very brief definition of historicism given in the last paragraph in some more detail so as to think through what historicism generally might entail, and to explore what its consequences might be for criticism.

A key difficulty in providing a brief introduction to historicism is that, in the words of Stephen Greenblatt, one of the founding and most well-respected exponents of the movement commonly referred to as 'new historicism', 'it's no doctrine at all' (Greenblatt 1989: 1), or, as the British critic Alan Sinfield puts it, it 'is not . . . a single approach but a bundle of preoccupations diversely elaborated' (Sinfield 1992: 7). If new historicism, a particular branch of historicist theory which will be introduced later, is 'a bundle of preoccupations' with 'no doctrine', then historicism as an entire **genre** of thought and writing whose exponents can be traced at least as far back as the eighteenth century is even more diverse.

Critics associated with historicism have worked in a number of disparate fields, have numerous theoretical and political affiliations, explore many different sorts of topic, and can often come to markedly dissimilar conclusions about apparently similar texts and contexts. As Greenblatt and Catherine Gallagher point out, 'historicism is not a coherent, close-knit school in which one might be enrolled or from which one might be expelled' (Gallagher and Greenblatt 2000: 2), nor is it 'a repeatable methodology or a literary critical program' (Gallagher and Greenblatt 2000: 19). Because historicism is neither a univocal methodology nor the product of a single 'school', it does not have an entirely systematic or programmatic approach to culture based on the application of a set of pre-given theoretical premises that can simply be applied to texts to generate readings. Although contemporary historicist critics frequently cite the French theorist Michel **Foucault** (1926–84) as a key source for their work, and have drawn extensively on a range of other recent critical theories from structuralism and poststructuralism to **Marxism**, feminism and deconstruction, as well as the work of earlier historians such as Giambattista Vico (1668–1744) and Johann Gottfried von Herder (1744–1803), their readings tend to focus explicitly upon what Gallagher and Greenblatt identify as the 'encounter with the singular, the specific, and the individual' (Gallagher and Greenblatt 2000: 6) in order to explore the historically and culturally specific production of meaning in a text, and therefore shy away from (or explicitly refuse) generalized theoretical principles. Despite this, however, there do seem to be a number of methodological premises that are shared by many exponents of historicism that might helpfully be set out.

HISTORICISM

To gain a sense of what historicism is, it helps to begin by saying what it is not. The key idea from which historicism differentiates itself is the notion that there are natural, divine or other fundamental laws that define eternally the essential truths of human existence. The idea, for example, of an innate human nature given by God or biology presents a universal essence shared by us all, towards which rational thought must strive if everyone is to achieve the true knowledge of, and freedom to become, who they truly are. While versions of history might be, and have been, written on the basis of such laws to show, for example, the constancy of human identity over time, or the inevitable progress of knowledge towards a final religious or secular **enlightenment**, historical change tends in these accounts to be presented as comparatively superficial or contingent, and what is fundamental is continuity. In contrast to this, historicism sees change itself as fundamental and inevitable, liable to impinge upon a society's most fundamental beliefs about itself, and always capable of transforming what currently appears to be stable, fixed and continuous. While the non-historicist analysis of a culture will tend to judge how closely that culture comes to matching the fundamental laws to which the analysis holds, and judge its success or failure in relation to them, historicism refuses the very basis for such judgements. Historicism is therefore much more interested in examining the processes of change, and the ways in which particular periods or cultures construct the systems of **power**, morality and meaning through which they can understand themselves.

For historicism, then, a key point to explore is the ways in which meanings have changed through history. The twin ideas that meaning is not natural but is rather produced by the rules and structures inherent in a particular language or signifying system, and that these rules and structures are open to change, are perhaps two of the most crucial premises of both structuralism and poststructuralism. These ideas are developed explicitly in Ferdinand de **Saussure**'s structuralist theory in his *Course in General Linguistics*, where he argues that the meaning of a linguistic **sign** emerges from an arbitrary (and thus culturally – and historically – produced) relation between its **signifier** and **signified**, and that the meaning of a particular utterance (*parole*) is given by the language structure (*langue*) in which it occurs. Historicism as a critical practice, even in the forms that appeared before the linguistic theories of structuralism were first formalized by Saussure, also holds firmly to these premises, and sets out to explore the consequences of them for our understanding of history. We might straightforwardly say, then, that historicism is the practice of interpreting texts on the basis of the idea that their meanings are generated by the historical contexts in which they are located, and that these contexts change as history moves on. This relatively clear-cut claim, however, has a range of implications, not just for the study of particular cultural texts but for broader questions of identity, society, politics and interpretation.

In the introduction to his book *Historicism*, the critic Paul Hamilton provides a clear and straightforward definition of historicism, and argues that it has a double focus:

> Historicism . . . is a critical movement insisting on the prime importance of historical context to the interpretation of texts of all kinds . . . Firstly, it is concerned to situate any statement – philosophical, historical, aesthetic or whatever – in its historical context. Secondly, it typically doubles back on itself to explore the extent to which any historical enterprise inevitably reflects the interests and bias of the period in which it was written. On the one hand, therefore, historicism is suspicious of the stories the past tells about itself; on the other hand, it is equally suspicious of its own partisanship.
>
> (Hamilton 1996: 3)

The first point of focus that Hamilton identifies states clearly that nothing means in isolation: one cannot take a text or an idea and simply lift it out of the contexts in which it was produced so as to claim that it always has and always will mean 'this' in and of itself. Rather, any meanings that a text might have are always related to the much wider cultural, political, economic and social institutions and practices of its context. Even those ideas that appear to us as most natural and fundamental, such as 'humanity', 'truth' or 'justice', or most obvious, such as the difference between 'man' and 'woman', have acquired different meanings for different cultures and epochs, and are likely to continue to change in the new historical contexts of the future. For the historicist critic, then, there are no eternal meanings or truths that exist entirely outside the processes of historical change: all meaning is historically mutable because it is situated in and generated by its context. To properly understand a text from the past, we must explore it in terms of the meanings and ideas that were in circulation in the context from which it emerged, and the more rigorously we do this the more nuanced our understanding will become. So, to give just one brief example, the depiction of the protagonist of Charles Dickens' novel *Oliver Twist* (1838) as an angelic child who remains finally uncorrupted by the degradations and dangers to which he is subjected, might for the historicist best be understood by exploring the relationship between this representation and the wide range of other Victorian discourses about childhood, innocence, class and morality. This would not simply include other literary representations of childhood, although of course these would be important, but would also encompass legal, philosophical, theological, economic, educational, biographical and suchlike non-literary contexts which, through their similarities to and differences from *Oliver Twist*, might help us to understand the ways in which Dickens reflects, questions and challenges Victorian ideas of the child. Only in relation to this background, a historicist might claim, can we understand what sort of character Oliver is, and what the novel is actually about.

The second part of Hamilton's definition develops from the first to reveal some of its more complex ramifications for historicist practice. Our own processes of reading and understanding also take place in a particular historical context, which is tied up with its own social, economic and political pressures and investments. As critics we cannot simply stand outside of this context and adopt a 'God's-eye view' of a text; we must also question the historically produced assumptions of the contemporary culture in which our readings take place. It is therefore not just the meanings of ideas and texts from the past that are open to question, but also the meanings that those ideas or texts might have acquired today, which are no more 'natural' or 'true' than older ones. In other words, the historicist critic's approach to a text is not based upon a judgement of whether its meaning is any longer true or false, or whether its mode of representing the world is more or less 'correct' than our contemporary modes, but rather sets out to explore the extent to which the meanings the text produces appear to have changed or stayed the same, if they have remained central to contemporary debates or have become hidden assumptions that lie behind what today appear to be natural ways of experiencing and thinking about the world. To return to the example of *Oliver Twist*, the historicist critic might self-reflexively question contemporary representations of the child, explore the extent to which the Victorian ideals that the novel adopts and questions remain current in today's culture, discuss how it might disrupt modern discourses about childhood and education, and ask what we might learn from rereading Dickens at the beginning of the twenty-first century.

This twofold focus, on both the context in which the text was first produced and the contemporary contexts of its reception, lies at the heart of historicist criticism and forms the basis of its approach to history, literature, art, politics and identity. The political stakes of this are summed up succinctly by Jonathan Dollimore and Alan Sinfield in the foreword to what quickly became one of the founding texts of cultural materialism when it was published in 1985, *Political Shakespeare: New Essays in Cultural Materialism*:

> Cultural materialism therefore studies the implication of literary texts in history. A play by Shakespeare is related to the contexts of its production – to the economic and political system of Elizabethan and Jacobean England and to the particular institutions of cultural production (the court, patronage, theatre, education, the church). Moreover, the relevant history is not just that of four hundred years ago, for culture is made continuously and Shakespeare's text is reconstructed, reappraised, reassigned all the time through diverse institutions in specific contexts . . . That is why [cultural materialism] discusses also the institutions through which Shakespeare is reproduced and through which interventions may be made in the present . . . Cultural materialism does not, like much established literary criticism, attempt to mystify its perspective as the natural, obvious or right interpretation of an allegedly given textual fact. On the contrary, it registers its commitment to the transformation of a social order which exploits people on the grounds of race, gender and class.
>
> (Dollimore and Sinfield 1985: viii)

For Dollimore and Sinfield, what the historicist approach offers is a way of making available for criticism ideas that might at first appear natural by showing how they have been employed differently in earlier periods. By questioning the circulation of meanings in terms of their economic and institutional modes of production, literary and cultural texts can be read to explore the faultlines in a society's self-representations so that the ways in which that society's power to construct and control the identities, beliefs, aspirations and desires of its subjects can become explicit. In brief, then, we might say that the central aim of historicism is not to discover universal truths or eternal verities, but rather to open such ideas up to critique by exploring the ways in which they are products of specific historical circumstances and function as sources of political power and control both in those circumstances and in the present.

If the key aim of historicist analysis is to denaturalize the eternal and universal by investigating its historically mediated deployments and thereby making them available for critique, it is important to try to grasp precisely how this sort of reading might be undertaken. To this end, the aim of the next two sections of this chapter is to introduce in some more detail the ways in which the two key contemporary forms of historicism, new historicism and cultural materialism, set out to fulfil this task.

NEW HISTORICISM

New historicism first emerged in literary studies towards the end of the 1970s from a context in which **new criticism** was the dominant theoretical framework for the work of scholars and students in literature departments. New criticism, in its broadest sense, focuses on the formal production of meaning in a text and, through processes of close reading that investigate the text's use of imagery, metaphor, symbol and tone to produce accounts of a work as a richly textured but coherent organic unity, tends to conceive of literature as something best understood separately from its social or political context, and even from the context of everyday language and identity. The result of this sort of approach to literature is that new critics tend to see a text as a 'verbal icon' (Wimsatt 1970) or 'well wrought urn' (Brooks 1968) that is self-enclosed, self-sufficient, cut off from the day-to-day interests of the world, and whose meaning can be gleaned from an understanding of the formal interactions of the poetic or narratalogical devices it employs. In contrast to this, new historicism insists that texts are part of the everyday, are firmly embedded in the institutions and power relations of general culture, that there is no separate realm of poetic utterance, and that such formal isolation drains literature and culture of any political or social importance. Only by refusing to separate artistic expression from other forms of social and cultural interaction, new historicists have argued, can art or literature come to be meaningful or important to us at all.

Perhaps the most important theoretical source for new historicism's challenge to new critical orthodoxy can be found in the work of Michel Foucault. It is, in fact, difficult to overestimate his influence on either new historicism or cultural materialism. In a series of works that explore the ways in which identities are constructed, policed and subverted by investigating such aspects of society as the clinic and the prison and such groups as the insane, the criminal and the sexually deviant, Foucault's writing questions the ways in which our contemporary social order has been produced, is maintained, and might be transformed. New historicists have drawn three key premises from this work: the idea that history is discontinuous, the argument that a given period is better understood as a site of conflict between competing interests and discourses than as a unified whole, and the redefinition of the role and function of power. Foucault rejects the idea that history marks a single continuous progress or development, and sees it based on discontinuity: history, he claims, is made up of 'different series, which are juxtaposed to one another, follow one another, overlap and intersect, without one being able to reduce them to a linear schema', so that discontinuity 'has now become one of the basic elements of history' (Foucault 2002: 8). This, as I tried to show in the previous section, is the central premise of historicism: the idea that historical continuity as a unified and progressive movement must be replaced by the investigation of history's discontinuities, breaks and ruptures. Because of this non-progressive movement between and overlapping of different series of discursive 'world-views', Foucault argues, it is simply incorrect to reduce the ideas and practices of a particular moment to a single unifying vision. This means that the idea, for example, of an 'Elizabethan World Picture' (see Tillyard 1943) that can be described in terms of a closed set of overarching beliefs governing a particular period must be replaced by the description of a period as a site of conflict in which 'a multiplicity of discursive elements that can come into play in various strategies' (Foucault 1984: 100) must be disentangled and analysed. In order to do this, the critic or historian must explore this multiplicity in terms of the ways in which power is produced, deployed and harnessed for particular interests. Foucault's analysis of power is perhaps one of his most important contributions to contemporary theory, and is essential to both new historicism and cultural materialism. He argues that power 'is not something that is acquired, seized, or shared, something that one holds on to or allows to slip away; power is exercised from innumerable points, in the interplay of nonegalitarian and mobile relations' (Foucault 1984: 94). Power, in other words, is not simply something held by a ruling class of society and imposed upon those below them, but is at work in all interactions, conflicts and communications: 'Power is everywhere; not because it embraces everything, but because it comes from everywhere ... It is the name that one attributes to a complex strategical situation in a particular society' (Foucault 1984: 93). What Foucault means by this is that power is immanent to all of the experiences and interactions that take place in society, and yet always remains unstable because every deployment of power generates resistances. The aim of his work, then, is to carefully disentangle the myriad ways in which power is produced and organized in a society or period, how it circulates in that culture to generate particular identities and institutions, and how alternative ways of thinking and being, resistances, might be made available.

The immediate effect for new historicism's analyses of literature and culture of Foucault's insistence upon the idea of history as a discontinuous process of conflict as different social discourses and institutions struggle for power is that, as the American literary critic H. Aram Veeser puts it, 'every expressive act is embedded in a network of material practices' and that 'literary and non-literary "texts" circulate inseparably' (Veeser 1989: xi). In other words, art and literature do not merely reflect the ideas, beliefs and desires of a society in a disinterested manner; they are shaped by them and are actively involved in sustaining or challenging them. Like any other discourse, literature and culture are sites of power and resistance. To explore this slightly further, it is useful briefly to discuss three specific consequences that arise from this approach to history and culture: first, new historicism's rejection of the idea of **authorial** genius; second, its disruption of established **canons** of great works; and, third, the ways in which literary and non-literary texts are related to each other.

The first consequence of this argument is that the idea that a work of art or literature is solely created by an individual artistic genius is rejected. The author or artist does not create the work entirely from the resources of their own imagination, but employs the ideas, vocabularies and beliefs of her or his culture to produce a work which that culture can understand. According to Greenblatt, 'the work of art is the product of a negotiation between a creator or class of

61

creators, equipped with a complex, communally shared repertoire of conventions, and the institutions and practices of society' (Greenblatt 1989: 12). In this way, the act of imagination or inspiration that allows a work of art or literature to be created is to be analysed not as some mystical force belonging to a genius, but as a function of the circulation of social discourses in which the artist or writer is as deeply embedded as any other person.

A second consequence is that traditional ideas of a canon of art or literature, an established list of great works or books that depict universal human values for all time, are challenged and opened up to include other works that 'have been hitherto denigrated or ignored' and 'also change the account of those authors long treated as canonical' (Gallagher and Greenblatt 2000: 10). Under the influence of new historicist (as well as feminist and postcolonial) criticism, the range of texts studied in literature, art and cultural studies has expanded rapidly. To give just one brief illustration, literary study of the Romantic period has moved away from a focus entirely on the canon of the 'big six' (Blake, Wordsworth, Coleridge, Shelley, Keats and Byron) with a few 'lesser writers' as background material, to rediscover and explore the work of a much wider range of texts including those by women, working-class, British non-English and colonial writers, to investigate genres other than poetry, to discuss the ways in which aesthetic, social and political categories were defined, reproduced and subverted during the period, and to question the **ideological** power that a category such as Romanticism has come to carry. In other words, it is not just a question of historicism expanding the canon by 'discovering' new authors; rather, it is a matter of fundamentally redefining the ways in which art and literature were produced, experienced and valued during the period. On this basis, for example, the American new historicist Jerome McGann is able to argue that new criticism constructed an image of Romanticism as a unified movement to support its own ideological beliefs about the value and function of literature; put bluntly, its readings of the period's poetry did not reveal Romanticism's true nature but produced a 'Romantic ideology' (McGann 1985) that historicist criticism should question and contest.

As well as breaking away from the idea of a straightforward distinction between the canonical and non-canonical in art and literature, new historicism also explores the relations between artistic and non-artistic texts in ways that open both up to question. According to Gallagher and Greenblatt, this sort of approach can

> suggest hidden links between high cultural texts, apparently detached from any direct engagement with their immediate cultural surroundings, and texts very much in and of our world, such as documents of social control and political subversion. It can weaken the primacy of classic works of art in relation to other competing or surrounding textual traces from the past. Or, alternatively, it can highlight the process by which such works achieve both prominence and a certain partial independence.

(Gallagher and Greenblatt 2000: 10–11)

Instead of treating non-artistic material as factual background for a reading of literature, new historicism treats the contextual material as text: the critic reads and analyses the signifying practices of legal, social, political, economic and other non-literary documents such as diaries or letters in the same ways, and with similar attention to rhetorical structures and narrative strategies, that earlier critical approaches had employed in their discussions of literature. So, for example, Greenblatt's essay, 'Invisible Bullets: Renaissance Authority and its Subversion, *Henry IV* and *Henry V*', discusses Shakespeare's plays in the light of readings of a wide variety of texts including records of atheism trials, police reports, a tract entitled *A Manifest Detection of the Moste Vyle and Detestable Use of Diceplay*, and the Elizabethan mathematician Thomas Harriot's *A Brief and True Report of the New Found Land of Virginia* to explore the relations between sovereign authority, religious doctrine and the processes of colonization. Each of the texts included in Greenblatt's essay is read with close attention to its signifying practices, and his argument develops from the relations between these practices in the different texts to explore the rhetorical production of state power and its potential for subversion.

Some critics have charged new historicism with being simply anecdotal, in that it appears able to move freely and apparently arbitrarily between such different genres of writing and representation, and does not provide an entirely comprehensive account of a particular movement or period. In many ways this is true, as the list of texts in the last example might suggest, but it also seems to miss the point. If history is no longer conceived as an organized progress of coherent world-views but rather as discontinuous, then such comprehensive accounts become impossible at best or, at worst, repetitions of dominant ideologies. The anecdotal, by forging links between texts, becomes a means by which those ideas and voices excluded by such ideologies can be traced and analysed.

Another criticism of new historicism comes from a different perspective, that of cultural materialism. Alan Sinfield differentiates cultural materialism from new historicism by arguing that the latter 'has been drawn to what I call the "entrapment model" of ideology and power, whereby even, or especially, man-oeuvres that seem designed to challenge the system help to maintain it' (Sinfield 1992: 39). While this might be true of an essay like Greenblatt's 'Invisible Bullets', which closes with the claim that 'There is subversion, no end of subversion, only not for us' (Greenblatt 1985: 45), it is not a categorical differentiation between the two discourses which share a lot of common premises, but rather indicates a tendency of each to see its project slightly differently. It is through this tendency that I should now like to introduce cultural materialism.

CULTURAL MATERIALISM

Although there are numerous continuities between cultural materialism and new historicism, and a whole set of shared methodological premises, perhaps the key difference between the former and the predominantly British critics and theorists associated with the latter is cultural materialism's focus on the questions of class, ideology and economy that are associated with Marxism. The main reason for this is the influence on contemporary British theory of the thinker who coined the term 'cultural materialism', Raymond **Williams**. Like new historicists, Williams insists that art and literature 'may have quite specific features as practices, but they cannot be separated from the general social processes' of a society (Williams 1980: 44). However, he develops this insight from a broadly Marxist perspective to argue that 'no dominant social order and therefore no dominant culture ever in reality includes or exhausts all human practice, human energy and human intention' (Williams 1977: 125), and that the focus for criticism should be the ways in which such dominant orders are continually negotiating with residual and emergent orders that threaten to undermine them. This produces a materialist model of culture that sees it as continually in transition and makes space for the forms of subversion that Sinfield sees as lacking in new historicism.

Cultural materialist criticism frequently sees its task as identifying 'faultlines' in the dominant social orders: Sinfield writes 'Despite their power, dominant ideological formations are always, in practice, under pressure, striving to substantiate their claim to superior plausibility in the face of disturbance' (Sinfield 1992: 41), and exploring these moments of pressure is a way for criticism to allow other possibilities and distributions of power to become apparent. An example of the analysis of such 'faultlines' can be seen at work in Catherine Belsey's book *The Subject of Tragedy: Identity and Difference in Renaissance Drama* (1985). Here Belsey investigates the ways in which subjectivity and gendered identity were produced in the Renaissance by reading closely not just the rhetorical strategies of Elizabethan drama but also those of popular ballads, conduct books, political proclamations and legal documents. What this book develops is an account of the English Renaissance as a complex formation in which different discourses and institutions jostle for power over the definition of the newly emerging sense of modern identity, particularly female identity. Belsey analyses the ways in which Renaissance tragedy becomes a site of conflict between residual medieval ideas of identity and the burgeoning ideas of modern capitalism, and shows how the plays do not present coherent totalities but conflicting visions of different forms of subjectivity that borrow rhetorical strategies from other social documents and produce a sense of identity that is fragmented. The point of this, she argues, in a typically cultural materialist formulation, is to demonstrate that apparently natural ideas about identity handed down to us from the Renaissance are politically produced and therefore open to criticism, and that such criticism might allow us 'to begin the struggle for change' in our own culture (Belsey 1985: 221).

As I said at the beginning of this chapter, historicism has rapidly become one of the key methodologies of contemporary theoretical analysis. Although both new historicism and cultural materialism emerged in Renaissance literary criticism, with texts such as Greenblatt's *Renaissance Self-Fashioning: From More to Shakespeare* (1980), Belsey's *The Subject of Tragedy* and Dollimore and

Sinfield's *Political Shakespeare*, their impact can now be felt across the humani-ties. To cite just two of the most important points at which it has intersected with and influenced other areas, one might point to Gayatri Chakravorty **Spivak**'s postcolonial analyses of the distributions of knowledge, power and ideology in **colonialism** in her book *In Other Worlds: Essays in Cultural Politics* (1988) in which she discusses the ways in which the colonial subject is constructed in literature, culture and society. Equally, Jonathan Dollimore's *Sexual Dissidence: Augustine to Wilde, Freud to Foucault* (1991) investigates the 'perverse dynamic' at work in the construction of sexual norms and the idea of deviancy in a way that has been taken up by a number of critics working on questions of gender outside of specifically literary studies. What began, then, as a branch of Renaissance literary criticism has come to be one of the most important and influential critical methodologies in the humanities. Historicism in its various forms has redefined both literary critical practice and cultural studies to demonstrate the centrality of history to ideas of meaning, identity and politics.

FURTHER READING

Colebrook, Claire (1997) *New Literary Histories: New Historicism and Contemporary Criticism*, Manchester: Manchester University Press.

This clearly written and lucid book provides a helpful overview of the wide range of different theoretical currents in contemporary historicist criticism, and relates them to other forms of theory.

Gallagher, Catherine and Greenblatt, Stephen (2000) *Practicing New Historicism*, Chicago, IL and London: University of Chicago Press.

This book by two of the key exponents of new historicism sets out some of its key ideas by investigating both the theoretical premises on which it is based and providing a number of quite fascinating practical examples of new historicist criticism.

Hamilton, Paul (1996) *Historicism*, London: Routledge.

This is a very widely ranging study of historicism from its emergence in the eighteenth century to its contemporary forms. It is clear, insightful, and probably one of the best places to start to get a sense of the genre as a whole.

Sinfield, Alan (1992) *Faultlines: Cultural Materialism and the Politics of Dissident Reading*, Oxford: Clarendon Press.

This is probably one of the most lucid accounts of the political and textual strategies employed in cultural materialist criticism. Through a range of readings of Renaissance and contemporary texts, Sinfield investigates the ways in which criticism can identify and put to work disruption and dissidence to challenge modern ideologies.

Veeser, H. Aram (ed.) (1989) *The New Historicism*, London: Routledge.

This early collection of new historicist essays by a range of important critics provides a detailed picture of the different approaches critics have taken, as well as including key definitions of the genre by such thinkers as Veeser, Gallagher, Greenblatt and Spivak.

6

PSYCHOANALYTIC CRITICISM

ROB LAPSLEY

Many people are afflicted by forms of psychological distress: anxiety, depression, phobias and other ailments. Psychoanalysis attempts to ease their pain through talking, hence its description as 'the talking cure'. Patients are invited to free-associate: that is, to say whatever comes into their heads however silly or embarrassing it may be. In so doing they relive the formative experiences of their lives and discover different and happier ways of dealing with them. It was initiated as a therapeutic technique by Sigmund **Freud** (1856–1939) in Vienna at the end of the nineteenth century and was subsequently developed by a host of practitioners, most notably Jacques **Lacan** (1901–81). Since its inception its influence has extended far beyond clinical practice and has profoundly informed thinking in art, culture, philosophy, politics and society. After introducing the work of the pivotal figures of psychoanalytic theory, I will conclude by outlining the continuing debates around the value of psychoanalysis.

SIGMUND FREUD

Sigmund Freud, the founder of psychoanalysis, specialized in the treatment of what were then termed 'hysterics': patients, almost invariably women, who suffered from a variety of disabling conditions such as hallucinations, nervous tics, pains and paralyses. After failing to cure them through hypnosis, he simply let them talk. Listening to and learning from them, he made his first significant discovery, namely that in each case the source of the problem was sexual. Take the case of Elizabeth von R set out in *Studies in Hysteria* (1895). She was referred to Freud because pains in her leg, for which there was no evident physical cause, made walking difficult. While thoroughly examining the thighs of this 24-year-old woman, Freud noticed that she lay back, closed her eyes and seemed to be experiencing some sort of sexual pleasure. Alerted by this unexpected reaction, Freud began to investigate the nature of her sexuality. It quickly became apparent to him that she was passionately attached to her symptom; it afforded her some form of sexual satisfaction. This immediately raised the question: why did she have to find sexual pleasure in such an unhappy way? Freud hypothesized that it was because her **desire** had taken a form that was unbearable to her. This inference was confirmed when she confessed her desire for her brother-in-law.

Elizabeth's life had been very unhappy. She had exhausted herself nursing her beloved father through his long and fatal illness. After his death she became increasingly isolated when her two sisters married and left home. Lonely and despairing, she came to envy her younger sister's marital happiness. A conversation during a long walk with her brother-in-law only confirmed her sense that her sister was the most fortunate of women. Consequently as she stood watching her sister dying from complications attendant on her second pregnancy, she did not think 'How terrible for her, mother and her child', but 'Good, now I can marry him.' Horrified at the nature of her desire, she immediately repressed this thought. The result was the onset of her symptom in its most crippling form. Although she was no longer aware of the nature of her desire at a conscious level, Freud, reading between the lines of what she said, guessed the truth. During a long and difficult treatment Freud helped her remember that her symptom first emerged after the walk with her brother-in-law. When subsequently she recalled the thought at her sister's deathbed, which had so appalled her, the symptom gradually began to lift.

Freud had made his greatest discovery: the existence of the **unconscious** mind. Elizabeth von R. and other cases convinced him that there is a part of the human mind whose contents are unknown to us at a conscious level. In its developed form Freud's theory was as follows: a child is necessarily brought up in accordance with the ideals of its parents (it is impossible to rear a child without saying, 'Do this', 'Don't do that' and thereby holding out an ideal to it). As the child is helpless and totally dependent on its parents, it is desperate for their love. Consequently it identifies with what it takes to be their ideal, imagines that it can embody its parents' aspirations and represses the impulses and desires which are not simply at odds, but utterly incompatible, with being 'a good little girl or boy'.

Freud's elaboration of the notion of the unconscious constituted a Copernican revolution in European thought. Previously many thinkers, taking their lead from the French philosopher, René Descartes, had believed that, whatever our doubts about the nature of external reality, we knew with complete clarity the contents of our own minds. Freud disabused them of this illusion. Not only is there an unconscious, a part of the mind to which we have no conscious access, but unconscious irrational forces inform our thought and behaviour in ways of which we are unaware. We know not what we do.

Repression is the beginning not the end of the story. Every repressed representation of a sexual desire – for example, 'Good, now I can marry him' – is invested with sexual, what Freud termed libidinal, energy and that repudiated energy has to find an outlet. As its direct expression is inadmissible ('good' people are deemed not to harbour such wishes), it has to find a form of expression acceptable to the mind's censor: what Freud, at this juncture, called the **ego**. In the case of Elizabeth it found expression in her symptom. As Freud divined, her symptom afforded her sexual pleasure; while at a conscious level she experienced pain, at an unconscious level she enjoyed it. Her symptom was, therefore, a compromise between her desire and her sense of what was right; it allowed her desire expression but in a form so painful her guilt was attenuated and rendered bearable.

Symptoms are only one form of compromise formation. Jokes, slips of the tongue and most famously dreams also represent compromises between desire and the law. Superficially most dreams seem both trivial and absurd but in *The Interpretation of Dreams* (1900) Freud argued that this is mere appearance. Like the pain in the symptom the apparent nonsense disguises the sexual desires at work and enables those desires to circumvent the censoring ego. Dreams, like symptoms, allow repressed sexual desires a form of expression and thereby afford sexual satisfaction. For example, a patient dreamt he saw his brothers and sisters playing in a field when suddenly they grew wings and flew away. According to Freud this manifest content – what the patient remembered of the dream after waking – masked the hidden, latent content, namely the patient's unconscious desire for the death of his siblings (in the dream they became angels and went to heaven) so that he could have exclusive possession of his parents' love. Since this desire was as abhorrent to the patient's ego as 'Good, now I can marry him' was to Elizabeth's, it had been repressed, but, just as her repressed desire returned in the symptom, so his returned in the dream.

The repressed always returns. This is most evident in slips of the tongue. In the business of living people often say something other than what they intend. In many cases this is easily explained: something the speaker wishes to silence insists on being heard. For example, I recently attended a funeral during which the priest, overcome with emotion at the loss of a particularly close friend, said, 'The power of God draws grief, sorry, I mean joy, from the grief of death.' Thus, contrary to her intentions, her sorrow had its say. It is Freud's contention that unconscious desires find similar routes to expression. If, in the case of Elizabeth, repressed desire spoke in the symptom, in many other cases it is more audible in slips of the tongue.

Two objections will immediately be advanced in relation to Elizabeth: first, her case is a special one – not everyone is in love with an in-law and, second, her desire for her brother-in-law was not really unconscious because, with Freud's help, she was able to recall it. To understand a Freudian defence to these charges we must consider his theory of sexuality.

In his *Three Essays on Sexuality* (1905) Freud argued that human sexuality, unlike animal sexuality, is not biologically pre-programmed. Although from birth every human being is inhabited by sexual energy (libido) pressing for satisfaction, the modes of satisfaction found are not pre-determined. Rather the aims and goals of sexual desire are determined by each person's individual history (few people find sexual satisfaction in thigh pain). Thus for Freud at this period sexual desire was so malleable and mutable that it could assume a near infinity of forms.

Elsewhere, however, he conceived of desire as more narrowly channelled. Again his theory developed from 'listening' to his patients. A troubling number of them reported sexual abuse by their parents, usually the father. Appalled by the scale of abuse, Freud hypothesized that, although there was some truth in his patients' narratives, they were more fiction than fact; the overlay of fantasy was crucial. 'Confirmation' of this supposition came during his self-analysis, when the latent content of one of his own dreams revealed that he had been in love with his mother and been jealous of his father. He concluded that in many cases the reported rapes and seductions were not 'real events' but, like his dream, expressions of repressed sexual desires. Given that many of these patients were almost certainly abused, this, in a field of strong candidates, was arguably Freud's biggest mistake. However, it eventually lead him to formulate his most notorious concept: the **Oedipus complex**.

At its simplest the Oedipus complex is the notion that every child sexually desires a parent and wishes to be rid of its rival, the other parent. It provides the answer to the objections lodged earlier: behind Elizabeth's desire for her brother-in-law lay the desire for a more ancient transgressive love object, namely her father (the pain in her leg was situated at precisely the point where he had rested his diseased leg while she bandaged it). This desire remained unconscious but had its say in the form of her symptom.

Even today the notion of the Oedipus complex has the power to shock, but in certain aspects at least it is uncontroversial. Two aspects should be borne in mind. In the first place Freud uses the term 'sexuality' in a much broader sense than everyday usage; it encompasses not only the pleasures the **subject** takes in its own and other bodies but also all affective (roughly emotional) bonds and attachments. As such it is far from confined to genital activity. Second, the other subjects to whom the child relates are largely fantasy figures; the parental figures, who populate the child's **imaginary**, whether monstrous or quasi-divine, bear little resemblance to those perceived from the vantage point of adulthood. Thus to say the child sexually desires the mother is simply to say that the child has a profound and possessive emotional attachment to her. In other words Freud's theory is little more than a statement of the obvious: our most intense attachments occur in early infancy, are formed in relation to figures as seen at that age, and long after childhood continue to shape and orientate our subsequent emotional development. The disappointment of many men and women in each other is attributable to the failure of their partner to measure up to the unforgettable, idealized, imaginary figures of their psychic prehistory. Could Elizabeth ever meet a man comparable to her imaginary father?

That said, crucial details of Freud's hypothesis do remain highly controversial. Indeed it is arguable that Freud never succeeded in formulating an entirely plausible account. Relatively speaking the boy's trajectory is straightforward. He is set the task of mastering and repressing the desire for exclusive sexual possession of his mother and the death of his rivals, above all the father. This becomes possible when he perceives that the girl does not possess a penis. Interpreting this lack as the result of castration, he concludes that he may suffer a similar fate at the hands of his father unless he renounces his incestuous desire for the mother and assumes the social role and identity demanded by his father. He consequently abandons his desire to usurp the father and seeks another love object, while finding compensation in an identification with an idealized version of his father. However, resolution of the complex is never complete; repressed

Oedipal desires return in compromise formations such as dreams, jokes and symptoms and inform the boy's later sexual life. Freud claimed something analogous happens with girls but his argument faced an apparently insuperable problem: if, as he sees it, girls are already 'castrated', why should they renounce their first love object, the mother? Boys do so because of the threat of castration but as girls are already 'castrated' they face no such threat. No persuasive answer to this problem was forthcoming from Freud or any of his followers.

Implicit in the above is a theory of art and literature, for both can be viewed as compromise formations in which repressed desires find expression in a socially acceptable form. Texts are thus as much unconscious as conscious creations, articulating unconscious desires they struggle to contain. Freud himself used the example of *Hamlet*. Why, he asked, did Hamlet, who was so decisive in dealing with Polonius, Rosencrantz and Guildenstern, hesitate to kill Claudius? His explanation was that Hamlet too had desired his father's death. Therefore in striking Claudius he would be striking himself. Significantly, when Hamlet does enact his Oedipal desire to kill his mother's lover he too is killed. Thus the play, like Elizabeth's symptom, is a compromise formation: just as Elizabeth expressed her desire and at the same time punished herself for it so Hamlet acts on Shakespeare's Oedipal impulse and is in turn punished. Inspired by this reading and Freud's analyses of such artists as Leonardo da Vinci and Fyodor Dostoevsky, generations of psychoanalytic critics have discovered behind the manifest content of artworks a latent content of forbidden sexual desires. The problem with such analyses is that they sell texts short: at the latent level they predictably and tediously always find the same repertoire of castration motifs. It turned out that just about everybody – Shelley, Poe, Carroll, James, Woolf, Joyce *et al.* – had problems with their mothers or fathers or both. Texts in all their differences become the same.

Intelligent psychoanalytic criticism seeks to avoid such reductionism. First it acknowledges the importance of form. In so doing it follows Freud's own thinking in relation to jokes. For Freud jokes are compromise formations; most articulate repressed sexual and or aggressive impulses, but they do so in a disguised form which is socially acceptable. But form is even more important than this suggests. If any joke is reduced to its content the humour evaporates. Consider the apocryphal story of the Queen Mother visiting an old people's home. Disconcerted by their lack of respect, she asked one resident, 'Do you know who I am?' 'No', came the reply, 'but if you go to reception they'll tell you.' Whatever humour this story possesses disappears if it is reduced to either its manifest content – the Queen Mother was mistaken for a patient suffering from dementia – or its latent content – aggression towards an authority, i.e. parental figure. Similarly, if literary texts are reduced to their supposed content, whether manifest or latent, their 'magic' disappears. As Freud observed in 'Creative Writers and Daydreams' (1908), to be socially acceptable artworks have to disguise their articulation of the artists' conscious and unconscious desires through formal devices. Without what Freud termed the 'fore-pleasure' afforded by this

Borrowed Items 09/12/2018 15:19
XXXX1902

Item Title	Due Date
* Routledge companion to critical theory	18/01/2019
* Introduction to literature, criticism and theory	18/01/2019
Hawthorne's tragic vision	18/01/2019
New essays on The scarlet letter	18/01/2019
Hawthorne : a critical study	18/01/2019
Nathaniel Hawthorne : a biography	18/01/2019
Cat's eye	18/01/2019
Twentieth century interpretations of The scarlet letter (by Hawthorne) : a c	18/01/2019
Nathaniel Hawthorne : tradition and revolution	18/01/2019
scarlet letter : complete, authoritative text with biographical backgrou	18/01/2019
Critical reading and writing : an introductory coursebook	18/01/2019
Cambridge companion to Margaret Atwood	18/01/2019
How to read texts : a student guide to critical approaches and skills	18/01/2019

* Indicates items borrowed today

organization, there is no aesthetic satisfaction. If, as the French critic Roland **Barthes** claimed, every story is the story of Oedipus, not all such stories 'work' for every reader. Success depends on form, and this brings me to the second feature of worthwhile psychoanalytic criticism: a focus on the way the reader engages with the text.

Here the concern is less on the text itself than on the possible forms of exchange between the text and the reader. Rather than reducing the text to its supposed latent content it examines the relationship between text and reader. Identification provides the best example. As indicated above, identity is no more of a biological given than our desires. Our sense of identity develops in the course of our lives and never achieves a fixed and stable form. A child is not born with an innate identity; rather it identifies with the often imaginary and idealized figures around it. Such identifications are never final; new and different identifications can and do arise, not least in the encounter with texts. It is a commonplace that the identification of readers and spectators with the idealized heroes of narrative is a source of much of the pleasure to be derived from such texts. Where psychoanalysis advances on such readings is in its thesis that the reader or spectator can identify with several characters at once. The prototype for such analyses was provided by Freud's work on dreams and fantasies where he argued that the subject often identifies with very different figures at the same time. Take, as an example, his interpretation of what he claimed to be a frequent fantasy of his patients which they encapsulated in the phrase 'a child is being beaten'. As usual, Freud found an unconscious Oedipal wish at work: here the desire for a sexual relationship with the father. More interestingly, he claimed that the subject could simultaneously occupy the positions of the beater, the beaten and the spectator. Similarly dispersed and multiple identifications often characterize our involvement in artworks. In narratives we can identify with several characters, hoping at different times that the criminal will pull off the heist and that the cop will catch up with him. In this way the text affords the pleasure of both identification with and transgression of the law. In other works the audience can identify with two figures simultaneously. Part of the attraction of tragedy is that the spectator can be at once the tragic victim who could not have done otherwise, and the omniscient, compassionate witness to the victim's sufferings, at once the child for whom things have gone badly and the parent who loves him nevertheless.

Perhaps the most attractive feature of Freud's career was his willingness to change his mind. To cite just one instance, Freud initially hypothesized that the psyche was governed by the pleasure principle. Thus, as we have seen, dreams, fantasies and even symptoms, to the degree they fulfil our desires, afford us satisfaction. However, towards the end of the First World War Freud became troubled by evidence to the contrary: dreams in which the patient relived a trauma. While considering this, he one day noticed his grandson Ernst playing with a bobbin attached to a piece of string. As he threw it behind a curtain he said 'Ooooh' and when he retrieved it by pulling on the string he said 'Aaaah'. Freud interpreted this activity – now termed the Fort Da game – as a symbolic re-enactment of the comings and goings of the mother. And that posed a problem. Why, if subjects seek pleasure, should the child choose to recall a painful experience, namely the mother's departure. Freud's explanation in 'Beyond the Pleasure Principle' (1920) was that Ernst was seeking to regain the initiative by taking control of a situation where previously he had none. And this, in turn, suggested that survivors in their nightmares were engaged in a similar attempt to master a **trauma**.

If Freud's hypothesis holds, then artworks are more than merely the articulation of conscious and unconscious desires; they are also attempts to actively master distressing, even traumatic, situations. Narratives, for example, often enact the logic of the Fort Da game: an initial equilibrium is disturbed (the bobbin is lost, a murder is committed or whatever) and then restored (the bobbin is recovered, the murderer is unmasked, etc.) As such, art seeks a mastery as illusory as the pleasures harboured by its fantasies.

JACQUES LACAN

Psychoanalysis exists to treat patients' suffering. As different forms of suffering emerge at different times and places, psychoanalysis has to evolve to address new developments. The exemplar of this approach is Jacques Lacan. Emphasizing the individuality of each patient and the singularity of each session, he enjoined analysts to reinvent psychoanalysis in every session. To underline the point he ensured that each of his own seminars was, in at least some respect, different from its predecessors. There is consequently no Lacanian system. However, in the evolution of his teaching, two moments have proved particularly important for subsequent developments in critical and cultural theory.

THE INTER-SUBJECTIVE LACAN

The most significant notion from this period for critical theory is that of the famous **mirror stage**, Lacan's account of the formation of the ego. In his 'On Narcissism' (1914), Freud had suggested that the subject takes itself as its first love object and that, in consequence, the subject tends to have an idealized self-image. But later in his second topography, set out in 'The Ego and the **Id**' (1923), he had envisaged the ego as an agency negotiating between, on the one hand, the demands of the id (at its simplest the unconscious drives) and the **superego** (the socially constituted voice of conscience) and, on the other, the exigencies of external reality. Lacan returned to Freud's earlier conception of the ego as the site of narcissistic self-idealization and hence misrecognition. In his account of the mirror stage he claimed that before the child has achieved motor control it identifies with an image of unity and completeness, an ideal which it anticipates but which it will never embody.

As no human being can ever fully coincide with an ideal, in so far as the child imagines it coincides with this ideal it is lost to misrecognition: the child's 'self-understanding' is actually a form of misunderstanding. For Lacan in the early 1950s the implications of this imaginary identification were enormous; it skewed not only the terms of the subject's self-perception but also its perception of the world and, above all, others. Freud had already noted a similar phenomenon. While listening to his patients, Freud had observed that they often addressed him as though he was somebody else, most usually an idealized parental figure; they transferred this other identity on to Freud and then reacted to him as though he were this other figure. But it was Lacan who gave the transference its full weight, insisting that in analysis the question to ask is less 'What is the meaning of the patient's words?' than 'Who is speaking and to whom?' The import of what is said depends on the identifications in play. An example from cultural studies, which may illustrate the point, is the public's reaction to the death of Princess Diana. Instead of asking whether Diana was deserving of that outpouring of grief, whether she was at once the epitome of glamour and saintly compassion, a Lacanian analyst would enquire into the identifications in play. Who was mourning whom? Who did the mourners imagine her to be and who did they imagine themselves to be? Did they, for example, see her as a wonderful person who was undervalued and unfairly rejected by those around her (i.e. the royal family)? And did this perception arise from their misrecognition of themselves as similarly rather wonderful yet unappreciated?

This notion of misrecognition in the imaginary has been of enormous importance in the development of theories of **ideology**. A problem for those subscribing to the notion of a dominant ideology has been to explain why subjects were duped into believing something that was not in their own interests. Why, for example, did women accept their subordination within **patriarchy**? Lacan's notion of the mirror phase seemed to offer a solution. On this model there is not a pre-given individual who is then fooled, but rather there is a subject produced/constituted in such a way that she misapprehends herself and reality. The attraction of this theory was that it not only explained women's acceptance of their oppression, it also emphasized the possibility of things being otherwise. We shall return to this when considering the related topic of **interpellation**.

THE INTRA-SUBJECTIVE LACAN

In the later Lacan the emphasis shifts from the imaginary to the **symbolic order**: the social structures and laws embodied in language. To relate to others each subject must take up a place in the language of the symbolic order. But this is problematic. What Lacan sometimes terms the 'wall of language' at once joins and separates subjects. It joins them in that it enables them to communicate, but it separates them in that communication is never complete.

The difficulty is that meaning is unstable and constantly shifting. In large part this claim derived from Lacan's reading of the Swiss linguist, Ferdinand de **Saussure**. According to Saussure language works because it is a rule-governed system of signs and all language-users know the rules. However, matters do not always run as smoothly as this would suggest. Each **sign** comprises two components: the **signifier** which is the bearer of meaning and the **signified**, the meaning produced. But they do not stand in a one-to-one relationship. Signifiers are not mere labels attached to pre-existing meanings. Rather meanings (i.e. signifieds) are produced by the relations between signifiers. Lacan fastened on to the radical implications of this hypothesis, arguing that, as the relations between signifiers are constantly changing – for example, when new signifiers are added to the signifying chain – meaning too can change. Thus patients in analysis can ascribe entirely different meanings at different stages of the treatment to earlier episodes or utterances.

In developing this notion Lacan was indebted to Freud's notion of deferred interpretation (*Nachträglichkeit*). Freud had faced a problem in theorizing the onset of neurosis: why, if the cause of neurosis was an event in childhood, most usually some form of seduction, did the symptoms not emerge until much later? Freud's explanation was that the significance of the episode was revised. Only with puberty did the sexual nature of the seduction become apparent and traumatic. Thus, on Freud's account, episodes are always open to revision and deferred interpretation. Following Freud, Lacan argued that a patient's history is always open to, and indeed the result of, retroactive interpretation. Meaning is always changing.

This has obvious implications for our reading of art and literature. If reinterpretation is always possible, then there can be no final readings. In different contexts texts can assume different meanings. *Hamlet*, as we have seen, could be read very differently after Freud's elaboration of the Oedipus complex. Thus for Lacan the meaning of a text comes from the future.

Later Lacan stated the problems with language in starker terms. The **Other** (of language), he announced, is lacking. Put at its simplest this was the proclamation that the crucial signifiers – the signifiers that would enable the subject to express itself – are missing. The speaking subject, the subject of the enunciation, can never put everything into words, into the enounced of its utterances; it at once says less than it wants (there is an impossible to say) and more than it wants (the repressed always returns, the unconscious speaks). When Freud was treating Elizabeth, he believed that she would be cured once she had said everything, but he later realized that the unconscious could never be fully verbalized and that, consequently, analysis was interminable. Lacan similarly concluded that something always remains impossible to say – the subject is always between signifiers.

Beyond this the lack in the Other has a twofold effect on the subject:

(1) Alienation

If the signifier to express the subject is missing, there are no identities, only identifications. To gain a sense of identity and become a subject, the human infant has to identify with a signifier even though it can no more coincide with that signifier than it can with its specular image (itself a signifier). This signifier is not of the child's own choosing. Prior to its birth, the human infant is spoken of with hopes, desires and fears in the light of which it is assigned an identity: it is given a name. Such naming is no mere labelling. Rather it is an interpellation, a summons to the child to assume an identity not of its choosing, an identity which necessarily incarnates an ideal. Thus George W. Bush had to determine his father's conscious and unconscious aspirations in naming his son after himself. What ideal was 'George' supposed to embody? A difficult task for the future president, though arguably Brooklyn Beckham faces a greater one.

Such naming gives rise to a sense of alienation. Although there is no self prior to the subject's constitution within the signifying chain, prior to the conferral of an identity with its name, the subject feels that its true self has somehow been lost and betrayed. Hence subjects often protest at the identity assigned to them. Think, for example, of the way schoolchildren customize their school uniforms as a way of saying, 'I am not just a school pupil. I am more than that. I am in excess of the assigned identity.'

Unsurprisingly alienation is a central preoccupation of modern culture. Fantasies of authenticity and protests against a society which enforces inauthenticity are everywhere. Whether in James Joyce or the Sex Pistols, Samuel Beckett or Eminem, the cry is 'I am not who you call on me to be.'

(2) Separation

In entering society and accepting one's allotted role, one's existence is necessarily, in at least some respects, curtailed. Consequently, in becoming a subject the child feels that something of its being has been lost. It feels there must be more to life than the existence allowed by society. Desire is born. From the moment of its constitution in the symbolic order the subject is in search of what is lacking.

The quest is vain; the missing object of desire, which Lacan designates algebraically as the 'object a', can never be found. Everything the subject imagines might embody or produce the lost object ultimately disappoints. There is always a gap between the enjoyment (in Lacanian terms the *jouissance*) obtained and the *jouissance* anticipated. This is an everyday experience. All year, for example, a worker may look forward to his fortnight in the sun, may enjoy the holiday, yet still feel disappointed; the experience falls short of his imaginings.

Unless of course he is able to transmute the holiday in his imaginary as a result of, say, a holiday romance. As the object a does not exist, the tendency is to fantasize that it does and, in our culture, the commonest form of such fantasies is romance. Lovers imagine that the other embodies the lost object and can make good their lack. As the object a is irreparably lost, no lover can incarnate the lost complement; no lover can complete their partner. Lovers bring to each other not what will make good the lack but lack itself. Hence Lacan's bluntly stated axiom: there is no sexual relation. Rather than accept this, lovers take refuge in fantasy. As Lacan points out, courtly love provides an effective format. In the courtly love tradition of the high Middle Ages the beloved was an inaccessible love object: for example, the wife of the liege lord. This might appear a deeply frustrating situation but it had one considerable advantage: by choosing an unattainable and socially prohibited love object the lover is able to imagine that but for the contingent circumstances – his beloved is married – a sexual relation would be possible. Similar alibis are available in less elevated circles. One reason for the potency of holiday romances is that the couple does not have time to discover the lack in the other and hence can imagine that if only the holiday had not come to an end they would have lived happily ever after. Art and literature abound with such fantasies. *Pride and Prejudice* offers an example. For most of the narrative Darcy and Elizabeth are kept apart by their misreadings of each other. As in courtly love, this is at once frustrating and delightful for the reader, frustrating in that the longed-for consummation is deferred and delightful in that its absence allows belief in its existence. Significantly, when they do get together, the novel can do nothing but end. James Cameron's dreadful but briefly very popular film *Titanic* provides an example from popular culture. But for that iceberg . . .

Lacan's thinking on the lack in the Other has a reach well beyond the consulting room. Both alienation and separation operate in the socio-political sphere. Let us again take each in turn.

(1) Alienation

Subjects are not simply interpellated within the family. As indicated by the example of the school child, they are interpellated by other institutions: schools, workplaces, the state, the courts, etc. In so far as interpellation succeeds, those institutions continue untroubled; their authority is accepted and their viewpoint unquestioned. Hence Louis **Althusser**, the **Marxist** theoretician, claimed that the mechanism of interpellation was crucial to the success of dominant **ideologies**. If an individual misrecognizes an assigned identity as his true identity, he will misrecognize the ideology in which that identity is inscribed as the truth. For example, if under patriarchy he accepts his interpellation as a 'man', the terms of that identification will entail his misrecognizing women as inferior. Althusser did not appreciate that the Other, the symbolic order, is lacking and hence seems to have believed that interpellation necessarily always succeeded, thus imprisoning subjects in ideological misapprehensions, but of course there is no such necessity. As the subject never coincides with a signifier, resistance is always possible; interpellation can be refused. Hence feminists and others engaged in political critique have emphasized the possibility of resistance: as interpellation has no guarantee of success, as there are no identities, only identifications, a subject can always desist from any particular identification. For example, Homi **Bhabha**, a leading theorist of postcolonialism, has argued that the instability of identity and meaning is the opportunity for postcolonial peoples to explore and forge very different forms of subjectivity from those previously assigned. As the subject is always between signifiers, political struggles around questions of representation

(What is it to be a woman? What is it to be a black man?) are less a matter of enabling those suffering from discrimination and oppression to realize pre-given 'authentic' identities than of exploring the possibilities of developing new signifying forms and hence new subjective modes.

(2) Separation

It is not just romantic holiday-makers and other lovers who want to believe that the object a is not irrevocably lost. So do many of our fellow citizens. According to the Slovenian philosopher and psychoanalytic theorist, Slavoj **Žižek** the fantasy that the object is attainable subtends crucial aspects of racist ideology. Racists typically believe either that some particular ethnic group has access to modes of *jouissance* unattainable to others, or that but for the existence of some 'cancerous' racial group in the body politic they could live in harmony and experience plenitude. Both stratagems allow him to believe that the object a not only exists but is attainable. Just as patients obtain satisfactions from their symptoms because of the fantasies they embody (Elizabeth almost certainly took pleasure in unconscious fantasies about her idealized father at the core of her otherwise troubling symptom), so too racists enjoy their racism because of the underlying fantasies of absolute *jouissance*. Žižek therefore argues that it is not enough to point out to a racist that his perception is mistaken; he must be persuaded to forgo the fantasy he so much enjoys. For Žižek social harmony is as impossible as the sexual relation. Just as the sexual relation does not exist because lovers' desires are ultimately antagonistic (each lover is pursuing the idiosyncratic libidinal agenda shaped by his or her unique history), so society does not exist because its members have conflicting aspirations. Rather than accept the existence of this ineradicable conflict at the heart of social relationships, fascists cling to their fantasy of an organic society. Only if they can be brought to renounce their investment in such fantasies of social wholeness will they abandon their fascism.

CRITICS OF PSYCHOANALYSIS

The standing of psychoanalysis was disputed from the first. Despite Freud's ambitions, its scientific credentials have never been convincingly established, and many of its claims have proved unpersuasive. Fundamentally it has been objected that the findings of a small group of doctors working with a narrow social stratum in turn-of-the-century Vienna have, at best, limited validity. The charge that psychoanalysis has elevated *a* perspective to the status of *the* perspective has been echoed in the criticisms of recent philosophers.

Jacques **Derrida**, while not hostile to psychoanalysis per se, has argued that in practice its interpretations are pre-programmed to confirm its own findings. Although Derrida's central thesis – namely that the meaning of a text depends on its context and that, consequently, in different contexts a text can acquire different meanings – is indebted to both Freud and Lacan, he is at odds with both. He claims that although they pay lip service to the notion that a text can always be read otherwise, their own readings always come down to the same old story: castration, the woman as lacking. Psychoanalysis forecloses on what is new or other.

From a very different angle, Michel **Foucault** similarly argued that psychoanalysis promoted a very particular point of view as *the* truth. Psychoanalysis, he argued, did not discover the truth of sexuality but constructed a particular notion of sexuality within its discourses. As such it had restricted our notions of what desire could do. Foucault's erstwhile friend Gilles **Deleuze** echoed this call for the invention of new forms of desire. Freud, he claimed, had betrayed his own insight of 1905, namely that desire, as a mutable form of energy without any predetermined aim or goal, could assume an infinity of forms, and retreated into the belief that all desire is ultimately Oedipal, a question of mommy, daddy and me. Freud thereby opened the door to the miseries of Lacanian psychoanalysis and its equation of desire and lack. In place of psychoanalysis Deleuze and his co-author, Felix **Guattari**, argue for **schizoanalysis**, i.e. experimentation with new forms of desire.

These debates have informed projects and struggles far beyond the academy, most notably within feminism. Many women focusing on such Freudian notions as penis envy (the notion that all women aspire to the possession of a penis) have understandably found psychoanalysis utterly abhorrent. Others, while condemning the sexist and homophobic aspects have salvaged and mobilized other concepts. In particular they have taken up the thesis that there are no identities, only identifications, to argue that there is no essence of femininity, and new forms of feminine subjectivity are always possible. Judith **Butler**, for example, despite her hostility to what she sees as the ahistoricism and heterosexism of Freud and Lacan, has deployed and elaborated their emphasis on the instability of identity. As identity is never finally achieved, and as disidentification can always occur, she argues that contestation of existing normative sexual arrangements in the interests of as yet undreamt of subjectivities is always possible. Although there is an imperative for every human being to identify as a man or a woman according to prevailing social norms, the identification is never exhaustive; the subject is always in excess of the assumed identity and consequently what she terms 'compulsory heterosexuality' can be eluded.

Feminist thinkers with a greater commitment to psychoanalysis have innovated from within. Where Freud and Lacan insisted that there was something irreducibly enigmatic about femininity, they have sought to go beyond such masculine musings. Plainly much of psychoanalysis has failed to do justice to women. For example, many of Elizabeth's problems were almost certainly attributable to her position within a nuclear family structured around patriarchal norms, but Freud only touches on these issues. There is, therefore, an evident need for the revision of many psychoanalytic theses. It is this task that female analysts have undertaken Thus Luce **Irigaray**, arguing that the feminine in its difference is excluded from the Lacanian symbolic order, has sought to develop a space in which this repressed feminine can be reconceptualized and rearticulated, while Julia **Kristeva**, drawing on the notion of the subject as always in process, has investigated the potential of pre-Oedipal, pre-verbal rhythmic drives and energies (which she terms the semiotic) to disrupt existing forms of the symbolic order, allowing new forms of both male and female subjectivity to emerge.

Questions unavoidably press upon us. Who am I? What do I want? What does the Other want of me? On its own account, psychoanalysis cannot provide the answers. As the key signifiers are missing, the final word can never be pronounced. But, in so far as psychoanalysis has addressed such issues more directly than any other body of thought, it has proved an indispensable resource and become the most vital and far-reaching influence upon critical theory. Of course, concepts born of the nineteenth century and developed in the twentieth speak to us less and less. However, that is no reason to jettison psychoanalysis. Rather it is the imperative to continually re-invent it.

FURTHER READING

Feldstein, Richard, Fink, Bruce and Jaanus, Maire (eds) (1995) *Reading Seminar 11, Lacan's Four Fundamental Concepts of Psychoanalysis*, Albany, NY: State University of New York.
  Containing articles by such leading commentators on Lacan as Jacques-Alain Miller, Eric Laurent, Colette Soler and Marie-Hélène Brousse, this is a sometimes complex but always precise discussion of some of the most influential ideas in Lacan's psychoanalytic theory.
Freud, Sigmund (1991a) *Introductory Lectures on Psychoanalysis*, trans. James A. Strachey, Harmondsworth: Penguin.
  Freud's own account of the aims and processes of analytic practice, aimed at the layperson, is still the clearest and most reliable route into psychoanalysis.
Lacan, Jacques (1994) *Seminar 11: The Four Fundamental Concepts of Psychoanalysis*, ed. Jacques-Alain Miller, trans. Alan Sheridan, London: Penguin.
  The most accessible of Lacan's seminars, if only because there are more commentaries available than on any other, and the one in which he develops many of the ideas and arguments that have been taken up by theorists.
Leader, Darian and Groves, Judy (1995) *Introducing Lacan*, Cambridge: Icon.
  A very straightforward introduction to Lacan's life and work, with illustrations. Leader's accuracy and insight into psychoanalytic theory makes this an excellent place to begin.
Nobus, Dany (ed.) (1999) *Key Concepts of Lacanian Psychoanalysis*, New York: Other Press.
  This is a very useful collection of short essays explicating the basic concepts of Lacan's teaching.
Wollheim, Richard (1971) *Freud*, London: Fontana.
  A classic introduction to the life and work of Freud, which provides clear and helpful definitions of many of his key concepts.

Wright, Elizabeth (1984) *Psychoanalytic Criticism*, London: Methuen.

A useful starting-point for students interested in the range of psychoanalytical theories and the different ways in which they have been put to use by literary and cultural critics.

Wright, Elizabeth (ed.) (1992) *Feminism and Psychoanalysis: A Critical Dictionary*, Oxford: Blackwell.

This is an authoritative survey of the productive, even if sometimes fraught, relationship between feminist and psychoanalytic theory.

Žižek, Slavoj (1992) *Looking Awry*, Cambridge, MA: MIT Press.

This is probably one of the most accessible of Žižek's many books. By discussing contemporary popular cultural artefacts such as Hitchcock's films and horror fiction, the book provides a helpful introduction to Žižek's readings of Freud and Lacan.

7

DECONSTRUCTION

ANDREW BENJAMIN

AND DECONSTRUCTION – WHAT IS IT?

> Deconstruction is on the side of the yes,
> of the affirmation of life.
> > Jacques Derrida (2004)

> Generosity of the invisible.
> Our Gratitude is infinite.
> The criteria is hospitality
> > Edmond Jabès (1991)

Deconstruction is as much an intellectual and political movement as a position within philosophy. Deconstruction, in fact, complicates any clear distinction between such possibilities. At its inception deconstruction was the term for a specific philosophical project identified with the proper name Jacques **Derrida**. The impact of that name, plus the project associated with it, has had a profound effect on the humanities and the social sciences, with a recognition from the start that such disciplinary designations are automatically questioned by the practice of deconstruction. Indeed, so significant is the effect of deconstruction that both as a strategy and as a mode of inquiry it has acquired a life of its own. It has outlived Derrida, even though Derrida lives on within it. In the course of an interview given on 30 June 1992, Derrida addressed explicitly the question of deconstruction. The extract, which has only recently been published – and which is entitled 'What is Deconstruction?' (*'Qu'est-ce que la déconstruction?'*) – appeared as part of a special supplement to *Le Monde* published on the occasion of Derrida's death (*Le Monde*, mardi 12 Octobre 2004, p. 3: all translations are my own). Rather than try and offer an all-encompassing overview of Derrida's writings, the project of this introduction to deconstruction will involve a commentary on that particular interview. The force of Derrida's question – What is deconstruction? – and that force has to do with an automatic questioning of identity by posing the question of identity, the identity of deconstruction, resides in its allusion to the fundamental philosophical question, one posed with its greatest acuity by Plato – What is X? This point is, of course, noted in advance by Derrida. Equally, though now the reference is only ever implicit, it alludes to Martin **Heidegger**'s text *Was ist das die Philosophie?*, which, when translated word for word – asks what is the 'that' that philosophy is. In other words, the very form of the question has an innocence that is betrayed the moment it is asked.

Derrida begins his response to this question by distinguishing between 'deconstruction' on the one hand and either 'destruction' or 'dissolution' on the other. The latter two possibilities have different meanings and, as significantly, enjoin different philosophical tasks. Their 'way' (*sens*) is different. Deconstruction, Derrida argues, should be 'understood' as an 'analysis', the object of which is 'the sedimented structures which form the discursive element, the philosophical discursivity in which we think'. On one level the project identified in this description is straightforward. On a quick reading it suggests a form of conceptual analysis in which careful attention would be paid to the formation of arguments and the use of concepts. However, such an interpretation would be too hasty. Derrida adds immediately to his description of the object of analysis that the 'discursivity of thought' – the structure in which 'we' operate – occurs through language. Equally, it operates through 'western culture' and indeed through the 'ensemble' that pertains to the history of philosophy. This complex state of affairs means that taking a stand positioned within the history of philosophy – the stand that starts with 'analysis' – has implicated within it, at the very minimum, the interplay of language and culture. Equally, as will emerge, once it can be argued that the presence of 'language', 'culture' and the 'history of philosophy' have not just an ineliminable quality but an operative presence, then the question of the outside becomes necessary. If deconstruction works through the 'same language' as the history of **metaphysics** how could any other possibility emerge? Conceptual analysis may analyse concepts and thus be concerned with the relationship between the conceptual and forms of argumentation. However, it does so while remaining oblivious to the specific forms of language used and concepts deployed within the project that it intends to realize. Once this point is conceded, then rather than tying deconstruction to a form of destruction, it takes on a different quality. While it remains to be qualified, what arises is a form of affirmation. Derrida will, in the course of his response to the question of deconstruction, make use of affirmation as a way of describing deconstruction. However, prior to investigating the link between deconstruction and affirmation it is vital to take up Derrida's own attempts to contextualize deconstruction.

Deconstruction was always, amongst other aspects, a form of intervention. In the interview he describes it as the 'taking of a position in relation to structuralism'. More emphatically, it was an attempt to contest the claim prevalent within structuralism that 'everything is language' ('*tout est langage*'). In formulating this position Derrida makes repeated use of the term 'contestation'. Indeed, he locates part of the particularity of deconstruction as 'contesting, the authority of the linguistic, and of language and of **logocentrism**'. This position involves three elements that are fundamental. In the first place, a form of criticism is opened up. Contestation involves a refusal to accept. What is not being accepted, and thus contested, is the dominance of a certain conception of language and with it the traditional interplay of language and concepts (an interplay that can be designated 'logocentrism'). The second is that, unlike the traditions of criticism, the conventional distance between the object to be contested and the position of contestation is equally refused. A different space is inaugurated. Its significance lies in the implicit recognition that there is no outside, and so the language and terms that form part of the tradition being contested have to become the site of engagement and invention. Finally, the ineliminability of this site forms part of the definition of deconstruction. In so doing the nature of what counts as a definition is transformed. Definition becomes the defined place rather than that which identifies the essence of a concept. Place becomes therefore a locus of activity rather than the termination of a programme: a termination brought about by an already determined and thus already given definition. Once definition is linked to activity, rather than to finality, another setting for philosophical inquiry is given. Derrida locates this place between what he describes as 'closure' ('*clôture*') and 'end' ('*fin*'). The distinction between these terms is of fundamental significance.

One of the first effective uses of this distinction occurs in Derrida's 1966 paper on the French writer Antonin Artaud. In his treatment of the question of Artaud's relation to representation in theatre – working with the twofold move in which the French term '*la représentation*' is as much part of a philosophical vocabulary as it is a theatrical one (the same positioning also occurs in relation to the term '*répétition*') – Derrida delimits the impossibility of an end to representation in the following terms:

> Because it has always already started the representation does not therefore have an end [*fin*]. But one can think the closure [*clôture*] of that which does not have an end [*fin*]. The closure is the circular limit at the interior of which the repetition of difference is repeated/rehearsed indefinitely [*se répète indéfiniment*].
>
> (Derrida 1967: 367)

In the interview Derrida formulates the distinction in the following terms. As a beginning, he argues that he holds to the term 'deconstruction' since it provides a way of recalling the necessity of the location of philosophical activity as inescapably positioned in relation to the history of philosophy. As such, what have to be avoided are strategies that simply posit the end of this context. Such moves totalize the history of philosophy, turning it into a single, thus internally coherent, metaphysical tradition. Derrida claims the contrary, arguing that the 'idea that there is a metaphysics is itself a metaphysical prejudice'. In addition, it is a prejudice linked to the possibility – a possibility that for Derrida is simply counter to the thrust of deconstruction – that an end could either be established or taken as defining the task of philosophy. In contradistinction to the language and strategies of ends, Derrida argues for an inherently complex and diverse sense of metaphysics and thus the possibility of establishing 'closures' within such a setting. Closures become the enactment or realization of points of contestation. These points are not committed to the language of ends and thus the totalizing of a tradition that subtends the use of such a language.

The space opened between a strategy of ends and one of closure locates the place of deconstruction. Equally, it involves the experience of deconstruction as well as its experimental possibilities. Derrida describes that place as one in which there is a 'reaffirmation of philosophy', a movement which is identified as the 'opening of a question on philosophy itself'. However, it is essential to pause, since it could be the case that to identify deconstruction as a mode of questioning might amount to arguing that deconstruction has become a form of philosophical method. Method demands that it be followed. Method paves the way – a way set in advance – towards the discovery of a truth or series of occurrences that are known with certainty. This conception of method – one already analysed in considerable detail by Derrida – falls beyond the hold of deconstruction. Indeed, it is a mode of approach that takes the outside as definitive. In other words, in positing an end it allows for an approach in which the strategy of the question is effectively ruled out. It is possible therefore to see an important relationship between a conception of the definition defined in terms of the essence and a conception of method as a pre-determined path towards the 'discovery' of truth. There is an important complementarity between these two positions. In both instances there will be the effective presence of an assumption resisting any form of equivocation. In regards to the definition, the assumption is that its content must have a form of immutability. And in relation to the question of method, the assumption of applicability will have to have been given in advance. In other words, both create or demand assumptions that resist the strategy inaugurated by the question. There will always be the possibility either of abandoning a definition or altering a method. However, the adoption of another definition or the reformulation of method, while this will involve the reinscription of a different set of phenomenal conditions, will retain the effective presence of the immutable. This position not only informs the way deconstruction approaches the question of philosophy's self-definition – a definition that is always the site of interrogation – it structures the political and ethical dimensions of deconstruction as well.

In his recent text *Rogues: Two Essays on Reason* (published in French as *Voyous*), Derrida continues a strategy of reworking terms fundamental to the interplay of the ethical and the political. In this particular instance the term is 'responsibility'. Part of the position he develops pertains to the possibility of thinking a conception of responsibility that necessitates not just a different understanding of the 'concept' of responsibility, but another way of under-standing the relationship between conceptuality and action. Derrida formulates this position in the following terms:

> the responsibility of that which remains to be decided or done (as an act) does not consist in following, applying or carrying out a norm or rule. Where I make use of a determined rule, I know what it is necessary to do, and from then on such a knowledge makes the law, the action follows the knowledge as a calculable conse-quence. One knows what way to take and one no longer hesitates. The decision no longer decides, it is taken in advance, and consequently the advance is annulled, it is already deployed without delay, presently, with the automatisation that is

attributed to machines. There is no longer the place for any justice or any responsibility (juridical, political, ethical etc.).

(Derrida 2003: 123–4)

Where this leads is not to the abandoning of responsibility as though the juridical,
the political and the ethical no longer pertained. Rather the point is that an
effective sense of these terms is not found in the traditional relationship between
the determinations given in either a norm or a definition and the already assumed
conception of action and evaluation that would then follow. Loosening the hold
of traditional conceptions is, once again, to open the space in which it becomes
possible to take up responsibility. That act is, of course, already implicated in the
action described as responsible. That there is no way out of this situation defines
the interplay between what has already been identified as 'contestation' and
the affirmative. Affirmation here is the responsibility that is extended to
responsibility itself. There is a differing site: one determined by disjunctions or
connections which are not given in advance, but are there to be made. What is
opened is a place of activity. It is therefore the disjunctive relation that opens
the site in which the decision can be made. The site in question is the locus of
interrogation. As a site it is only possible because notions of strict entailment –
the entailments that would follow from definitions or from a certain conception
of method – are held in abeyance and thus effectively distanced. Distancing is not
destruction, it is an opening up: a rethinking of place.

In more general terms, to insist on the centrality of the question is to begin to
locate the activity of philosophy as an internal investigation into its own
conditions of possibility. This incorporates the question of philosophy's formal
presence. Indeed, this must occur precisely because of the presence and necessity
of language within (and as) the construction of the philosophical. What this
means is that the philosophical is not merely implicated in the use of language,
but in its already having its own language. Related to the primordial presence of
logocentrism – understood as the already present entanglement of language in
the history of metaphysics – is the related impossibility of positing an outside. In
operating *in medias res* the question that must always be addressed is the *res*
('thing') within which philosophy operates. Here the question of the 'thing' is not
the question of style as such. On the contrary it is the recognition that philosophy
takes place within writing, and thus draws the question of style into consideration.
Rather than pursue this question through the realm of style, it can be linked,
more productively, to the interplay of strategy and writing. That interplay is not a
new realm of the pragmatic. Rather, it is the acknowledgement that the philosophical 'thing' is itself the site of contestation.

In strategic terms this will account, in part, for the formal presence of a work
such as Derrida's *The Post Card* (*La carte postale*). The book itself – a book
comprised of letters (*envois*) as well as more traditionally constructed academic
texts – begins as follows: 'You might [*pourriez*] read these letters [*envois*] as the
preface to a book that I have not written.' (Prior to any attempt to interpret this

opening it should be noted that *The Post Card* is a book of 552 pages, of which the *'envois'* comprise 273 pages; hence the question of what a 'preface' consists in is already raised.) While opening a book of this nature – and it should be remembered that this book is a work of philosophy – might prompt a comparison with other openings, it can be assumed that the 'tone' of such openings is in general declarative. A position is announced and then worked from, and this will be true even if it is one that is worked through. Through these 'letters', remembering that they form a 'preface' to a series of papers on psychoanalysis even though the letters themselves are already immersed in a discussion of the psychoanalytic, the status of the person writing, and thus the security of authorship, is continually staged. In a letter dated 11 August 1979, the lines take the following form:

Evident-
ly when under my public signature they will read these words
they will be right to (to what, indeed) but they will be
right; it is not at all like that (*ça*) that it [*ça*] took place,
you know well, my intonation at this moment is completely other
I could
always say 'this is not me'.

(Derrida 1980: 225)

What is at work in these lines is 'detail'. In other words, this is the work of a form of particularity. Part of what is meant by detail is that the actual presence of this extract has to be taken into consideration. Presence here refers as much to its being a letter as to its layout on the page. In addition, its reiteration of impersonal formulations – the use of 'that' and 'this' – opens up as a question the status of personal formulation, e.g. 'my', 'I', 'me'. While the questioning of these formulations and the permanence secured though dates, modes of address and authorial presence can always be undertaken discursively – **Freud**'s pretensions towards a form of science could be interpreted in precisely this way – the continual refusal, though it is a refusal that also deploys the opposition between the public and the private, a deployment complicated in this 'letter' by the public having been linked to a signature rather than to an actualized public presence, means that the status of what is said is opened up ('I could always say "this is not me"'). Interrogation and contestation work together. Rather than in the tradition of the epistolary novel in which the letters have to be read as fictions, or in a correspondence in which the letter precisely because it is taken to be a personal expression may be given a greater sense of truth for that very reason, these letters give rise to a different sense of positioning. Two related demands are brought into play. In the first there is the demand that the letters be comprehended and thus explicated. A second set of demands arises accordingly. These are linked to the difficulties occasioned by the first. As such they are the relationship between detail and a more general expectation concerning comprehension.

In sum, what is at work here is the following. The first demand is a mark of the inescapable. The letters, due to the simple fact of their presence, make a demand. The nature of that presence, however, makes a further demand. Taken together these two demands can be interpreted as 'contesting' not just the tradition of the letter but all that its contents then stage. Contesting occurs while retaining the mark of '*clôture*' – because of the refusal of the conventions of the letter – while at the same time bringing an exigency into play. This exigency is of course bound up with the letter's presence – the fact of its presence.

The opening words of *The Post Card* – 'You might read . . .' ('*Vous pourriez lire . . .*') already complicate any approach and thus any expectation that might be taken to a work. The use of the conditional tense establishes a form of equivocation. Not only 'might you' read these letters in a certain way, equally you might not. The status of reading and the status of the 'I' already announced in the closing words of the sentence 'I have not written' ('*je n'ai pas écrit*') is brought into play, especially since what was not written is the book – this is a definite statement – to which these letters might or might not have been a 'preface'. Even if they had been (or not) the option remains whether to read them in that way (or not). The locus of deliberate equivocation – though also equivocal deliberation – begins a work whose work is with psychoanalysis. The status of that site – psychoanalysis – its impact upon thought and the impossible possibility of the simple declarative statement is already under investigation in *The Post Card*'s extraordinary opening sentence, although, as a sentence written after psychoanalysis, it should not have been thought to be at all extraordinary.

It should be added here that this reference to *La carte postale* should not be read as an argument concerning examples. In fact the contrary is the case. This work needs to be understood as enjoining a specific form of particularity; the nature of the 'letters', and there is an insistence that they be read as letters which, as was indicated, brings both the history of the epistolary novel as well as the *après coup* publication of a putatively private correspondence into play, cannot be separated from the topics they are addressing. Their address in part constructs that topos. When writing about the 'washes' (*lavis*) of the contemporary French artist Colette Deblé, Derrida's approach works in sympathy with the subject matter (see Derrida 1993c), thereby leaving open the question of that subject matter (and moreover that subject's matter). Inquiring into the work necessitates scrupulous attention to the detail of its particularity. Any claim about '*le dessin*' (the general term through which these works are addressed) is itself always already implicated with '*le dessin*' in question. Addressing the particular is already to address painting or art in general. Therefore the approach taken has to be worked out in relation to the demands of the particular. To begin to write is to begin to negotiate those demands. Not knowing their detail in advance nor subsuming particularity under a universal whose content is itself already determined, means allowing – within and through the act of writing – that detail to emerge. This could be described as the situation of deconstruction.

As part of his response to the question of deconstruction in the interview, and prior to providing what he describes as an 'economical and elliptical description' of deconstruction, Derrida locates its situation in relation to **Heidegger**. In positioning deconstruction in relation to Heidegger's 'question of Being' (*'La question de l'Être'*) Derrida counters with the proposition that, 'in a certain way it [deconstruction] is nothing' (*'elle n'est rien'*). To the determination of Being comes the counter 'nothing'. And yet this is not the naiveté of nihilism. The 'nothing' here is most productively read in relation to the work of the French writer and critic Maurice **Blanchot**. Blanchot's treatment of the poet Mallarmé in *The Space of Literature* (*L'espace littéraire*) introduces a productive sense of the nothing:

> when there is nothing [*il n'y a rien*], it is this nothing itself which can no longer be negated. It affirms, keeps on affirming, and it states nothingness [*dit le néant*] as being, as the unworking of being [*le désouvrement de l'être*].
>
> (Blanchot 1982: 110, translation modified)

While Derrida does not refer to Blanchot in the course of this published extract from the interview, there is a real possibility of situating his juxtaposition of Heidegger's sense of Being with the 'nothing' of deconstruction within the site opened up by Blanchot's connection of 'nothing' and affirmation. While Blanchot is writing for Mallarmé and against his (Mallarmé's) Hegelianism, this positioning of the 'nothing' will have a greater sense of productivity than this one use. Affirmation occurs at that moment in which, and this despite an ineliminable relationality, there is still the possibility of an irrecuperable moment. If there is a strategy that captures that moment then it is one defined by interrogation. It is not surprising therefore that the working definition of deconstruction provided by Derrida is 'a thought of the origin at the limits of the question, what is it?'. Hence he will go on clarifying this position to argue that integral to deconstruction is 'an interrogation of all that which is more than an interrogation'. Not only does this original act of interrogation hold open the continuity of philosophy as a mode of inquiry and thus of thinking, it has the more emphatic consequence, as Derrida indicates at the end of the interview, of calling into question any necessity that gets to be attributed to the questions 'What is it?' or 'Who/What are you?'

The interrogation of this form of questioning works in at least two directions. In the first instance it works against the hold of pre-determined definitions and thus functions as a form of contestation within the philosophical. On the other hand, precisely because there are, for example, certain forms of humanity that are accepted as given, an instance of which is the form that defines the being of being human on the necessary sacrifice of animality; or there is the tacit acceptance of interventions that define patriotism on the basis of legislative acts; or moves that structure identity in the form of citizenship in terms of boundaries established by acts of political **power**, any resistance to the exclusivity of these designations, and it will be a resistance that is to begin with the philosophical, has an inherently political orientation. The politics in question, however, maintain the status of an interrogative force. Once a politics of this nature is allowed, then asking the question of the politics of deconstruction involves an inbuilt redundancy. Deconstruction, precisely because of the inscription of an ineliminable conception of contestation, will always overlap with the political. This will be the case no matter how the latter is defined. Either there will be a politics of deconstruction or there will be a deconstruction of the conventions of the political. That both are connected means that the place of contestation is always at hand.

If there is an end point, the point at which deconstruction continues to turn, then it concerns affirmation. For Blanchot the 'nothing' that resists its own negation and thus continues as a source of productivity – a productivity, however, that is positioned beyond any reduction to a form of instrumentality – affirms. That affirmation is the saying of 'nothing'; its being said, however – perhaps its saying – is then the 'unworking of being'. That 'unworking' can be read as the reiteration of what Derrida has already identified as 'closure' (*clôture*), the site where difference repeats itself indefinitely: always new and always the same, never new though never the same. The chiasmatic intersection of these points reiterates the place of deconstruction: the place of activity and thus a place that is always active. Affirmation becomes the continuing working out of that site.

FURTHER READING

There are many good works on deconstruction. Among the most significant are:

Bennington, Geoffrey (1999) *Jacques Derrida*, Chicago, IL: University of Chicago Press.
    Bennington provides a clear, accessible and systematic account of many of Derrida's key texts and ideas. Running alongside his commentary, and responding to it, is a text written by Derrida himself. This is a very useful introduction to the latter's work, produced by one of his most insightful readers.
Critchley, Simon (1992) *The Ethics of Deconstruction: Derrida and Levinas*, Oxford: Blackwell.
    This book provides a detailed and nuanced introduction to the ethical questions raised by Derrida's work, explores the relationship of this work with that of the philosopher Emmanuel Levinas, and argues that deconstruction should be viewed as an ethical mode of criticism.
Gasché, Rodolphe (1988) *The Tain of the Mirror: Derrida and the Philosophy of Reflection*, Cambridge, MA: Harvard University Press.
    Although quite a complex text, this is probably one of the best introductions to the ways in which deconstruction, and Derrida's work particularly, emerges from and actively engages with the history of European philosophy.
Naas, Michael (2002) *Taking on the Tradition: Jacques Derrida and the Legacies of Deconstruction*, Stanford, CA: Stanford University Press.
    Another text that explores deconstruction's relations with the traditions of philosophy; in this case, though, the focus is on the performative rhetorical structures of

Derrida's work, and the ways in which his readings of philosophy are, at the same time, arguments about literary language.

Royle, Nicholas (1995) *After Derrida*, Manchester: Manchester University Press.

This text explores Derrida's work through a series of discussions of literary and cultural texts, as well as topics such as surprise, telepathy, ghosts and laughter.

Royle, Nicholas (2003a) *Jacques Derrida*, London: Routledge.

This is probably one of the most accessible introductions to Derrida's work. Aimed at undergraduate students, it sets his work in a broad literary, cultural and philosophical context, discusses its contemporary significance and provides a range of helpful examples of deconstructive reading.

Wood, David (1991) *The Deconstruction of Time*, Atlantic Highlands, NJ: Humanities University Press.

Another complex but important and useful text, Wood's book examines the ways in which deconstruction opens up crucial questions about how we experience and understand time by exploring the work of Nietzsche, Husserl, Heidegger and Derrida.

8

FEMINISM

SUSAN HEKMAN

Contemporary feminism began in the late eighteenth century as a social movement to achieve political equality for women. Since its inception it has passed through a number of different stages. In the nineteenth and early twentieth centuries liberal feminism and socialist feminism allied feminism with the dominant political theories of the day. Beginning in the 1960s, however, feminists developed approaches that did not depend on male-defined theories. Radical feminism, psychoanalytic feminism, the feminisms of women of colour, and postmodern feminism are attempts to develop analyses of women's role in society from a woman's perspective. These approaches analyse how gender is constructed and maintained as one of the central meaning structures of society. Feminism today provides a comprehensive analysis of the social meaning of gender that forms a fundamental aspect of contemporary critical theory.

In the late eighteenth and early nineteenth century Western Europe was engaged in an effort to enfranchise people previously excluded from political participation. The vehicle that political activists employed to achieve this goal was the political theory of liberalism. Liberalism involves the belief that government is formed by rational, autonomous individuals for the purpose of serving these individuals' interests. Liberals argued that all citizens should participate equally in government and that all should be treated equally under the law. Some women of the era embraced these liberal theories. Beginning in 1798 with the publication of English writer Mary Wollstonecraft's *A Vindication of the Rights of Women* women argued that the movement toward a more egalitarian society should include an equal place for women. English philosopher John Stuart Mill's *The Subjection of Women* published in 1869 made this case as well. To these authors and the women and men who agreed with them it seemed obvious, first, that women should be enfranchised, and, second, that giving women the vote would be all that was required to secure their equality in society.

In the first decades of the twentieth century women were granted the franchise in most nations in Western Europe and North America. As far as liberal theory was concerned, this should have solved the problem of women's inequality: women were now equal citizens. But the status of women in Western nations was little changed by their enfranchisement. Most women continued to occupy an inferior status politically, legally, economically and socially. Consequently, in the 1960s women began to push for more extensive changes in society. They organized to remove laws that discriminated against women and challenged barriers to certain kinds of employment. Liberal feminists such as Betty Friedan, in *The*

Feminine Mystique (1963), argued that women should seek full political and legal equality and that this would remove their inferior status in society. Underlying the approach of liberal feminism is the assumption that the inferiority of women is solely a function of their political and legal status. Liberalism rests on the presupposition that equal participation and equality before the law are sufficient to secure freedom. Once this equality has been achieved, freedom should be the inevitable result. Liberal feminists thus had no way of explaining or rectifying the continued inequality of women under the conditions of political equality.

Another feminist movement arose on the basis of the political theory that opposed liberalism: **Marxism**. While liberalism locates **power** in the government, Marxism locates it in the economy. For Karl Marx, power resides with those who control the means of economic production; consequently changing the locus of that power will change the structure of society. What this means for women was developed by Marx's collaborator, Friedrich **Engels**, in *The Origins of the Family, Private Property, and the State* (1845). Engels argued that the domination of women by men arose with the advent of private property in human society. He concluded that the overthrow of private property, and specifically capitalism, will result in the liberation of women. It follows that women, like the proletariat, should work for the overthrow of capitalism.

In the twentieth century a number of feminists used Marx's theories to formulate a Marxist/socialist feminism. Juliet Mitchell developed 'dual-systems theory': the position that women are oppressed not only by capitalism, as Engels had argued, but by **patriarchy** as well. Dual-systems theorists concluded that the liberation of women requires the dismantling of both of these structures. Nancy Hartsock took Marx's concept of the proletarian standpoint and used it to develop what she called the 'feminist standpoint'. Hartsock asserted that women's oppression gives them a unique and truer view of the realities of society. Like Mitchell, she argues that women must attack both patriarchy and capitalism to achieve liberation.

Marxist/socialist feminism goes beyond liberal feminism in exploring the societal rather than the strictly political and legal roots of women's subordination. By arguing that it is the structure of patriarchy that oppresses women it expands the understanding of the causes of women's oppression. But, like liberal feminism, Marxist/socialist feminism is still limited to an examination of the objective structures of society. It was only with the advent of the next stage of feminism that feminist thought developed as a critical theory of society. Radical, psychoanalytic and postmodern feminism explore, although in different ways, how women become 'women' in our society. They look beyond the economic, legal and political structures of society to analyse how the meaning of gender is created and perpetuated in all aspects of society.

Simone de **Beauvoir** began her classic analysis of women, *The Second Sex* (1988), with a statement that sets the tone for contemporary feminism: 'One is not born, but rather becomes, a woman'. Beginning in the late 1970s feminists looked beyond the economic, political and legal structures of society to the deeper levels of meaning production to explain and rectify the inferior status of women. A central element of this movement was the effort to analyse women's role in reproduction. Radical feminists turned their attention to the practices surrounding mothering, sexuality and the definition of gender roles. What these feminists argued is that it is women's role in these processes that both defines and perpetuates their subordination to men. A significant element of the argument of radical feminists is their assertion that it is not the biological fact that women have children that is the cause of women's subordination but, rather, the cultural construction of mothering and sexuality that defines women's status.

Shulamith Firestone's *The Dialectic of Sex* (1970) was one of the first clear statements of the radical feminist position. Firestone argued that it is the fact that women bear children and are responsible for raising them that keeps women in a subordinate position. It follows that even if legal, economic and political barriers to women's equality are removed, women's status will not change. Women will still be mothers, and hence subordinate. Firestone's argument with regard to the organization of reproduction was persuasive to many women; the logic of her argument was compelling. The solution that she proposed, however, was not. Firestone argued that only if women abandoned the role of mothering altogether could true emancipation be achieved. She thus advocated a form of artificial reproduction – test-tube babies – that many feminists found bizarre and unacceptable.

While other radical feminists rejected Firestone's conclusions, they continued to explore questions of reproduction and sexuality. In an almost complete reversal of Firestone's position, many radical feminists asserted that, far from abandoning motherhood, women should embrace it as a positive good. Essential to such an affirmation is taking control of the process of reproduction away from the powers of patriarchy. The theme of Mary O'Brien's *The Politics of Reproduction* (1981) is that men control women's reproductive process through medical, social and cultural structures. O'Brien argues that women should reclaim this control and positively affirm the role of mothering. Adrienne Rich offers a compatible argument. Rich emphasizes the positive role of mothering and identifies it as the distinctive contribution of women. These and other radical feminists argue that mothering is a uniquely feminine activity that women should affirm rather than deny. What we need to do, they argue, is to redefine mothering as a positive, life-affirming activity rather than the source of women's oppression.

At the root of these and other arguments offered by radical feminists is the thesis that it is the cultural creation of the concept 'woman', not biological or structural forces, that define her subordination. Although they assert that the central aspect of this definition is sexual, they also assert that it extends into every aspect of social life. Radical feminists developed a wide-ranging body of literature that explores these myriad aspects. Kate **Millett** argues that literature is suffused with sexual meanings that demean women. Mary Daly takes on the institution of Christianity, arguing that the patriarchal structure of the church has been a major factor in women's oppression. Marilyn Frye looks at everyday events such as men opening doors for women and analyses the significance of these events for the ongoing subordination of women.

One of the most controversial aspects of radical feminism is its stance on pornography. The now infamous work of legal theorist and activist Catharine MacKinnon on the subject of pornography has become synonymous with radical feminism itself. MacKinnon argued, along with other radical feminists, that if women's subordination is a result of how the identity 'woman' is constructed in our society, then we must expose the roots of that construction. The root that MacKinnon identified is pornography. In our society, MacKinnon asserted, sex is what women are *for*. And the sexual function of all women is most clearly evident in the practice of pornography. Pornography reveals the essence of the construction of 'woman': that the purpose of women's existence is to satisfy the sexual desires of men. Thus, she concluded, if women want to overthrow patriarchy that effort must begin with the eradication of pornography.

MacKinnon's attack on pornography was controversial even among radical feminists. Many did not agree with her thesis that pornography is the essential element of women's subordination. Others argued that her position entails a stance that is anti-sex and pointed out that some women enjoy pornography. In the 1990s, a 'pro-sex' movement developed as a counter to MacKinnon's position. Some feminists also objected to MacKinnon's efforts to outlaw pornography through legal strategies, arguing that pornography is protected speech under the First Amendment. In the American context an attack on First Amendment freedoms is regarded as a serious issue. The public character of these strategies brought the ideas of radical feminists to the attention of a broader public, frequently with negative results.

Radical feminism represents an important juncture in the history of feminist thought. Liberal and Marxist/socialist feminism focused on the objective structures of society, law, politics and economics as the cause of women's oppression. Radical feminism shifted the focus to the production of meaning. They argued that women's oppression is rooted not in objective structures, which can be and had been changed by the 1970s, but in how 'woman' is constructed in our society. The cause of women's subordination is not the political/economic/legal structures or even biology, but the meaning conferred on the identity 'woman' in all aspects of cultural life. Radical feminists turned the lens of feminism beyond politics and economics to the processes by which cultural life is structured and perpetuated.

Radical feminism represents another change as well: a shift in feminist thought from equality to **difference**. Liberal and Marxist/socialist feminisms are about equality: bringing women up to the standard set by men. Critics of these approaches point out that this privileges men. It forces women to conform to the standard set by men; equality is defined in terms of women being equal to men. Radical feminism, in contrast, emphasizes difference. Women are different from men, they claim, not in a negative but a positive sense. Radical feminists want to positively affirm women's difference and, most importantly, to remove women's subordination without erasing their difference.

The shift from equality to difference led a number of feminists in the 1970s to turn to psychology to explore this difference. Since the work of nineteenth-century psychoanalyst Sigmund **Freud**, the question of how women differ from men had been cast in psychological terms. Freud's account of the psychological differences between men and women, however, was not one feminists could accept. For Freud, woman's psyche was a problem. He defined women as unable to successfully resolve the **Oedipus complex**, a failure that created difficulties for their mature sexuality. He concluded that this problem accounts for the psychological dilemmas many women encounter. As feminists began to explore the differences between men and women from a psychological perspective, however, they developed a very different understanding of the origin of these differences. In the late 1970s two feminist theorists, Dorothy Dinnerstein and Nancy Chodorow, argued that women differ from men in our society not because their psyches are innately different but because they are raised by their mothers to conform to a specific image of 'woman' that pervades society.

In order to make this argument Dinnerstein and Chodorow employed a theory developed by child psychologists, object relations theory. They asserted that mothers raise boys and girls according to very different patterns. Mothers treat boys as little men: they keep them at a distance, they encourage them to go out and play competitively, they discourage expressions of emotion. Girls are treated in exactly opposite ways: they are kept in the house, discouraged from engaging in competitive play, taught how to 'mother' dolls and to deal with emotional relationships. The result is that when these boys and girls become men and women they have very different psychological makeups. Men are good at competition and autonomy and bad at relationships and emotion. Women excel in relationships and emotions and are bad at competition and autonomy.

Chodorow goes on to argue that it might be possible to move beyond these differences. She asserts that since the difference between men and women is caused by the parenting style of mothers, that difference can be erased by a practice she calls 'dual parenting'. Dual parenting entails, first, that both parents are equally involved in raising their children and, second, that boys and girls are not treated according to different gender patterns. Thus both girls and boys learn both autonomy and relatedness; these qualities are not associated with one gender or another. The result, Chodorow hopes, will be a world in which an individual's characteristics are not gender-defined: that is, a world beyond gender.

In 1982 a moral psychologist from Harvard, Carol Gilligan, published an analysis of women's processes of moral decision-making, *In a Different Voice*. Gilligan's book had a profound effect on the feminist movement. In a strict sense it is an empirical study of the processes by which women arrive at moral decisions. The broader implication of Gilligan's thesis, however, extends far beyond the empirical and accounts for the pervasive influence of her book. Like many radical and psychological feminists Gilligan emphasized women's difference from men. Exploring this difference from the perspective of moral reasoning, Gilligan came to the conclusion that women typically approach moral decisions from a relational and contextual perspective, while men abstract from the concrete situation and appeal to universal principles. The (male) psychologists who studied moral development classified women's moral process as deficient, men's as the model and norm. Gilligan's thesis was that women's style of moral reasoning, although different from that of men, is not deficient but equally valid as a moral practice.

Much of the influence of Gilligan's analysis in *In a Different Voice* is due to her ability to speak to the experiences of women. Gilligan's descriptions of women's moral decisions resonated with women; women saw themselves in the situations Gilligan described. But the most significant aspect of Gilligan's analysis is that she validated those experiences. She argued that women's relational approach to moral decision-making was not inferior or inadequate but, rather, a legitimate approach to moral situations. It is this aspect of Gilligan's argument that moves her discussion beyond the empirical realm. The 'difference' in women that Gilligan valorizes, their relational, contextual nature, is precisely the difference that has been identified as the source of women's inferiority since Plato. By valorizing this difference, and arguing that women are different but equal, Gilligan is in effect challenging nothing less than one of the founding assumptions of the Western tradition.

Object relations theory is not the only psychological theory employed by feminists. Some feminists argued that Freud's theory can be useful to women despite its masculinist bias. Others looked to the work of other psychologists such as Jacques **Lacan** to formulate a feminist approach. Despite these differences, however, two themes dominate psychoanalytic feminist approaches. First, most psychoanalytic feminists replace biological and essentialist explanations of sexual difference with social and cultural explanations. For most psychoanalytic feminists women are, in de Beauvoir's sense, made rather than born. Psychoanalytic feminists argue that the psyche is a social product, a result of formative influences early in childhood rather than the expression of an innate nature. Thus, as with radical feminists, the focus is shifted from nature and biology to nurture and culture. For psychoanalytic feminism women's 'difference' is a social product.

Second, psychoanalytic feminists emphasize difference rather than equality. With the exception of the argument for dual parenting these theorists are not interested in exploring how men and women can become equal. Rather, they are interested in exploring how the differences that characterize the sexes have been formed and the implications of those differences. One of the results of this focus is that in psychoanalytic as well as radical feminism differences *between* women tend to be obscured. In both of these feminist approaches 'woman' becomes a monolithic category; the emphasis is on the difference between men and women, not the differences between women.

As the feminist movement gained momentum in the 1970s and 1980s women of colour who participated in the movement began to protest against the dominance of white, middle-class women. In both theory and practice, the 'woman' of the women's movement was a white middle-class woman; other women were defined as 'different'. Women of colour resisted this dominance in a number of ways. One means of resistance was political. Women of colour began to split off from the established feminist organizations and form organizations to meet their specific needs. Thus African-American women, Chicanas, Asian-American women and others formed political organizations around their specific ethnicities.

Women of colour also argued that they needed a theory that speaks directly to their situations and that the theories of white middle-class women are not applicable to those situations. In an influential book published in 1988, *Inessential Woman*, Elizabeth Spelman argued that the use of the concept 'woman' is the 'Trojan Horse' of feminist theory. She asserted that using the concept 'woman' necessarily privileges a certain definition of woman, in this case white heterosexual middle-class women, and defines all other women as different and hence deficient. As a counter Spelman advocated a feminist theory and practice that eschews general categories and acknowledges the differences between women.

The feminist community has heeded Spelman's advice. Since the 1980s differences between women, particularly differences of race, ethnicity and sexual orientation, have been at the forefront of feminist theory and practice. Women of colour, lesbians, bisexuals and transgendered women have formed feminist organizations to promote their interests. Women from each of these groups have also developed theories specific to their situation or, in some cases, rejected theory altogether, arguing that it is a product of Western patriarchal thought that has no relevance for them.

Some feminists have regarded the movement toward an emphasis on differences with apprehension, fearful that it fragments the feminist community. Most feminists, however, agree with Spelman that we must recognize and accommodate diversity. The controversy is primarily over how to practise that recognition. Another aspect of the emphasis on differences comes into play as well. Acknowledging differences between women is a direct corollary of the basic insight of the contemporary feminist movement: identity categories are socially constructed. Radical and psychoanalytic feminists argued that the category 'woman' is socially constructed and that resistance to that identity involved a fundamental change in society. Feminists are now arguing that other categories are socially constructed as well. Race, ethnicity and sexual orientation are identity categories to which individuals are assigned and which carry specific meanings. In order to challenge those meanings we must explore these differences along with the difference of gender.

The theme of differences was also at the forefront of another major influence on the feminist movement in the 1980s and 1990s: postmodernism. The postmodern movement is a wide-ranging phenomenon that has affected almost all areas of academic life. It has also reached into the realms of art, architecture and literature. The aspect of postmodernism that has had the most effect on feminism has its roots in the work of a number of French thinkers in the late twentieth century. The psychoanalytic theories of Jacques Lacan and the philosophical approaches of Jacques **Derrida** and Michel **Foucault**, among others, have been embraced by a significant number of feminists. Postmodern feminism has had a major impact on the direction of contemporary feminist thought.

The root of postmodern thinking, as the name indicates, is a rejection of **modernism**, a tradition of philosophical thought with its roots in the seventeenth century. Modernism presupposes a rational, autonomous **subject** who attempts to find universal, absolute truth. Postmoderns declare this attempt to be at best futile, and at worse dangerous. They claim that absolute truth does not exist and that the subjects who pursue this truth are neither rational nor autonomous. Against this postmoderns claim that everything is continually in flux. Truth is a metaphor; its definition changes with styles of **discourse**. Individual identity is a fiction; it is created by the discourses that structure society.

One of the key aspects of postmodern thought is the claim that modernist thought is dualistic: it divides the world according to entities and their opposites. These opposites are always hierarchical and, most significantly, also gendered. For the modernist the privileged side of the opposites that comprise the world is gendered masculine; the feminine is always the disprivileged '**other**'. The masculine is the standard; entities defined as feminine are inferior. It is this element of postmodern thought that constitutes its appeal for many feminists. Postmodernism makes it possible to identify the source of women's subordination in the basis of Western modernist thought itself. From a postmodern perspective the answer to the question of why women have been and continue to be subordinated is that they are always defined as 'other', the opposite and inferior to the masculine standard.

The postmodern feminists who first developed these ideas were a group of French writers, Luce **Irigaray**, Julia **Kristeva**, and Hélène **Cixous**. The 'French feminism' that these writers developed began to move feminism in a postmodern direction. Although the work of these writers is far from identical, all focus on the major theme of postmodern thought: the rejection of modernist dualisms. Irigaray argues that the modernist dualisms that define women as 'other' create a trap for women. The only solution, she argues, is to embrace a pluralistic epistemology that defies dualisms. She advocates developing a feminine writing (*écriture féminine*) that opens up what the postmoderns call **phallocratic** writing: the masculinist, dualistic discourse that characterizes modernism. Kristeva approaches the issue of modernist dualities from the perspective of the psychoanalytic work of Lacan. Lacan's thesis is that in phallocentric language woman is not just the 'other', she is a lack; she is quite literally not present in discourse. Kristeva uses this theory to argue that women's position outside of discourse provides her with the radical potential to disrupt and transform discourse. Thus, like Irigaray, she advocates a distinctively feminine writing. Cixous's discussion of feminine writing leads her in another direction. She defines what she calls a 'feminine **imaginary**' that can escape the dualism of the masculine subject.

Although French feminism had a significant impact on feminist thought, it is the work of Judith **Butler** that has been the definitive influence in postmodern feminism. The publication of Butler's *Gender Trouble* in 1990 brought postmodern feminism to the forefront of feminist thought. Although Butler builds on the theories of Derrida, Foucault and the French feminists, her version of postmodern feminism is distinctive. Butler's thesis is that gender, the identity of 'woman', is a fiction. She asserts that there is no essential subject, 'woman', but, rather, that this subject is created and maintained by the actions that are dictated by the concept. 'Woman' exists because women act in accordance with this identity; there is no essence of 'woman' beyond the acts that constitute gender identity.

Butler's book hit the feminist community like a storm. Its most immediate impact was to question the viability of feminist identity politics, a politics united around the concept 'woman'. The implications of Butler's argument were clear. If there is no 'woman', then 'women's liberation' makes little sense. What Butler advocates in lieu of feminist identity politics is 'gender trouble': engaging in actions that subvert gender identity. If 'woman' is created by the acts that define gender, then acting subversively will destabilize that identity. Such acts were Butler's prescription for feminist politics.

The theoretical implications of Butler's work are similarly revolutionary. Butler's theory is the radical culmination of a trend that began with radical and psychoanalytic feminism: the turn away from biology and essences and towards language and meaning production. Radical and psychoanalytic feminism emphasized how 'woman' is constructed by the meaning structures of our society. Butler takes this one step farther by arguing that 'woman' herself is a fiction. For Butler it is not the case that there is an entity, 'woman', that is shaped by social meanings. Rather, there is no there there: 'woman' is a fiction produced by the actions that constitute gender. The identity 'woman' is quite literally created, not shaped or influenced, by the discourses that define it.

Postmodern feminism has generated an ongoing controversy in the feminist community. Its defenders claim that the radical approach of postmodernism is precisely what feminism needs. Postmodern thought has revealed the dualistic, hierarchical and gendered structure of modernist thought. It has also revealed that unless we dismantle those dualisms that gendered hierarchy will remain in place. Thus, they argue, it is only by employing postmodern strategies that feminists can successfully challenge patriarchy. The critics of postmodernism, on the other hand, argue that by declaring 'woman' a fiction postmodernism destroys the possibility of a feminist politics and, for that matter, feminism itself. If there is no 'woman' then there can be no women's liberation. Both 'woman' and 'liberation' are anathema to postmodernism. They conclude that the nihilism at the heart of postmodernism is inappropriate for feminism, a movement that, by definition, must focus on improving women's lives.

How this dispute will be resolved is not yet evident. It is significant, however, that the most recent development in feminism, a movement loosely organized under the rubric 'third-wave feminism', is defined primarily by its rejection of theory. Third-wave feminists, women in their twenties and thirties who have grown up in a feminist era, are not interested in taking sides in the theory wars of their mothers' generation. Nor are they interested in developing a theory of their own. Rather, they are concerned with living feminist lives in today's society. Third-wave writings focus on differences between women, the different ways in which women today negotiate their lives as feminists. But what emerges from these writings is not a new theory of differences but descriptions. These writers argue that there is no one answer to the question of how to live as a feminist. Rather, each woman must confront the unique problems of her particular life. Theories only get in the way of this task.

Feminism in the early twenty-first century is not a monolithic movement. Feminists disagree on many issues encompassing the full range of theory and practice. Despite these differences, however, a number of significant commonalities unite contemporary feminism. First, most feminists agree that the subordination of women in our society cannot and has not been eradicated by political and legal means alone. Securing the vote and legal equality has not produced an equal societal status for women. In order to achieve this equality other strategies must be employed. Second, most feminists agree that the subordinate status of women is a product of the meanings associated with 'woman' in our society. It is because 'woman' is defined as irrational, closer to nature, more emotional and dependent that women occupy an inferior role in society. Addressing these issues, however, is much more complex than changing laws. Altering societal meanings entails employing strategies that must permeate every aspect of society. Feminists must fight their battles everywhere, not just in the political arena. Third, most feminists agree that we must emphasize and continue to explore the differences between women. Focusing on the difference between men and women was a useful strategy at the beginning of the feminist movement. But most feminists now agree that treating 'woman' as a monolithic category does more harm than good. We need to recognize and examine the differences between women in order to create a feminism for all women. The challenge for feminism is to continue to promote the cause of women without losing sight of the differences between them. Feminists must find a common ground that does not presuppose a homogeneous concept of 'woman'.

Feminism has been and continues to be at the forefront of contemporary critical theory. How society produces and maintains the distinction between men and women is one of the central elements, if not the central element, of meaning production in society. The concerns of feminism are thus closely linked to the concerns of critical theory. These two movements will continue to influence each other as each explores new issues and problems in the contemporary world.

FURTHER READING

Butler, Judith (1990) *Gender Trouble: Feminism and the Subversion of Identity*, London: Routledge.

The definitive statement of postmodern feminism.

Findlen, Barbara (ed.) (1995) *Listen Up: Voices from the Next Feminist Generation*, Seattle: Seal Press.

A collection of third-wave feminist writings.

Gilligan, Carol (1982) *In a Different Voice*, Cambridge, MA: Harvard University Press.

The influential argument for women's different moral voice by a psychoanalytic/ difference feminist.

Hekman, Susan (1990) *Gender and Knowledge*, Cambridge: Polity Press.

An overview of the relationship between postmodernism and feminism.

hooks, bell (1989) *Talking Back: Thinking Feminist, Thinking Black*, Boston, MA: South End Press.

An argument for a black feminist position.

MacKinnon, Catharine A. (1977) *Feminism Unmodified*, Cambridge, MA: Harvard University Press.

The radical feminist position against pornography.

Spelman, Elizabeth (1988) *Inessential Woman*, Boston, MA: Beacon Press.

An argument for acknowledging the differences between women.

9

GENDER AND QUEER THEORY

DONALD E. HALL

Though commonly used, the term 'gender theory' is something of a misnomer or, at best, a euphemism. In reality, gender theory could more accurately be termed 'sexuality theory', because it explores the variety of ways that 'gender', our assignment to social roles in ways related to our biological sex, is connected intimately and variously to our experience of sexuality, and how that experience bears on our own and others' identity. While gender theory is deeply indebted to feminist theory (see Chapter 8), it takes students and critics in very different directions. Building on its origins in the analysis of the differential valuations of women's and men's social roles, its specific interests are the ways that sexuality, in its myriad forms, has been variously defined, valued, prescribed and proscribed across time periods, social groups and world cultures. In short, gender theory examines critically the *identity politics* of sexuality.

As all entries in this companion discuss, or certainly imply, critical theory argues generally that there is always a theory underlying cultural expression and interpretation, even if and perhaps especially when such expression and interpretation denies adamantly or ignores wholly its theoretical positioning. Thus gender theory is not a twentieth- and twenty-first-century phenomenon alone, even if the term would hardly have been used or recognized in previous centuries. There always already was a gender theory in use, even millennia before the rise of identity politics as we know it today. Thus gender theory is a body of work as applicable to the study of classical literature as it is to the study of aesthetic expression and popular culture in the twenty-first century.

Indeed, the first explicit expressions of a gender theory occurred during the classical era. In early Greek poetry, for example, one finds an idealization of the beauty of youth, with an implicit theory of intergenerational desire embedded therein that allows for erotic attachment between adult men and boys or adolescents; often this is placed in a context of tutelage in which the younger individual receives education from the mature man and in return offers some form of emotional attachment and physical affection (precisely what form is vague and open to much dispute). Even more explicitly, in Plato's *Symposium* (*c*.380–367 BC), a collection of differing perspectives on love offered by a group of men at a banquet, we find one of the most influential theorizations of desire between men and women, men and men, and women and women, ever written. Aristophanes, a character in the *Symposium*, attempts to account for the diversity of sexual desires manifested in his society. In his theorization of the origins of what we would today call homosexuality and heterosexuality (though such terms were unknown then), he claims that human beings descended from primordially conjoined beings, some comprised of male and male halves, others female and female, and still others half male and half female. After Zeus divided them, to diminish their strength and humble them, they forever after sought their missing half. Longing for completion through erotic attachment to an individual of the same or other sex is thus theorized as wholly natural by Aristophanes; no one at the banquet disagrees with his perspective, though each has his own theory of ideal love and ideal lovers. As I have suggested elsewhere (Hall 2003), we find therein the origins of the still persistent myth of the 'soulmate', in which a dyadic partnering is the primary means through which personal fulfilment is achieved. As I mention below, queer theory today questions all such assumptions, even those such as Aristophanes' that do not validate male/female couplings alone.

Yet any such tolerance of diversity in sexual desire expressed in Plato and in the erotic poetry that Sappho wrote to other women during the Greek era gave way to ever tightening regulations of proper and improper desire during the Christian era. Numerous social forces and factors contributed to this change. One of the ways that Judaism, and then Christianity, differentiated itself from paganism and Greco-Roman culture generally was in the strictness of its moral teachings and increasing specification of rules governing domestic relationships. The hedonism and social chaos of the late Roman empire was what Christianity used to define itself against, emphasizing, in contradistinction, temperance, stable domestic arrangements based on well-defined marital rules, and strict obedience to church doctrine and political/religious hierarchy. And it is important to emphasize here that the era's 'gender theory' was one of an ever tightening regulation of male/female relationships and couplings, as well as a proscription of male/male and female/female sexual relationships. Indeed, students of 'gender theory' today should never assume that it is relevant only to the lives of lesbians, transgendered people, gays and other oppressed sexual minorities. The prevailing gender and sexual paradigms of an era regulate everyone's lives, working to curtail possibilities and relentlessly push sexual/erotic relationships into socially acceptable channels.

Of course, this affected individuals in highly differential ways. John Boswell, in *Christianity, Social Tolerance, and Homosexuality* (1980) has demonstrated how the late Middle Ages in particular saw an increasing and harsh stigmatization of same-sex activity as a threat to social and religious order. One might connect this desire to track down and clearly delineate all forms of potential impropriety to any number of social changes occurring: a shift from agrarian to increasingly urban social organization that brought with it new potentials for social chaos; an increasing emphasis on individualist interpretations of biblical truth (resulting finally in the Protestant revolution of the early sixteenth century) with its concomitant anxiety over regulating strictly just how far that individualism could extend; and new socio-economic demands for population growth and stability that meant domestic, reproduction-based, and rigidly patriarchal male/female relationships became ever more highly valued. Thus all manifestations of sexual nonconformity posed complex multidimensional threats to vested social and religious authority. Gender theory urges us to recognize that erotic relations were and always have been heavily imbricated within diverse and far-reaching networks of **power**. For an example we need look no farther than the case of Henry VIII, whose domestic, though certainly politically involved, sexual needs and demands during the early sixteenth century led to massive social upheavals and renegotiations of power that stretched over centuries. While marital and other intimate relationships are usually termed 'private', they often have far-reaching public implications and consequences.

In acknowledging that complexity, gender theory today (especially as influenced by Michel **Foucault**, whom I discuss below) urges us always to multi-dimensionalize such power relationships, to resist reducing them to a simple top/down model of socio-sexual regulation. Thus in the Renaissance, even as sexual relationships between men became newly regulated as a capital crime, subcultures (specifically houses of male prostitution) began to flourish, demonstrating how indications of increasingly intense attempts at social control often signal the emergence of vibrant and threatening new manifestations of social nonconformity. Again, urbanization is one key to understanding this phenomenon. Only when populations reached a critical density did individuals establish communicative and erotic relationships that led to the emergence of new forms of group self-identification (see John D'Emilio's essay in Abelove *et al.* (1993) for a related argument). While undoubtedly same-sex desiring individuals throughout history (even those in rural and sparsely populated areas) had always had erotic contact with each other, only in the 'modern', or post-medieval, era could those individuals encounter sufficient numbers of other, similarly desiring people to self-identify as a group, as something other than an aberration or individual sinner. New technologies today further complicate this dynamic as individuals no longer even need to be in physical proximity to find each other, discover common ground, and privately or publicly proclaim a shared identity.

Yet certainly paradigm shifts occur very slowly. Even with gradual processes of urbanization, for the many centuries leading up to the dramatic changes of the Victorian era, religious definitions held sway. In particular, 'sodomy', a vague term that often refers to anal sex between men and sometimes to any sexually deviant activity at all, was the prevailing mode of defining non-normative sexuality. This cast same-sex desiring men as one subset of that broader category of 'sinner', not unlike thieves, adulterers or blasphemers. It also meant that social discourse largely ignored same-sex desiring women, a fact which reminds us that 'gender theory' demands a recognition of the gender differentials always circulating in society. Yet all of this changed in the nineteenth century with the flourishing of the natural and social sciences, with new emphases on philosophical reasoning, and with the rise of identity politics (the women's movement and the anti-slavery movement in particular). Traditional forms of social hierarchy were newly abraded by the rise of a market economy (which emphasized social change and renegotiation of social roles and rights) and by increasing literacy and new communication technologies (the rise of journalism and the popular press, the circulation of erotic fiction and poetry, the rise of a postal system that allowed inter-regional and international sharing of information, etc.). Changes in prevailing sexuality theories thus cannot be separated from the socio-cultural changes that led to the rise of the workers' rights movements, the abolitionist movement and the feminist movement. All were reflective of and participating in the Enlightenment and post-Enlightenment emphasis on human (rather than divine) agency in determining social roles and definitions of the normal and abnormal, and group demands for social justice and recognition of equal status.

Michel Foucault writes famously in his *History of Sexuality, vol. 1* that 'The nineteenth-century homosexual became a personage, a past, a case history, and a childhood', continuing, 'The sodomite had been a temporary aberration; the homosexual was now a species' (Foucault 1984: 43). Foucault's observation has been influential and deserves some close analysis here for what it tells us about how and why gender theories changed and what 'gender theory' means today. His emphasis on the nineteenth century bears explanation first. The Victorian era (1837–1901) saw an explosion in new scientific knowledge and quasi-scientific movements. In particular, the rise of the so-called social 'sciences' meant that individual human beings, discrete social groups and entire populations were scrutinized intensely in efforts to describe them accurately and, more importantly, prescribe their proper functioning. Psychology, anthropology, sociology and analytical history all provided perspectives, and implicit judgments, on social subsets such as non-whites, women, the working classes, religious minorities and criminals. All were examined and valued against an idealized 'norm' of white, bourgeois, Christian, law-abiding men. The social sciences were determined to track down all of the causes and qualities of deviance.

This was extended by the end of the century to the category of the 'homosexual', as a subset of other sexual deviants, by the new discipline of sexology. In a sense, Foucault oversimplifies when implying that it was only the 'homosexual' that became a separate, highly individuated 'species' or quasi-biological category. The 'heterosexual' also became a category, as did other groupings of like-acting sexual beings: prostitutes, flagellants, fetishists, etc. As Sigmund **Freud** explored in historically unparalleled fashion around the turn of the twentieth century, all human beings became 'case histories', with adult personalities and sexual proclivities that could be traced back to childhood experiences, developmental processes and peculiarities, and variously channelled drives and desires. What is clear also about Freud, as well as other psychologists and sexologists of the era, however, is that underlying their desire to 'understand' is also the drive to classify, contain and perhaps cure abnormality. While sodomy had been a sin that any individual might find tempting, sexual deviance originated in social, familial and biological processes that could be understood and potentially regulated or remedied.

Therefore, key to understanding the legacy of nineteenth-century social science and the importance of Foucault's analysis of it is the recognition that classification systems are always hierarchical. Heterosexual/homosexual, white/ non-white, male/female exist as binary pairings in which the first term of the binary is the norm and value-generating term against which the second is judged and found to be inferior and lacking (see Chapter 8). Claims of objectivity, both scientific and social scientific, always mask a thorough, even if unwitting, imbrication of the sciences within the value systems of a given time and place. Key then to gender theory of the late twentieth and early twenty-first century is a meta-commentary on such contextual embeddedness and, one could say, arbitrariness, which allows the gender theorist and political activist to challenge discriminatory laws, popular perceptions and offensive discursive common-places. All such theoretical categorizations and their at once enabling and resulting (or, in other words, self-reinforcing) lived, interpersonal systems of behaviour became newly perceived as socially constructed and therefore poten-tially deconstructable through concerted analytical work and political action.

Gender theory as a subset of identity political theory is thus heavily indebted to and intertwined with feminist theory. Early twentieth-century feminist writers such as Virginia Woolf, and later Simone de **Beauvoir**, questioned the differ-ential nature of socially prescribed gender roles, probing the narrow rules that limited the ways women could express themselves and live their lives. Beauvoir's famous observation in *The Second Sex* is that 'One is not born, but rather becomes, a woman' (Beauvoir 1988: 301). This sums up the social constructionist perspective: that one's biology, body, and bodily functionings are not inherently meaningful; they are interpreted and inscribed upon by society and social value systems. For most feminist theorists, this means a complete repudiation of any reference to 'natural' or essential qualities of womanhood or femininity, with an emphasis instead on an iconoclastic questioning of the extent to which everything having to do with gender difference is a human construct, created to reflect and reinforce a set of power dynamics privileging men.

The same thorough iconoclasm animates the work of most recent theorists examining the identity politics of **desire**, sexuality and sexual expression. Wherever and however desire originates (see Bristow 1997, which examines the perspectives of Freud, Jacques **Lacan**, and others in some detail), gender theorists of the twentieth and twenty-first century redirect our critical attention to the question of how and why certain forms of desire and sexual expression have become privileged and others denigrated as deviant, unhealthy and/or criminal. In this way gender theory is political theory, and is certainly bound up with the lesbian, bisexual, gay and transgender social rights movements of the last century. Just as feminist theorists renegotiated the valuations of the binary male/female, and theorists of race renegotiated the social values ascribed to white/black/brown, so too have gender theorists attempted to undermine the judgements and seeming timelessness of the concepts heterosexual/homosexual. Applied gender theory then examines how such social constructions and normalized valuations are represented in diverse modes of cultural expression: the law, media, literature, art, interpersonal interaction, and individual self-representation and social presentation (i.e. fashion, physical mannerisms, verbal inflections, etc.).

Indeed, among the first impulses in twentieth-century gender theory, as in feminist theory, was to argue for equal treatment and equal rights for lesbian and gay individuals. This often involved the recovery of historical information concerning the important work of sexual nonconformists in the past and an attendant argument for a liberalization of laws today. Thus important foundational works of gay analysis such as Boswell's *Christianity, Social Tolerance, and Homosexuality*, from 1980, argued that gay men have always existed, have always contributed importantly to culture, and have been treated with varying degrees of tolerance over time. Similarly, two important early works of lesbian analysis, Judy Grahn's *Another Mother Tongue* (1984) and *The Highest Apple: Sappho and the Lesbian Poetic Tradition* (1985), argued for the transhistorical and transnational importance of lesbian and gay cultural expression. In doing so, these works tended to use twentieth-century terms and uniquely Western constructs in ways that sometimes sacrificed historical and cultural nuance for the sake of political impact.

An attention to nuance and a deep commitment to the specificity of social categories and identity constructs are key characteristics of the critical movement known today as 'queer theory', even as the umbrella term 'queer' also seeks self-consciously to bridge categories and identity groups for the sake of political coalition-building. 'Queer', long a term of opprobrium and even hatred, was reclaimed in the late 1980s as a political term of radical coalition-building by AIDS activists. As the 'norm' of conservative politics, bourgeois decorum and popular media banality became perceived as contributing significantly to the climate of fear and hatred of AIDS sufferers, queer activists proclaimed the end to their complicity with deadly silence and status-quo confirming niceties. 'We're here, we're queer, get used to it!' became the rallying cry of a social movement loudly demanding an end to the smug self-congratulation of a heterosexual population itself fractured by divorce, economic turmoil and various other crises and hypocrisies. 'Queer theory', beginning in the 1990s, has taken such radical political energy and translated it into philosophical/academic language and applied it to the interpretation of a variety of cultural forms. It is radically anti-essentialist theory, arguing that everything – desire, sexual norms and gender, certainly – is interpretable as social construction and open to challenge and change.

The anthropologist Gayle Rubin was one of the first to signal the need for such iconoclasm in sexuality studies in her 1984 essay 'Thinking Sex: Notes for a Radical Theory of the Politics of Sexuality' (reprinted in Abelove *et al.* 1993). In it she argues that 'it is essential to separate gender and sexuality analytically to reflect more accurately their separate social existence' (Rubin 1993: 33), and goes on to catalogue the hypocrisies and horrors of the persecution of sexual nonconformists during the 1980s; she ends with the injunction 'It is up to all of us to try to prevent more barbarism and to encourage erotic creativity . . . It is time to recognise the political dimensions of erotic life' (Abelove 1993: 35). Throughout her influential essay, she urges a de-sensationalization of sexuality and a commitment to challenging all forms of hierarchy in sexual valuation and variation.

Rubin's work was foundational to that of Judith **Butler**, who has been one of the leading voices in queer theory and who provides yet another bridge between gender theory and feminist theory. In *Gender Trouble: Feminism and the Subversion of Identity* (1990, 1999) and the essay 'Imitation and Gender Insubordination' (1991; also reprinted in Abelove *et al.* 1993), Butler emphasizes 'performance' as an analytical category that also allows for radical political and critical intervention. Speaking out of and also participating in an era of spectacular protests by AIDS activist groups (such as ACT-UP and Queer Nation), Butler suggests that all identities – gendered and sexual, in particular – are forms of scripted performance that are always available for subversive reinterpretation. She implies, thereby, an exciting potential for individual or group agency in the possible rewriting of such performances:

> if heterosexuality is compelled to *repeat itself* in order to establish the illusion of its own uniformity and identity, then this is an identity permanently at risk, for what if it fails to repeat, or if the very exercise of repetition is redeployed for a very different performative purpose? If there is, as it were, always a compulsion to repeat, repetition never fully accomplishes identity.
>
> (Abelove 1993: 315)

This implication of fragility, however overstated it may be, certainly helped energize political activism and queer critical/intellectual activity. It also implies that mundane subversions of received gender and sexual norms, such as queering one's clothing or hair colour, or one's appearance through piercings or tattooing, could at the very least contribute to a destabilization of traditional hierarchies. While Butler has long argued that readers might grossly oversimplify the idea of **performativity** by overemphasizing one's ability to choose a new sexuality or gender at will, her emphasis on identity roles open to subversion has had the positive consequence of allowing for connections among high theory, political activism and quotidian choices. It is rare that a theorist can cross those divides.

Similarly revolutionary in theoretical implication was the work of Eve **Sedgwick** in the 1980s and 1990s. In *Between Men: English Literature and Male Homosocial Desire* (1985), Sedgwick first explored how patriarchal structures of male bonding – the homosocial order – have in modern Western culture increasingly depended upon the virulent, violent suppression and exclusion of homosexuality. Her intriguing analysis of the oppression encountered similarly by gay men and all women in a regime of sexist and heterosexist men has remained highly influential and laid the foundation for queer theory's argument that tactical linkages among the oppressed could be achieved while not erasing differences and divergences in political interest. She embraces that inclusivity in *Tendencies* (1993), arguing for a definition of 'queer' that brings under its umbrella 'the open mesh of possibilities, gaps, overlaps, dissonances and resonances, lapses and excesses of meaning when the constituent elements of anyone's gender, of anyone's sexuality aren't made (or *can't be* made) to signify monolithically' (Sedgwick 1993: 8).

At the same time, of course, gender theory as a body of work could be seen as subsuming and potentially diluting the political and critical interests of a host of identity-related causes. This bears some discussion. To the extent that gender theory (especially in its manifestation as queer theory) emphasizes useful, if limited, linkages among various identity bases and interest groups, it has also struggled with the possibility that it might become a rigidly and narrowly regulatory regime of its own. At its best, gender theory offers opportunities for collective action among heterosexual feminists, lesbians, gay men, transgendered people, bisexuals, and a host of others defined as 'other' by the forces of tradition and conservatism. Michael Warner argues in his introduction to *Fear of a Queer Planet* (1993) that:

'queer' represents, among other things, an aggressive impulse of generalization; it rejects a minoritizing logic of toleration or simple political interest-representation in favour of a more thorough resistance to regimes of the normal ... For both academics and activists, 'queer' gets a critical edge by defining itself against the normal rather than the heterosexual.

(Warner 1993: xxvi)

This cuts a very wide swathe, of course, though it also suggests a potentially huge coalition of those opposed to 'normal' values, practices and ways of thinking.

Yet certainly scepticism by those traditionally disenfranchised within the larger social collective remains warranted. At what point does coalition-building and common-ground finding begin to do violence to the specificity of individual struggles and the nuances of the experience of oppression? Gender theory retains a useful but also dangerous murkiness in its assumed relationship between the exterior performance of and social mandates concerning binarily defined 'gender' (masculinity and femininity, even as those hardly capture the fully range of human lives and potentials), binarily defined biological sex (XX and XY chromosomal differences, the physiological manifestations of those differences, and the ways inter-sexed individuals challenge such distinctions), binarily defined sexual 'orientation' (heterosexual and homosexual, as well as the criss-crossings and complexities undercutting such a binary), and finally the ways all of the above get differently interpreted and performed across and within races, classes, regions, cultures, linguistic groups and a host of micro-social spaces. So much specificity gets lost in this process of aggrandizement and subsumption that vigilance and incessant self-interrogation are not only necessary, but also inevitably insufficient.

Indeed, something is lost and something gained in each instance of coalition-building. In linking theories of oppression on the basis of *sexuality* to those of oppression on the basis of *sex* (and, especially, the gender roles associated with one's biological sex) the critic/theorist certainly risks losing an awareness of how sexually nonconforming men are treated very differently from women (whether heterosexual or lesbian). Thus when Michael Warner, in a foundational statement concerning queer theory, writes 'For academics, being interested in queer theory is a way to mess up the desexualised spaces of the academy, exude some rut, reimagine the publics from and for which academic intellectuals write, dress, and perform' (1993: xxvi), one is not only struck with the uninterrogated masculinism of the language ('exude some rut'), but also the lack of nuanced awareness of how one's experience of writing, dressing, and otherwise perform-ing differently on a university campus can be significantly different if one is a physically large, perhaps muscular, man or a physically smaller woman. Rape, assault and other forms of violence are often threatened and carried out against women who refuse to gender-conform in dress or appearance; that fact gets wholly lost in Warner's bravado. Gender theory and queer theory more speci-fically are not necessarily inattentive to the dramatically different experiences of oppression on the basis of sexuality confronted by women and by men, but the fear remains palpable (and understandable) that 'a generic masculinity may be reinstalled at the heart of the ostensibly gender-neutral queer' (Jagose 1996: 3). Repeatedly calling attention to this possibility at least mitigates the likelihood that it will happen automatically or uniformly.

Similarly, gender theory in its titular nod toward naturalized roles of femin-inity and masculinity, but underlying focus on sexuality, has a complicated but potentially synergistic relationship to theories of transgenderism, transsexuality and inter-sexuality. Judith Halberstam is a leading advocate of drawing fully on that dynamism. Near the beginning of her influential study *Female Masculinity*, she writes:

> I am using the topic of female masculinity to explore a queer subject position that can successfully challenge hegemonic models of gender conformity. Female masculinity is a particularly fruitful site of investigation because it has been vilified by heterosexist and feminist/womanist programs alike ... I want to carefully produce a model of female masculinity that remarks on its multiple forms but also calls for new and self-conscious affirmations of different gender taxonomies.
>
> (Halberstam 1998: 9)

Thus, for Halberstam, transgender theory can enrich and be enriched by a queer political and theoretical movement that, à la Butler, finds in performative nonconformity the possibility for radical social change.

But for activists and social workers speaking out of their own experiences of oppression and first-hand knowledge of the horrific experiences of clients and friends, such linkages and potentially subsumptive moves are highly problematic. Viviane Namaste articulates the concerns of many when writing that in Anglo-American gender theory, 'transgendered individuals are conceived as a function of a lesbian/gay identity politics' (Namaste 2000: 64). She takes particular issue with Halberstam's Butler-inspired queer theory model:

This framework does not respect the diverse ways transsexual and transgendered people make sense of themselves . . . [It] does not respect the identities and lives of heterosexual FTMs [female to male], assuming that one cannot be politically progressive and heterosexual, and that transsexuals need lesbian and gay communities to advance their collective situation.

(Namaste 2000: 64)

One of Namaste's specific concerns as a sociologist is that folding all gender nonconforming individuals into a single field of study – 'queer theory' or 'gender studies' – means losing the specificity of individual experiences of oppression:

Critics in queer theory write page after page on the inherent liberation of transgressing normative sex/gender codes, but they have nothing to say about the precarious position of the transsexual woman who is battered and who is unable to access a woman's shelter because she was not born a biological woman.

(Namaste 2000: 9–10)

Such a reminder about the hard daily struggles of those actively challenging or otherwise abrading the predominant 'gender theory' should complicate thoroughly, challenge fundamentally, the tendency among theorists and students alike to textualize and thereby objectify (and grossly oversimplify) the lives of differentially oppressed individuals. Gender theory as practised by academics is articulated within and out of specific institutional positions, ones that often ignore or actively hide their own ideological inflections and identity political exclusions.

Indeed, gender theory's relationship to class identity, struggles and inherent complications has often gone under-theorized. As Linda Garber explores in *Identity Poetics*, 'Early on, the women's movement and lesbian feminism were informed by the class consciousness and materialist analysis inherited from prevailing leftist movements of the 1960s' (Garber 2001: 33). Similarly, the very early gay rights movement had important ties to the American Communist Party in Harry Hay's Los Angeles-based Mattachine Society during the 1950s. Yet such attempts to link oppression on the basis of sexuality with an awareness of class dynamics was always problematic given the ways that social recognition and validation in American society has long been linked with the acquisition of material goods and the pursuit of wealth. Just as other oppressed peoples (African Americans, new immigrants, etc.) have often sought social standing and a sense of having 'made it' through growing economic security and a movement into the middle and upper classes, so too at times have lesbians, gays and other sexual nonconformists found a source of validation in class advancement and the trappings of class status. Both Alexandra Chasin in *Selling Out: The Gay and Lesbian Movement Goes to Market* and Donald Morton in *The Material Queer: A LesBiGay Cultural Studies Reader* contribute to the slowly growing body of work that now attempts to theorize the class blindness, and sometimes even overtly repugnant class politics, of a queer consumerism (marketed openly today through glossy magazines and advertising campaigns) that has often been overlooked in the broad strokes of gender theorization.

The African American lesbian feminist writer Audre Lorde first pointed out the dangers of overgeneralization in the early 1980s. In 'Age, Race, Class, and Sex', she wrote from the position of 'a forty-nine-year-old Black lesbian feminist socialist mother of two, including one boy, and a member of an inter-racial couple' (Lorde 1984: 114), to call attention to the fact that '[u]nacknowledged class differences rob women of each others' energy and creative insight' (Lorde 1984: 116); she added that 'white women ignore their built-in privilege of whiteness and define *woman* in terms of their own experience alone' (Lorde 1984: 117). Race, in particular, continues (and should always continue) to undermine the fiction of a single gender theory that describes a uniform experience of sexuality and oppression on the basis of sexuality. Twenty years after Lorde wrote the above words, José Esteban Muñoz reiterates them for a queer generation in *Disidentifications*, saying that 'Most of the cornerstones of queer theory that are taught, cited, and **canonized** in gay and lesbian studies classrooms, publications, and conferences are decidedly directed toward analysing white lesbians and gay men' (Muñoz 1999: 10).

Responses to the omissions that Lorde and Muñoz pointed out have taken several dynamic forms. In *Borderlands/La Frontera*, Gloria Anzaldúa spoke eloquently out of the position of one who crosses numerous boundaries of difference: sexual, racial, linguistic and geographical. She explores how some individuals inhabit and negotiate a multifaceted cultural and sexual identity:

> For the lesbian of color, the ultimate rebellion she can make against her native culture is through her sexual behaviour. She goes against two moral prohibitions: sexuality and homosexuality. Being lesbian and raised Catholic, indoctrinated as straight, I *made the choice to be queer* ... It's an interesting path, one that continually slips in and out of the white, the Catholic, the Mexican, the indigenous, the instincts. In and out of my head. It makes for *loqueria*, the crazies.
>
> (Anzaldúa 1987: 41)

In *Black Gay Man* Robert Reid-Pharr also emphasizes such multiplicity and its dynamism:

> I attempt to bring together various elements of my political, cultural, and social identities – Perverse, Modern, American, Negro, Queer, Progressive – not as problems to be solved but as potentially fruitful ground for the articulation of American left identity. I do not wish to evoke anxiety or to demonstrate the difficulty of living with multiplicity, but rather to present its pleasure.
>
> (Reid-Pharr 2001: 9)

Of course, gender theory often, necessarily, isolates a single aspect of what is inevitably a multifaceted social identity. However, Anzaldúa and Reid-Pharr remind us that such academically useful partitionings have little to do with the way many people, perhaps all people, must live their lives.

Indeed, if there are some discernible emerging challenges in the field of gender theory, they reflect that multiplicity and the need for critical reflection on the continuing, naturalized assumptions that we bring to sexuality and identity. One obvious blind spot that many working in the field of gender theory today evince is that of their own positioning vis-à-vis the variety of world cultures, even as those cultures also continue to metamorphose. Anglo-American and Western European paradigms of gay and lesbian identity and queer resistance do not translate easily or even relate necessarily to the experiences of individuals living in India, Africa and many parts of Asia. And while I acknowledge below the complications that new technology brings to sexuality today, these also do not pertain to the lives of the vast majority of peoples across the globe who do not have access to computers or the internet. Yet, at the same time, the forces of globalization and continuing cultural imperialism mean that Western paradigms are working relentlessly to reshape local structures of meaning, through movies, television, advertising, and ever-increasing tourism. This hybridity, to borrow a term from postcolonial theory (see Chapter 11), will continue to complicate gender theory and sexuality itself in important ways. If I travel to a 'foreign' place and find a startling easiness and openness about certain forms of sexual behaviour that are anxiety-producing in my home country, I may be changed. However, when I bring with me not only my own vocal judgements concerning that behaviour, but also films and television shows mocking it or rendering it shameful, I also change the place I visit. Thus 'theory' itself can provide only a snapshot of a moment in time; it will always lag behind the dynamism attributable partially to those interminglings and other diachronic changes.

And of course these exchanges are made far more rapid and unpredictable because of the explosion of new technologies and media. Web-based support groups, information-sharing, erotica and even sexual encounters mean that potentially anyone anywhere can experiment with or at least find out about practically any form of sexuality or gender possibility imaginable. Since we are very much in the early days of this particular technological paradigm shift, it is impossible to say how this will alter our experience of sexuality or necessitate changes in current gender theory. However, that unpredictability does mean that there are enormous opportunities for inventive work in gender theory in the coming years.

That dynamism is infectious and hopefully will energize the readers of this book. Even if we are never able to exercise the type of agency first implied by Judith Butler over our genders and sexualities, we do possess a certain type of analytical agency. We choose whether or not to engage critically with the world around us and with our own identities, we choose to ally ourselves dogmatically or more supplely with certain theories or methods, and we choose finally to experiment or not experiment with new ideas and different eroticisms. Furthermore, we choose the care with which we interact with others and with their identities and positions in the world. Gender theory, at its best, urges us to see these choices as not always 'free' or easy, but certainly as worthy of ample discussion and careful, non-sensational consideration.

FURTHER READING

Abelove, Henry, Barale, Michèle Aina and Halperin, David (eds) (1993) *The Lesbian and Gay Studies Reader*, London: Routledge.

This is still the best collection of essays covering the theorization of sexuality and its relationship to theories of gender. See especially essays by Gayle Rubin, Judith Butler and John D'Emilio.

Bristow, Joseph (1997) *Sexuality*, London: Routledge.

This book's attention to the origins of desire as theorized by Freud and Lacan will provide useful information for students new to the discussion of sexuality and psychoanalytic theory. Bristow also provides an important historical overview of the origins of the field of sexology during the nineteenth century.

Garber, Linda (2001) *Identity Poetics: Race, Class, and the Lesbian-Feminist Roots of Queer Theory*, New York: Columbia University Press.

This book does a superb job of looking at the origins of queer theory and its relationship to the work of feminists from the 1970s and 1980s. Garber usefully complicates any notion of a uniform body of work termed 'gender theory' with an examination of the class and racial politics underlying broad strokes of theorization.

Glover, David and Kaplan, Cora (2000) *Genders*, London: Routledge.

This book examines first the broad body of work in feminist and masculinity studies. It then usefully examines recent work in queer theory as it relates to earlier theoretical interests. This accessible book complements Bristow's above. The two will be helpful to all beginning students of theory.

Hall, Donald E. (2003) *Queer Theories*, Basingstoke: Palgrave.

For students eager to explore the emergence of queer theory and its usefulness in applied literary and cultural criticism, this book may provide helpful information and examples. In particular, its last section of readings of literary texts including *Dr Jekyll and Mr Hyde*, *Giovanni's Room*, and *The Color Purple* offer some useful models of how queer theory can be applied by students and scholars.

10

POSTMODERNISM

LINDA HUTCHEON

DEFINING THE POSTMODERN

In the final decades of the twentieth century and even into the new millennium, the term 'postmodern' has appeared to be more casually bandied about than carefully defined. For some it was a mere 'moment', while for others it was a more general 'condition'. Some denigrated it to just a 'style'; still others elevated it to a historical 'period'. These variations do not only signal differences in critics' perspectives, however; they also mark the multiplicity and complexity of the cultural phenomena gathered together under this heading. There is certainly no shortage of differing opinions and competing models of postmodernism, but the critics are not the only ones to blame for the sometimes confusing number of explanations and descriptions. Although the word existed before, it first gained wide acceptance (and its current meaning) in the field of architecture in the 1970s, and referred to works that were 'doubly coded', as the influential architecture theorist Charles Jencks (1986: 7) put it: that is, new and modern(ist), but also historical, although in a parodic or ironic way. These hybrid buildings self-consciously took advantage of all the technical advances of modernist architecture, but their historical echoes of earlier traditions challenged the anti-historical emphasis on purity of form alone that had resulted in those familiar stark, undecorated skyscrapers typical of what was called modernism's International Style.

It was not long before the term 'postmodern' spread to other art forms that also demonstrated a paradoxical mixing of seeming opposites: the traditional (though ironized) and the new, and history and the self-conscious quoting of other art. Literature, the visual arts (especially photography), dance, film, theatre and music (classical and popular) all defined their own postmodernism, as did philosophy, sociology, historiography, psychoanalysis and theology. This move from the realm of the arts into what the French call the 'human sciences' was inevitable, given the very close connections between theory and practice in the postmodern. As we shall see, the impulse of postmodern art both to exploit and then to undermine the conventions upon which it depended – from formalism (or a concern for artistic form) to **mimesis** (with a focus on the imitation of nature or life) – was matched by the urge of poststructuralist theory to call attention to and then deconstruct our unexamined assumptions about basic things like meaning in language or even human identity. Art and theory clearly had overlapping concerns and at least one common method of operation:

that is, looking for and then exposing contradictions in what appeared at first to be a totally unproblematic, coherent and unified whole. In a sense, the conflation of theory and practice came about because of shared responses to common provocations.

The conflating process was helped along by the fact that there were a good number of postmodern artists who doubled as theorists: witness the Italian semiotician-novelist, Umberto **Eco**; the British literary theorist and writer of 'academic' novels, David Lodge; the American novelist and influential essayist, John Barth; the British photographer and cultural theorist, Victor Burgin; the list could go on. The postmodern artist was clearly no longer the inarticulate, silent, alienated creator figure of the Romantic or even modernist tradition. Nor was the theorist the dry, detached, dispassionate writer of the academic tradition, however. From the Slovenian psychoanalytic theorist, Slavoj **Žižek**, to the American cultural analyst, Michael Bérubé, theorists showed they could write with sharp wit, verbal play and anecdotal verve.

The borders between theory and practice were not the only ones to be crossed in what many saw as the democratizing push of the postmodern. The boundaries between popular and high art, between mass and elite culture, were frequently blurred or simply ignored, be it in the populist theorizing of American critic Leslie Fiedler or in German photographer Hans Haake's documentary exposés of the capitalist roots of the (high) art world. This border-crossing did not involve the uncritical or celebratory espousing of the commercial (as many accused American Pop Art such as that of Andy Warhol of doing), but rather offered a critical confrontation with the definitions of and assumptions underlying our concepts of both the popular and the elite. In a novel like Eco's *The Name of the Rose* (*Il nome della rosa*), with its bringing together of the popular detective story format, medieval monastic history and philosophy and contemporary semiotic theorizing, this mixing of levels of culture created a strange state of 'in-between-ness'. The resulting formal and thematic hybrid challenged any simple notions we might have had of homogeneity or uniformity in either art or theory.

This postmodern way of thinking – which many see as paradoxical – can be characterized as displaying a 'both/and' kind of logic. Making *distinctions* but not making *choices* (which would be an 'either/or' kind of logic) between the popular and the elite, the postmodern offered instead a model that would force us to consider equally both sides of this (or any other) binary opposition, and in effect to undo or to 'deconstruct' the seeming opposition between its two terms. There is an obvious parallel here with the theorizing of Jacques **Derrida**, the French philosopher and founder of the theory known as deconstruction. Demonstrating how every binary conceals within it an implied hierarchy of values, Derrida strove not to reverse but, more radically, to undo both the opposition and its implicit evaluation of one term as superior. In the process he made us rethink the relationship between not only the oral and the written (his main interest) but also such familiar binaries as high art/popular, white/black, male/female, and so on. For the poststructuralist Derrida, as for most postmodern artists and theorists, any seemingly coherent whole (say, the 'self') carries within itself the deconstructable **traces** of its own contradictions (in this case, the '**other**'). Of course, the very word 'postmodern' illustrates this, for it carries within itself the 'modern' – from which it both derives and deviates. It is 'post' in the sense of both temporally 'after' and conceptually 'beyond'.

SITUATING THE POSTMODERN

POSTMODERNISM

Within cultural and aesthetic history, it is modernism – the art and theory of the primarily Europeanized West of the first third of the twentieth century – that offers the initial defining relationship for 'postmodernISM', the word now used to describe a certain kind of art and theory born in and flourishing after the infamous counter-cultural sixties. But that relationship is a complex one of both similarity and difference, or (to put it in historical terms) of both continuity and rupture. In architecture, postmodernism gained public recognition through the 1980 Venice Biennale exhibition with its descriptive but provocative title: 'the presence of the past'. Italian architect Paolo Portoghesi analysed the twenty façades comprising the exhibit's 'Strada Novissima' (the newest street), arguing that their very newness lay paradoxically in their parody of historical traditions such as classicism, thereby showing how architecture was rethinking **modernism**'s famous (and defining) purist break with history. For revolutionary modernist architects like Mies van der Rohe, buildings had been considered pure form and thus new (i.e. modern) in the sense of not being repositories of the past. For equally revolutionary postmodern architects who contested modernism's stranglehold on the world's cityscapes (think of all those blocks of high-rises), the past of our built environment had to be revisited, but critically and from the perspective gained after (that is, post) modernism. With the aid of distancing techniques like irony and parody, they could recall a shared vocabulary and a history of architectural forms (banished by modernists) without falling into the trap of nostalgia or antiquarianism. 'The past whose presence we claim is not a golden age to be recuperated', argued Portoghesi (1983: 26). Its artistic forms and its social meanings alike were to be reconsidered through critical reflection. But what is important to remember is that postmodern architecture could not have happened without modernism: there was clear continuity, even as there were equally obvious differences.

Although modernism in literature and visual art, for example, meant something else – related but not exactly the same – there are analogies to be drawn. American critic Ihab Hassan was one of the first to make the link between postmodernism in literature and a certain kind of modernist avant-garde writing, and was one of the many (including Jean-François **Lyotard**, the French philosopher and early definer of the postmodern) to see in *Finnegans Wake*, the radically experimental novel by Irish arch-modernist James Joyce, the precursor or even epitome of the postmodern. But Hassan became best known for his later typology or categorization of modernism and postmodernism in terms of contraries, creating a long list of (very un-postmodern) binary oppositions. For instance, in his terms, if modernism stood for form, purpose and hierarchy, postmodernism represented anti-form, play and anarchy (Hassan 1987: 91–2).

Modernism, of course, was no more a unified movement or concept than postmodernism. To risk generalizing, however, the postmodern openly broke from three high modernist tenets: its concentration on form; its belief in the autonomy of the work of art and thus its willed separation of art from the social and historical world; its insistence on the firm distinction between high art and consumer or mass culture (what Andreas Huyssen (1986) called 'the great divide'). But there were other sides to modernism, as Hassan saw early on, from which postmodernism learned much – namely, the various avant-gardes' attempts to break down the borders between art and life as well as between the popular and the elite, and also their experimental challenges to the existence of any single Truth – be it in defining what 'art' was or how to live one's life in society. Such challenges, of course, were among the reasons modernism was rejected by twentieth-century totalitarian regimes: both Hitler and Stalin perceived only too clearly its threats. There were other continuities too, however, with modernism in all its forms: the ironic parody of Joyce would find its echo in that of the elusive American novelist, Thomas Pynchon, and the controversial British feminist writer Angela Carter. Works of art that self-consciously contained within themselves their own first critical commentary – that is, works that were called self-reflexive or metafictional – proliferated in the modernist period and continued into the postmodernist. Because of the nineteenth-century historical focus of much postmodern culture, and the fashion in the 1990s for Victorian film and television adaptations, it has been argued that 'post-Victorian' might be a more accurate term than postmodern (Sadoff and Kucich 2000). But in fiction, as in visual art or film, the postmodern has actually ranged more widely in its appropriation and critical reconsidering of the past: from German writer Patrick Süskind's fictional exploration of the olfactory life of eighteenth-century France in his novel *Perfume* (*Das Parfum: die Geschichte eines Mörders*) to American photographer Cindy Sherman's ironic self-insertion into Renaissance painting scenarios.

The complicated relationship of the 'post' to the 'modern', therefore, is one of critical rethinking, leading either to a continuation and often intensification (of irony, parody, self-reflexivity) or a rejection (of ahistoricity, barriers against the popular). This cultural and artistic relationship, however, is itself based upon another broader one that is social and political in nature, and has its roots in a series of earlier German thinkers whose work was revisited (and reinterpreted) by French poststructuralist theorists: the philosopher Friedrich **Nietzsche**; the articulator of political revolution, Karl **Marx**; and the founder of psychoanalysis, Sigmund **Freud**.

POSTMODERNITY

Although there is considerable slippage between the two terms, postmodernISM is usually used to talk about cultural and artistic dimensions, while post-modernITY usually connotes the more general social and political context. The two are clearly not easily separable, however. (For one thing, both carry within themselves their defining modern 'other'.) In most accounts, the movement from Renaissance humanism to the start of what German philosopher Jürgen **Habermas** calls the 'project of **modernity**' began with seventeenth-century French philosopher René Descartes' infamous phrase *cogito ergo sum* – I think, therefore I am – a concept that placed human reason at the centre of human existence. In Anglo-American philosopher Stephen Toulmin's terms, this move entailed a shift 'to a higher, stratospheric plane, in which nature and ethics conform to abstract, timeless, general, and universal theories' (Toulmin 1990: 35). On this plane, connections among our knowledge of Nature, of ourselves, and of history and society are said to be objectively determined. This then provides us with a foundation for ordering our understanding of our world and for progressing towards what is called Truth. Rational knowledge is therefore not dependent on our particular culture and is totally value-free; it exists in the form of what Lyotard called '**grand narratives**' (*grandes histoires*) or '**metanarratives**' which, in effect, centre or orient and make sense of the world for us (Lyotard 1984: 26).

Postmodernity, on the other hand, saw these grand explanatory schemes as simply some among many possible narratives. There are countless 'little narra-tives' (*petites histoires*), argued Lyotard, that jockey for position, begging for our attention and allegiance. There is no single Truth; there are, instead, multiple truths, thus causing what he called a crisis of legitimation. What the postmodern did was deprive the modern of its idea of a single anchoring centre (it was thus 'de-centred') and of any certainty (as rationally established). This was the effect of what Lyotard calls the postmodern 'incredulity toward metanarratives' (Lyotard 1984: xxiv). Not surprisingly, there has been considerable negative reaction to this unsettling and deconstructing move, and from a wide variety of political and philosophical positions. Habermas argued that the project of modernity, with its roots in the eighteenth-century **Enlightenment** faith in rationality, was still unfinished and required completion – not destruction (1980). (For Lyotard, that particular grand narrative of modernity, on the contrary, had been ended by history – by which he meant the Nazi concentration camps (1992: 18).) American Marxist critic Fredric **Jameson** saw in the postmodern only the negative 'cultural logic of late capitalism' (Jameson 1984; 1992). For French sociologist Jean **Baudrillard**, postmodernity brought with it a crisis in how we represent and understand the world around us.

Why, we might well ask, was the postmodern perceived as such a threat? One reason may lie in its social and political history. The calling of attention to little narratives could be seen, in part, as the result of a series of oppositional movements, primarily in Europe and North America, which arose during the 1960s and 1970s. Students, workers, women, gays and lesbians, African and Native Americans, and many others took to the streets to make sure their little narrative was heard; the civil rights and anti-Vietnam war movements were protests against the tyranny of the grand narratives of repressive **power**. In other parts of the world, decolonization brought with it a generalized awareness not only of challenges to imperial metanarratives but also of the limitations of a purely Euro-American focus. Out of all this came what African American theorist Cornel **West** aptly called 'the new cultural politics of difference' (1990). Those who had been ignored by the grand narratives now demanded to be heard. Herein lay the roots of the postmodern focus on those who have been excluded, those variously referred to in the theory as the marginal, the ex-centric, the **different** or the other.

This historical context also explains the very real threat to modernity's belief in the value of the universal and the general, or what came to be called the 'totalizing'. One of the lessons to be learned from the differing views of (post)modernity held by the German Habermas and the French Lyotard was that one's particular national culture and history had a determining effect on one's theorizing. So too, some argued, did things like religion, gender, race, ethnicity and sexual choice. The local and the particular became the anchors of post-modern 'situated knowledges' (**Haraway** 1991: 195) in a more generic way than they were in the more focused theories of identity politics just listed (to which we shall return shortly).

In an even broader sense of the word, 'identity' became another point of contention in postmodernity. In fact, the very word came to be replaced by the term 'subjectivity'; the 'individual' became the '**subject**'. The core of modernity's idea of human identity had come from two sources: liberal humanism and capitalism. From the Renaissance on, humanism had placed 'Man' at its centre and granted 'him' a unique, coherent, rational, autonomous identity. However, the individual was still said to partake of a general and universalized essence called 'human nature'. Capitalism (or so German critical theorist Theodor W. **Adorno** argued (1978: 280)) both needs and yet manipulates 'him' into mass conformity in the name of democratic ideals. Postmodernity de-centred these concepts of selfhood, and substituted for this monolith of 'Man' the ambiguity of the 'subject'. Under the influence of poststructuralist theory's view of human consciousness as not the source of language, but as constructed in and by language, the postmodern adoption of this idea of the 'subject' was also meant to suggest both the 'subject' of a sentence (the agent of a verb) and the idea of being 'subjected to' the language that constructs one's identity.

What was clear in the postmodern notion of the subject as divided within itself, and as anything but a coherent and independent source of reason and meaning (*cogito ergo sum*), was the strong impact of the thinking of a number of French poststructuralist theorists: literary semiotician Roland **Barthes**' analysis of how we come to accept the 'doxa' – public opinion, the 'Voice of Nature', the given, what goes without saying (1977a: 47); the related theorizing of how we are recruited as 'subjects' by **ideology** (that is, how we are subjected to social values and made to internalize them as 'natural') that was carried out by Marxist philosopher Louis **Althusser**; psychoanalyst Jacques **Lacan**'s rereading of Freud's theories of the unconscious through the lenses of structuralist linguistics; philosopher Gilles **Deleuze**'s provocative reconsideration of Nietzsche's idea of the will to power. However, French theorist Michel **Foucault** was paramount in calling attention to the subject in relation to this idea of power and in rethinking the nature of power relations. For Foucault, power is not imposed from above and it is not something outside us. Power is everywhere, he argued; but so too is resistance. The aim of his work, he said, was to 'locate the forms of power, the channels it takes, and the discourses it permeates . . . in short, the "polymorphous techniques of power"' (Foucault 1984: 11). And the result was an interrogation of the power that lies inherent in the language we use daily (and thus daily gets perpetuated by it) as well as the power of the institutions that support and are supported by that language.

Out of this intersection of poststructuralist theories came not only a linking of the self to the world (through language and power) but also a postmodern sense of selfhood or subjectivity that flatly contradicted everything about identity defined by modernity's humanism and rationalism. This postmodern self was not seen as a coherent whole, but rather as always having traces of the other within itself. Once again, 'both/and' thinking replaced 'either/or'. Binary oppositions were deconstructed; implied hierarchies were challenged, as Derrida said they should be. Like its cultural and artistic form (postmodernISM), postmodernITY as a social and political condition appeared fundamentally contradictory, or at the very least paradoxical: it was both a break from and a continuation of what had come before. But there were other, even more basic, postmodern paradoxes as well.

POSTMODERN PARADOXES

BOTH INWARD-LOOKING *AND* OUTWARD-LOOKING

Like poststructuralist theory, postmodern art self-consciously looked inwards to examine critically the concepts and conventions that underpinned the very idea of 'art', but it did not do so in the way some modernist art had: that is, arguing for art's self-sufficient autonomy from the world. On the contrary, Barthes' analysis of what he called 'mythology' and Althusser's theorizing of **Ideological State Apparatuses** had had their impact: both theories had worked to reveal and then 'denaturalize' what seemed 'natural' in society and culture. So too did photographic artists like the American Barbara Kruger and novelists like Canadian Timothy Findley (in a work such as *Famous Last Words*). Using the deconstructing tools of parody, irony and self-reflexivity, they critically considered the structures and conventions of their art, but always in terms of the relation of these formal elements to **ideology**. While Jameson saw in postmodern parody only emptiness and pastiche (Jameson 1992: 17), others saw in it the very embodiment of a postmodern paradox (Hutcheon 1988: 11). Parody both continues the life of the work it parodies (by the very act of parodying it), but in a sense it also abducts it for its own critical purposes; it both installs and subverts at the same time. As an ironic form of **intertextuality**, parody engages the history of art, and through it a larger social and cultural history.

But the postmodern was historical in other ways as well. In contrast to Jameson's assertion that the victory of capitalist commodification meant a loss of 'genuine historicity' and therefore a 'random cannibalization' of the styles of the past (1984: 65), novels like American writer E. L. Doctorow's *Ragtime* or Canadian poet and novelist Michael Ondaatje's *In the Skin of a Lion* were not only parodic (though certainly not randomly so) of past literary works but they also dealt directly with both the past and its recording – that is, with history and historiography. While the novel has, from its very inception, been a genre that is both fictive and worldly, the particular form of it that has been labelled 'historiographic metafiction' (Hutcheon 1988: 5) was perhaps the most obvious of the postmodern paradoxical forms that were both self-consciously fictive ('metafiction') and yet directly addressing historical issues, events and personages. Again the overlap between theory and practice made itself felt. In the discipline of history, theorists like the Americans Hayden V. **White** and Dominick LaCapra and the French Paul Veyne and Michel de **Certeau** raised the same issues as the fiction, issues such as the implications of the fact that novels and historiography share a narrative form, or the role of language in the construction of fictional and historical 'worlds'. The postmodern was not ahistorical, despite Jameson's assertion to the contrary, but instead was obsessed with history (Elias 2001: 1). But because poststructuralism and postmodernism together had challenged Western cultural assumptions about totalities and coherent unities, logic and reason, consciousness and subjectivity, representation and truth(s), the history with which the postmodern concerned itself was not the single, neutral or objective Truth assumed of empirical History (with the capital letters symbolizing here the status as 'absolutes' held by these concepts). The claim that historical knowledge is always partial, provisional and in the end indeterminate was not new to postmodernism. But what both postmodern historiographic theory and literature taught was that both history and fiction are equally '**discourses**', that is, ways of speaking about (and thus seeing) the world that are constructed by human beings; both are systems of meaning by which we make sense of the past – and the present. The meaning of history is not therefore in the events but in the narrative (or, quite simply, the story) that makes those past events into present historical 'facts'.

Blurring the boundaries between history and fiction, between the documentary and the self-reflexive, postmodern writing was also paradoxically both serious and playful. This was what attracted American Indian writer Gerald Vizenor to it, for he argued that the postmodern condition found its correlative in native oral cultures, especially in their trickster figure (Vizenor 1989: x–xii). Both narcissistically self-reflexive and yet engaged with the real world of history – as known through its historiographic narratives – postmodern writing was both ironically intertextual and historically engaged. It managed this feat by putting into the foreground (and thus challenging) the conventions and the unack-nowledged ideology of these various discourses, asking us to question the process by which we represent our selves and our world to ourselves, and thereby making us aware of the means by which we literally *make* sense of and construct order out of experience in our particular culture (see Ermarth 1992). These 'repre-sentations' (another central postmodern concept) therefore do not so much *reflect* us and our world (as realist fiction implied) as grant meaning and value to both. And that meaning is never considered single, authentic, pure, closed and homogeneous – and guaranteed by the author's authority and originality; instead it is plural, hybrid, shifting, open and heterogeneous – and thus inviting collaboration with the reader (Trachtenberg 1985: xii): again, both inward-looking and outward-looking.

BOTH POLITICIZED *AND* FENCE-SITTING

Another paradox involved postmodernism's ability to engage and even deconstruct political issues and yet – precisely because of its inclusive both/and logic – still remain sitting on the fence, in a sense, when it came to moving from analysis to action. This was where various politically interventionist movements and postmodernism parted company. Australian cinema theorist Barbara Creed articulated the difference for feminism, but her remarks could apply equally well to any other group, including the more recent 'post' – the postcolonialist:

> Whereas feminism would attempt to explain that crisis [of legitimation described by Lyotard as defining the postmodern] in terms of the working of patriarchal ideology and the oppression of women and other minority groups, postmodernism looks to other possible causes – particularly the West's reliance on ideologies which posit universal truths – Humanism, History, Religion, Progress, etc. While feminism would argue that the common ideological position of all these 'truths' is that they are patriarchal, postmodern theory . . . would be reluctant to isolate a single major determining factor.
>
> (Creed 1987: 52)

The kind of strategic focusing on a single issue that is usually needed for political action was not really possible within postmodern 'both/and' thinking. But this did not stop postmodernism from being seen as a threat to more politically engaged groups.

Fearing the absorption of their own specific interventionary oppositional agendas into those of the generic category called postmodernism, and deeply suspicious of the postmodern's apparent lack of a theory of political action or what was called agency, feminists in the 1980s were among the first to attack postmodernism's complicitous form of critique, that is, its tendency to deconstruct cultural monoliths (a positive) but never to reconstruct (decidedly a negative). Postmodernism, 'in its infinitely skeptical and subversive attitude toward normative claims, institutional justice and political struggles, is certainly refreshing. Yet it is also debilitating' (Benhabib 1992: 15). For oppositional critics, the value of postmodern theory's suspicion of truth-claims and its 'denaturalizing' and deconstructing impulses was compromised by its eventual canonization as a kind of super-discourse of opposition (Heble 1996: 78). For some, postmodernism's deliberate open-endedness, its 'both/and' thinking, and its resolute lack of resolution risked immobilizing oppressed people. Others responded, however, by arguing that postmodernism was as liberating and empowering as it was disturbing: it all depended on whose power was being challenged. The act of installing but then subverting those grand narratives had the potential to fulfil what African American writer bell **hooks** called a 'yearning' for a critical voice in those who had been silenced by the dominant powers (1990).

Yet, as postcolonial theorists insisted (echoing feminists before them), it can be hard to achieve activist ends (with firm moral values) in a postmodern world where such values are not permitted to be grounded in some firm and single Truth, where no utopian possibility of change is left untouched by irony and scepticism. Without a coherent unified notion of the human subject, others argued, no 'significantly transformative action' could take place (Eagleton 1996: 16). In contrast, Catherine Belsey has argued at length that poststructural theory offers a way – through critical reflection – of acting in the world for change (Belsey 2002b: 89–107). Be it Foucault writing about resistance and power or Lyotard theorizing postmodern language games – in which power shifts with whoever has the word in a dialogue – there have been theorists who have focused on the contradictions within ruling ideologies which allow room for not only resistance but real change. Postmodernism's critique, however, remained somewhat more complicit.

While it is obvious that 'both/and' thinking need not make us 'paralyzed or helpless' because we have to give up 'the luxury of absolute Truths' for the 'local and provisional truths' of postmodern 'situated knowledge' (Marshall 1992: 3), it is also the case that its inclusivity can result in the uncomfortable position referred to above as sitting on the fence. Seeing all sides of an issue, deconstructing oppositions, exposing the traces of the other in the same – these critical activities taught that we can never escape implication in what we are critiquing, and that goes for everything from humanism to capitalism. This was postmodernism's paradox. On the one hand, by the very act of critiquing, it granted seriousness and importance to what it was taking on. And in so doing, it revealed that there was no 'outside' from which to launch any 'objective' attack. The theory that grew out of gay and lesbian identity politics and known as 'queer theory' illustrates the same awareness of position in its very name. 'Queer' was originally a term of abuse, but when appropriated by gays and lesbians themselves, the word changed meaning through irony, while still retaining the traces of its history. Not surprisingly, postmodern and queer theory and practice share both a theoretical base (in poststructuralist theory) and artistic techniques (irony and parody).

Lamenting the substitution of the 'micropolitics' of race, gender and sexuality for 'more classical forms of radical politics, which dealt in class, state, ideology, revolution, material modes of production' (Eagleton 1996: 22), British Marxist Terry Eagleton blamed the postmodern for this transformation (by which he meant reduction) of the concept of the political (Eagleton 1996: 24) and the move away from 'far-reaching political action' (Eagleton 1996: 9). But, as we have seen, these micro-political shifts, on the contrary, may have made the postmodern possible in the first place. But for years the Marxist left joined the neo-conservative right and even the liberal centre to attack or simply to dismiss the postmodern, as much for its politics as for its threatening deconstruction of Truth and reason, History and individuality. Yet postmodernism continued, and its impact is still felt today, although some have argued that electronic technology and globalization have moved us into another 'ism' – one yet to be given a name. Anglo-American cultural critic Dick Hebdige's memorable summing up of the situation over a decade ago still holds today: 'the degree of semantic complexity and overload surrounding the term "postmodernism" at the moment signals that a significant number of people with conflicting interests and opinions feel that there is something sufficiently important at stake here to be worth struggling and arguing over' (Hebdige 1991: 182).

FURTHER READING

Belsey, Catherine (2002b) *Poststructuralism: A Very Short Introduction*, Oxford: Oxford University Press.
  A brief and easy-to-digest introduction to difficult theories.
Bertens, Hans (1986) 'The Postmodern *Weltanschauung* and its Relation to Modernism: An Introductory Survey', in Douwe Fokkema and Hans Bertens (eds), *Approaching Postmodernism*, Amsterdam and Philadelphia, PA: John Benjamins.
  A comprehensive survey of the history of the uses and meanings of the term 'postmodern'.
Creed, Barbara (1987) 'From Here to Modernity: Feminism and Postmodernism', *Screen* 28.2: 47–67.
  A clear and powerfully argued placing of postmodern alongside (and against) feminist theory and practice.
Elias, Amy J. (2001) *Sublime Desire: History and Post-1960s Fiction*, Baltimore, MD: Johns Hopkins University Press.
  An excellent study of the interrelations of history and the genre of romance in postmodern fiction.
Hassan, Ihab (1987) 'Toward a Concept of Postmodernism', in *The Postmodern Turn*, Columbus, OH: Ohio State University Press.
  A later and more developed version of Hassan's early and influential listing of the differences between the modern and the postmodern.

Hebdige, Dick (1991) 'Staking Out the Posts', in Dick Hebdige, *Hiding in the Light*, London: Routledge.

'Stakes out' all the major concepts and theorists in an entertaining manner.

hooks, bell (1990) *Yearning: Race: Gender and Cultural Politics*, Boston, MA: South End Press.

Places postmodern theory and practice in the context of American race and gender politics in a balanced yet critical way.

Hutcheon, Linda (1987) 'Beginning to Theorize Postmodernism', *Textual Practice* 1.1: 10–31.

Derives a theory of the postmodern from artistic practice in various arts, using architecture as a model for the paradoxes of 'both/and' thinking.

Huyssen, Andreas (1986) *After the Great Divide: Modernism, Mass Culture, Post-modernism*, Bloomington, IN: Indiana University Press.

A thorough study of the defining differences between modern and postmodern attitudes to popular or mass culture.

Jameson, Fredric (1984) 'Postmodernism, or the Cultural Logic of Late Capitalism', *New Left Review* 146: 53–92.

The canonical argument against the postmodern for being apolitical and ahistorical pastiche.

Marshall, Brenda K. (1992) *Teaching the Postmodern: Fiction and Theory*, New York: Routledge.

An accessible and engaging example of the overlapping of postmodern theory and practice in action.

Russell, Charles (1985) *Poets, Prophets and Revolutionaries: The Literary Avant-Garde from Rimbaud Through Postmodernism*, New York and Oxford: Oxford University Press.

Clarifies the complex political and artistic relations between the modernist avant-gardes and postmodernism in terms of their double orientation – inward and outward.

Slemon, Stephen (1989) 'Modernism's Last Post', *Ariel* 20.4: 3–17.

A lucid analysis of the differences between postmodernism and postcolonialism, arguing the latter's need to retain modernist foundations for strategic political reasons.

11

RACE AND POSTCOLONIALITY

APOLLO AMOKO

Like all other fields of study and/or modes of critique in contemporary human-ities, 'postcoloniality' and 'race' defy easy definition or summation. Whether conceived of singly or in tandem, each term holds together, in sometimes uneasy if not conflictual co-existence, a diverse range of critics working from a vast array of theoretical, ideological, aesthetic, historical and regional perspectives. What I present here is a particular partisan argument in the full knowledge that someone else working in the same field(s) would, in all likelihood, present the argument differently, if not present a different argument altogether. In short, I want to convey the sense that postcoloniality and race are sites of contestation and debate rather than clearly defined and readily summarized fields.

This chapter addresses three broad areas. First I seek to define two conjoined terms: 'race' and 'postcoloniality'. What does each term signify and what, if any-thing, does each have to do with the other? Why are they conceived of together in this instance? My suggestion is that, though the two terms refer to separable concepts, each of them is, in a fundamental sense, unthinkable without the other. Second, I trace the implications of race and postcoloniality for the discipline of English literature. Polemically, I suggest that, properly understood, the entwined terms, postcoloniality and race, spell the death of English literature as we have historically known it. The postcolonial/race critique renders untenable the idea of English literature originating in medieval England and radiating outwards, in the fullness of time, to the rest of the English-speaking world; it renders suspect, in the words of the postcolonial theorist Simon Gikandi, the 'common period-ization of English studies in epochs such as Medieval, Renaissance, Augustan, or Victorian' (Gikandi 2001: 648). Third, I close by tempering the inflated rhetoric of my prior contentions. I attempt to account for the fact that the discipline of English literature seems to have remained remarkably unchanged in the wake of the postcolonial critique. The discipline seems to have reduced postcoloniality/race, for its radical rhetorical claims, into a mere field of study. The discipline seems to have simply tucked the field of postcolonial/race studies at the tail end of a largely unreconstituted English periodization.

To begin with a self-consciously hyperbolic statement: in conjunction with innovations in gender, sexuality, disability and cultural studies, postcolonial and race studies have, over the last 40 years, come to radically reconfigure the traditional discipline of English literature. (My statement is hyperbolic because it accepts the rhetorical claims made by various radical movements within English literature without taking into account the institutional context that both enables and constrains such claims.) Forty years ago, race and postcoloniality were simply not part of the critical vocabulary; a volume such as this would not have included these concepts. Today the two terms seem to pervade all aspects of literary study. Not only have race and postcoloniality come to constitute legitimate fields of inquiry, but they have also brought new modes of critique to bear on the discipline as a whole. Questions regarding racial difference and colonial history are now routinely asked of all other fields within the discipline. There are two ways to account for this rapid, ostensibly radical, shift, the one 'positive', the other 'negative'. From the positive perspective, one could argue that, as modes of critical inquiry, race and postcoloniality have helped redefine the discipline by challenging its ethnocentric foundations. So radical has that challenge been that the very traditional-ness of traditional English literature has lately been called into question by studies claiming to uncover the discipline's colonial origins. From the negative perspective, however, one could argue that race and post-coloniality are but the latest in a series of fields of inquiry that has been gradually accommodated by an infinitely elastic but fundamentally unchanged discipline.

RACE

In attempting to define the concept of race, one is immediately confronted by a series of paradoxes. Race turns out to be a false idea that has had, and continues to exert, powerful global consequences even after its fundamental falseness has been recognized. There can be no question that *race* (that is, the belief that human beings can be divided into a limited number of morphological categories) and *racism* (that is, discrimination on the basis of race) remain two of the principal forces organizing the modern world. (Race is a necessary condition for, but at least in theory not an inevitable cause of racism.) In much the same way that everyone is thought to 'have' a gender, sexuality and nationality, everyone is thought to 'have' a race. For a long time, this way of thinking about race was validated by mainstream intellectual opinion; to deploy the sexist vocabulary of a bygone era, 'the races of man', were for more than two centuries thought to constitute a legitimate science. But the consensus of intellectual opinion today, both in the humanities and the sciences, seems to be that race is an irredeemably dubious concept: its boundaries are notoriously unreliable and its identity categories ('white', 'black', 'brown', etc.) are internally incoherent. There is greater variation, we are told nowadays, between the members of each so-called race than among the various races. Furthermore, everyone is thought to experience race as an identity that comes from deep within: that is, as a natural expression of one's fundamental identity. But we now know that race is socially constructed from without, and that, like sexuality, nationality and gender, it is a peculiarly modern invention. For all that we claim to know today, everyone is still thought to have a race. Official state documents routinely insist that we declare our race (even if they now may allow for such declarations to be multiple and/or mixed). University officials proclaim their commitment to diversity on campus, by which they mean, among other things, a desire that the faculty and student body comprise different races. In the practice of everyday life, race continues to be one of the principal ways by which we identify each other – and ourselves. In short, lived reality seems daily to belie current academic knowledge. Indeed, in a world in which the spectres of racism still loom large, self-assured academic assertions about the inventedness and falseness of race may seem oddly beside the point, if not reactionary.

For a concept that dominates so much of the modern world, race proves surprisingly difficult to define. Indeed, in the memorable words of Robert Sherman, a character in *Fires in the Mirror* (1991), 'we have sort of lousy language / on the subject [of race] . . . I think we have very, very bad language' (Smith 1991: 66). *Fires in the Mirror*, a compelling drama by the African American performance artist, Anna Deavere Smith, addresses contemporary American racial identities. (The irony is not lost on me that, by way of introducing her to potentially unfamiliar readers, I have, naturally enough, identified Smith by race and nationality.) Based on interviews with a diverse set of real-life characters, the play seeks to come to terms with race riots that rocked New York City in August 1991. *Fires in the Mirror* depicts several instances in which various characters strive, not altogether successfully, to stabilize the identities 'Jewish American' and 'African American' in the volatile context of Crown Heights, a racially mixed immigrant neighbourhood. The characters deploy a number of ostensibly innate physical characteristics, principally skin colour and hair texture. Generally speaking, the characters assume that African Americans have dark skin, while Jewish Americans have light skin. But it emerges that skin colour is a wholly unreliable indicator of race, since some African Americans have light skin. Confronted with the lightness of Smith's racially ambiguous skin, to cite but one example, a young dark-skinned African American's schoolgirl sense of racial identity is thrown radically into doubt. Smith informs us that the girl in question is a teenager of Haitian descent. 'How did I find out I was Black?' she asks herself (Smith 1991: 16). Her entire monologue is an attempt to answer that ostensibly self-evident question. She knows that she is black and has a strong sense of racial pride. 'Black is beautiful', she asserts (Smith 1991: 16). But she is also quick to proclaim that '[w]hite is beautiful too'; her sense of racial pride is clearly not racist. She is at first quite self-confident, perhaps even impatient at the obviousness of the issue: 'When I grew up and I look [sic] in the mirror and saw I was / Black' (Smith 1991: 16). But that was not quite right. She offers a second account that seeks to deepen without invalidating the first: 'When I look at my parents, / That's how I knew I was Black [sic]' (Smith 1991: 16). On this second account, her parents provided the intersubjective reflection on the basis of which she emerges to herself as a racial subject. Race, in other words, is neither self-evident nor self-defined. 'Look at my skin', she says (Smith 1991: 16), still striving to explain how she found out that she was black. She invites her interlocutor, that is, Anna Deavere Smith (a light-skinned black woman), to affirm her blackness. Reversing the interlocutor's gaze she asks, as if suddenly in anxiety and self-doubt, 'You black?'

(Smith 1991: 16). Smith, by her physical ambiguity, confuses the young girl's sense of racial self.

In addition to being inherently unstable, the characters in *Fires in the Mirror* show that both skin colour and hair texture can be radically modified. Instructively, in one of the text's most memorable moments, the African American civil rights leader, Al Sharpton, forcefully defends himself against charges that he had straightened – which is to say 'whitened' – his hair. Moreover, the two identities – Jewish and black – are not necessarily mutually exclusive. As one of the characters – a Jewish housewife as it happens – hesitantly concedes, one can be both black and Jewish. In order to come to the conclusion that a young man she met in the streets was not Jewish, she adds to the fact of his blackness the reality that he was not wearing a yarmulke (Jewish religious headgear). She implies that the young man could have been both black and Jewish. When ostensibly innate physical characteristics fail them, some of the characters in *Fires in the Mirror* turn to the extra-morphological: hairstyle and headgear are thought to embody race as much as, if not more reliably than, skin colour and hair texture. Race, apparently the most interior of identities, comes to rely on superficial external markers.

One of the clearest attempts to define the concepts of race and racism is found in the work of the philosopher and literary scholar Kwame Anthony Appiah. (It is instructively difficult to classify this scholar by race and nationality. The son of a Scottish mother and a Ghanaian father, he initially wrote as a self-identified 'African', but has become self-consciously 'American' in his subsequent scholarship.) In an essay aptly titled 'Racisms', Appiah avers that there are at least three distinct doctrines that express the theoretical content of race and racism: *racialism*, *intrinsic racism* and *extrinsic racism*. Appiah defines racialism as the belief

> that there are heritable characteristics, possessed by members of our species, that allow us to divide them into a small set of races, in such a way that all the members of these races share certain traits and tendencies with each other that they do not share with members of any of other race.
>
> (Appiah 1990: 4–5)

These distinct characteristics are thought to constitute 'racial essences'. Appiah contends that racialism (which he considers a dubious concept) need not be dangerous or destructive *even if* the various races were assigned moral and intellectual dispositions. As long as such assignment is impartial and equitable, race would remain a harmless foible.

The second doctrine that expresses the theoretical content of racism in Appiah's model is extrinsic racism. He defines extrinsic racists as people who 'make moral distinctions between members of different races because they believe that the racial essence entails certain morally relevant qualities' (Appiah 1990: 5). 'The basis for the extrinsic racists' discrimination between people', he continues, is their belief that members of different races differ in respects that *warrant* the differential treatment, respects – such as honesty or courage or intelligence – that are uncontroversially held (at least in most contemporary cultures) to be acceptable as a basis for treating people differently.

(Appiah 1990: 5)

Extrinsic racism rests on claims that are subject to empirical verification or falsification. As Appiah argues,

[e]vidence that there are no such differences in morally relevant characteristics – that Negroes are not especially lacking in intellectual capacity or that Jews are not especially avaricious – should thus lead people out of their racism if it is purely extrinsic.

(Appiah 1990: 5)

The final doctrine in Appiah's model is intrinsic racism. Intrinsic racists are people who 'believe that each race has a different moral status, quite independent of the moral characteristics entailed by its racial essence' (Appiah 1990: 5–6). Unlike the extrinsic variety, intrinsic racism does not hinge on empirical claims. In much the same way that many people think that biological relatives are entitled to preferential treatment as a matter of course, intrinsic racists believe that people of the same race are naturally entitled to special consideration.

Racialism (as well as extrinsic racism) was prominently at work in the formulation of the modern idea of literature in general and English literature in particular. As Appiah puts it, a new – and ultimately false – theory of race, inaugurated in the eighteenth and nineteenth centuries, colours 'our modern understanding of literature – indeed of most symbolic culture – in fundamental ways, and this despite the fact that many of these assumptions have been officially discarded' (Appiah 1992: 47). He argues that the terms race, nation and literature are bound together in the modern intellectual history of the West by the

dual connection made in the eighteenth- and nineteenth-century Euro-American thought between, on the one hand, race and nationality, and, on the other, nationality and literature. In short, the nation is the key middle term in understanding the relations between the concept of *race* and the idea of literature.

(Appiah 1992: 48)

Put simply, the nation was conceived of as united by race, and the grandeur of each nation was thought to be powerfully manifest in its culture, specifically its 'high' literature. At the heart of the idea of English literature, for instance, were nationalist, if not racist, arguments regarding the supremacy of the 'Anglo-Saxon race'. These arguments were first articulated during the Victorian age by such writers as Martin Farquhar Tupper, the now forgotten but once famous English poet and novelist. Appiah suggests that it was on account of the idea of an 'Anglo-Saxon race' that the origins of English literature were identified:

not in its antecedents in the Greek and Roman classics that provided the models and themes of so much of the best known works of English 'poesy'; not in the Italian models that influenced the drama of Marlowe and Shakespeare; but in *Beowulf*, a poem in the Anglo-Saxon tongue, a poem that was unknown to Spenser and Shakespeare, the first poets to write in a version of the English language that we can still almost understand.

(Appiah 1992: 51)

Appiah points out that when English literature was instituted as an academic discipline in English universities in the nineteenth century 'students were required to learn Anglo-Saxon in order to study *Beowulf*. Anglo-Saxonism thus played a major role in the establishment of the **canon** of literary works that are to be studied in both British and American colleges' (Appiah 1992: 51–2). In short, race was at core of the modern idea of English literature.

Arguments such as Appiah's have helped breach the self-evidence of the system of classification and periodization that continues to govern English literature. His argument is motivated by the desire to contest the normalization of race as a ground in aesthetic inquiry whether that normalization takes the form of jingoistic imperialism or anti-colonial nationalism. As such, there is a contemporary – 'postcolonial' if you will – dimension to his critique. If English literature rests on a dubious conjunction of race, nation and culture, then later attempts to inaugurate other literatures in English – such as American literature in the nineteenth century and postcolonial African literature or African American literature in the second half of the twentieth century – rest on similarly dubious premises. If the idea of an English literature that embodied an Anglo-Saxon essence was predicated on a historical fallacy, then later attempts to propagate the idea of an African or African American literature that embodied a black essence are predicated on an imitative fallacy.

POSTCOLONIALITY

Postcolonial studies refer to an effort by scholars in such diverse disciplines as literature, cultural studies, history and anthropology to come to terms, from a global perspective, with the legacy of European **colonialism**. In the wake of the voyages of exploration and 'discovery' from the fifteenth century onwards, a few European powers (England, Belgium, France, Spain, Portugal and the Netherlands) came gradually to exercise sovereignty over vast territories covering roughly 80 percent of the world. In political, social, economic and cultural terms, the colonial situation effected epochal transformations of not only the conquered societies but also imperial Europe. The colonial encounter resulted in the consolidation of the idea of European or Western modernity at the apex of human civilization. It also resulted in incomplete, chaotic and traumatic attempts forcibly to transform other societies in the image of that modernity.

By the end of the twentieth century virtually all formerly colonized territories had become independent nations, but the effects of colonial rule continue to be powerfully felt at multiple levels. The practice of everyday life in vast sectors of both the ex-colonizing and the ex-colonized worlds continue to be governed, often with devastating consequences, by ideas about racial, national, continental, gender, sexual and other identities invented in the context of the colonial encounter. The political economies of many formally independent nations also continue to be characterized by fundamental contradictions, inequalities and dependencies brought about by colonial rule. Finally, the global economic, political and cultural order continues to be organized in terms of a contest pitting the interests of a handful of wealthy and disproportionately powerful nations against a multitude of poor and relatively powerless nations.

As a field within (but by no means limited to) English literature, postcolonialism studies the history and legacy of colonialism from the disciplinary perspective of literary and cultural studies. The field explores a rich variety of cultural objects (including literary texts) from a range of theoretical and critical perspectives. It traces the vexed historical and enduring relationship between culture, race, nationality and imperialism. There are, to my mind, two dimensions to postcoloniality, the one 'historical', the other 'contemporary'. The historical critique proposes a rereading of the canonical texts and paradigms of so-called traditional English or Western literature from the standpoint of race and colonialism. Edward **Said**'s books, *Orientalism* (1978) and *Culture and Imperialism* (1993), have proved foundational for this mode of postcolonial critique. Postcoloniality traces the history of the institutions specifically designed to organize and promote the study of culture, such institutions as English departments in the university. Many of these institutions trace their historical origins to the colonial moment and were profoundly affected by that context. In a way that would seem to complement Appiah's trenchant theoretical critique, a number of historical studies have recently emerged to challenge the ethnocentric foundations of English literature. These studies have sought to establish the origins of English literature elsewhere than early modern England. The most famous of these studies is probably Gauri Viswanathan's *Masks of Conquest* (1989). At the heart of Viswanathan's project is the contention that, as an academic discipline, English literature traces it origins not to imperial England, but rather to colonial India. In pointed rebuttal of the link presumed between the history of English literature and the national history of England, she writes:

> The amazingly young history of English literature as a subject of study (it is less than a hundred and fifty years old) is frequently noted, but less appreciated is the irony that English literature appeared as a subject in the curriculum of the colonies long before it was institutionalised in the home country.
>
> (Viswanathan 1989: 2–3)

Not only was the discipline founded on questionable racial premises, but it was also inaugurated in the context of colonialism. English literature sought, by means of an aesthetic education, to 'Anglicize' subject populations designated as racial others. In an instructive irony, it apparently sought to do so prior to the formal Anglicization of the English themselves.

The contemporary dimension of postcoloniality seeks paradigms and parameters for reading global culture in the wake of colonialism. Perhaps the earliest attempt to codify postcoloniality into a coherent theory in the context of English literature is found in *The Empire Writes Back*, a ground-breaking book by three Australian scholars, Bill Ashcroft, Gareth Griffiths and Helen Tiffin published in 1989. The three writers attempt to provide the rules for all the objects, operations, concepts and theoretical options for a field of study they named 'english literature', the postcolonial writing from former British colonies, in contradistinction to 'English literature', the literature of Imperial England (see Ashcroft *et al.* 1989: 1–13). The latter discourse, according to Ashcroft, Griffiths and Tiffin, is a condition of possibility for the emergence of the former. The mediating circumstance between the two discourses is colonial history:

> More than three-quarters of the people living in the world today have had their lives shaped by the shared experience of colonialism. It is easy to see how important this has been in the political and economic spheres, but its general influence on the perceptual frameworks of contemporary peoples is often less evident. Literature offers one of the most important ways in which these new perceptions are expressed and it is in their writing, and through their other arts such as painting, sculpture, music, and dance that the day-to-day realities experienced by colonised peoples have been most powerfully encoded and so profoundly influential.
>
> (Ashcroft *et al.* 1989: 1)

Elaborating on what such a general theory of 'english literature' would entail, the three authors proceed to cite examples from the entirety of the English-speaking postcolonial world across vast historical, geographical and cultural contexts – African countries, Australia, Bangladesh, Canada, Caribbean countries, India, Malaysia, Malta, New Zealand, Pakistan, Singapore, South Pacific countries and Sri Lanka.

In Ashcroft *et al.*'s formulation, literary production in the USA is not just 'postcolonial' but, in its relationship with the metropolitan centre, is 'paradigmatic for post-colonial literatures everywhere' (Ashcroft *et al.* 1989: 2). What holds together the diverse national contexts of educated literary consumption discussed by the three authors is the fact of British colonialism *as well as* the particular conception of national culture that is a product of that colonialism. What holds English literature together is the reality of university pedagogies within which literature is understood as representative, in the first instance, of national cultures. As the title suggests, the central argument in *The Empire Writes Back* is the claim that formerly colonized peoples across the globe are writing new national cultures and writing back to the imperial centre in gestures of literary self-affirmation at once nationalist (in their specific expressions) and global (in their cumulative scope).

In *The Empire Writes Back*, postcoloniality is not another name for the so-called third world. The postcolonial world here includes such developed and world dominant countries as the United States, Canada and Australia alongside the impoverished economies of Africa, Asia and the Caribbean. Nor is postcoloniality determined by race. 'White' settler communities are conceived to be postcolonial in the same breadth as 'black' and 'brown' ex-colonies in Africa and Asia. These two points are worth underscoring because, in its canonization in the Anglo-American academy in the late 1980s and early 1990s, the concept of postcoloniality seemed to change quite considerably. In the British and American academy postcoloniality largely came to stand for underdeveloped, displacing thereby earlier paradigms such as 'neo-colonialism' and 'dependency theory', which sought to explain the failures of third world nationalism and the persistence of imperial relations after the end of colonialism. These earlier paradigms were rejected because of their grandness and one-sidedness. In the Anglo-American academy, postcoloniality is centrally concerned with questions of race especially as it pertains to the mass migration of people of colour from the ex-colonies of Africa, Asia and the Caribbean to the imperial centres of Britain and America. As such, émigré intellectuals such as Homi **Bhabha,** Simon Gikandi, Edward Said and Gayatri **Spivak** came to play a defining role in the codification of postcolonial theory in Anglo-American literary studies. Beyond literary studies, other émigré intellectuals, including the cultural critic Stuart **Hall**, the anthropologist Arjun Appadurai and the historian Achille Mbembe, helped define the field.

In its Anglo-American incarnation, the dominant strain of postcolonial theory has been allied with two apparently antithetical intellectual forces namely **globalization** and poststructuralism. From its affiliation with poststructuralist thought (most notably the work of French philosophers like Jacques **Derrida**, Michel **Foucault** and Jean-François **Lyotard**), postcolonialism in its Anglo-American incarnation has adopted an attitude, in Lyotard's famous words, of 'incredulity towards **metanarratives**' (Lyotard 1984: xxiv). Lyotard designates as modern 'any science that legitimates itself with reference to a metadiscourse . . . making an explicit appeal to some **grand narrative**, such as the **dialectics** of the Spirit, the **hermeneutics** of meaning, the emancipation of the rational or working subject, or the creation of wealth' (Lyotard 1984: xxiii). The modern age was the age of grand narratives: universal reason, rationality, race, nationality and so on. The postmodern age exposes the limits of these grand narratives without positing new ones in their place. From this perspective, 'english literature' as Ashcroft *et al.* conceive of it may be regarded as a narrative as grand as the myth of English literature that it seeks to replace. In its dominant Anglo-American tradition, postcoloniality tends to reject grand narratives of all sorts. For such critics as Bhabha, the postcolonial is an exemplary instance of postmodernity. Drawing from poststructural thought, Bhabha sees the postcolonial subject as radically decentred, hybrid and fluid. Even as his theory seems to depend on such foundational categories as 'race', 'nation' and 'empire', he seeks to contest rather the authority of these terms. He rejects the binary oppositions – between self and other, margin and centre – that attach to these terms.

Apropos of the link between globalization and postcoloniality, Gikandi contends that:

> *Globalization* and *postcoloniality* are perhaps two of the most important terms in social and cultural theory today. Since the 1980s, they have functioned as two of the dominant paradigms for explaining the transformation of political and economic relationships in a world that seems to become increasingly interdependent with the passing of time, with boundaries that once defined national cultures becoming fuzzy.
>
> (Gikandi 2001: 627)

In harmony with poststructuralist thought, globalization tells of a world coming together without a defining centre. Globalization refers to the emergence of a world economy characterized, among other things, by the recent phenomenon of mass migration, increasingly rapid telecommunication, and the rapid flow of both capital and economic goods across national boundaries. More directly germane to literary studies, discourses of globalization suggest that the production, circulation and consumption of the objects of culture – movies, books, electronic texts, clothing, food and so on – occur in excess of or outside the logic and bounds of the nation-state. These developments are thought to have undermined, or at any rate diminished, the authority of the nation-state. Bhabha argues: 'The very concepts of homogenous national cultures, the consensual or contiguous trans-mission of historical traditions, or "organic" ethnic communities – *as the grounds of cultural comparativism* – are in the process of profound redefinition' (Bhabha 1994: 5). He suggests that 'there is overwhelming evidence of a more trans-national and translational sense of the hybridity of imagined communities' (Bhabha 1994: 5). In short, the postcolonial subject comes to proclaim the death of national literature.

In an argument that neatly summarizes the cultural logic of the discourses of globalization, Bhabha posits a new internationalism whose demography 'is the history of postcolonial migration, the narratives of cultural and political diaspora, the major social displacements of peasant and aboriginal communities, the poetics of exile and the grim prose of political and economic refugees' (Bhabha 1994: 5). On the face of things, the evidence for transnational and translational imagined communities seems compelling:

> Contemporary Sri-Lankan theatre represents the deadly conflict between Tamils and the Sinhale through allegorical references to State brutality in South Africa and Latin America; the Anglo-Celtic canon of Australian Cinema is being rewritten from the perspective of Aboriginal political and cultural imperatives; the South African novels of Richard Rive, Bessie Head, Nadine Gordimer, John Coetzee, are documents of a society divided by the effects of apartheid that enjoin the international intellectual community to meditate on the unequal, asymmetrical

worlds that exist elsewhere; Salman Rushdie writes the fabulist historiography of post-Independence India and Pakistan in *Midnight's Children* and *Shame*, only to remind us in *The Satanic Verses* that the truest eye may now belong to the migrant's double vision; Toni Morrison's *Beloved* revives the past of slavery and its murderous rituals of possession and self-possession in order to project a contemporary fable of a woman's history that is at the same time the narrative of an affective, historic memory of an emergent public sphere of men and women alike.

(Bhabha 1994: 5)

The mobile, hybrid, and fluid postcolonial subject would seem to be the global subject par excellence.

CONCLUSION

My argument may have seemed to cast the effect of race and postcoloniality in contemporary literary studies in a 'positive' light. From the 'negative' perspective, however, I want to suggest, in closing, that race and postcoloniality may well be but some of the latest in a series of fields of inquiry that have gradually and cumulatively been accommodated by a bewilderingly capacious discipline. Like any other field, the two conjoined fields now have their respective slots within the discipline. Like every other field, race and postcoloniality have now generated canonical authors and courses, systems of coherence, rules for evidence, and protocols for readings as well as a growing army of faculty, graduate and undergraduate students. Notwithstanding the radical claims made *within* this entwined field, the discipline of English literature remains largely unchanged by the addition of race and postcoloniality at its margins.

Why has the discipline proved hospitable to the new field but indifferent to its radical central claims? The answer to this question is to be found in the compartmentalized nature of knowledge production in the discipline of English literature. As the American literary scholar Gerald Graff asserts,

For reasons having to do equally with ensuring humanistic breadth and facilitating specialized research, the literature department adopted the assumption that it would consider itself respectfully staffed once it had amassed instructors competent to 'cover' a more or less balanced spread of literary periods and genres, with a scattering of themes and general topics.

(Graff 1987: 6–7)

What Graff calls 'the field-coverage principle' allowed the English department to operate in a model of self-regulating efficiency:

By assigning each instructor a commonly understood role – to cover a predefined period or field – the principle created a system in which the job of instruction could proceed as if on automatic pilot, without the need for instructors to debate aims and methods.

(Graff 1987: 7)

Graff's model of the English department is analogous to the model of perfect competition under capitalism propounded by the Scottish moral and economic philosopher Adam Smith (1723–90). According to Smith, optimal production is ensured not by careful government regulation and centralized planning, but rather by the free, seemingly chaotic, flow of goods and services in conditions of perfect competition. Although each actor is guided by narrow self-interest, the free flow of goods and services will eventually ensure, as if guided by an invisible hand, optimal social outcomes with no need going unfulfilled and no wasteful production. If the English department were understood as a marketplace of aesthetic ideas, then the field-coverage principle would seem to reproduce Smith's fantasy. Individual actors driven by narrow self-interest might specialize in specific fields. But the totality of their apparently chaotic efforts would eventually ensure a self-regulating discipline in which all fields as they currently existed were optimally represented and in which new fields could be efficiently accommodated.

As Graff argues, however, the field-coverage principle produces efficiency at a steep price. Under the guise of efficacious knowledge production and dissemination, questions regarding the fundamental coherence of the discipline are infinitely deferred. Questions regarding the internal coherence of each field are similarly deferred. Finally, also deferred are questions regarding the connections between the various fields. There is, in fact, created between the fields what Graff terms 'systematic non-relationship' (Graff 1987: 8). In a sense, this volume demonstrates Graff's point: postcoloniality and race have been assigned a prominent slot. But, as I write this chapter, I am blissfully unaware what claims my co-authors – experts in other fields – may be making and how their claims relate to mine. In Graff's estimation, the range of questions effaced include:

> what connections or contrasts the different periods and genres might bear to one another, what was meant by a particular periodization or by 'period' in general, or what it might mean to approach literature in a historical or generic (and later a 'New Critical' way). It was as if these categories existed in order to make it unnecessary to think about them and to recognise that they were the product of theoretical choices.
>
> (Graff 1987: 8)

The constitution of race and postcoloniality as fields within the discipline of English literature accounts for their at once radical and limited impact. Graff avers that the field-coverage principle simultaneously encourages and disables novel scholarship: 'innovation even of a most threatening kind could be welcomed by simply *adding* another unit to the aggregate of fields to be covered' (Graff 1987: 7). Innovation, he observes, was welcomed precisely because it did not entail change in other fields. The conclusion seems as dismal as it is inevitable:

It is only the field-coverage principle that explains how the literature department has managed to avoid incurring paralyzing clashes of ideology during a period when it preserved much of its earlier traditional orientation while incorporating disruptive novelties such as contemporary literature, black studies, feminism, Marxism, and deconstruction.

(Graff 1987: 7)

I began my essay by assessing the prospects of postcoloniality and race optimistically; I end, alas, pessimistically. English literature giveth and English literature taketh away.

FURTHER READING

Appiah, Kwame Anthony (1992) *In My Father's House: Africa in the Philosophy of Culture*, New York: Oxford University Press.
   A trenchant philosophical examination of a number of important issues including race, culture, literature, nation and identity from the perspective of contemporary Africa.
Bhabha, Homi K. (1994) *The Location of Culture*, London: Routledge.
   A dense and provocative elaboration of some of the key issues in postcolonial studies, in particular such concepts as 'hybridity' and 'ambivalence'.
Gikandi, Simon (2001) 'Globalization and the Claims of Postcoloniality', *South Atlantic Quarterly* 100.3: 627–58.
   A thoughtful and provocative piece challenging the radical claims made on behalf of 'postcoloniality' and 'globalization' within the discipline of English literature.
Godberg, David Theo (ed.) (1990) *Anatomy of Racism*, Minneapolis, MN: University of Minnesota Press.
   An impressive set of essays addressing race and racism from a broad range of disciplinary, ideographical, historical and geographical standpoints.
Said, Edward (1978) *Orientalism*, New York: Vintage.
   One of the earliest and most influential examinations of the relationship between culture and imperialism in the modern history of the West.
Williams, Patricia and Chrisman, Linda (eds) (1994) *Colonial Discourse and Postcolonial Theory: A Reader*, New York: Columbia University Press.
   An anthology of some of the foundational essays in the field of postcolonial studies. From diverse perspectives, the essays address a wide range of cultural, social, historical and political issues pertaining to European colonialism and its aftermath.

Part II
NAMES AND TERMS

CONTENTS

A

ABJECTION A term drawn from psycho-analytic theory that refers to specific acts of exclusion. Etymologically derived from the Latin *abjectus* meaning to throw out, it is Julia **Kristeva** in *Powers of Horror: An Essay on Abjection* (1982) that most comprehensively addresses its complexity.

For Kristeva, the widely held view that the acquisition of language sees the child enter the **symbolic order** and sever their pre-symbolic maternal connection is too simplistic. In *Powers of Horror* she argues that prior to this developmental stage being reached, a preceding state must already have been attained. For Kristeva, entrance to the symbolic order is dependent upon a rejection of the mother *before* the acquisition of language and the child's **unconscious** drives to expel or reject her. Only when this act of abjection has taken place, and the mother becomes the 'object of primal repression', can the child's formation of the *I* proceed.

Following progression into the symbolic order, acts of abjection continue to determine the individual's personal development. In this secondary role, abjection manifests itself as a 'narcissistic crisis', embodying everything we do not wish to see in ourselves, an antithesis of the **ego** ideal.

Ultimately, for Kristeva, the abject represents those ambiguous elements that challenge the boundaries of our experience. She demonstrates this by outlining the sense of horror we feel when our lips touch the *solid* skin on the surface of *liquid* milk. Abjection is that which challenges order and identity and must be continuously jettisoned from the psyche. [PSW]

See also Chapters 1, 6.

Further reading

Kristeva, Julia (1982) *Powers of Horror: An Essay on Abjection*, trans. Leon S. Roudiez, New York: Columbia University Press.

ADORNO, THEODOR WIESENGRUND (1903–69) A German sociologist, philosopher, music theorist and composer. He was a prominent member of the **Frankfurt School** along with Max **Horkheimer**, Walter **Benjamin** and Herbert **Marcuse**, amongst others. Adorno is primarily known for his rigorous analysis of post-war capitalist culture and for coining the term '**culture industry**'.

Having had to emigrate in 1934 because of his Jewish ancestry, Adorno was deeply affected by his experiences in pre-war Germany and the subsequent rise of fascism. For Adorno, fascism, far from being the opposite of civilization, was generated by the rationalization of human society. In *Dialectic of Enlightenment* (1947), Adorno and Horkheimer located civilization's impulse towards self-destruction in the notion of reason itself, which the **Enlightenment** and modern scientific thought had transformed into an irrational force. Adorno concluded that rationalism offers little hope for human emancipation, turning instead to art and the prospects it offers for preserving individual autonomy and fulfilment.

Allied to this, Adorno and Horkheimer viewed modern culture as a degradation of the individual. This is detailed in *The Culture Industry: Enlightenment as Mass Deception* (1947). Their dynamic application of **Marxist** theory introduced **dialectics** as a tool for a critical analysis of consumer culture. They argue that in post-war capitalist culture the commodification and standardization of art has led to the suppression of individuality.

Adorno developed this approach in the posthumously published *Negative Dialectics* (1970), in which he outlines a methodology for deciphering capitalist structures. Adapting Marx's dialectical logic, Adorno argued that multinational capitalism could only be challenged with a multinational dialectic, providing a series of strategies and concepts for that purpose. For Adorno, without a global solidarity transcending nationality, capitalism would become impossible to displace. In *Aesthetic Theory* (1970) Adorno offers a framework for his preceding discussions of art, arguing that art is the ultimate translation of the range of human experience.

Adorno remains significant to Marxist and poststructuralist thought. Most notably his methodology can be seen in the work of the prominent contemporary dialecticians Fredric **Jameson** and Pierre **Bourdieu**, two of the most strident critics of global capitalism. [RW]

See also Chapter 3.

Further reading
Adorno, Theodor and Horkheimer, Max (1992) *Dialectic of Enlightenment*, trans. John Cumming, London: Verso.
Jameson, Fredric (1990) *Late Marxism: Adorno, Or, the Persistence of the Dialectic*, New York: Verso.

AGAMBEN, GIORGIO (1942–) Professor of Aesthetics at the University of Verona in Italy. Influenced by the German philosopher Martin **Heidegger**, with whom he studied, Agamben's work explores the history of European thought to trace the development of contemporary ideas of aesthetics in texts such as *The Man Without Content* (1999), which explores the profound redefinitions of the meaning of art at the beginning of the nineteenth century,

and politics and community in his most influential book *Homo Sacer: Sovereign Power and Bare Life* (1998), which sets off from Michel **Foucault**'s analyses of **power** to analyse sovereignty, the concentration camp and the refugee as the key sites of contemporary political theory. His work produces powerful readings of philosophers and theorists such as Hannah **Arendt**, Walter **Benjamin**, Michel Foucault and Martin Heidegger. [SM]

Further reading
Agamben, Giorgio (1998) *Homo Sacer: Sovereign Power and Bare Life*, trans. Daniel Heller-Roazen, Stanford, CA: Stanford University Press.
Agamben, Giorgio (1999) *The Man Without Content*, trans. Georgia Albert, Stanford, CA: Stanford University Press.

ALTERITY One of the central pillars of contemporary postmodern thought. The term itself is liberally used in literary criticism, referring to otherness either as specific cultural otherness or as otherness in general. In philosophy and critical theory alterity can be found in such concepts as Immanuel Kant's **sublime**, Emmanuel **Levinas**' **other** (*autrui*), Jean-François **Lyotard**'s **event** and Jacques **Lacan**'s Other. The common link between these concepts is the insistence on the existence of something or somebody outside or prior to conceptualization and understanding. Consequently, alterity is what remains irreducible to the **subject**'s conscious experience. In other words, it cannot be intended as something or somebody. In **phenomenological** terms one might say that alterity can never be situated within a horizon of familiarity. Since it transcends (goes beyond) the realm of the already known, it is also that which threatens sameness, the realm of the subject's known world, exposing it to an experience of the unknown. The ethical dimension of alterity lies precisely in this interruption of what

Jacques **Derrida** calls 'the economy of the same' in which the subject is considered the underlying foundation of meaning. [RS]

See also Chapters 7 and 10.

Further reading

Docherty, Thomas (1996) *Alterities: Criticism, History, Representation*, Oxford: Clarendon Press.

Gibson, Andrew (1999) *Postmodernity, Ethics and the Novel: From Leavis to Levinas*, London: Routledge.

ALTHUSSER, LOUIS (1918–90) Althusser is best known for his radical rereading of the works of Karl **Marx**. Marx believed that the economic mode of production (often referred to as the '**base**') determined both the political system and **ideology** (or '**superstructure**'). Capitalism, for instance, produced democratic politics and humanist values. Althusser argues, however, that this relationship is not one of simple cause and effect. Instead, the three 'levels', the economy, politics and ideology, exist in a state of 'relative autonomy'. In other words, they might change independently of one another, so that an ideological shift, such as the rise of humanism, might be the condition, rather than the effect, of the rise of capitalism. The mode of production, however, is determining 'in the last instance'.

His most influential theory is his reinterpretation of the Marxist concept of ideology. For Althusser, ideology is not what Marxists had called 'false consciousness'. Instead, in Althusser's view, it is better understood as a partial relationship to the facts, both limited and partisan. Ideology invites us to accept the cultural and political system we inhabit as natural, unchanging and 'commonsensically' better than any other. It does this by incessantly inviting, cajoling and flattering us into accepting its values as self-evidently true through a process which Althusser calls **interpellation**. As subjects of ideology we are neither pre-programmed robots that regurgitate dominant values, nor the dupes of some elaborate capitalist conspiracy.

Althusser was mainly concerned with the *economic* exploitation of subjects under capitalism, but his theory of ideology is equally useful to an understanding of how people are complicit with their own subjection to racist, sexist or any other ideologies. Examining ideology and the way it works involves politicizing our understanding of culture, denaturalizing 'common sense' notions of how that culture should operate, and resisting, or not consenting to, our own subjection by that culture's rules. [AW]

See also Chapter 3.

Further reading

Althusser, Louis (1996) *For Marx*, trans. Ben Brewster, London: Verso.

Althusser, Louis (2001) 'Ideology and Ideological State Apparatuses', in *Lenin and Philosophy and Other Essays*, trans. Ben Brewster, New York: Monthly Review Press.

APORIA A Greek term that denotes an insoluble problem or paradox; etymologically it comes from *aporos* meaning *impassable* (*a-*, *without*; *poros*, *passage*). In rhetoric and literary theory, it is often used to indicate those moments in a text where meaning becomes ambiguous or appears self-contradictory. In his book *Aporias*, Jacques **Derrida** differentiates an aporia from a problem, arguing that the former is 'the experience of the nonpassage ... What, in sum, appears to block our way or to separate us in the very place where *it would no longer be possible to constitute a problem*, a project, or a projection' (Derrida 1993: 12). In other words, while a problem can be resolved within the rules of logical argument, an aporia calls those very rules into question and remains impossible to incorporate into a straightforward logic. [SM]

See also Chapter 7.

ARENDT, HANNAH (1906–75) A German-American philosopher best known for her post-Second World War political analysis, *The Origins of Totalitarianism* (1951). *Origins* traces the steps toward the unique twentieth-century authoritarianisms of Hitler and Stalin, delineating the broad concept of 'totalitarianism' as an emergent form of dictatorship from within European society. Essentially, Arendt's concept of totalitarianism captures the common factors in fascism and communism, characterized by fantasies of control from within the party – and in the public domain – that led to the transformation of a community into a mass, the end result being the evil of the Holocaust and the gulag.

Arendt was a German Jew living in Germany during the rise of fascism. She originally studied theology; however, the rising anti-Semitism affecting Germany turned her attention to history and politics. Having escaped the Gestapo in 1941, Arendt moved to the USA where she continued to develop her political theory and publish on Jewish politics. Later publications include *Eichmann in Jerusalem: A Report on the Banality of Evil* (1963), an account of Nazism that emerged from her coverage of the trial of Adolph Eichmann in 1961, and the posthumously published *Life of the Mind* (1978), a discussion of politics and democracy. [DD]

Further reading

Arendt, Hannah (1999) *The Origins of Totalitarianism*, Orlando, FL: Harcourt Brace.

AURA A concept that plays a key role in Walter **Benjamin**'s analyses of the impact of technical reproducibility (the photograph, film, compact disc, etc.) upon works of art. In 'Little History of Photography', he defines aura as a 'strange weave of space and time: the unique appearance or semblance of distance, no matter how close it may be' (2000: 518). What he means by this is that the uniqueness for which a work of art is valued, its originality, sets it at a distance from us as something singular. In his essay 'The Work of Art in the Age of Mechanical Reproduction' Benjamin argues that the onset of new technologies has fundamentally changed our relation to artworks as they remove this aura by allowing potentially infinite numbers of identical copies to be produced. He argues that this liberates art from ritual and moves it into the political realm. This account of the loss of aura in a technological age is taken up by a number of postmodern thinkers, particularly Jean **Baudrillard** in his analyses of the infinite interchangeability of **simulations**. [SM]

See also Chapters 3 and 10.

Further reading

Benjamin, Walter (1999) 'The Work of Art in the Age of Mechanical Reproduction', in *Illuminations*, ed. Hannah Arendt, London: Fontana, pp. 211–44.

Benjamin, Walter (2000) 'Little History of Photography', in *Selected Writings*, vol. 2: *1927–1934*, ed. Michael W. Jennings, Howard Eiland and Gary Smith, Cambridge, MA: Harvard University Press, pp. 507–30.

AUSTIN, JOHN LANGSHAW (1911–60) Former White's Professor of Moral Philosophy at Oxford University, Austin was one of the so-called 'ordinary language philosophers' of the 1950s, a group which also included G. E. Moore, and which sought to tackle large philosophical problems via an examination of everyday language use.

His influence, however, extends beyond anglophone philosophy into the realms of linguistics and literary studies. In particular his *How to Do Things with Words* (1962) is viewed as a seminal contribution to **speech act theory**, and sets out his analysis of 'performative' utterances – literally words that 'do' something, perform an act, such as 'I do' in a marriage ceremony, or 'I promise' in all sorts of situations. In more recent years this work has received reappraisals at the hands of J. Hillis **Miller** and Jacques **Derrida**, amongst others. [KM]

See also Chapters 1 and 4.

Further reading

Austin, John Langshaw (1962a) *How to Do Things with Words*, Oxford: Oxford University Press.

Austin, John Langshaw (1962b) *Sense and Sensibilia*, Oxford: Oxford University Press.

Derrida, Jacques (1982) 'Signature Event Context', in *Margins of Philosophy*, trans. Alan Bass, London: Prentice Hall.

Miller, J. Hillis (2001) *Speech Acts in Literature*, Stanford, CA: Stanford University Press.

AUTHOR No longer simply the creator of a literary artefact, the concept of the author has been the site of significant theoretical debate in the twentieth century. The 'common sense' position, which suggests that a reader should learn more about the intentions or life of an author in order to understand the author's creative works, was first challenged by a group of scholars known as the **New Critics** in the 1930s and 1940s. The New Critics argued that meaning did not lie with the author but in the literary text, which was an entity complete in and of itself. Poststructuralism similarly has no interest in the author as origin or guarantee of meaning, but whilst New Criticism effectively sought fixity by attributing to the text an ultimate and immutable meaning, poststructuralists would argue that texts in fact contain an inexhaustible multiplicity of meanings. This view was famously expounded by

Roland **Barthes** in his essay 'The Death of the Author'. For Barthes, the author's only power in composing a text is the power of quotation, and if the author wished 'to *express himself*, he ought at least to know that the inner "thing" he thinks to "translate" is itself only a ready-formed dictionary, its words only explainable through other words, and so on indefinitely' (Barthes 1977a: 146). The real power lies with the reader, who is able to interpret the text from any number of different perspectives and thus activate meanings not necessarily recognized or understood by the author. Michel **Foucault**, in his essay 'What is an Author?' (1977), usefully introduced the term 'author-function' as a way of drawing attention to the fact that the concept of the author has altered throughout history. Foucault charts the connection between authorship and the legal and institutional contexts within which it is asserted, concluding that the concept of the author is nothing more than a way of limiting the dizzying proliferation of meaning inherent in the poststructuralist view of language. [CMa]

See also Chapter 2.

Further reading

Barthes, Roland (1977a) 'The Death of the Author', in *Image Music Text*, trans. Stephen Heath, London: Fontana.

Burke, Sean (1998) *The Death and Return of the Author*, Edinburgh: Edinburgh University Press.

Foucault, Michel (1977) 'What is an Author?', in *Language, Counter-Memory, Practice*, ed. Donald F. Bouchard, trans. Donald F. Bouchard and Sherry Simon, Ithaca, NY: Cornell University Press.

B

BACHELARD, GASTON (1884–1962) French scientist, philosopher and literary critic. The development of Bachelard's early work is evident in his career path which saw him move from the University of Dijon (1930–40), where he lectured on mathematics and physics, to the Sorbonne where he became Professor of the History and Philosophy of Science (1940–62). In the latter role Bachelard undertook an investigation into the formation of scientific knowledge which, he argued, develops not so much by way of a gradual accumulation of facts but rather through a combative process that repeatedly challenges current 'fixed' modes of thinking and perception. This argument, which is often described as an account of history based on 'epistemological breaks', has two significant implications: first, that the pre-existing 'reality' may lead the scientist or observer to be predisposed towards certain ideas/hypotheses; and second, that shifts in scientific knowledge may result in the reformulation of that reality. Bachelard's revolutionary approach to knowledge is best expressed in his *The Philosophy of No*. Bachelard also produced a large volume of literary criticism, much of which emphasizes the role of the imagination. [PW]

Further reading

Bachelard, Gaston (1968) *The Philosophy of No: A Philosophy of the New Scientific Mind*, trans. G. C. Waterston, New York: Orion Press.

Bachelard, Gaston (1971) *On Poetic Imagination and Reverie: Selections from the Works of Gaston Bachelard*, trans. Colette Gaudin, Indianapolis, IN: Bobbs Merrill.

McAllester Jones, Mary (1991) *Gaston Bachelard: Subversive Humanist*, Madison, WI: University of Wisconsin Press.

BADIOU, ALAIN (1937–) French novelist, playwright and philosopher. Starting out as a Maoist communist, Badiou remains a committed political theorist and activist whose philosophical work explores the possibilities for radical transformation and revolutionary action inherent in any situation. Influenced by thinkers such as Jacques **Lacan** and Gilles **Deleuze**, his works explore the ways in which thought and action occur in response to what he calls an '**event**': 'a hazardous, unpredictable **supplement**, which vanishes as soon as it appears' (2001: 67). The task of theory, he argues, is to respond to what is unique in each event, what challenges existing conceptions of the way the world works, and to activate the event's revolutionary potential for change. This, he claims, is to produce the truth of the event rather than reducing it to what is already known and losing what makes it 'hazardous'. As a materialist thinker, Badiou's work also critiques the theological basis of contemporary theories of **ethics**, particularly those that develop from the work of Emmanuel **Levinas** and Jacques **Derrida**. Rather than an ethics based on infinite respect for a transcendent **Other**, he argues that 'genuine ethics is of truths in the plural – or, more precisely, the only ethics is of processes of truth, of the labour that brings *some* truths into the world' (2001: 67). It is, in other words, an ethics that is based on the recognition of the material singularity of each event. [SM]

Further reading

Badiou, Alain (2001) *Ethics: An Essay on the Understanding of Evil*, trans. Peter Hallward, London: Verso.

Badiou, Alain (2004) *Infinite Thought: Truth and the Return of Philosophy*, trans. Oliver Feltham and Justin Clemens, London: Continuum.

BAKHTIN, MIKHAIL MIKHAYLOVICH (1895–1975) Russian literary historian, critic and philosopher best known for his theories about language and the novel. Bakhtin's output was remarkably diverse, but critics have noticed his sustained interest in 'dialogism', the way in which meaning and artistic form always emerge in the social world, as part of a dialogue.

Bakhtin's discussions of language stress that all utterances are socially situated. In his influential essay 'Discourse in the Novel' (in *The Dialogic Imagination*, 1981), he describes language as a rich dialogue of voices, each permeated with its own **ideology** and culture. In this dynamic account, the unity of national languages such as Russian is intersected by a multiplicity of other languages, such as dialect, jargon and generational differences. Bakhtin calls this diversity 'heteroglossia', a term which signals the social conflict over values built into all speech. According to Bakhtin, the novel exploits this linguistic dynamism, replicating the social tensions between the elite and the popular within the apparent unity of a national language.

Interest in dialogism also shapes Bakhtin's literary criticism. *Problems of Dostoevsky's Art* (1929) praises Dostoevsky for inventing the 'polyphonic novel'. Bakhtin uses this term not simply to indicate multiple voices in the novel, but also to characterize the relationship between the characters and the narrator. According to Bakhtin, what is distinctive about Dostoevsky's fiction is that the characters are given voices in their own right and granted as much authority as the narrator. A further version of this dialogism is Bakhtin's attention to popular rather than learned sources through his ideas on **carnival/carnivalesque**.

Bakhtin's theories are important because they offer a way of discussing the novel in social terms, as a space where differing views of the world collide and conflict. This emphasis on multiple voices has been picked up by theorists eager to recover marginalized voices. Henry Louis **Gates** Jr, for instance, adopts a Bakhtinian approach to theorize a distinctive African-American vernacular tradition in *The Signifying Monkey* (1987). [RF]

See also Chapter 2.

Further reading

Bakhtin, Mikhail (1981) *The Dialogic Imagination: Four Essays*, Michael Holquist (ed.), trans. Caryl Emerson and Michael Holquist, Austin, TX: University of Texas Press.

Dentith, Simon (1995) *Bakhtinian Thought: An Introductory Reader*, London: Routledge.

Holquist, Michael (2002) *Dialogism: Bakhtin and his World*, London: Routledge.

BARTHES, ROLAND (1915–80) Barthes studied French literature and classics at University in Paris, and after working as a schoolteacher and as a lecturer in universities in Romania and Egypt, he returned to Paris to work at the Centre National de Recherche Scientifique, and became chair of Literary Semiology at the Collège de France.

Mythologies, published in French in 1957, launched Barthes' career as one of the most important cultural critics of the twentieth century. It is also one of the foundational texts of modern cultural studies. A series of short essays about such diverse topics as amateur wrestling, steak and chips, and literature and criticism, the book applies a **Saussurean** account of language and the linguistic **sign** to a series of readings of the objects that constituted French culture. The essays are incisive and witty explorations of cultural meanings that Barthes calls 'myths'. The preface to the book states: 'I resented seeing nature and history confused at every turn, and I wanted to track down, in the decorative display of *what-goes-without-saying*, the **ideological** abuse which, in my view, is hidden there' (Barthes 1993: 11). In each essay, Barthes draws attention to the ways in which historically contingent cultural *meanings* are continually passed off as common-sensical, unchanging or natural *truths*.

One essay reads a famous photographic exhibition called *The Great Family of Man*. The exhibition's aim is to 'show the universality of human actions in the daily life of all the countries of the world' (Barthes 1993: 100). It invites the visitor to suppose that birth, death, work and play are shared practices which unite us all. However, for Barthes, such calls for the recognition of a universal human essence always elide, or mask, existing social injustices, or seek to preserve existing power structures. The cultural reproduction of '**myths**' like the 'family of man' ignores race, gender and class inequalities. The seemingly natural, or innocent, cultural object is shown to have political and cultural significance.

Throughout the 1960s Barthes continued to develop the new discipline of **semiology**. He did this by analysing popular cultural objects, by reading **canonical** texts, and by writing theoretical books (such as *Elements of Semiology*). One of Barthes' boldest theoretical arguments came in his famous 1968 essay 'The Death of the **Author**' in which he states that the literary critical institution has controlled the meanings of texts by insisting on identifying the author as their primary explanation and guarantee. Once the author no longer fixes interpretation, the literary text becomes open to new readings. No longer understood as determined by one privileged mind,

the text is seen as a 'tissue of quotations drawn from the innumerable centres of culture' and therefore open to a range of different readings (Barthes 1977a: 146).

His most influential work of literary criticism, *S/Z* (published in French in 1970), takes these ideas further. It starts by distinguishing two kinds of text: 'writable' and 'readable'. The reader of writable texts is invited to produce meaning, whereas the reader of the readable text is invited to consume it. Writable texts draw attention to their own intertextuality, reject the kind of coherent plot that usually characterizes fiction, and invite the reader to understand the *plurality* of meanings connoted by the many cultural 'quotations' which constitute the work. Readable texts, such as classic realist nineteenth-century novels and current works of popular fiction, meet the expectations of the reader, limit multiple interpretations and invite the reader to accept a single, stable meaning. Despite the restricted and restricting way in which the readable text addresses the reader, however, these works *can* actively be read in order to draw attention to the plural meanings and **intertexts** which constitute all writing. Barthes demonstrates this with a dazzling, imaginative, and extremely detailed, reading of Honoré de Balzac's short story, 'Sarrasine'. This reading mimics some of the characteristics of Barthes' writable text in the way it does not construct a linear critical narrative that ends in an easily identifiable conclusion. Instead it identifies a number of very different ways of tracing the problems the text is obliged to confront, including the unsavoury origins of wealth and the instability of gender. One of the most striking things about Barthes' work is the range of the cultural objects he reads. As well as the things already discussed, he also focuses on films, photography and biography as part of this cultural semiotic analysis. [AW]

See also Chapters 1, 2 and 4.

Further reading

Barthes, Roland (1977) 'The Death of the Author', in *Image Music Text*, trans. Stephen Heath, London: Fontana.

Barthes, Roland (1990) *S/Z*, trans. Richard Miller, Oxford: Blackwell.

Barthes, Roland (1993) *Mythologies*, trans. Annette Lavers, London: Verso.

BASE / SUPERSTRUCTURE A **materialist** conception of the relationship between economics and culture. 'Base' refers to the economic modes of production at the basis of any society. This economic base determines the 'superstructure', or the public, political and intellectual configuration of that social system.

Karl **Marx** proposed this system in his 'Preface' to *A Contribution to the Critique of Political Economy* (1859). For Marx the individual is subject to external forces 'independent of their will' which are shaped by the modes of production. This principle forms the basis for the everyday formation of judicial and religious institutions. Marx contended that this produced 'definite forms of social consciousness' which, in a capitalist society, were 'false', or an illusion to secure social compliance.

These early formulations are now generally regarded as excessively deterministic. In place of the base/superstructure dichotomy, subsequent Marxist theorists have elaborated more refined conceptions of the material construction of society. These include Antonio **Gramsci**'s theory of hegemony, Louis **Althusser**'s outline of the **Ideological State Apparatus** and Theodor **Adorno**'s work on the **culture industry**. [RW]

See also Chapter 3.

Further reading

Elster, Jon (1986) *Karl Marx: A Reader*, Cambridge: Cambridge University Press.

Williams, Raymond (1977) *Marxism and Literature*, Oxford: Oxford University Press.

BATAILLE, GEORGES (1897–1962) French **Marxist** cultural philosopher, essayist and novelist renowned for his incorporation of orgiastic excess into both theory and fiction. Along with the surrealist André Breton and theorist Roger Callois, he developed the anti-fascist publication *Contra-Attaque*. Together they helped found Acephale, an intellectual forum that gave rise to the significant theoretical body, the College of Sociology.

Bataille was primarily interested in sex, death, transgression, the sacred and the power of the obscene. Although notoriously contradictory, his books *Literature and Evil* (1957) and *Eroticism* (1957) expound the rejection of traditional literature. His novels detail stories of orgies, degradation, sadism and torture, usually culminating in a definitive act of sacrilege. Bataille considered that the ultimate aim of all intellectual, artistic, or religious activity should be the annihilation of the rational individual in a violent, transcendental act of communion.

In general, Bataille rejects the acquisitive principle of capitalism, arguing that it is inhibitive to individual fulfilment, and his work continues to offer a route into the complex, unspoken and repressed world beneath the façade of modern civilization. [RW]

See also Chapters 3, 6 and 10.

Further reading

Bataille, Georges (1990) *Literature and Evil*, trans. Alastair Hamilton, London: Marion Boyars Publishers.

Bataille, Georges (1991) *Eroticism*, trans. Mary Dalwood, San Francisco, CA: City Lights.

BAUDRILLARD, JEAN (1929–) Cultural theorist, sociologist and philosopher whose most recent work is highly controversial. Accusations of 'demonic genius' and 'cerebral coldbloodedness' have greeted his essays on the (first) Gulf War and the events known as 9/11. Whilst his thinking originally emerged from **Marx** and post-structuralism, it is fair to say that – unlike many of his contemporaries (**Jameson, Lyotard, Deleuze**) – he has entirely embraced the discourse of postmodernism. Many critics have come to regard him as a media *agent provocateur*, a role he both embraces and reviles. He increasingly tends to concentrate on writing short pieces, posting many of his essays on the internet, and is perhaps the only philosopher whose work is referenced in a series of Hollywood blockbusters: the Wachowski Brothers' *Matrix* trilogy (1999, 2003, 2003).

Baudrillard began his academic career as a Professor of German. However he continued to study philosophy and sociology, completing his Ph.D. thesis under the guidance of Henri Lefebvre in 1966. He eventually became a Professor of Sociology at the Université de Paris-X Nanterre, and during this time he was influenced by the work of Marx, particularly the discourses around commodity fetishism. His earlier writing provided an analysis of the objects, **signs** and codes of twentieth-century consumer society through a post-Marxist framework (the synthesis of political economy with structuralism). Many see *Symbolic Exchange and Death* (1976) as being his distinctive break with Marxism.

Baudrillard became more widely known in the late 1970s for his investigations into what he called **hyperreality** (which can be seen to be related to Herbert **Marcuse**'s concept of one-dimensionality). In *Simulations* (1975), for instance, he argues that America has constructed the perfect imaginary representation of itself in the form of Disneyland. Disneyland is neither a real nor an unreal version of America: rather, its unreality is a ruse. Disneyland functions as an imaginary space in order to guarantee the authenticity of the America outside its gates. However, 'real America' is as imaginary as Disneyland. It is just

those living 'within' the illusion that are unable to see this.

It was with the essays on the Gulf War that Baudrillard received international notoriety. In January 1991 he wrote in the French daily *Libération* that 'The Gulf War Will Not Take Place'. During the conflict he wrote 'The Gulf War: Is It Really Taking Place?' After hostilities had ceased, he followed up with the essay 'The Gulf War Did Not Take Place'. According to Baudrillard, the reality of the war (where men and women engage with an enemy, fighting and dying for a cause) had been superseded by the televised conflict. For the Western televisual spectator the war became a form of marketing, as its presentations of Western values, might and technology became indistinguishable from the advertisements for other commodities that occurred during breaks in the coverage. Further, video game methodologies meant that, even on the battlefields of the Gulf, the American military experienced little more than a virtual war – rarely seeing the enemy and annihilating him at a distance with the push of a button. While an estimated 15,000 Iraqi military and civilians were killed during the conflict, American casualties were comparatively minimal, many caused by 'friendly fire'. For Baudrillard, war is experienced by the majority of Americans as broadcast via CNN. Further, CNN is broadcast around the world, so the majority of the world now engages with warfare via the television.

For Baudrillard, then, what is always at issue is the status of the '**real**'. Once upon a time the image was a direct reflection of reality. Now, however, this is no longer the case. Simulations and simulacra predominate, and these have no **referent**: no real object-in-the-world to which they relate. The traditional boundaries between different domains of information (such as entertainment and politics) have collapsed. Additionally, there has been both an escalation in the amount of information available (leading to information over-load) and an increase in the speed at which information can be exchanged. All of this means that any sense of what is real has been irretrievably lost in the postmodern world. Many of these arguments can be seen as having been developed from the media studies of Marshall **McLuhan** allied with the nihilism of Friedrich **Nietzsche**. [DD]

See also Chapters 3, 4 and 10.

Further reading

Baudrillard, Jean (1994) *Simulacra and Simu-lation*, trans. Sheila Glaser, Ann Arbor, MI: University of Michigan Press.

Baudrillard, Jean (1995) *The Gulf War Did Not Take Place*, trans. Paul Patton, Indian-apolis, IN: University of Indiana Press.

Baudrillard, Jean (2002) *The Spirit of Terrorism*, trans. Chris Turner, London: Verso.

Lane, Richard J. (2000) *Jean Baudrillard*, London: Routledge.

BEAUVOIR, SIMONE DE (1908–86) Philosopher, novelist and essayist, who is at once remembered for her feminist treatise, *The Second Sex* (1949) and for her relation-ship with fellow French philosopher Jean-Paul Sartre.

In *The Second Sex*, de Beauvoir summar-izes her analysis of male–female relations in the famous statement that 'One is not born, but rather becomes, a woman'. By this she means that femininity is socially constructed rather than innate. This rejec-tion of biological determinism exerted a lasting influence on feminists, particularly in the mid-twentieth century.

De Beauvoir argued, further, that whereas men define themselves by com-parison with the feminine **Other**, women are conditioned to adopt a femininity that is equally Other to themselves. She recognized women's complicity in this process, criticizing acceptance of their inferior position and eagerness to conform to the feminine ideal. De Beauvoir has herself been criticized for the unresolved conflict in her work between the recog-nition that woman is a social construct, and her simultaneous belief that she is free to change her situation. [CC]

See also Chapters 8 and 9.

Further reading

Beauvoir, Simone de (1988) *The Second Sex*, trans. H. M. Parshley, London: Picador.

BENJAMIN, WALTER (1892–1940) Influ-ential German philosopher and **Marxist** cultural theorist who was an important member of the **Frankfurt School** before taking his own life whilst fleeing the Gestapo in 1940. He is widely acknow-ledged as being crucial to the development of critical theory, especially through his acquaintance with Theodor **Adorno**, and for his work on modern culture, art and architecture.

Benjamin's philosophy is a combination of Marxist analysis, Jewish mysticism and an aesthetic sensibility. In his essay 'The Work of Art in the Age of Mechanical Reproduction' he engages closely with diff-erent art forms, exploring how commodi-fication and reproducibility had destroyed the unique sense of originality and authen-ticity of art, or its '**aura**'. He argues that this has liberated art from its 'parasitical' dependence on ritual, moving it into the arena of politics. For him this plays an important role in resisting totalitarian systems culminating in the essay's final phrase, 'This is the situation of politics which Fascism is rendering aesthetic. Communism responds by politicizing art' (Benjamin 1999: 235).

Of equal importance to Benjamin is how history is conceived and constructed. He criticizes linear conceptions of chronicling the past, preferring the metaphor of a constellation to describe a spatial relation of contexts in which the historian should relate the present to the past. In this formulation, socio-cultural phenomena, such as ideas, models and events, are delicately configured around a common organizing factor. If any one element of the constellation were altered, the entire configuration would have to be modified accordingly. This prompts him to contend that 'There is no document of civilization that is not at the same time a document of barbarism' (1999: 248). In his view of history, rationality has resulted in the justification of horrific acts, which can only be understood through an analysis of certain specific historical circumstances.

Although criticized by various members of the Frankfurt School, Benjamin's theories remained highly influential on their thought. His re-evaluation of history, politics, aesthetics and architecture pioneered new critical approaches and have proved invaluable to both philosophy and cultural theory confronted with the monopoly capitalism of the late twentieth century. [RW]

See also Chapter 3.

Further reading
Benjamin, Walter (1999) *Illuminations*, trans. Harry Zohn, London: Pimlico.

BENVENISTE, ÉMILE (1902–76) French linguist who taught at the École pratique des Hautes Études and later the Collège de France. Influenced by the linguistic practices established by Ferdinand de **Saussure**, Benveniste was an important figure in early structuralism. His best-known work is *Problems in General Linguistics* in which he makes a distinction between 'discourse' and 'histoire' – terms which roughly correspond with 'narrating' – which assumes the presence of a speaker and a listener, and 'story' which denotes the events that are the subject of that discourse. In its emphasis on the role played by the speaker of discourse Benveniste's work can be seen to diverge from Saussure's notion of language as a purely

formal system. His work explores the connections between linguistics and psychoanalysis, arguing that the **subject** is constituted by, or through, language. In this respect the influence of his work can be seen in that of Jacques **Lacan** and Julia **Kristeva**. [PW]

See also Chapter 1.

Further reading
Benveniste, Émile (1971) *Problems in General Linguistics*, trans. Mary E. Meek, Miami, FL: University of Miami Press.

BHABHA, HOMI (1949–) The theories of Homi Bhabha, along with those of Gayatri Chakravorty **Spivak** and Edward **Said,** have dominated postcolonial theory over the last two decades. Bhabha's major work, *The Location of Culture* (1994), brings together essays in which he formulates and discusses the theoretical concepts for which he is best known: ambivalence, mimicry and hybridity.

Bhabha is interested in the gaps and disturbances that exist within colonial texts. He argues that colonial discourse is agonistic, split and contradictory, so that it never fully manages to assert a fixed and stereotypical knowledge of the colonial **Other** as it sets out to do. Even in the most confident colonial text, Bhabha suggests that there are moments of ambivalence: moments when it is possible to discern that the argument is contradictory.

Bhabha argues further that not only the resistance of the colonial **subject**, but also his compliance with colonial strictures, endangers the fragile stability of imperialist knowledge and power. Through his theory of mimicry, Bhabha contends that even the most slavish attempts of the colonial subject to imitate his master result in an inadvertent threat to the colonial order. As the colonial subject begins to resemble the colonizer, the differences between the two are reduced. This lessening of the distance between the two groups exposes an example of ambivalence. Colonial discourse is predicated on the assumptions that the colonized subject is alien, dangerous and essentially different from the colonizer, while at the same time he is seen as educable and capable of being remade in the colonizer's image. Colonial texts anxiously seek to hide or disavow these mutually exclusive suppositions, but mimicry exposes their internal conflict.

Finally, the borders that are conventionally assumed to exist between colonizer and colonized, East and West, self and Other, are refigured in Bhabha's theory of hybridity. Bhabha argues that borders presuppose a no-man's land, an in-between space that simultaneously divides and connects two areas. This space, he suggests, is productive and enabling. Using the biological term 'hybrid' to denote the liminal position of the migrant, Bhabha celebrates the intermingling of cultures and contests the idea of cultural purity. [CC]

See also Chapter 11.

Further reading

Bhabha, Homi K. (1994) *The Location of Culture*, London: Routledge.

Huddart, David (2005) *Homi Bhabha*, London: Routledge.

BLANCHOT, MAURICE (1907–2003) French philosopher and literary theorist, who wrote and contributed to numerous forms of publication including political journals, novels, reviews and philosophy. This varied output makes it notoriously difficult to classify his work within a particular **genre**. His eclectic style of thought has been influential for the development of poststructuralist theory and to the work of such notable figures as Jacques **Derrida**, Roland **Barthes** and Michel **Foucault**.

Blanchot's early work included contributions to right-wing political journals during the mid 1930s. However, during the war his views swung more to the left in the light of the horrors perpetuated by Nazi Germany. During this time he also wrote a number of novels, critical reviews and essays which were to have a significant impact on the development of French literature and theory.

Arguably the central tenet to Blanchot's work is the idea that there is no clear distinction between philosophy and literature (a theme later taken up by, amongst others, Derrida). In this sense, his work has been influenced by a variety of literary and philosophical writers including Stéphane Mallarmé, Franz Kafka, G. W. F. Hegel and Martin **Heidegger**. Further, Blanchot's understanding of literature argues for a multitude of interpretations. In other words, there is not just one singular meaning within a text, an argument that was to become a central concern of poststructuralist thought.

Blanchot's later work also developed a concern with **ethical** issues alongside his usual preoccupation with philosophy, literature and politics. This coincided with a rise in his political activities associated with the radical left. From the 1970s, however, Blanchot became more reclusive and his literary output less frequent. He was a very enigmatic character, and arguably his greatest significance has been his influence on the emergence of poststructuralist thought. [JS]

See also Chapters 4 and 7.

Further reading

Blanchot, Maurice (1982) *The Space of Literature*, trans. Ann Smock, Lincoln, NE: University of Nebraska Press.

Blanchot, Maurice (1995) *The Blanchot Reader*, ed. Michael Holland, Oxford: Blackwell.

Haase, Ullrich and Large, William (2001) *Maurice Blanchot*, London: Routledge.

BLOOM, HAROLD (1930–) American theorist best known for his work on Romantic poetry and more recently in biblical and theological studies. Bloom is notable for *The Anxiety of Influence* (1973), and *Deconstruction and Criticism* (1979), a collection of essays which also features contributions by Paul **de Man**, Jacques **Derrida**, Geoffrey Hartman and J. Hillis **Miller**, a group of writers who came to be known collectively as the 'Yale critics'. Bloom's more recent work, from *The Western Canon* (1995) onwards, has challenged the various critical schools that de-emphasize the **canonical** notion of a tradition of great writers.

Bloom's key ideas are set out in *The Anxiety of Influence*, which draws on Sigmund **Freud**'s **Oedipal** model, arguing that poets strive to assert their own vision without being creatively directed by the influence of earlier poets. The art of creation requires an act of denial of that influence, a 'misprision', misunderstanding or misinterpretation, of those precursors. The poet is 'belated', a latecomer to the world of creativity, inheriting a linguistic system from those who have gone before. The 'strong poet', however, will achieve an individual voice through an ability to revise the tradition. Each revision becomes, therefore, 'antithetical' to earlier poems. It is through such acts of creative misinterpretation that the poet finds a voice. Bloom argues that critics of poetry also follow this misreading model, an argument that has associated him with deconstruction.

As he distanced himself from colleagues of the Yale School, particularly in *The Western Canon*, Bloom's critical writings have challenged Marxist, feminist and new historicist readings of literature as a social, **ideological** product, and have retained his focus on reading for signs of the originality of great writers, notably Shakespeare and Milton. Bloom's 'anxiety of influence' theories have, paradoxically, been extremely influential in destabilizing traditional approaches to literature, whilst supporting the tradition itself. [TES]

Further reading

Allen, Graham (1994) *Harold Bloom: Poetics of Conflict*, New York: Harvester Wheatsheaf.

Bloom, Harold (1995) *The Western Canon: The Books and Schools of the Ages*, New York: Harcourt Brace.

Bloom, Harold (1997) *The Anxiety of Influence: A Theory of Poetry*, New York: Oxford University Press.

BODY WITHOUT ORGANS Borrowed from the surrealist poet Antonin Artaud, the concept of a 'body without organs' is taken up by French poststructuralist philosophers Gilles **Deleuze** and Félix **Guattari** in *Anti-Oedipus* (1972), *Kafka: Toward a Minor Literature* (1975) and *A Thousand Plateaus* (1980). Following Friedrich **Nietzsche** and the Jewish philosopher Baruch Spinoza, the nature, **powers**, and potentials of the body are considered to be largely unknown and unthought by philosophy. Rather than trying to define the body, however, Deleuze and Guattari take a **nomadological** and **schizoanalytic** approach. A 'body without organs' is a body that exists and coheres without the structuring articulations which reduce the plurality of its parts (or organs) to the unity of a single organ*ism*. It is not a body defined in terms of the identity of a **subject** or object but solely by its power to affect or be affected in a variety of different external relations. In other words, like a **rhizome**, a 'body without organs' is a pure multiplicity of **unconscious differences** which constitute desire in an active process. However, it is not itself a productive element, nor does it function as either the cause or effect of **desire**. Rather, the 'body without organs' expresses the *immanence* of desire to itself. [DH]

BOURDIEU, PIERRE (1930–2002) French sociologist, philosopher and anthropologist whose work explored a wide range of subjects including art, education, language, the mass media and **globalization**. He analyses society as a series of fields (for example, the literary field or the field of popular culture) that are in continual struggle to accumulate economic and cultural capital, and hence **power**. **Subjects** exist within these fields, are constructed in terms of their categories, perpetuate their conflicts, and judge the world and others according to the tenets the fields produce. A central theme in his work is that education and art perpetuate class division by producing identities in terms of distinctions between more and less valuable positions or works. In his best-known book, *Distinction: A Social Critique of the Judgement of Taste* (1984), he uses these categories to explore the social and economic production of a distinction between high art and popular culture, arguing that one is not intrinsically better than the other, but that such a distinction is produced by the conflict between social fields. [SM]

Further reading

Bourdieu, Pierre (1984) *Distinction: A Social Critique of the Judgement of Taste*, trans. Richard Nice, London: Routledge.

Bourdieu, Pierre (1993) *The Field of Cultural Production: Essays on Art and Literature*, ed. Randal Johnson, Cambridge: Polity Press.

BRICOLAGE A term used by the anthropologist Claude **Lévi-Strauss** to describe the mentality of the non-industrialized **subject**, or 'primitive man'. In *The Savage Mind* (1966), Lévi-Strauss compares primitive man to the *bricoleur*, or DIY enthusiast. The *bricoleur* employs whatever is at hand – scraps, odds and ends, fragments – adapting their original function to tackle each new problem. Mythical thought, he argues, similarly 'expresses itself by means of a heterogeneous repertoire which, even if extensive, is nevertheless limited' (Lévi-Strauss 1966: 17). In contrast, Lévi-Strauss compares post-industrial man to an engineer who fashions specific tools to tackle each different project.

Derrida has responded to Lévi-Strauss's theory, pointing out that *bricolage* is also characteristic of literary criticism, since the critic similarly borrows concepts from 'the text of a heritage which is more or less coherent or ruined' (Derrida 1978: 285). Yet Derrida challenges Lévi-Strauss's notion of the engineer who stands outside society and creates cultural practices from scratch, and contends that all forms of knowledge and cultural expression – whether post-industrial or '**mythic**', Western or 'savage', scientific or artistic – are products of *bricolage*, of a magpie-like collection of fragments, intertexts and influences. This interpretation of *bricolage* has proved influential in postmodernism, with many postmodernists celebrating the idea of knowledge as fragmented, rather than being organized according to so-called **grand narratives**. [CC]

See also Chapters 1 and 10.

Further reading

Derrida, Jacques (1978) *Writing and Difference*, trans. Alan Bass, London: Routledge.

Lévi-Strauss, Claude (1966) *The Savage Mind*, London: Weidenfeld and Nicolson.

BURKE, KENNETH (1897–1993) The influence of this North American critic on contemporary theory is incalculable. Its emphasis on the way social reality is built up through language is indebted to his pioneering work on 'symbolic action' (Burke 1989: 77–85). 'Symbolic action' refers to the notion that every 'saying' is also a 'doing': when we produce words, whether in conversations or in poems, we are trying to engage with the world. Similarly, its assumption that the human **subject** is always situated and never quite complete owes much to his theory of 'dramatism' (Burke 1989: 135–8). If, in Shakespeare's words, 'All the world's a stage', then 'dramatism' is Burke's account of what is involved when we treat language and thought as activities within the theatre of society. In philosophical terms, he is a pragmatist (one who assesses statements in terms of their consequences); he is interested in the uses to which language is put, whether in literary or in everyday **discourse**. One tendency which he documents particularly closely is the way our 'words' inevitably build up to imply one absolute 'Word' – some ultimate idea, or rather ideal. According to Burke, it is in pursuit of this perfection, and in consolidating our societies, that we create scapegoats – a process he describes as 'victimage' (Burke 1989: 280–90). Literature and **mythology** are useful means of dealing with this urge symbolically; religion, politics and ideology need watching carefully, as they have a tendency towards literal, violent enactment. Enjoying a tragedy whose protagonist acts as scapegoat is preferable to succumbing to propaganda which victimizes a racial minority. But here too a literary form can help: Burke commends the 'comic corrective' as a means of learning from the structure and mood of comedy how to conduct ourselves in society (Burke 1989: 261–7). In his later writings, however, Burke becomes more pessimistic: he focuses increasingly on nature as the victim of human aggression – by way of our misguided 'cult of technology' (Burke 1989: 200) – and he wonders whether our obsessive perfectionism might not end in disaster for the planet and for ourselves. In this respect, he anticipates some of the concerns of **ecocriticism**. [LC]

Further reading

Burke, Kenneth (1989) *On Symbols and Society*, ed. Joseph R. Gusfield, Chicago, IL: University of Chicago Press.

Coupe, Laurence (2005) *Kenneth Burke on Myth: An Introduction*, New York: Routledge.

BUTLER, JUDITH (1956–) One of the most influential American critics in poststructural feminist and queer theories. Butler's work draws on a wide range of preceding theories of gender, **subjectivity** and sexuality, from **Foucault**'s genealogical approach to **Lacanian** psychoanalysis and **Derrida**'s deconstruction. She is best known for proposing the notion of gender **performativity**.

In her most influential book, *Gender Trouble* (1990), Butler maintains that gender is not the cultural meaning of a pre-given sex, but rather is the cultural means to produce sexes, which are then referred to as the 'natural' ground for gender. Gender is performatively constituted: that is, it is naturalized and substantialized only through repeatedly citing normative gendered practices. Feminism, then, should not ground its politics on the presumed category of 'woman', but should instead find ways to subversively open up the category and undermine the existing norms.

One of the major criticisms of her theory of gender performativity is that it renders feminism impossible by deconstructing the category of 'woman'. However, instead of negating the category per se, Butler is arguing against the predetermination of what can legitimately fall into the category. Other critics have questioned whether Butler's theory gives enough consideration to the materiality of the body/sex, and have argued that one cannot freely take up whatever sex one wants. The expectation for the voluntary construction of sex/gender was ironically also the reason that 'gender performativity' became widely popular, although Butler's notion of performativity refers to the construction of gender through the system's self-repetition, and has nothing to do with individual choices.

In *Bodies That Matter* (1993a), Butler explores how materiality of the body itself is performatively constituted through deeper deliberation on psychoanalysis. She introduces history and politics into psychoanalytic understandings of **desire** and subjectivity, and offers various psychoanalytic readings of cultural and political practices that concern not only sex/gender but also race. Butler went on to theorize, in *Excitable Speech* (1997), how performativity, or the repetitive citation of the norms, can result in displacing the very norms through repetition, inadvertently bringing about an agency for a radical political change.

Following her analysis in *Bodies That Matter* and *Excitable Speech*, Butler has recently increased her commitment to investigating how the psychoanalytic understanding of an agency as the constitutive outside of symbolic operation relates to the concept of agency or subject in politics.

This attempt at the mutual intervention between politics and (psychoanalytic) theory manifests itself in *Contingency, Hegemony, Universality* (2000), in which she collaborated with Slavoj **Žižek** and Ernesto Laclau. [AS]

See also Chapters 4, 8 and 9.

Further reading

Butler, Judith (1990) *Gender Trouble: Feminism and the Subversion of Identity*, London: Routledge.

Butler, Judith (1993a) *Bodies That Matter: On the Discursive Limits of Sex*, London: Routledge.

Butler, Judith (1997) *Excitable Speech: A Politics of the Performative*, New York: Routledge.

C

CANON In its narrowest sense, the term canon means the works of an **author** that are considered to have been genuinely written by that author. But the term is used more often in critical theory in relation to its wider meaning, which refers to texts that have been considered by the literary establishment to be the most valuable examples of the literature produced by a particular culture or tradition. In short, the canon is composed of those books that a graduate of English literature would be expected to have read. Critical theory challenges the canon by objecting to what it sees as the **ideologically** motivated selection of texts and authors that gain access to it. The convenient fact that the canon is largely made up of texts written by dead, white, straight, European men has been challenged by theorists of all persuasions, with the most notable attacks coming from feminist critics. Consequently, the traditional notion of a fixed canon has in recent years come to be seen as outmoded, and the canon is perhaps best understood today as a category that is in a permanent state of contestation, and which perpetually reconstitutes itself around newly canonized and de-canonized texts. [CMa]

See also Chapters 1, 8 and 11.

CARNIVAL/CARNIVALESQUE A term that came to prominence after the publication of Mikhail **Bakhtin**'s *Rabelais and his World* (1965). Bakhtin identifies a shift from popular festive life to literary culture, arguing that Rabelais's grotesque representation of the human body, linguistic diversity and taste for parody derive from the popular practices of carnival in Renaissance Europe. Bakhtin conceives of carnival as a utopian moment when dominant constraints and hierarchies are temporarily overturned: authority figures are parodied, routines are disrupted, and the body is celebrated. Rabelais's writing, with its focus upon the grotesque body, draws its subversive energy from carnival practices and, in this sense, it can be described as 'carnivalesque'.

Bakhtin's ideas about carnival are valuable because they provide a framework for assessing the influence of popular forms on literature. Critics have explored the relationship between the historical carnival and the political uses of popular culture in Renaissance literature; but the term 'carnivalesque' has also been stretched beyond the actual historical moment of carnival to describe writing that reproduces the inversions of carnival. This approach has been used to study writers such as the British novelist Angela Carter, who employ popular against elite forms, mixing a variety of styles and voices. [RF]

Further reading

Bakhtin, Mikhail (1984) *Rabelais and his World*, trans. Hélène Iswolsky, Bloomington, IN: Indiana University Press.

Dentith, Simon (1995) *Bakhtinian Thought: An Introductory Reader*, London: Routledge.

CERTEAU, MICHEL DE (1925–1986) French cultural theorist who originally trained in theology. He became a member of the Jesuits in 1950 although his later work was to branch out considerably from religious concerns. Certeau's interdisciplinary work covers a wide range of topics including history, theology, cultural theory, philosophy, politics and sociology. Arguably his most famous work is the two-volume *The Practice of Everyday Life* written in collaboration with Luce Giard and Pierre Mayol.

The events in France in 1968, centred on student unrest, had a significant influence on Certeau's thought, especially with regard to the area of politics and culture. After 1968 Certeau received a grant in order to complete a research project to investigate the current cultural climate. This research eventually led to *The Practice of Everyday Life*. In the first volume Certeau looks at the conditions of social behaviour and investigates possibilities for the redemption of society from the restraints of contemporary capitalist society. The second volume, subtitled *Living and Cooking*, analyses these ideas further to show how society can resist the **hegemonic** order through the very simple and practical means of daily life. Through this work, Certeau's use of micro-histories to investigate the discursive practices underlying our conception of everyday life can be seen to follow a similar strategy to that of Michel **Foucault**. [JS]

Further reading

Certeau, Michel de (1984) *The Practice of Everyday Life*, trans. Steven Rendall, Berkeley, CA: University of California Press.

Certeau, Michel de (1988) *The Practice of Everyday Life Volume 2: Living and Cooking*, trans. Timothy J. Tomasik, Minneapolis, MN: University of Minnesota Press.

Certeau, Michel de (2000) *The Certeau Reader*, ed. Graham Ward, Oxford: Blackwell.

CHORA Julia **Kristeva**'s concept of the **semiotic** chora is developed out of **Lacanian** psychoanalysis and attempts to account for the repressed linguistic and libidinal excesses of the speaking **subject** that originate in the pre-**Oedipal phase**. Kristeva appropriates the chora from Plato's *Timaeus* (*c*. 360 BC) to denote an unnameable space or receptacle formed by the **drives** which are anterior to identity. This chora refers to the earliest stage in psychosexual development in which the child is dominated by the drives and is unable to distinguish boundaries between itself and its mother. At this stage the child experiences its body as an undifferentiated, ungendered space across which chaotic and rhythmical drives of physical and psychic impulses flow. These drives form the basis of the semiotic chora, which is the alternative non-signifying element of meaning within language. Although it is repressed by the **symbolic**, this semiotic chora remains active beneath the rational discourse of the speaking subject and manifests itself in the 'vocal or kinetic rhythm' of poetry and other non-rational discourses, threatening to disrupt the stability of meaning and subjectivity (Kristeva 1984: 26). [CM]

See also Chapter 6.

Further reading

Kristeva, Julia (1984) *Revolution in Poetic Language*, trans. Margaret Waller, New York: Columbia University Press.

CHRONOTOPE Term coined by Mikhail **Bakhtin** in the 1930s to describe the way in which time and space are represented and connected in literature. In his essay 'Forms of Time and the Chronotope of the Novel', Bakhtin offers a history of the novel, which aims to show that different novels are structured according to different ideas of time and space. Moreover, Bakhtin argues that changes in chronotopes, or dominant metaphors of time and space, can be explained by broader historical developments.

The concern of Bakhtin's work, such as in his discussions of language and **carnival**, is to explore the relationship between forms and structures, and the transformations of history. His approach is useful not only because it identifies links between the metaphorical significance of motifs such as 'the path of life' and the narrative progress of a character, but also because it encourages analysis of time and space in the context of specific socio-historical conditions. [RF]

See also Chapter 2.

Further reading

Bakhtin, Mikhail (1981) *The Dialogic Imagination: Four Essays*, ed. Michael Holquist, trans. Caryl Emerson and Michael Holquist, Austin: University of Texas Press.

Dentith, Simon (1995) *Bakhtinian Thought: An Introductory Reader*, London: Routledge.

CIXOUS, HÉLÈNE (1937–) Feminist poststructuralist, literary critic, poet, novelist and playwright, Cixous is most famous for her essays 'Sorties' and 'The Laugh of the Medusa' which explore the links between female sexuality, the psyche and language. Her main theoretical concern is expressed in 'Sorties' where she attempts to find 'ways out' of a masculine **phallocentric** binary system that excludes the 'feminine' and exiles women from their bodily pleasures. Hierarchical binaries, based on the heterosexual couple, construct language as a 'battlefield' in which one term must be destroyed to make 'sense': an act structured in terms of a (masculine) victory and a (feminine) defeat (1986: 64). Cixous' deconstructive approach is influenced by Jacques **Derrida**'s theory of **differance**, which demonstrates that meaning resides in language and is a temporary effect of **difference**, infinitely deferred along a chain of **signifiers**. As the only source of meaning is linguistic difference, there is always a '**trace**' of the excluded term within the signifier. Cixous' alternative to the masculine **symbolic** is 'feminine' writing, or *écriture féminine*, located in the pre-**Oedipal imaginary**, and is closely aligned with the (female) body and the unconscious as the site of the repressed '**other**'. Cixous' aim is to explode the myth of binary logic, thus transforming sexuality and subjectivity through an encounter with difference and the 'other' situated within the signifying gaps or '[in] the between' of writing (1986: 86). This 'between' space is closely associated with the '*other bisexuality*' which is radically opposed to unity and allows for the free play of differance within gender construction: sexual differentiation relies on the presence (or *trace*) of the 'other' sex within the self (1986: 84). This interplay between the 'self' and the 'other', or 'I/play of bisexuality' moves beyond dualism and gestures towards the possibility of multiple, mobile subjectivities, open to infinite transformation (1986: 84). [CM]

See also Chapters 4, 8 and 9.

Further reading

Cixous, Hélène (1986) 'Sorties: Out and Out: Attacks/Ways Out/Forays', in Hélène Cixous and Catherine Clément *The Newly Born Woman*, trans. Betsy Wing, Minneapolis, MN: University of Minnesota Press.

COLONIALISM The practical acquisition of, and the maintenance of a hold over, colonies. It is distinct from imperialism, although the two terms are sometimes used interchangeably. Whereas imperialism is the policy, belief or practice that a nation should be able to extend its power over other territories, colonialism involves settlement and an often **traumatic** encounter between indigenous peoples and newcomers. While colonialism has arguably had some positive outcomes, bringing cultural interchange, intellectual developments and economic rejuvenation, it has also led to appalling abuses, typified most starkly by the slave trade.

Colonialism is not a homogeneous phenomenon, and great variations exist between colonial systems in different historical and geographical locations. Temporally, while many civilizations have had colonial enterprises, most commentators agree that a new brand of colonialism began to be practised by Western European nations from the Renaissance onwards. According to **Marx** and his followers, its novelty lies in economics. Empires run by such peoples as the Romans, Aztecs and Mughals were pre-capitalist, whereas from the sixteenth century Europeans were moving towards a capitalist colonial model. Rather than engaging in straightforward plunder, capitalist colonizers aimed at entirely restructuring the economies of the occupied countries. They destroyed indigenous manufacturing and handicraft industries by using exploitative tariffs to prevent the exportation of colonial goods. Simultaneously, the raw materials, labour power and markets available in the subjected countries of Asia and Africa fed the European colonizers' burgeoning industries and economies.

Geographically, there are two main types of colonialism. In settler colonies, such as Australia and the Americas, newcomers violently displaced the indigenous population to set up permanent homes in the chosen country. In colonies of occupation, which include India and Nigeria, the white rulers were vastly outnumbered by the local population and rarely chose to stay in the colonies.

Colonialism is not simply about economic and political domination, however; it also involves what **Spivak** terms 'epistemic violence' (1988a: 281). The West's economic and political ascendancy in the eighteenth and nineteenth centuries meant that ideas travelled with goods along the trade routes, in a similar process of imperial appropriation and imposition. The British, for example, justified their occupation of vast areas of Asia and Africa using the rhetoric of the 'civilizing mission'. Policy-makers such as Thomas Macaulay

(1859) argued that British colonizers brought sophisticated science, technology, literatures and geography to barbaric or declining non-Western civilizations. Macaulay's argument, while oversimplistic, is supported by the fact that many non-Western peoples found their colonizers' ideas useful and insightful. Yet the colonizers' 'civilizing mission' also met with resistance, and each culture was constantly fertilized with new ideas from the other. This was never an equal exchange, however, and the colonizers' insistence on the correctness of their world-view has wreaked lasting damage on colonized countries' infrastructures, institutions, and the individual psyches of their citizens.

Not all colonial subjects were treated the same under colonialism. There was a vast difference, for example, between the 'cultural cringe' that many white settlers adopted towards metropolitan standards, the racial oppression experienced by the inhabitants of occupied colonies, and the decimation of indigenous occupants of settler colonies. Within individual occupied colonies, the British promoted the creation of a privileged group of middle-class 'mimic men' (see Macaulay 1995). This class internalized British values and acted as an intermediary between the rulers and the colonized masses. As part of their policy of 'divide and rule', the British also favoured certain religious, regional and linguistic groups over others.

Finally, women experienced what has been termed a 'double colonization' (Petersen and Rutherford 1986), whereby they were oppressed by both colonial and patriarchal practices. Colonial **discourse** tended to represent non-Western women as exotic temptresses, whereas white women were depicted as the epitome of colonial virtues. The 'plight' of Asian and African women was used as another justification for Empire. Practices such as *sati* (the self-immolation of Indian widows), child marriage and *purdah* (the seclusion of women from strangers' eyes) were roundly censured in 'civilizing mission' texts, while the colonizers' treatment of women was assumed to be exemplary. Despite the contextual variations in the treatment of colonial subjects, the idea of Empire had a unifying effect on the different classes in Britain, and provided a method of self-definition in relation to the colonial **other**.

From the early twentieth century, colonialism began to be challenged by colonized elites. The anti-colonial struggle was at first characterized by a tendency to romanticize the pre-colonial past as a golden age that could be recreated once colonialism was overthrown. The Negritude movement of francophone Caribbean and African nations, for example, created texts that celebrated blackness and African social models. Such idealized representations of colonial societies and history were necessary strategies in the anti-colonial movement, contributing to the demise of the British Empire from 1947. Yet colonialism has arguably been replaced by a neo-colonial world order, in which the formerly colonized countries continue to be oppressed by the First World's economic, social and political **hegemony**. [CC]

See also Chapter 11.

Further reading

Loomba, Ania (1998) *Colonialism/Postcolonialism*, London: Routledge.

Spivak, Gayatri Chakravorty (1988a) 'Can the Subaltern Speak?', in Cary Nelson and Lawrence Grossberg (eds), *Marxism and the Interpretation of Culture*, Basingstoke: Macmillan Education.

CULTURAL MATERIALISM This British 'school' of criticism is centrally concerned with the role of historical context in interpreting texts, but what is distinctive about the approach is the examination of literature of the past in the context of contemporary power relations. Key proponents of cultural materialism include

Catherine Belsey, Jonathan Dollimore and Alan Sinfield. These theorists rejected the formalist and liberal humanist criticism that had dominated literary studies in Britain since the 1950s, and developed new ways of thinking about the relationships between literature, history and politics. Paying particular attention to works central to the British literary **canon**, including Shakespeare and Wordsworth, they sought to historicize and politicize their readings. Their analysis is underpinned by an overt political aim to undermine conservative **ideologies** in the present.

Cultural materialism came to prominence when Dollimore and Sinfield used the term as the subtitle for their edited collection of essays *Political Shakespeare: New Essays in Cultural Materialism* (1985). Dollimore and Sinfield saw themselves in opposition to the liberal humanist criticism that had prevailed in Shakespeare studies prior to the 1980s, and their attention to historical context represents a direct challenge to the idea that literature is 'timeless'. Using historical contextualization to reveal that literary texts are always implicated in the ideology of the moment of their production, they undermine the theory that texts have transcendent significance, suggesting that there can be no separation of text and context. While they are careful to show that literary texts do not simply reflect their context, Dollimore and Sinfield show that texts participate in the production of ideology, particularly as it exists in a material form through institutions such as churches, theatres and schools.

This analysis of the formation of ideology leads to one of the distinctive features of the approach: its bifocal historical perspective. Cultural materialists locate their work in a double historical context: the moment in which the text was produced, and also in the context of its **reception**, when the text is adapted, reproduced and reinterpreted. For these critics, analysis of how the present adapts and recasts the past exposes contemporary politics, showing that texts always have a political function in the power structure. In *Political Shakespeare*, for instance, half the essays are devoted to discovering what is at stake politically in late twentieth-century reinterpretations of Shakespeare in education, film, theatre and tourism.

Dollimore and Sinfield express distrust of critical approaches that claim political neutrality. The humanist tradition, for instance, treated Shakespeare as part of a great English heritage without recognizing the political investment in such a stance; for Dollimore and Sinfield, apparently neutral approaches serve to naturalize conservative values. By contrast, their method is polemical. As suggested by their title *Political Shakespeare*, which highlights a commitment to politicizing literature, the editors view representation as inevitably involved in political struggle. This results in a double focus upon how literature is deployed to reinforce ideology, on the one hand, and a search for possible dissident readings that challenge conservative interpretations, on the other. While acknowledging literature's central role in the preservation of the status quo, cultural materialists look for ways in which the literature of the past can be mobilized to challenge exploitation on grounds of race, gender and class in the present. They read with an explicit political aim to destabilize contemporary conservative values. This is best illustrated by Sinfield's *Faultlines* (1992), in which he suggests that it is possible to read against the grain of dominant culture by analysing the contradictions, conflicts or 'faultlines' that are seeded through ideologies as they attempt to sustain themselves. Placing emphasis on the reader's active pursuit of political meaning, 'faultlines' enable the critic to notice the dissidence that has been contained by the text: they can extract it from the text to contest dominant ideology.

Cultural materialism has exerted a strong influence on contemporary critical practices. Largely as a result of cultural materialism and its American counterpart new historicism, it is now a matter of routine to ask questions of historical context and political attitude. [RF]

See also Chapters 3 and 5.

Further reading

Dollimore, Jonathan and Sinfield, Alan (eds) (1985) *Political Shakespeare: New Essays in Cultural Materialism*, Manchester: Manchester University Press.

Sinfield, Alan (1992) *Faultlines: Cultural Materialism and the Politics of Dissident Reading*, Oxford: Oxford University Press.

CULTURE INDUSTRY The commercial system that commodifies and standardizes art, identified by German Marxist theoreticians Theodor W. **Adorno** and Max **Horkheimer**. Adapting ideas cultivated in the Institute of Social Research, or **Frankfurt School**, especially by Walter **Benjamin**, they objected to the trend of consumerist society that limits cultural diversity and promotes homogeneity.

In their chapter 'The Culture Industry: Enlightenment as Mass Deception', from *Dialectic of Enlightenment* (1947), Adorno and Horkheimer argue that with monopoly capitalism the powerful few had engineered the social system to provide the individual with an illusion of spontaneity, choice and diversity. Consequently, individuals become complicit in their own coercion, making the possibilities of emancipation increasingly difficult. They contend that only through intense critical thinking can the banality of mass culture be exposed.

Contemporary theorists such as Pierre **Bourdieu**, Fredric **Jameson** and Jean **Baudrillard** have used aspects of this interpretation to decode the cultural formations of modern capitalism. In the context of **globalization** and the increased power of multinational corporations over broadcast media, the 'culture industry' proves an especially potent concept in analysing modern instances of mass culture. [RW]

See also Chapter 3.

Further reading

Adorno, Theodor W. (2001) *The Culture Industry: Selected Essays on Mass Culture*, ed. J. M. Bernstein, New York: Routledge.

CYBERSPACE As a concept, cyberspace owes its 'birth' to the American author William Gibson (1948–) and his science fiction novel *Neuromancer* (1984). The term is generally employed to designate 'virtual reality'; however, this virtual terrain ultimately emerges from the physical hard drive of a computer, either locally or online. Accordingly, the concept cannot be considered in isolation, but only in relation to the terms 'network', 'internet' and 'world wide web'.

The network is the infrastructure upon which telecommunication is built, and has been in existence in one form or another for over 100 years. When a human being sitting in front of a personal computer goes online, they connect their PC over their local network to an internet service provider which gives them access to the network of networks. It is this that is known as the internet.

The world wide web is simply one service amongst many. Specially formatted documents in a script called HTML (**hypertext** mark-up language) support connections to other documents via 'hot' links. To view these documents a special application is needed (e.g. an internet browser). There are many other protocols which support many other services, such as email, newsgroups and instant messaging. These services are constituents of cyberspace. [DD]

See also Chapter 10.

CYBORG A contraction of 'cybernetic organism', a cyborg is any self-organizing system which combines organic and mechanical parts.

The term often refers to humans who have been technologically adapted, for example with pacemakers or artificial limbs, but cyborgs can take many forms. Examples include laboratory rats implanted with remote-control devices, and fictional entities such as the giant computer intelligence that is fuelled by organic human bodies in the film *The Matrix*.

The word was coined by Manfred E. Clynes and Nathan S. Kline in their 1960 *Astronautics* article 'Cyborgs and Space'. They argue that, instead of altering conditions in space for human habitation, human bodies should be adapted to the environment. For example, they suggest implanting astronauts with an 'inverse fuel cell' which would replace the lungs, 'making breathing, as we know it, unnecessary'. Clynes and Kline's theory was groundbreaking because it suggested that the human body could be fundamentally altered by technology and that the human was not the centre of the universe. (For more on this, see **posthumanism**.)

However, critical theory did not explore the implications of the cyborg until the American socialist-feminist Donna **Haraway** wrote her seminal 'Cyborg Manifesto' (1985). Haraway reinscribed the cyborg as a political and theoretical idea which could disrupt conventional binary oppositions, such as human/animal and organism/machine. Because the cyborg is a hybrid or mixture, it suggests an alternative to unifying, homogeneous concepts, such as 'Woman'. For Haraway, the cyborg is a liberating myth which represents 'transgressed boundaries, potent fusions, and dangerous possibilities which progressive people might explore as one part of needed political work'.

Many theorists have responded to Haraway's essay, and the last 20 years have seen an explosion of cyborg theory – 'cyborgology' – examining subjects as diverse as IVF, the *Terminator* films and dog training. Cyborgology becomes more relevant every day, as real and fictional cyborgs prolifer-ate around us, changing our bodies, our homes and our lives. [JM]

See also Chapter 10.

Further reading

Haraway, Donna (1985) 'A Manifesto for Cyborgs: Science, Technology, and Socialist Feminism in the 1980s', *Socialist Review* 80: 65–108.

Kirkup, Gill, Janes, Linda, Woodward, Kathryn and Hovenden, Fiona (eds) (2000) *The Gendered Cyborg: A Reader*, London: Routledge.

D

DEATH-DRIVE (Also 'death-instinct' or 'Thanatos') A term that **Freud** introduces in his later writings, which emerges from his work on sadism and the compulsion he discovered patients had to repeat **traumatic** events.

In *Beyond the Pleasure Principle* (1920) and *The Ego and the Id* (1923) Freud posits two contending drives: 'the *sexual instincts* or *Eros* ... not merely the uninhibited sexual instinct proper ... but also the self preservative instinct' (Freud 1991b: 380) and the death-instinct, 'the task of which is to lead organic life back into the inanimate state' (Freud 1991b: 380). Accordingly, life itself is the conflict and compromise between these two drives.

Whilst this duality of instincts was, by Freud's admission, speculative ('I do not know how far I believe in them' (Freud 1991b: 332)), and while the idea has met with mixed reactions in the work of subsequent psychoanalysts, the death-drive has been discussed in great detail by psychoanalytic theorists such as Jacques **Lacan** and Julia **Kristeva**, as well as forming the central focus for Jacques **Derrida**'s discussion in *The Post Card: From Socrates to Freud and Beyond* (1987). In literary theory, the category is usefully employed by Peter Brooks in his analysis of narrative in *Reading for the Plot* (1984). [PW]

See also Chapter 6.

Further reading
Freud, Sigmund (1991b) *On Metapsychology: The Theory of Psychoanalysis, Beyond the Pleasure Principle, The Ego and the Id, and Other Works*, London: Penguin.

DEBORD, GUY (1931–94) A key member of the Situationists, a group of French radical writers of the 1960s who set out to critique the ways in which contemporary capitalism is as much concerned with the commodification of spectacle as it is with material goods. His most influential text *The Society of the Spectacle* was first published in French in 1967. Here he argues that 'the whole life of those societies in which modern conditions of production prevail presents itself as an immense accumulation of *spectacles*. All that was once directly lived has become mere representation' (Debord 1995: 12). This argument produces a **Marxist** critique of contemporary forms of representation, and has been extremely influential for postmodernist critics, perhaps most notably Jean **Baudrillard** whose analyses of **simulation** and **hyperreality** owe a good deal to Debord's arguments. [SM]

See also Chapter 10.

Further reading
Debord, Guy (1995) *The Society of the Spectacle*, trans. Donald Nicholson-Smith, New York: Zone Books.

DELEUZE, GILLES (1925–95) French poststructuralist philosopher best known for his books *Anti-Oedipus* (1972) and *A Thousand Plateaus* (1980), co-written with psychoanalyst Félix **Guattari**. After studying at the Sorbonne and teaching at the University of Lyon, Deleuze was appointed Professor of Philosophy at the University of Vincennes in Paris, the city in which he was born and lived most of his life.

Accorded the highest praise by contemporaries such as Jacques **Derrida** and Michel **Foucault**, Deleuze's most influential single-authored texts are *Nietzsche and Philosophy* (1983), *The Logic of Sense* (1968) and *Difference and Repetition* (1994). With Foucault, he also edited an authoritative French edition of the works of German philosopher Friedrich **Nietzsche**.

Despite its formidable difficulty, Deleuze's work has become an increasingly important point of reference for critical theory since his suicide in 1995. This is particularly true in film and cultural studies, architectural theory, and feminism, where his texts have most frequently been taken up. His writings on French novelist Marcel Proust and (with Guattari) German author Franz Kafka, as well as many other essays and references to literary authors such as Irish dramatist Samuel Beckett and English writers D. H. Lawrence and Lewis Carroll, are now beginning to attract the attention of literary and cultural critics.

Deleuze's thought draws on the work of what are traditionally considered a fairly disparate set of philosophers. These include Immanuel Kant, Scottish empiricist David Hume, French vitalist Henri Bergson, Jewish philosopher Baruch Spinoza, and Nietzsche. In a series of original, frequently difficult, and occasionally rather eccentric texts on the work of these and other thinkers, Deleuze radically reconstructs the concerns of both **phenomenology** and existentialism, movements which dominated French thought in the mid twentieth century. Instead of privileging a transcendental **subject** or the notion of a free individual who understands and thereby masters the world, Deleuze's work focuses on ontological questions concerning the place of **difference** in philosophical thinking. Like Derrida and Foucault, he strongly rejects Hegelian **dialectical** models that treat difference as negative or as the binary opposite of a naturally whole

and unified identity. Deeply influenced by Nietzsche, Deleuze embraces a pluralist approach that treats difference as primary and constitutive of identity or being. This destabilizes, rather than simply inverting, the conventional oppositions of Western philosophy. For Deleuze, identity is never unified or fixed but always in a process of becoming and thus subject to endless variation and change. Similarly, origins are never absolute or ideal but relative to and affected by what they produce. As in deconstruction, placing difference at the origin upsets traditional **logocentric** ideas of what an origin is. Consequently, all ideas of a pure, unified presence or transcendent truth are utterly rejected in Deleuze's work. Instead, it follows in the footsteps of the Greek pre-Socratic philosopher Heraclitus (*c.* 480 BC), who graphically emphasized the ephemeral, flowing nature of things by suggesting that 'You cannot step into the same river twice.'

In *Anti-Oedipus*, Deleuze's first book co-authored with Guattari, the ideas of non-dialectical difference and a constant Heraclitean flux are linked to a radical critique of **psychoanalysis** which is named **schizoanalysis**. Psychoanalysts Sigmund **Freud** and Jacques **Lacan** are criticized in a polemical and stylistically exuberant text that continues to provoke either strong praise or distaste among readers today. Deleuze and Guattari attack the metaphysical and totalizing nature of the **Oedipus complex**, using both Nietzsche and **Marx** to produce a deeply atheistic and **materialist** reading of **desire** and the **unconscious**. The book is by no means a synthesis of these two thinkers, however, but a creative appropriation and reconstruction of particular trajectories opened up by their thought. Deleuze's earlier reading of the concepts of difference and force in Nietzsche's work is transformed into a new way of thinking about desire in terms of active production and flows, rather than negativity and lack. While *Anti-*

Oedipus seems to champion a Marxist idea of production above all other concepts, the later *A Thousand Plateaus* develops more complex ideas such as **rhizomes** and multiplicities as ways of thinking about active difference, change and plurality. In both texts, as in all Deleuze's writings, there is an attempt at making philosophical thinking into a **nomadology** or 'nomad thought' – a fluid, mobile approach to thinking that refuses to privilege identity, unity or the subject. [DH]

See also Chapter 4.

Further reading

Deleuze, Gilles (1983) *Nietzsche and Philosophy*, trans. Hugh Tomlinson, New York: Columbia University Press.

Deleuze, Gilles and Guattari, Félix (1984) *Anti-Oedipus: Capitalism and Schizophrenia*, trans. Robert Hurley, Mark Seem and Helen R. Lane, London: Athlone Press.

DE MAN, PAUL (1919–83) Literary theorist born in Belgium. His works include *Allegories of Reading*, *Blindness and Insight* and *The Rhetoric of Romanticism*. De Man was an influential figure within what came to be known as the Yale School of deconstruction along with other notable critics such as J. Hillis **Miller** and Harold **Bloom**.

De Man's work has much in common with the deconstructive theory of French philosopher Jacques **Derrida**. According to De Man, deconstruction is not simply a form of literary criticism that can be applied to a text in order to generate a certain understanding. Rather, deconstruction already inhabits a text, and it is the task of the critic to analyse how the contradictions within the text itself contribute to its overall meaning.

De Man's work also engages the question of language within works of philosophy and literature. He observes how the **genre** distinction between literature and

philosophy collapses through the use of analytic and rhetorical language in both disciplines, and his readings of philosophers such as Kant, Hegel and **Heidegger** have proved as influential as his readings of Romantic poetry.

The reception of De Man's work suffered in the late 1980s with the revelation that he had written for a pro-Nazi publication during the war. Despite this, his work remains an important contribution in the ongoing debate of deconstructive strategy. [JS]

See also Chapter 7.

Further reading

De Man, Paul (1982) *Allegories of Reading*, London: Yale University Press.

De Man, Paul (1983) *Blindness and Insight*, 2nd edition, London: Routledge.

De Man, Paul (1984) *The Rhetoric of Romanticism*, New York: Columbia University Press.

Norris, Christopher (1988) *Paul De Man: Deconstruction and the Critique of Aesthetic Ideology*, London: Routledge.

DERRIDA, JACQUES (1930–2004) Algerian-born French philosopher whose work has been extremely influential within literature and philosophy departments in Europe and America, giving rise to a philosophy and method of reading known as deconstruction.

Derrida was an enormously prolific writer, and first came to attention with a spate of publications in 1967 (*Speech and Phenomena*; *Of Grammatology*; *Writing and Difference*) and again in 1972 (*Positions*; *Dissemination*; *Margins of Philosophy*). These early works established his fundamental concern with language, text and meaning, and displayed his distinctively playful, 'literary' style which continually draws attention to the rhetorical, figurative and metaphorical potential of language and the ever-present possibility of misapprehension and miscommunication.

Derrida's self-consciously 'difficult' style has earned him praise and condemnation in equal measure: his work is often seen as blurring the boundaries between philosophical and literary discourse. His most vociferous critics have been analytic philosophers seeking to maintain the alleged purity of their discipline and its modes of expression.

Deconstruction is primarily directed against what Derrida has called the '**metaphysics** of presence' or **logocentrism**; by this he means the dominant tradition of Western philosophy and the logic upon which it is founded – a logic which he consequently attempts to reveal as dependent upon certain founding metaphors, rhetorical gestures and self-fulfilling assumptions. His own emphasis is upon **difference** rather than identity, absence rather than presence, although he concedes that he is still working within the system of philosophy which he criticizes.

Much of Derrida's work involves close readings of texts by thinkers as diverse as Plato, **Heidegger**, Husserl, **Nietzsche**, **Austin**, **Marx**, Rousseau, **Saussure** and **Freud**. In such readings he often picks out an apparently marginal comment or motif and makes it central to his account, showing a text's internal tensions and contradictions, the moments when it undermines its own central messages and meanings. It is not that he deconstructs texts; rather they deconstruct themselves, hence his claim that deconstruction defies definition and is not, strictly speaking, a 'method' at all. For example, in a reading of Plato's *Phaedrus* in *Dissemination*, Derrida explores the double (and contradictory) meanings of '*pharmakon*' as both 'remedy' and 'poison', and shows how this undermines Socrates' apparent attack on writing.

While structuralist criticism generally looks to identify and reinforce the binary oppositions underpinning a text, Derrida, as a poststructuralist, sets out to deconstruct binaries such as presence/absence, sensible/intelligible, ideal/real and speech/writing. He reveals the dependence of one term upon the other (their fundamental inextricability) and also the hierarchical and asymmetrical nature of the binary (the fact that one term will be privileged, the other seen as derivative or secondary, as with white/black, man/woman). Poststructuralist feminist critics such as Hélène **Cixous** and Judith **Butler** reveal Derrida's influence in their interrogation of such binaries.

His recent work has been demonstrably political and ethical in its concerns, ranging from an examination of Marxist philosophy in *Specters of Marx* (1993) to more personal works on Jewish theology, death, mourning, forgiveness and friendship; the former is perhaps in response to critics of deconstruction who have regarded it as worryingly apolitical in its refusal to privilege any form of knowledge and its tendency to treat all truth and knowledge claims as more or less textual constructions. The latter more ethically minded works put him in dialogue with philosophical contemporaries such as **De Man** and **Levinas**. [KM]

See also Chapters 3, 4 and 7.

Further reading

Derrida, Jacques (1973) 'Differance', in *'Speech and Phenomena' and Other Essays on Husserl's Theory of Signs*, trans. David B. Allison, Evanston, IL: Northwestern University Press.

Derrida, Jacques (1976) *Of Grammatology*, trans. Gayatri Chakravorty Spivak, Baltimore, MD: Johns Hopkins University Press.

Derrida, Jacques (1987) *The Post Card: From Socrates to Freud and Beyond*, trans. Alan Bass, Chicago: University of Chicago Press.

Derrida, Jacques (1994) *Specters of Marx*, trans. Peggy Kamuf, London: Routledge.

Norris, Christopher (1987) *Derrida*, London: Fontana Press.

Royle, Nicholas (2003a) *Jacques Derrida*, London: Routledge.

DESIRE This term has long been central to Western culture, but its contemporary theoretical importance derives from the French psychoanalyst Jacques **Lacan**'s elucidation of **unconscious** desire. Sigmund **Freud** observed that the human sexual **drive** is never wholly satisfied. For Lacan, this is because desire is produced by the subjection of the human organism to the law of language, which is for him the fundamental organizing principle of consciousness. Desire, which he differentiates from bodily need, is conceivable as the structural effect of the split that language introduces between our animal and speaking selves.

Desire comes from the '**Other**', the place of speech, which is both outside and inside us. We internalize speech by learning it, but it never truly becomes 'ours' as its meanings are not generated by individual **subjects** but by the arbitrary differences between **signifiers**. Lack results from this awkward compromise between the general and the specific, the linguistic and the organic, in which something of the latter is consistently lost. Desire, which is not only sexual, relentlessly attempts to fill this lack, settling on various objects which seem to offer fulfilment: hence the appeal of a different lover or new car. The lack cannot be filled, and so desire keeps going, finding new objects, and making the grass appear greener on the other side of the fence. It is effectively the desire of nothing, of no thing that exists, which is why its sign is the **phallus**. Though Lacan's account may appear pessimistic, desire's energy can be vital, revolutionary and exciting. Founded upon lack, its restless dissatisfaction drives change. However, it can also be destructive. Desire could only be satisfied in the end, which is to say in death: it can thus become the desire for annihilation of self and other.

Lacan's definition has been critiqued and extended by the philosophers Jacques **Derrida**, Gilles **Deleuze** and Félix **Guattari**

among others, but remains of central importance to accounts of subjectivity, sexuality and culture. [RLS]

See also Chapter 6.

Further reading

Belsey, Catherine (1994) *Desire: Love Stories in Western Culture*, Oxford: Blackwell.

Lacan, Jacques (1977) *Écrits: A Selection*, trans. Alan Sheridan, London: Routledge.

DIALECTIC Derived from the word 'dialogue', meaning the pursuit of truth through debate or discussion, the term denotes the belief that change is driven by contradiction. The ancient Greek philosopher Plato's dialogues represented discussions in which the truth of a proposition was tested, and its contradictions revealed, by question and answer.

The late eighteenth-century German philosopher, G. W. F. Hegel developed a form of dialectical logic that influenced a group of mid-nineteenth-century German philosophers known as the 'Young Hegelians', which included the political philosopher Karl **Marx**. Marx's theory of 'historical **materialism**' applied the dialectic to the study of human history, while his collaborator Friedrich **Engels** controversially attempted to develop a scientific method of 'dialectical materialism', founded on 'three Laws' applicable to human history and the natural world. The first of these is the unity of opposites, which simply refers to the interdependence of two contradictory principles; an example of this kind of relationship is that between capitalists and workers. The second is the transformation of quantity into quality, whereby gradual quantitative change brings about a fundamental qualitative change. To take a proverbial example: placing a single straw on a camel's back will effect no qualitative change; continue to do so and eventually the load will be so heavy that the camel's back will break. The third is the negation of the negation, which occurs when elements of a prior stage of development subsequently recur in a modified form; Engels gives the example of evolution as it takes place in plants.

Though the dialectic is primarily associated with Marxist thought, it was Hegel's contemporary Johann Fichte who detailed the most common explanation of the dialectic: two competing terms ('thesis' and 'antithesis') generate a third (the 'synthesis'), which incorporates aspects of both. Marx, for example, believed conflict between bourgeoisie and proletariat would lead to revolution and a new, productive but classless society. The dialectical conception of change continues to influence contemporary theorists of culture and society, although its universalizing premises have been challenged by many thinkers associated with poststructuralism. [CRC]

See also Chapter 3.

Further reading

Rees, John (1998) *The Algebra of Revolution: The Dialectic and the Classical Marxist Tradition*, London: Routledge.

DIFFERANCE A term coined by Jacques **Derrida**, which forms a central strand of his attack on the logic and values of traditional Western philosophy – what Derrida calls '**logocentrism**'.

Perhaps unhelpfully, Derrida claims in *Margins of Philosophy* (1972) that differance is 'literally neither a word nor a concept' and that it 'has neither existence nor essence'. What is clear, however, is that differance derives from the Latin verb *differre* and the French *différer*, which in English have given rise to two distinct verbs: to defer and to differ. Differance incorporates both of these meanings and thus serves to emphasize two key Derridean concerns: with absence rather than presence (full meaning is never present, but is instead constantly deferred because of the differance characteristic of language); and with **difference** rather than identity (Derrida

focuses on the difference between terms, and the spaces between words, rather than on the terms in themselves and any positive value they might otherwise be thought to have).

In describing differance as the 'systematic play of differences' which is built into language, and highlighting the dependence of language upon 'intervals' (spaces between words) without which words could not function, Derrida carries **Saussure**'s theory of language as a system of differences to its most extreme conclusion. He also develops and expands the emphasis upon difference which has been central to the work of **Nietzsche** and **Heidegger**.

In addition, differance reiterates Derrida's desire to assert the primacy of writing over speech, because the 'a' which makes it distinguishable from difference is only detectable when the word is written or read, not when it is spoken or heard (*différance* and *différence* are pronounced in exactly the same way in French); so differance is also an attack on the perceived phonocentrism of Western philosophy, i.e. its privileging of speech over writing. [KM]

See also Chapters 4 and 7.

Further reading

Culler, Jonathan (1983) *On Deconstruction*, London: Routledge.

Derrida, Jacques (1982) 'Différance', in *Margins of Philosophy*, trans. Alan Bass, London: Prentice Hall.

DIFFERENCE A concept which took on its now generally recognized theoretical meaning in the early twentieth century in the work of Ferdinand de **Saussure**. According to Saussure's **semiology**, language is made up of **signs**, and each sign gets its meaning only because of its *difference* from every other sign: a sign has no inherent value in and of itself. Thus, the written word 'mouse' does not have any intrinsic relationship with the small rodent that eats cheese; rather, its meaning emerges from the fact that it differs from other possible graphic images such as h-o-u-s-e, d-o-u-s-e, m-o-u-t-h, etc. If there was any intrinsic relationship between this small cheese-eating rodent (either the real world animal or the mental image of the thing) and the word 'mouse', then all languages would use the same word. The same is true of the spoken word. For example, if the word 'mouse' is used in a phrase such as 'by moving the mouse, the pointer on the screen moves', then the precise meaning attributed to 'mouse' emerges from the words surrounding it.

It is this notion of difference that underpins structuralism. First, the **sign** has an arbitrary relationship to the **referent**: a sign has meaning only through the way it is related to other signs and not through reference to a real world object. Second, the sign itself can be divided into **signifier** (an acoustic or written image) and **signified** (mental concept). Again, the relationship between the sound and the mental image is arbitrary: in this way the concept can only emerge in difference from other concepts, and, equally, the written/acoustic image can only emerge in difference from other written/acoustic images.

Poststructuralism, however, tends not to accept any distinction between signifier and signified. In this way, concepts are words and words are concepts. Signifiers are signs that refer to other signs, and 'meaning' (in the loosest possible sense of the word) is the play of this difference. Accordingly, Jacques **Derrida** established the neologism **differance** to designate the relation between signifiers as one of difference *and* deferral – a slippage from word to word, in which each word keeps a **trace** of the words that differ from it. Derrida's notion of differance, however, comes from at least two sources: one being the work of Saussure, the other of which is the philosophy of Martin **Heidegger**. Heidegger's notion of difference refers to the difference between Being (*Sein*) and particular entities (*Seindes*). These concepts of Being and beings are central to Heidegger and appear not as a synthesis, but rather as having an interdependence (in that all beings have Being and yet Being is not simply reducible to the sum of beings). Difference is what tears Being apart, yet at the same time is what draws beings together.

Another notion of difference that emerges from philosophy is that put forward by the early work of Gilles **Deleuze**. Deleuze attempts to sidestep Saussure completely by citing **Nietzsche** as an origin for the concept of difference, though arguably this is in part to subvert the accepted tradition and re-energize the term. In *Nietzsche and Philosophy* (1983), Deleuze interprets Nietzsche's philosophy to engage with a concept of difference in order to mount an attack upon **dialectics** and its implied dualism (in Plato, Hegel and **Marx**). In *Difference and Repetition* (1994), Deleuze describes a 'non-dialectic philosophy of becoming' in order to deny that that which is different can in any way be unified. Jean François **Lyotard**, like Derrida, invents a new concept to approach difference, that of the **differend**, though similarly to Deleuze it is a difference that can never be resolved. Poststructuralist notions of difference, then, are multifarious and emerge from a number of sources. Most recent applications however, have been in the domain of social studies in order to activate an anti-essentialism. Particularly successful has been work in the domains of gender and ethnicity. [DD]

See also Chapters 1, 4 and 7.

DIFFEREND Communities have language regimes which are based on the shared rules for meaning within the group. According to Jean-François **Lyotard** in *The Differend*, phrases are units of language in which the shared understandings of a particular group are embedded. Any individual phrase possesses rules for meaning which are shared by the particular group to whom the phrase belongs. When two such groups come into contact, the differend expresses the condition of irreconcilable **difference** between the two language regimes. As the meaning of any particular phrase is dependent on the shared understanding of one group, a differend occurs when the meanings shared in one group collide – inevitably – with the meanings shared by the other group. This difference is incommensurable because the generic rules of one language regime are quite literally not commensurate – immeasurable or untranslatable – with the rules of another group's language regime. Cases of differends exist at points of dispute – for example, where the laws of one group must pronounce judgement over another. In *Introducing Lyotard*, Bill Readings illustrates this by reference to cases of Australian aborigines pursuing land rights under the Australian state legal system whereby the aboriginal understanding of property collides with the meaning shared by the court. Thus in order to win rights, the aborigines have to succumb to a language regime other than the one to which they subscribe – they had to lose their 'land' in order to try to gain land. The two meanings of the term were incommensurable and so gave evidence of a differend. For Lyotard, the persistence of active differentiation is crucial in a world which places so much emphasis on an impossible consensus. While consensus may be desirable, it typically involves the imposition of one language regime (and set of cultural meanings and norms) over all others. This would lead to totality which, at the end of his essay 'Answer to the Question: What is the Postmodern?', Lyotard entreats us to wage war on as it equates to totalitarianism. To guard against this we must 'activate the differends' – bear witness to the irreconcilable differences of culture. [AT]

See also Chapter 10.

Further reading

Lyotard, Jean-François (1991a) *The Differend: Phrases in Dispute*, trans. Georges Van Den Abbeele, Minneapolis, MN: University of Minnesota Press.

Lyotard, Jean-François (1992) 'Answer to the Question: What is the Postmodern?', in *The Postmodern Explained to Children: Correspondence 1982–1985*, London: Turnaround.

Readings, Bill (1991) *Introducing Lyotard: Art and Politics*, London: Routledge.

DISCOURSE   This term refers to the use of language as it is embedded in social practice. In emphasizing the social and functional aspects of language, discourse analysts seek to examine the rules governing language use as it is deployed within wider social structures of regulation and control. Within critical theory, this study is related, most importantly, to the work of French structuralist Michel **Foucault**, who understood discourse to be part of the social structure itself. Any language community, such as medicine, will share a methodology, phraseology and a body of thought which makes up their discourse. This discursive field contains within it rules governing language use within the community; thus certain usages will be prohibited as unacceptable or excluded altogether. By examining the historical formation of, for example, medical discourse, Foucault shows that the rules governing acceptable language use amount to a discursive regime which determines not only what can be said but, ultimately, what can be known. Discourse is thus a site of **power** as it constitutes both the sphere of knowledge and the community perceived to be in possession of it: 'It is in discourse that power and knowledge are joined together' (Foucault 1984: 100). While Foucault's earlier work focused primarily on the institutionalization of certain discourses, hence certain knowledge regimes, in the service of social control, his later work on sexuality refined the concept somewhat. Here, the medical and juridical discourses concerning homosexuality in the nineteenth century are shown to give rise to a 'reverse' or counter-discourse which allows for the possibility of resistance. The writings around homosexuality, which were designed to define the excluded category of the homosexual, also guaranteed the emergence of a new identity which 'began to speak on its own behalf . . . often in the same vocabulary, using the same categories by which it was medically disqualified' (1984: 101). Discourse here remains a channel for power but this is no longer understood to be controlling, rather strategic. The reworking of discourse becomes a tactical force within the ongoing strategies of power and resistance. [AT]

See also Chapters 3 and 5.

Further reading

Foucault, Michel (1984) *The History of Sexuality, vol. 1: An Introduction*, trans. Robert Hurley, Harmondsworth: Penguin.

DISSEMINATION Term coined by Jacques **Derrida** in a text of the same name. *Dissemination* consists of three important essays: 'Plato's Pharmacy', 'The Double Session' and 'Dissemination'. These include readings of Plato, Stéphane Mallarmé and Philippe Sollers.

The concept of dissemination has much in common with other Derridean terms, including **differance**, **trace** and **supplement**. According to Derrida, the notion of dissemination is primarily concerned with how texts can produce a variety of different meanings as opposed to just one. This draws on the literal meaning of the term which is the dispersal of information. As with other aspects of Derridean thought, dissemination refers to the undecidable elements that prevent a text settling down into a clear, stable meaning. For example, in 'Plato's Pharmacy', Derrida demonstrates how, in Plato's *Phaedrus,* Socrates

privileges speech over writing. However, Derrida identifies Plato's use of the word '*pharmakon*' to refer to writing, a term which can mean both remedy *and* poison. The undecidable, double nature of the term problematizes Socrates' argument that writing is inferior to speech. This uncertainty within a text is what Derrida terms 'dissemination'. [JS]

See also Chapter 7.

Further reading

Derrida, Jacques (1993a) *Dissemination*, trans. B. Johnson, London: Althone.

DRIVE The theory of drive needs to be sharply distinguished from the category of instinct, which is a biological term. Many English translators of **Freud** have interpreted the German term *Trieb* to mean instinct, while other interpretations, perhaps most notably that of Jacques **Lacan**, have insisted on drive as the more accurate rendition of Freud's intended meaning. Drive differs from animal instinct in that, in the case of the human **subject**, bodily needs are experienced not purely in terms of physical compulsion but through the **symbolic** dimension of language and meaning. Basic animal instincts such as sexual procreation are transmuted into sexuality, whereby pleasure and gratification are intimately bound up with images and objects that have become symbolic stand-ins for the biological act. Drive is what continually compels human subjects to seek pleasure and satisfaction precisely within the domain of symbols and images, not as a relatively simple biological imperative. It is important to note that, for psychoanalysis, drive is the basis of the circular or endlessly reproductive core of human subjectivity. Drive also differs from the psychoanalytic idea of **desire** in that while drive compels the subject to seek pleasure from the symbolic as a general category, desire can designate a yearning for or focus upon one particular symbolic object. [HJ]

See also Chapter 6.

Further reading

Lacan, Jacques (1994) *Seminar 11: The Four Fundamental Concepts of Psychoanalysis*, ed. Jacques-Alain Miller, trans. Alan Sheridan, London: Penguin.

DU BOIS, WILLIAM EDWARD BURGHARDT (1868–1963) The work of the African-American scholar, journalist and activist W. E. B. Du Bois has been massively influential in many fields of study, including cultural studies, postcolonial studies and, most obviously, various strands of American historical studies. In particular, *The Souls of Black Folk* (1903) has provided powerful models of racial thinking since its original publication, and is generally credited with initiating the bold challenge which African-American writers and other artists and thinkers would offer to the supremacy of Eurocentric models of 'culture'. Although avowedly influenced by European '**Enlightenment**' notions of history and nationhood, *The Souls of Black Folk* asserts the equal cultural worth of specifically 'black' cultural products, most specifically the 'Negro spirituals' descended from slave songs.

Just as crucially, *The Souls of Black Folk* introduced powerful conceptualizations of the effects of racial segregation/demarcation on the individual African-American *and* the ways in which he/she is represented by the dominant white culture. In the key metaphor of 'the Veil', Du Bois captures the sometimes ambiguous but always present barrier between the black and white world in the USA in the late nineteenth and the early twentieth centuries; it is a metaphor which resonated through African-American writing in particular throughout the twentieth century. The notion of 'double consciousness' – 'this sense of always looking at one's self through the eyes of others' – which Du Bois insists permeates the African-American's sense of self, is a precursor to such postcolonial notions as '**othering**', the objectification of the **colonial** subject, the fracturing of the native self, and so on.

In the years following the publication of *The Souls of Black Folk*, Du Bois's ideas were radicalized and attention turned from black to white America, and the white world. In *The Souls of White Folk* (1920), the racial 'problem' across the globe is seen as a product of 'the discovery of personal whiteness ... a very modern thing'. In switching focus onto the problematics of 'white' culture and history, Du Bois's work would be key in the development of Panafricanism and its political manifestation in the colonial national liberation movements. The autobiographical *Dusk of Dawn* (1940) exemplifies the increasingly internationalist stance taken by Du Bois, in which 'race' becomes just one aspect – if a very important one – in the global struggle for economic and cultural power: again, Du Bois' work might be seen as prefiguring subsequent developments in **Marxist** approaches to 'race and class'. And some late twentieth-century critical approaches such as 'black Atlanticism' are heavily dependent upon Du Bois as an example of transnational, interdisciplinary and cross-cultural theory and practice. [KH]

See also Chapter 11.

Further reading

Du Bois, W. E. B. (1995) *Dark Princess*, Jackson, MS: University Press of Mississippi.

Du Bois, W. E. B. (2001) *The Negro*, University Park, PA: University of Pennsylvania State Press.

Gilroy, Paul (1993) *The Black Atlantic: Modernity and Double Consciousness*, London: Verso.

Zamir, Shamoon (1995) *Dark Voices: W.E.B. Du Bois and American Thought, 1888–1903*, Chicago, IL: University of Chicago Press.

E

Eco, Umberto (1932–) Italian author and theorist, Eco is Professor of Semiotics at the University of Bologna. His early work has much in common with reader-response theory, arguing in *The Open Work* (1989) (*Opera aperta*, 1962) that texts should be regarded as dynamic and open to numerous, but not limitless, interpretations. His theoretical writings explore the application of **semiotics** to both high and low culture (see *A Theory of Semiotics*, 1976), rejecting **Saussure**'s emphasis on linguistic study, and taking in a wide range of texts from outside the literary **canon**. Eco's semiotic theory is perhaps most engagingly expressed in *The Role of the Reader* (1979) in which he develops the arguments set out in *The Open Work* to discuss the role of the **author**, the text and the 'model' reader – the reader that the author attempts to 'create'.

Eco's first novel, *The Name of the Rose* (1983), a medieval crime novel, is a prime example of the 'open' work, operating on several levels and containing a fictional embodiment of the reader, and of reading practices, in the form of the detective-monk William of Baskerville. *The Name of the Rose* was, as Eco indicates in his *Postscript to 'The Name of the Rose'* (1994), a deliberate attempt to write a postmodern novel and it has, along with his subsequent novels, *Foucault's Pendulum* (1989) and *The Island of the Day Before* (1995), been taken up by postmodern theorists as a prime example of the form. [PW]

See also Chapter 10.

Further reading

Caeser, Michael (1999) *Umberto Eco:* *Philosophy, Semiotics and the Work of Fiction*, Cambridge: Polity Press.

Eco, Umberto (1979) *The Role of the Reader: Explorations in the Semiotics of Texts*, Bloomington, IN: Indiana University Press.

Eco, Umberto (1983) *The Name of the Rose*, trans. William Weaver, London: Vintage.

Ecocriticism At the very least, 'ecocriticism' may be seen as a sustained attempt to redress the balance after decades of what we might call 'culturalism'. That is, where structuralism and poststructuralism seem generally to concur in seeing nature as a cultural – specifically, linguistic – construct, ecocriticism demands that we take nature seriously, as far as is possible, in its own right and for its own sake. As Kate Soper observes: 'It is not language which has a hole in its ozone layer' (Coupe 2000: 124). If it has become a truism in literary and cultural studies that 'there is no such thing as nature', then ecocritics wish to challenge this, without taking us back to a naïve **realism**. If Raymond **Williams** is right that 'Nature is perhaps the most complex word in the language' (1976), then the task is to restore its centrality as a site of struggle. Ecocriticism 'debates "Nature" in order to defend nature' (Coupe 2000: 5). Far from wishing to evade the problem of 'the **real**', ecocritics wish to make it central to critical thinking and practice.

It was in the USA that an explicitly ecological approach to literature and culture was first developed. As to an exact starting-point, opinion is divided. Some point to an ambitious article by William Rueckert, a disciple of Kenneth **Burke**: 'Literature and Ecology: An Experiment in

Ecocriticism' (1978); the very use of the word has all the air of drafting a critical programme. Others point to a slightly earlier article by Karl Kroeber: '"Home at Grasmere": Ecological Holiness' (1974). This is ostensibly a more modest piece of writing, being a commentary on a poem by William Wordsworth, but it certainly raises all the main issues. Whatever its origin, ecocriticism was firmly established by the early 1990s, when Cheryll Glotfelty and Scott Slovic launched the Association for the Study of Literature and the Environment. This enterprise was consolidated in the middle of that decade, when Glotfelty edited, with the help of Harold Fromm, *The Ecocriticism Reader* (which significantly included Rueckert's article). Her introduction firmly establishes nature as an essential referent of contemporary critical theory, not only complementing race, class and gender but also comprehending them, since the destruction of the planet would render them incidental.

The philosophical origins of American ecocriticism lay in the North American movement known as 'transcendentalism'. It had been Ralph Waldo Emerson and Henry David Thoreau who had, in the mid nineteenth century, insisted on the fundamental human need for nature, for wilderness, for something beyond the human sphere. Thoreau, whose experiment in living close to the land was documented in his *Walden* (1854), became especially important for ecocritics. Emerson had perhaps been too concerned with the 'transcendental' aspect of the appreciation of nature; Thoreau seemed much more down to earth, to use a particularly apt phrase. Lawrence Buell's ambitious study of American cultural history in relation to ecological thinking is centred on his work, his reputation and his influence: Buell's book, published in 1995, is entitled *The Environmental Imagination: Thoreau, Nature Writing, and the Formation of American Culture.*

Mention of the category of 'nature writing' is a reminder that one of the main contributions of ecocriticism has been the extension of the literary **canon** to include **genres** that hitherto have been regarded as non-literary. This has been especially true in the USA. In the UK, the tendency has been to make central hitherto marginal writers in established genres. For example, the early nineteenth-century poet John Clare's sensitive evocation of the minutiae of English rural life and of the natural world is now widely respected and celebrated, whereas once he was treated as something of a curiosity.

Mention of Clare suggests the chief reference point for British ecocriticism. If the movement in the USA drew on American transcendentalism, then the movement in the UK drew on English Romanticism. Particularly important is Jonathan Bate's book, *Romantic Ecology: Wordsworth and the Environmental Tradition* (1991), which defends Wordsworth's preoccupation with nature against the Marxist challenge that 'Romantic ideology' involved using the natural world as a refuge from proper political engagement. In doing so, Bate lays down his own challenge: that the time has come for politics to take on a 'green' aspect as well as a 'red' – thus extending the prophetic work done by the **cultural materialist** critic, Raymond Williams in *The Country and the City*, with its case for a 'socialist ecology'.

It has been particularly evident in the reading of the English Romantic writers – by both British and North American critics – that the ecological approach to literature allows not only for extending the literary canon but also for radically rereading canonical works. Kroeber's account of Wordsworth's 'Home at Grasmere' is one instance. Another is Bate's essay, 'Major Weather', included in his *Song of the Earth* (2000): this analyses John Keats' 'To Autumn' and Lord Byron's 'Darkness' in relation to hitherto neglected information about climate, geography and agricultural practice. What previous critics have regarded as incidental becomes imaginatively and critically crucial.

Ecocriticism seems to have taken hold in the North American academy much more systematically than in the British. Here, a broader and looser approach to the ecological aspect of literature, culture, philosophy and politics seems to be adopted. In the UK, the preferred term is 'green studies'. In both versions, however, there has been a sustained interest in the connection between ecology and feminism, since the privileging of nature over culture has been thought to parallel the privileging of the male over the female. As always, the task is to challenge this process without reliance on an equivalent dualism. [LC]

Further reading

Coupe, Laurence (ed.) (2000) *The Green Studies Reader*, London: Routledge.

Garrard, Greg (2004) *Ecocriticism*, London: Routledge.

Glotfelty, Cheryll and Fromm, Harold (eds) (1996) *The Ecocriticism Reader: Landmarks in Literary Ecology*, Athens, GA: University of Georgia Press.

ÉCRITURE FÉMININE The leading practitioner of *écriture féminine* is the French poststructuralist Hélène **Cixous** whose works, 'The Laugh of the Medusa' and 'Sorties' (originally published in French in 1975), are manifestos of the practice. This form of writing attempts to inscribe femininity by challenging the **phallocentric** discourses of sexuality and subjectivity posited by the psychoanalysts Sigmund **Freud** and Jacques **Lacan** in which women are marked as deviant on account of their lack of a penis. Cixous makes a close link between sexuality and writing and focuses on the **imaginary** mother/child dyad of the pre-**Oedipal** phase, which forms the repressed **'Other'** within the unconscious upon entry into the **symbolic**. Cixous

argues that writing is the place of the 'Other' and the feminine text attempts to *write through the body* the unconscious polymorphous drives of the child and its closeness to the body of the 'm/other'. The subversive potential of this 'what-comes-before-language' (1986: 88) is expressed through the use of puns and metaphors which attempt to foreground the polysemic, literally 'multiple meaning', nature of signification. Cixous refuses to define the feminine, insisting that it must remain an open question and that the writer must actively search for gaps, disruptions or excesses in language, not in order to 'master' otherness, but 'to see it, to experience what she is not, what she is, what she can be' (1986: 86). The connections between the female body and the 'feminine' remain ambiguous. Whilst she does not attempt to fix the 'feminine' biologically, her maternal metaphors of writing in 'white ink' suggest a female biological essence (1981: 251). However, this *seeming* impossible logic is strategic in its attempt to *displace* (masculine) binary logic, formulated on the principle of Oneness and the effacement of the feminine, by gesturing towards the (im)possiblity (within phallocentric logic) of articulating an 'other' discourse of heterogeneity and **difference**. [CM]

See also Chapters 8 and 9.

Further reading

Cixous, Hélène (1981) 'The Laugh of the Medusa', trans. Keith Cohen and Paula Cohen, in Elaine Marks and Isabel de Courtivron (eds), *New French Feminisms: An Anthology*, New York: Harvester Wheatsheaf.

Cixous, Hélène (1986) 'Sorties: Out and Out: Attacks/ Ways Out/ Forays', in Hélène Cixous and Catherine Clément, *The Newly Born Woman*, trans. Betsy Wing, Minneapolis, MN: University of Minnesota Press.

EGO A concept defined by Sigmund **Freud**, who conceived the human subject as being divided between the ego, the **superego** and the **id**. In the Freudian schema the ego represents the **subject**'s conscious self-image, a defensive space from which the violence and irrationalism of the id is excluded. The ego thus provides a vantage point, in terms of the reciprocal gaze between spectator and image outlined in the **Lacanian mirror stage**, from which the subject can view the ego as both a unified formation and, crucially, as an object worthy of love. The ego is that component of subjective identity that, in terms of 'normal' psychical development, is what represents the subject in social, intersubjective relations. What the ego represents is how the subject would like to be viewed, minus the **unconscious**, destructive and anti-social urges of the id and the punitive sadism of the superego. [HJ]

See also Chapter 6.

EMPSON, WILLIAM (1906–84) British critic, poet and former Professor of Literature at Sheffield University who is best known for the work of literary criticism written whilst he was still a student, *Seven Types of Ambiguity* (1930).

The close textual analysis of passages of poetry that Empson performs in *Seven Types of Ambiguity* has often led to him being connected with the school of **New Criticism**, but in fact he contested the anti-intentionalism of the New Critics as well as their doctrine of textual autonomy. *Seven Types of Ambiguity* analyses meaning, rather than determining literary value – although ambiguity itself emerges as a kind of value in Empson's rendering of it.

In *Some Versions of Pastoral* (1935), Empson considers the simple presentation of complex ideas in pastoral literature, and in the linguistic criticism of *The Structure of Complex Words* (1951) he examines the meaning of particular words within particular works – such as 'all' in *Paradise Lost*. The long-term influence of his work, particularly *Seven Types of Ambiguity*, may

be discerned in the increasing emphasis, throughout the twentieth century, on active and productive reading, and on the continuity of ordinary and poetic language. [KM]

Further reading
Empson, William (1995a) *Seven Types of Ambiguity*, London: Penguin.
Norris, Christopher (1978) *William Empson and the Philosophy of Literary Criticism*, London: Athlone Press.

ENGELS, FRIEDRICH (1820–95) German (Prussian) socialist philosopher best known for his close association with Karl **Marx** and the early stages of the Marxist movement. Engels' socialist principles are set out in his account of industrialization and poverty, *The Condition of the Working Classes in England in 1844* (1845).

Engels developed a theory of 'scientific socialism', which located social change as inspired by class antagonisms. Engels argued that there was an intrinsic, **dialectical**, opposition between the interests of the middle and the working classes. The apparent pity exhibited by the middle class for the conditions of the working class was a pretence; the middle classes, Engels contended, addressing the working class directly, would 'make you believe in their most hearty sympathy with your fates', drawing a distinction between the materiality of real life and the **ideology** that attempts to conceal the material facts of life as it is lived. Engels' work on dialectics would later be developed in collaboration with Marx, most notably in *The German Ideology* (1844) and *The Communist Manifesto* (1848).

Although Engels is generally discussed alongside Marx by critics, it is important to stress his individual contribution to the development of socialist theories and also to consider the influence of his dialectical theories on the development of Marx's own critical paradigms. [TES]

See also Chapter 3.

Further reading

Engels, Friedrich (1987) *The Condition of the Working Classes in England in 1844*, London: Penguin

Engels, Friedrich and Marx, Karl (1985) *The Communist Manifesto*, London: Penguin.

ENLIGHTENMENT Although its origins can be traced back as far as the late middle ages, Enlightenment thinking derives its name from the philosophical revolution of 1720–80 whose participants aimed to 'enlighten' their less forward-thinking peers. Influenced by pioneering thinkers such as Francis Bacon, René Descartes, and Jean-Jacques Rousseau, philosophers including Voltaire and Immanuel Kant mounted a direct challenge to the dominant religious doctrines that determined and organized 'knowledge'. Disputing the church's pre-eminence in governing common societal wisdom, and the myth of the 'natural' rights of the hereditary aristocracy, the Enlightenment encouraged individualism, reason and freedom. It was a combination of these doctrines that resulted in the French Revolution of 1789, where the partnership between church, state and gentry was so manifestly challenged and defeated.

One of the leading pioneers of 'enlightened' thinking was Galileo Galilei, who in 1632 advanced his Copernican assertion that the earth orbits the sun. Because his account directly contradicted the biblical notion that God's earth is the dynamic celestial body, Galileo's teaching was denounced, and he was forced to publish his later works clandestinely. In spite of the papal edict against Galileo's theory, the revolution of thought that his work initiated could not be disparaged. And so, in the mid eighteenth century, scholars such as Diderot and Voltaire published 17 volumes of the seminal *Encyclopédie ou Dictionnaire Raisonné des Sciences, des Arts et des Métiers*, commonly known as *The Encyclopedia*. Intrinsic to the work of the 'Encyclopedists' was a promotion of the attributes of science and measurability over the Christian revelations of nature and moral *truth*.

Whilst 'enlightened' thinking continues to influence contemporary critical theory, it does have its critics. In *Dialectic of Enlightenment*, Theodor W. **Adorno** and Max **Horkheimer** present an acute Marxist critique of its limitations. For Adorno and Horkheimer, all 'enlightened' societies are unreservedly repressed, and within *Dialectic of Enlightenment* they examine how the apparatus of the culture industry manifests an 'enlightenment of mass deception'.

In addition to the Marxist critique, postcolonial theorists argue that the Enlightenment idealized its European notions as universal truths and subsequently allows little or no 'speech gap' for the subaltern. Critics aside, the Enlightenment revolutionized the way we think in terms of critical interpretation and general cognition; it also continues to uphold the belief that knowledge should be impartial, neutral and objective. [PSW]

Further reading

Adorno, Theodor and Horkheimer, Max (1992) *Dialectic of Enlightenment*, trans. John Cumming, London: Verso.

Schmidt, James (ed.) (1996) *What is Enlightenment?: Eighteenth-Century Answers and Twentieth-Century Questions*, Berkeley, CA: University of California Press.

ETHICS In one of its many senses, ethics refers to a set of principles or codes which stipulate how one should behave in a certain field of practice. Doctors and lawyers, for example, are bound by the ethical principles in their respective disciplines. The rules of conduct within a Christian ethics are laid out in the Ten Commandments. More recently, ethical debates have been held in the field of genetics, in particular stem-cell research. Generally, ethics here can be characterized as an 'ethics of' since it only refers to a certain discipline or practice. However, there have also been more general interrogations into the meaning of ethics. Ethical theories attempt to define generally 'how one ought to behave' or 'what a good life is'. In nineteenth-century England, a movement called utilitarianism tried to determine those principles which would decide whether an action is right or wrong. The main representatives, Jeremy Bentham (1748–1832) and John Stuart Mill (1808–73), thought that an action is right if it achieves the greatest happiness for the greatest numbers. The principle of utility thus separates the rightness of an action from the good or bad intentions of the agent who performs the action. The German philosopher Immanuel Kant (1724–1804) produced an ethics that differs from Mill's utilitarianism by pointing out that a moral action is performed on the basis of respect for duty and that a moral action is good if it is performed out of this respect. Here the result of the action, the achievement of happiness, is secondary. What is one's duty in a particular situation, says Kant, is determined by the categorical imperative. This imperative stipulates that every action must be judged as if it were to become a universal code of behaviour. Kant calls this ability to use practical reason in order to generate rules of conduct the autonomy of the will and regards it as constituting a person's dignity. In modified forms, Kant's ethics still enjoys a wide currency. Contemporary French philosophers such as Emmanuel **Levinas** and Jacques **Derrida** reject Kant's universalizability thesis and emphasize that ethics is generated in the singular encounter with the **other**. [RS]

Further reading
Grayling, Anthony C. (ed.) (1997) *Philosophy: A Guide Through the Subject*, Oxford: Oxford University Press.

ETHNOCENTRICITY A term originally coined by the American sociologist William Graham Sumner (1840–1910). Ethnocentrics believe their own ethnic group to be the standard against which to judge all **other** cultures. Whether consciously or **unconsciously**, they assume that their own ideas and customs are superior to those of other ethnic groups. Ethnocentricity also often involves the assumption that the concepts of one's ethnic group are universally applicable.

To the ethnocentric, the ideas of her own culture appear so natural that they are taken to be facts. Western ethnocentricity, currently one of the most prevalent and potent manifestations, is often known as Eurocentricity. Eurocentrics hold such values as individual freedom and democracy to be universal verities. Looked at from the perspective of many non-Western societies, however, these supposedly culturally neutral principles seem weighted in favour of the developed world.

Ethnocentricity relies on homogenizing stereotypes of the other. These stereotypes tend to reveal more about the society that holds them than the stereotyped group. This is confirmed by the fact that different cultures have vastly different preconceptions about the same nationality. Stereotypes of course also change over time, so that, for example, the British caricature of Russians as Cold War paupers is being overlaid with a new myth of extravagant Russian millionaires. [CC]

See also Chapter 11.

Further reading
Sumner, William Graham (1906) *Folkways: A Study of the Sociological Importance of Usages, Manners, Customs, Mores, and Morals*, Boston, MA: Ginn.

EVENT One of the key concepts of contemporary critical thought that has been dealt with by an array of thinkers such as Friedrich **Nietzsche**, Jean-François **Lyotard**,

Gilles **Deleuze**, Jacques **Derrida**, Emmanuel **Levinas** and, recently, Alain **Badiou**. The event is best characterized by the French phrase '*il y a*' or the German '*Es gibt*' both referring to an occurrence or happening which cannot be circumscribed within a situation or an identifiable state of affairs. In other words, it denotes the moment when something happens but we do not yet know what. As such it is very close to Kant's notion of the **sublime** which interrupts the **discourse** between the faculty of imagination and understanding and thus prevents conceptualization. Lyotard argues that in the event the **subject** is fundamentally dispossessed and consequently no longer able to structure and control the world from its subject position.

The genuine postmodern condition is precisely that of the event where existing rules and traditional modes of behaviour no longer suffice to render the world meaningful. The avant-garde artist, above all, is aware of this condition and expresses it in a type of art which can no longer be said to be beautiful in the Kantian sense. Instead postmodern art offers the experience of a specific postmodern sublime. In the writings of Levinas, the loss of the subject position and the concomitant loss of mastery in the event opens the subject to an unpredictable or messianic future and thus receives a specific ethical dimension. [RS]

See also Chapter 10.

F

FANON, FRANTZ (1925–61) Psychiatrist and anti-colonial activist, born in the French colony of Martinique, Fanon was the author of *Black Skin, White Masks* (1952) and *The Wretched of the Earth* (1961), as well as numerous clinical writings on psychiatry.

Black Skin, White Masks, deals with the psychology of racism and the dehumanization generated by **colonialism**. The book's central themes of alienation and dislocation reflect its author's experience as a French-educated Martiniquan and Algerian Nationalist. Fanon argues that the psychological and cultural effects of colonialism on black individuals engender a complex of inferiority. In her or his subsequent desire to be white, the black subject adopts a 'white mask'. This is a schizophrenic identity from which, according to Fanon, black people must be liberated. *The Wretched of the Earth* is a more militant work. By this time, Fanon had become directly involved in the Front National de Libération, fighting for Algeria's independence against French occupation. The book explores the revolt of the oppressed and the negative psychological effects of colonialism.

Fanon's life and work have inspired many, including the American activists of the Black Power movement in the 1960s. He is now considered to be a leading thinker in postcolonial theory. [SP and CHC]

See also Chapter 11.

Further reading

Fanon, Frantz (1986) *Black Skin, White Masks*, trans. Charles Lam Markmann, London: Pluto Press.

Fanon, Frantz (2001) *The Wretched of the Earth*, trans. Constance Farrington, London: Penguin.

FISH, STANLEY (1938–) Prominent American theorist working on matters of interpretation within literary and legal studies, Fish is a key figure in reader-response theory. Associated with the neo-pragmatism of thinkers like Richard **Rorty**, he is famous for his accessible yet argumentative writing style.

Fish highlights the role of the reader in interpretation, arguing that the reader's understanding of the text to a large extent constructs that text. However, this does not imply that a text can mean whatever we want it to mean, because every reader is part of some 'interpretive community' which significantly structures their expectations of and responses to any text. Emphasis on pragmatic agreement and the importance of convention runs through his work – including his influential studies of Milton – and leads him to conclude that 'literature' itself, rather than having any settled or inherent formal properties, is just what we as a 'community' agree it to be. [KM]

See also Chapters 1, 2 and 4.

Further reading

Fish, Stanley (1980) *Is There a Text in This Class?*, Cambridge, MA: Harvard University Press.

Fish, Stanley (1989) *Doing What Comes Naturally*, Oxford: Clarendon Press.

Fish, Stanley (2001) *How Milton Works*, Cambridge, MA: Harvard University Press.

FOUCAULT, MICHEL (1926–84) French historian whose diverse studies presented theoretical concepts and approaches that were among the most influential of the poststructuralist moment and have continued to stimulate and inform analyses in many disciplines.

In texts that constituted historical studies and theoretical explorations, Foucault returned repeatedly to the questions of **power** and identity. His exploration of the ways in which power exists as a historically situated relationship, is exercised rather than possessed, and can be viewed as productive as well as oppressive, constituted an extremely useful departure from dominant **Marxist** models. His various analyses of how the human being is constituted as an object of knowledge, and as a knowing **subject**, within and by changing and contingent **discourses** and practices, tempered the apparently transhistorical, and sometimes ahistorical, aspects of psychoanalytic models of subject formation.

Foucault described his early work as 'archaeology', seeking the invisible cultural formations that produced the practices and representations he analysed. This work has been subsequently related to structuralism, as it seems to propose a model of deep structures beneath a surface. His first major theoretical work was *The Order of Things*, which posited the idea that history is composed of discrete epochs, characterized by epistemes, or sets of relations that govern the discursive and epistemological practices of the time. He had already offered an example of this in *Madness and Civilisation*, which explored the varying conceptions of madness in different epochs, not as examples of linear development from age to age but as discrete products of specific epistemic contexts.

Foucault's own work can also be categorized, albeit reductively, by methodological and epistemological shifts, as his 'archaeological' practice was supplanted by an approach which he termed '**genealogy**'.

Heavily influenced by **Nietzsche**, Foucault turned to analyse the practices and technologies of power, subjection and subjectification. This would be the dominant concern of his later work.

In *Discipline and Punish* he examined the operation of power in what is assumed to be its most obvious form – punishment – contrasting the pre-eighteenth-century display of the operations of power on the body, revealing the power of the state in spectacular punishments, with subsequent practices of discipline and surveillance that aimed at the production of a regulated and ultimately self-regulating subject, the prisoner.

In the volumes of his ambitious *History of Sexuality* that were completed before his death, he analysed the ways in which the individual subject was constituted in, and defined by, networks of power and knowledge about sex, sexual practices and sexuality. Overturning the popular misconception that the modern age is the culmination of a history of the incremental liberation of sexuality, Foucault's analysis established the idea of sexuality as a construct of the knowledges and discourses that are assumed to have repressed it. In his examination of the discourses and practices of sex, Foucault's theories about the operation of power were further developed with a greater emphasis than hitherto on the production of resistance and oppositional or alternative subject positions. So whilst his later work posited the idea that the operations of power suffuse all aspects of human activity, they also insisted on the instability in the power relations that such operations sought to maintain.

Foucault's studies of Western culture focused on what he deemed to be key historical epochs: Hellenic Greece and Classical Rome, or 'antiquity'; the seventeenth and eighteenth centuries, or the 'classical period'; and the nineteenth century or '**modern** period'. Although this was most schematic in his early writings, it was judged by many historians to be a serious limitation. His concentration in his studies of the classical and modern epochs almost exclusively on France was also the subject of considerable criticism.

His influence has been very wide-ranging, and although his methods and findings have been repeatedly and convincingly criticized, his impact on the development of critical thinking and methods within and across diverse academic disciplines cannot be overestimated. [TS]

See also Chapters 3, 4, 5 and 9.

Further reading

Foucault, Michel (1967) *Madness and Civilisation: A History of Insanity in the Age of Reason*, London: Tavistock.

Foucault, Michel (1977a) *Discipline and Punish: The Birth of the Prison*, trans. Alan Sheridan, London: Penguin.

Foucault, Michel (1978) *The History of Sexuality, vol. 1: An Introduction*, trans. Robert Hurley, Harmondsworth: Penguin.

Foucault, Michel (1980) *Power/Knowledge: Selected Interviews and Other Writings, 1972–1977*, ed. Colin Gordon, New York: Pantheon.

Foucault, Michel (1991) *The Foucault Reader: An Introduction to Foucault's Thought*, ed. Paul Rabinow, Harmondsworth: Penguin.

FRANKFURT SCHOOL This name refers to the Institut für Sozialforschung (Institute for Social Research) in Frankfurt and is commonly used to describe an influential current in twentieth-century theory. The Frankfurt School was founded in 1923, and attracted a diverse faculty of mostly Jewish, left-wing intellectuals, committed to the interdisciplinary study of society, grounding generalized philosophical thought in concrete sociological research. Those associated with the Frankfurt School include the philosophers Max **Horkheimer**, Theodor **Adorno**, Herbert **Marcuse** and Walter **Benjamin**. When Adolf Hitler came to power in 1933, Jewish intellectuals were forbidden to teach in Germany and by 1934 the Frankfurt School had gone into exile, reconvening in the USA. The experience of Nazi Germany and consumerist America was a formative influence on the work for which the Frankfurt School is best remembered.

Walter Benjamin played a central role in the development of the Frankfurt School's pessimistic brand of philosophy, famously stating in his 'Theses on the Philosophy of History' that 'There is no document of civilization which is not at the same time a document of barbarism' (1999: 248). This insight influenced Adorno and Horkheimer's argument in *The Dialectic of Enlightenment* that rationality, far from being progressive, could be employed in the service of barbarism.

The body of thought that emerged from the Frankfurt School was called 'Critical Theory', as distinct from the more generalized modern sense that is common in literary and cultural studies. Horkheimer first used the term in his paper 'Traditional and Critical Theory' (1937), in which he detailed the Frankfurt School's agenda. Horkheimer considered 'traditional theory' to be complicit with capitalism, whereas 'Critical Theory' would specifically aim to critique capitalist social relations.

Frankfurt School thinkers used the term 'advanced industrial society' to describe capitalist and fascist societies, which tended towards both centralization and standardization of culture. In general, they championed esoteric, avant-garde or 'modernist' forms of art, which they believed to express a critique of the dominant culture. Adorno and Benjamin debated this issue throughout the 1930s, and the vision of modern culture set out in *The Dialectic of Enlightenment* was both influenced by, and a critique of, the position advanced by Benjamin in his famous essay 'The Work of Art in the Age of Mechanical Reproduction'. Adorno and Horkheimer considered that Benjamin had placed too much emphasis on the technology involved in mass production and reproduction, and not enough on the economic power that drove the industrialization of culture. This, they felt, had caused Benjamin to be too optimistic about the emancipatory potential of reproducible media such as film. For Adorno and Horkheimer, mass-produced forms of entertainment such as films, radio and magazines were products of the '**culture industry**', which they saw as an instrument of ideological domination that promoted the acceptance of existing social conditions.

Though the Frankfurt School was extremely cynical about the prospects of social transformation, it was opposed to the mechanistic economic determinism (see **materialism**) that characterized some interpretations of Marxism. One antidote to this tendency was close engagement with the recently published early works of Karl **Marx**, in which the influence of the idealist philosopher Hegel is most evident. Benjamin sought to achieve a synthesis of Marxist politics and Jewish mysticism, and Marcuse's *Eros and Civilization* (1955) attempted to reconcile **Freudian** and Marxist approaches to society.

Marcuse shared the pessimism of his Frankfurt School colleagues but became a major influence on the radical and countercultural movements of the 1960s. Marcuse argued in *One Dimensional Man* (1964) that the working class in Western societies had become integrated into the capitalist system, and that there was more revolutionary potential to be found in struggles against other kinds of social oppression such as the campaign for African-American civil rights. More positive was Jürgen **Habermas**, Adorno's research assistant from 1956 to 1959 and the most prominent member of the Frankfurt School's second generation. Habermas considered the implications of the first generation's theories to be too discouraging, and endeavoured to recuperate the concept of rationality as a constructive force in

society. He argued that 'communicative rationality' could disclose and combat existing forms of oppression, and become the basis of a more democratic public sphere.

Frankfurt School 'Critical Theory' is an important tradition within Western philosophy. Though its cultural and political stance has been criticized as elitist and pessimistic, the Frankfurt School retains its interest, often invoked in the continuing debates in which its members engaged but also as a subject of study in its own right. [CRC]

See also Chapter 3.

Further reading

Bottomore, Tom (2002) *The Frankfurt School and its Critics*, London: Routledge.

Jay, Martin (1973) *The Dialectical Imagination: A History of the Frankfurt School and the Institute of Social Research, 1923–1950*, London: Heinemann.

Kellner, Douglas (1989) *Critical Theory, Marxism, and Modernity*, Cambridge: Polity Press.

Wiggershaus, Rolf (1995) *The Frankfurt School: Its History, Theory and Political Significance*, trans. Michael Robertson, London: Polity Press.

FREUD, SIGMUND (1856–1939) The founder of psychoanalysis, a field of psychology that attempts a scientific conception of the individual based upon **unconscious** processes. This conceptual framework destabilized the dominant Western mode of thought regarding the conscious human **subject**, captured by René Descartes' proposal: 'I think therefore I am.'

Freud began his study of the human mind by practising hypnosis as a clinical technique after a secondment to the Salpêtrière Hospital in Paris in 1885–6. Here he studied with Jean-Martin Charcot (1825–93), Professor of Neurology, who demonstrated that the symptoms of hysteria could be reproduced using hypnotic techniques. Freud returned to Vienna and in

1895 he published *Studies on Hysteria* with his colleague Josef Breuer. This book was essentially a publication of patient case-notes in which they traced the emergence of hysteria in puberty back to a sexual encounter with an adult during childhood. This 'seduction theory' was later abandoned by Freud (apparently due to him not being able to comprehend that such a high incidence of incest could occur in a civilized society). Freud also came to reject hypnosis as a tool, seeing no real need for it. Rather, he began to concentrate upon aspects of the mind that presented themselves to the subject involuntarily and over the ten years that followed he inaugurated what would become his lifetime's work, the mapping out of a new theory of the mind.

The publication of *The Interpretation of Dreams* in 1900 and *The Psychopathology of Everyday Life* in 1901 conferred on him international recognition. Central to this was his 'discovery' of the unconscious. The idea of an unconscious had been evoked before, most significantly by the Romantic poets; further, the concept of a non-conscious agency had been explored many times throughout the history of philosophy, most recently by **Nietzsche**. However, it was Freud who formulated the distinction between the conscious and the unconscious as being the central structure of human subjectivity, where consciousness *came into being* through the primary repression of the **drives**. It was this fundamental activity within the infant's mind that formed the unconscious. Freud continued to develop his theories through reflection on the outcomes of a clinical practice of psychoanalysis over several years with a great number of analysands (patients). Perhaps the most controversial aspect of this was his theories of infant sexuality and the **Oedipus complex**. It was this account of how the male infant's mind developed into adulthood that made Freud notorious throughout Europe and the United States, taking psychoanalysis into the domain of the general public. Over the next few years Freud published a number of books and papers mapping out a complete topography of the mind.

The First World War, cancer and the death of his daughter have all been cited as marking the beginning of a change of tone in Freud's work. In 'Beyond the Pleasure Principle' (1920) he developed further the concept of a **death-drive** opposing the life-drives of narcissism and sexuality. In 'The Ego and the Id' (1923) he re-evaluated his first topography of the mind (the binary agencies of the conscious and the unconscious) preferring a tripartite division of the **ego**, **superego** and **id**. This reworking allowed him to explore the internal conflicts of the mind more cohesively. In 'Civilization and its Discontents' (1930) he applied psychoanalysis to contemporary society, foretelling dark times for humanity. In 1938, when Hitler's troops invaded Vienna, Freud escaped to London. He died on 23 September 1939 when – on Freud's demand due to the constant pain of his cancer – his doctor gave him a lethal injection.

Jacques **Lacan** went on to develop Freud's theories in light of **Saussure**'s structuralism. Louis **Althusser** opened up psychoanalysis to wider political concerns through a development of the theories of Marx. Much Lacanian and Althusserian work was co-opted into film theory during the 1970s through journals such as *Screen*. Freud, however, remains highly controversial, having many opponents. Amongst these are the writers of various feminisms (sometimes even working within the domain of psychoanalysis) such as Kate **Millett** and Luce **Irigaray**, who take issue with much of his work (particularly the series of papers from around 1931 on female sexuality). More recently, studies and clinical work by Gilles **Deleuze** and Félix **Guattari** have challenged Freud's psychoanalysis with the less structural theory of **schizoanalysis**. [DD]

See also Chapter 6.

Further reading
Easthope, Antony (1999) *The Unconscious*, London: Routledge.
Freud, Sigmund (1991c) *The Essentials of Psycho-Analysis*, trans. James Strachey, London: Penguin.

FRYE, HERMAN NORTHROP (1912–91) Canadian literary theorist who is best known for his work on archetypes and 'myth. Frye saw myth as the underlying cyclical paradigm, analogous to the cycle of seasons, uniting all works of literature. The medium of this unification Frye defined as *archetypes* (Greek, *arche* = original, *typos* = figure or image): symbols or images recurring frequently enough within literature to be understood as unifying our experience of the whole of literature.

The central archetype is that of a poem's protagonist. His relation to the reader, be it superior, inferior or analogous, decides the literary *mode* into which the poem fits. Myth, as paradigm, is the primary mode, characterized by divine beings. If the hero is superior to men and the world, the poem is a 'romance'. If superior to men, but not the world the poem is 'high **mimetic**'. If analogous, the poem is 'low mimetic'; if inferior, 'ironic'.

Myth finds its distillation in literature in romance, which contains the patterns of tragic descent and comic ascension of the other modes. This takes the form of a hero, who must overcome a demonic foe in order to be united with his lover and redeem the land which his foe has laid waste. This, according to Frye, is the pattern underlying all literature: a secular variant on the scriptural myth of Christ the redeemer. The rhetorical motivation of myth and literature, therefore, is analogous to the vision, or *myth of deliverance* of the Bible, which Frye posited as their ultimate source. [MB]
See also Chapters 1 and 2.

Further reading
Frye, Northrop (1982) *The Great Code: The Bible and Literature*, London: Routledge and Kegan Paul.
Frye, Northrop (1990) *Anatomy of Criticism: Four Essays*, Oxford: Princeton University Press.

FUKUYAMA, FRANCIS (1952–) American political scientist whose 'end of history' thesis continues to polarize opinion more than a decade after its first articulation in 1989. Fukuyama argues that history, envisaged by Hegel and **Marx** as a process moving towards perfection, ends its evolution with the advent of liberal democracy. Although he acknowledges flaws in its practical implementation, Fukuyama suggests that liberal democracy as an ideal cannot be improved upon. He also argues that liberal democracy goes hand in hand with market capitalism, controversially writing that 'the world's most developed countries are also its most successful democracies'.

Although critics acknowledge the prescience of Fukuyama's arguments with regard to the collapse of the Soviet bloc, some have pointed out that endism is not a new idea, but one that has recurred throughout the twentieth century. Fukuyama has also faced widespread criticism for the alleged naïvety and **ethnocentricity** of his views. Samuel Huntington counters his belief in an increasingly cohesive global system with the notion that the world is caught up in a 'clash of civilizations', in which divergent cultures (particularly Islam and Western secularism) fight for supremacy. Huntington has interpreted 9/11 as proving his theory, but Fukuyama's response to the terrorist attacks is that modernity will not be derailed by what he sees as Islam's inherently retrograde tendency. [CC]
See also Chapter 10.

Further reading
Fukuyama, Francis (1992) *The End of History and the Last Man*, London: Penguin.
Huntington, Samuel P. (1998) *The Clash of Civilizations and the Remaking of World Order*, London: Touchstone.

G

GADAMER, HANS-GEORG (1900–2002)
One of the most important twentieth-century German **hermeneutic** philosophers who argues vehemently against the notion that finding the truth is a matter of applying the right method. In his groundbreaking and ironically titled study *Truth and Method*, Gadamer delineates and complicates German hermeneutics in a compelling engagement with Wilhelm Dilthey, Friedrich Schleiermacher and Martin **Heidegger**. The basis of Gadamer's argument consists in recognizing that perspectivity or horizonality cannot be avoided. In other words, there is no neutral perspective that would reveal the world or a text as it really is. Instead, one is always already situated within a horizon of familiarity (such as tradition, what Stanley **Fish** calls interpretive communities, and **Jauss** identifies as horizons of expectations). Friedrich **Nietzsche** would say that there is always interest and never neutrality; and, because this is so, the act of explaining of how things really are must give way to an act of understanding which is always limited and interested. Hermeneutics is consequently the theory of the fore-structure of knowledge. In order not simply to assimilate different horizons of understanding, Gadamer suggests that we must always examine our prejudices and pre-formed habits. [RS]

Further reading

Gadamer, Hans-Georg (1993) *Truth and Method*, trans. Joel Weinsheimer and Donald G. Marshall, London: Sheed and Ward.

GATES, HENRY LOUIS, JR (1950–)
Influential African-American critic, editor and essayist. An early achievement in his project of **canon** formation was to establish that the novel *Our Nig; or, Sketches from the Life of a Free Black* (1859) was written by an African-American, Harriet Wilson. He has also edited several groundbreaking compendia of essays, including *Black Literature and Literary Theory* (1984) and *'Race', Writing, and Difference* (1986), which analyse aspects of black culture using theories drawn from poststructuralism and postmodernism.

In his own writing, Gates draws attention to the formal features of African-American writing, which he suggests have been overlooked due to earlier critics' narrow focus upon identity. In *The Signifying Monkey* (1988), Gates argues for the acknowledgement of a separate and distinctive tradition of African-American letters in the United States, notable for its deployment of oral forms. He contests that the black vernacular tradition is characterized by 'signifyin[g]', or 'repetition with a signal difference' (Gates 1988: xxiv). Through verbal play, imitation and invention, then, African-American writers signify onto white texts and literary codes to forge a space of freedom in an oppressive society. [CC]
See also Chapter 11.

Further reading

Gates, Henry Louis Jr (ed.) (1984) *Black Literature and Literary* Theory, New York: Routledge.

Gates, Henry Louis Jr (ed.) (1986) *'Race,', Writing, and Difference*, Chicago, IL: University of Chicago Press.

Gates, Henry Louis Jr (1988) *The Signifying Monkey: A Theory of Afro-American Literary Criticism*, New York: Oxford University Press.

GEERTZ, CLIFFORD (1926–) American cultural anthropologist best known for his ethnographic studies of Southeast Asia and North Africa, and for his writings about the interpretation of cultures. Geertz's key contribution to cultural theory is *The Interpretation of Cultures* (1973).

Geertz argues that the aim of anthropology is not to discover scientific laws, but rather to search for meaning in cultures which may initially appear inaccessible to the anthropologist. He develops the term 'thick description' to suggest that anthropology should move beyond neutral observation of surface meanings towards the analysis of layers of cultural implication. To illustrate the term, he takes winking as an example. If we simply describe the mechanical action of opening and closing one eye, we use 'thin' description. By contrast, 'thick' description seeks to untangle complex layers of cultural inference, association and meaning that the wink can acquire.

Geertz's redefinition of culture as a complex structure that should be interpreted rather like a literary text has been influential in literary studies. His argument that culture is integral to humanity, and that humans require cultural symbols and signs to function, has heralded a productive relationship between the disciplines of literature and anthropology. [RF]

See also Chapter 1.

Further reading

Geertz, Clifford (1993) *The Interpretation of Cultures*, London: Fontana.

GENEALOGY (Greek *genea* meaning race) The study of an entity's lineage, which within critical theory is primarily associated with the work of Michel **Foucault**.

Developing Friedrich **Nietzsche**'s *On the Genealogy of Morality*, it is Foucault's *The Archaeology of Knowledge* (1970) that serves as the key text for understanding genealogy in relation to analytical thinking. For Foucault, genealogical investigation should not be a passive programme of simply looking at the archaeology or architecture of discourse, but one that actively interrogates it in order to uncover its hidden values. Adopting a Nietzschean refusal of the notion of truths outside their contextual setting, Foucault argues that discourses and 'what we know' can only be fully understood when their genealogical development is addressed. Such analysis will reveal the hidden structures that support not just the knowledge base of society but also its ideology and power relations. Genealogical investigation reveals that discourse, ideas, and 'universal truths' are riddled with human intervention and implicated within the maintenance of society's conformity. [PSW]

Further reading

Foucault, Michel (1989) *The Archaeology of Knowledge*, trans. A. M. Sheridan Smith, London: Routledge.

Nietzsche, Friedrich (1994) *On the Genealogy of Morality*, ed. Keith Ansell-Pearson, trans. Carol Diethe, Cambridge: Cambridge University Press.

GENETTE, GÉRARD (1930–) French literary theorist best known for his work on narratology and poetics. His major essays in French are collected in *Figures I, II* and *III* (1966, 1969, 1972); a selection of these essays have been translated into English and collected as *Figures of Literary Discourse* (1982). For the English reader Genette's key ideas can be found in *Narrative Discourse* (1980).

Genette identifies three aspects of narrative. He calls these: 'story' (*histoire*), the succession of events that are recounted; 'narrative' (*récit*) which is the story-telling structure of the text itself; and 'narrating', the event of recounting that produces the narrative. In order to discuss the ways in which story, narrative and narrating relate to each other he introduces the idea of levels of narrative: the diegesis refers to the events of the main story, whilst events that occur within that story are described as metadiegesis, or, in more familiar terms, metanarrative. Genette suggests a scale of narratorial involvement from 'reported' discourse, where the narrator is largely absent from the text, to 'narratized' discourse in which the narrator's presence as source and commentator of the narrative is clear.

The concern of Genette's work, like the structuralism of **Barthes** and **Todorov**, is not with interpreting individual texts but with investigating their forms, structures and devices. His work is therefore invaluable in that it offers a systematic theory of narrative and generates the appropriate vocabulary required for such analysis. [PW]

See also Chapter 2.

Further reading

Genette, Gérard (1980) *Narrative Discourse*, trans. Jane E. Lewin, Oxford: Basil Blackwell.

Genette, Gérard (1982) *Figures of Literary Discourse*, trans. A Sheridan, New York: Columbia University Press.

GENRE Originating from the French meaning 'kind' or 'type', genre is used to classify different artistic forms that share common features. One of the earliest sets of definitions, found in Aristotle's *Poetics*, distinguishes between three generic types: lyric, epic and drama. Each was distinguishable from the other on the basis of who spoke or narrated the work. The lyric was told in the first person; the epic also features a first-person narrator, but allows the characters to speak for themselves; whilst in drama the characters

are responsible for all speech. A range of subgenres were also recognized within this division, such as comedy, tragedy and satire.

Until the eighteenth century, these genres were treated as rigid categories, as 'species' of literary works, and neo-classicists argued that there should be no intermingling of genres, attempting to construct a set of universal dictums to govern all genres for all times. With the emergence of different literary categories such as the novel in the eighteenth century, the reliance on fixed generic categories was undermined. The Romanticist emphasis on expression and organicism, which incorporated terms applicable to all literary productions of whatever genre, largely removed the need to locate literary works within classes. With the emergence of media studies, such as television and film criticism, genre theory has once more become a useful critical tool. Contemporary genre theory focuses on the ways in which genre categories lead to certain sets of expectation in the reader or audience. For example, a programme described as a 'soap opera' will give rise to a very different set of expectations from a 'documentary' – although it has been noted that certain categories overlap.

Rather than arguing in favour of fixed definitions of genres, structuralist and poststructuralist critics look at the ways in which genres overlap. Other critics, appropriating Ludwig Wittgenstein's theory of family resemblance, have argued that the group of works that constitute a genre share some features with the others of that group, but there is no essential feature that would fix an essential generic quality. Genre is an often uncertain theoretical tool, but in providing a set of distinctions that have become central to literary debate, remains the subject of extensive analysis. [TES]

See also Chapters 1, 2, 4, 7 and 9.

Further reading

Freedman, Aviva and Medway, Peter (eds) (1994) *Genre and the New Rhetoric*, London: Taylor and Francis.

Todorov, Tzvetan (1977) *The Poetics of Prose*, trans. Richard Howard, Oxford: Blackwell.

GILBERT, SANDRA M. (1936–) and **GUBAR, SUSAN** (1944–) Feminist literary critics best known for their extensive and highly influential work on nineteenth-century women writers, *The Madwoman in the Attic* (1979). This study was one of the first to identify a tradition of women's writing rather than merely looking at representations of women in the work of male **authors**. Gilbert and Gubar employ Harold **Bloom**'s idea of 'The Anxiety of Influence' but apply it to an exploration of the problems faced by female authors writing in a **patriarchal** society where authorship is defined as male and patrilineal. They argue that this 'anxiety' is reflected in the figure of the 'mad woman' in women's work, such as Bertha Mason in *Jane Eyre* or Catherine in *Wuthering Heights*. These 'monstrous' characters become a repository for those aspects of femininity suppressed and/or denied by patriarchy. Gilbert and Gubar are concerned with exploring how women writers work to challenge this patriarchal binarism of woman as either subservient angel or resisting monster. Later critics have pointed out that this thesis both essentializes the female writer and assumes that the creation of textual meaning resides with the author, but despite this *The Madwoman in the Attic* remains a key text in the development of feminist literary theory.

Gilbert and Gubar have also co-written *No Man's Land* – a three-volume study of the woman writer from the mid nineteenth century to the present – and co-edited, amongst others, *The Norton Anthology of Literature by Women*. [GC]

See also Chapters 8 and 9.

Further reading

Gilbert, Sandra M. and Gubar, Susan (1979) *The Madwoman in the Attic*, New Haven, CT and London: Yale University Press.

Gilbert, Sandra M. and Gubar, Susan (1985) *The Norton Anthology of Literature by Women: The Traditions in English*, New York and London: W. W. Norton.

GILROY, PAUL (1956–) British cultural and social theorist whose *The Black Atlantic: Modernity and Double Consciousness* (1993) has become a key text across many academic disciplines. Taking its cue from W. E. B. **Du Bois**'s formulation of African-American 'double consciousness' – 'this sense of always looking at one's self through the eyes of others' (Du Bois 1903: *The Souls of Black Folk*) – Gilroy's text argues that '**modernity**' is largely constituted along racial, ethnic and more broadly 'cultural' grounds. *The Black Atlantic* privileges the cultural products of black Europeans and Americans in the formulation of modernity, precisely because they mediate between Euro- and Afro-centric models of cultural authority: and it is that mediation which, Gilroy argues, gives rise to a productive 'ambivalence'. Exile, homelessness, hybridity, mobility: these are key concepts in black atlanticist thinking, concepts that Gilroy's book seeks to view positively. Other works, including *There Ain't No Black in the Union Jack* (1987), *Between Camps* (2000) and *Against Race* (2000), exhibit the breadth of Gilroy's work in sociology and cultural studies – he is currently Professor of Sociology and African-American Studies at Yale University – with an increased scepticism about the inviolability of what Du Bois termed 'the color-line'. [KH]

See also Chapter 11.

Further reading

Gilroy, Paul (2004) *Between Camps: Nations, Cultures, and the Allure of Race*, London: Routledge.

Rice, Alan (2002) *Radical Narratives of the Black Atlantic*, New York and London: Continuum.

Walvin, James (2000) *Making the Black Atlantic*, New York and London: Continuum.

GLOBALIZATION A term drawn from economics to refer to the dominant model of contemporary manufacture, consumption and political systems within capitalist societies. Rather than focusing upon the needs of a local or national market, the globalized approach considers the world or 'global village' as its end user. Because such an audience encompasses a wide range of peoples and values, globalized practices inevitably use models of 'best fit'. Many times these values reflect a corporation's Western origin, with the result that some critics accuse globalization of favouring Western interests and norms. In addition to the global corporations, regulatory bodies such as the World Trade Organization (WTO) are also criticized for their perceived role in maintaining a global Western dominance.

Whilst numerous events and inventions could be associated with the advent of globalization, perhaps it main facilitators have been the creation and embracing of mass communication media such as satellite television and the internet. Only through the development of this **cyberspace** revolution do the key features of globalization become attainable: the eradication of the boundaries of time, space and culture. With information now able to travel at the speed of light and cross international borders unhindered, these modern communications are crucial to globalization – the global dissemination of money, trade and ideas. Developments within these media are of increasing interest to cultural theorists for their impact on identity, and the postmodern transgression of previously bounded space, both national and personal. [PSW]

See also Chapters 10 and 11.

Further reading

Bauman, Zygmunt (1998) *Globalization: The Human Consequences*, Cambridge: Polity Press.

Held, David and McGrew, Anthony (eds) (2000) *The Global Transformations Reader: An Introduction to the Global Debate*, Cambridge: Polity Press.

GRAMSCI, ANTONIO (1891–1937) Italian politician and cultural theorist. A founder in 1921, and General Secretary from 1924, of the Italian Communist Party, Gramsci was imprisoned by Mussolini's fascist government in 1926. While in custody, he was allowed to read and keep notebooks, which were posthumously published.

Gramsci identified two levels on which authority is exercised. The first – 'political society' – denotes institutions traditionally identified with the state, such as the judiciary and military. Gramsci calls their coercive enforcement of discipline 'direct domination'. The second – 'civil society' – consists of institutions usually considered to be private, such as churches and schools. These induce in citizens seemingly spontaneous consent. This process, which Gramsci calls '**hegemony**', is exercised by intellectuals, the 'functionaries' of the dominant group in society. A group wishing to transform society must therefore cultivate 'organic' intellectuals whose affiliation is to the 'subaltern' (dominated) group, in order to institute an alternative hegemony.

Gramsci's work has been an important influence on the continuing debate about the role of **ideology** in inducing citizens to accept social systems that dominate or exploit them. [CRC]

See also Chapter 3.

Further reading

Gramsci, Antonio (1988) *A Gramsci Reader: Selected Writings 1916–1935*, ed. D. Forgacs, London: Lawrence and Wishart.

GRAND NARRATIVE An all-encompassing theory which claims to provide an explanation for all of the narratives in circulation in a culture. For Jean-François **Lyotard**, grand narratives (*grands récits*) have characterized **modernity**, and he refers to examples such as Christianity, socialism, capitalism and **hermeneutics** in the introduction to *The Postmodern Condition*. Any theory which claims to account for the true meaning of all social and cultural forms can be considered to be a grand narrative. Thus it could be seen that even an oppositional philosophy such as feminism becomes a grand narrative when it claims to offer a totalizing account of woman, thereby subsuming the differences between women. Grand narratives typically offer the subject a specific role in relation to the future revelation of a singular social or aesthetic truth. Thus, in the case of Marxist thought, all social formations, including art, literature, etc., are considered as outcomes of the capitalist system, whose inconsistencies bear the seeds of the future revolution, which will ultimately emancipate the working subject – the hero of the socialist grand narrative. Crucially, Lyotard finds that the postmodern condition is characterized by a new scepticism towards the grand narratives of modernity. [AT]

See also Chapter 10.

Further reading

Lyotard, Jean-François (1984) *The Postmodern Condition: A Report on Knowledge*, Manchester: Manchester University Press.

GREIMAS, ALGIRDAS JULIEN (1917–92) Lithuanian **semiotician** who worked in France. Influenced by the work of, among others, Ferdinand de **Saussure**, Claude **Lévi-Strauss**, Vladimir **Propp** and Maurice **Merleau-Ponty**, Greimas set out to find the underlying grammar, or 'deep' structure, of narrative. Greimas's main contribution to narratology is the 'actant'. Distinguished

from a novel's actors, or characters, the actant is a basic structural unit of narrative defined in terms of what it does, as opposed to what/who it is. In other words, all narratives, however different they may appear at the surface level, can be described in terms of a finite group of possible actions/actants. Greimas identified six actants which he arranged in oppositional pairs, each of which is linked to a different aspect of narrative. These are: **Subject/Object** (**desire**); Sender/Reviewer (communication); and Helper/Opponent (secondary support/conflict). This emphasis on binary oppositions is also apparent in Greimas's notion of the 'semiotic square', an idea that ultimately draws on the Saussurean argument that signs are meaningful because they differ from one another. Accordingly each seme, or basic unit of communication, entails its opposite and what he terms its 'contradictory pair': for example, happy/sad/not happy/not sad would be the four constituents for the word happy.

In works such as *The Semiotics of Passion* (1991), Greimas sought to extend his semiotic theory to account for all signifying practices, arguing that all forms of human articulation, in direct contrast to the arbitrary relation between signs and the real world, must conform to structural rules. In this emphasis on the disjunction between language and reality, Greimas's work prefigures much that is central to contemporary theory: for example, Jacques **Lacan**'s work on the **real** or Jean **Baudrillard**'s work on **simulation**. [PW]

See also Chapters 1 and 2.

Further reading

Greimas, Algirdas Julien (1987) *On Meaning: Selected Writings in Semiotic Theory*, trans. Paul Perron and Frank Collins, Minneapolis, MN: University of Minnesota Press.

Schleifer, Ronald (1987) *A. J. Greimas and the Nature of Meaning: Linguistics, Semiotics and Discourse Theory*, Lincoln, NE: University of Nebraska Press.

GUATTARI, FÉLIX (1930–92) Radical French psychoanalyst trained by Jacques Lacan, Félix Guattari advocated a schizoanalytic approach to thought that traversed philosophy, linguistics, politics, ecology and aesthetics. Guattari's work at the experimental La Borde clinic in France reveals a sympathy with R. D. Laing and the British anti-psychiatry movement. This is evident in his single-authored texts, *Psychoanalyse et transversalité* (1972) and *La Révolution moléculaire* (1977) – partially translated in a single edition entitled *Molecular Revolution: Psychiatry and Politics* (1984). However, he is best known in English-speaking criticism for the more radical and far-reaching *Anti-Oedipus* (1972) and *A Thousand Plateaus* (1980), written in collaboration with French poststructuralist philosopher Gilles Deleuze. Often silently erased in scholarship focused solely on Deleuze's work, Guattari's machinic approach to the unconscious in *Anti-Oedipus* and his role in emphasizing pragmatics and linguistics in *A Thousand Plateaus* are, nonetheless, essential. Later texts such as *Communists Like Us* (1990) – written with Italian Marxist Antoni Negri – and *Chaosmosis* (1992) consider questions of subjectivity, ecology, globalization and resistance. [DH]
See also Chapter 6.

Further reading
Guattari, Félix (1996) *The Guattari Reader*, ed. Gary Genosko, Oxford: Blackwell.

H

HABERMAS, JÜRGEN (1929–) German social philosopher best known for his work on the project of **Enlightenment** and communicative theory in the public sphere. Habermas is perhaps the best known of the so-called second-generation **Frankfurt School** critical theorists. He was a student and assistant of Theodor **Adorno** and significant influences on his early work and thought, which was more concerned with sociology rather than philosophy, included Karl **Marx** and Max Weber. However, from the 1960s his work has become more concerned with philosophical issues. His most important texts include *Knowledge and Human Interests* (1968), *The Theory of Communicative Action* (1981) and *The Philosophical Discourse of Modernity* (1987).

In *Knowledge and Human Interests*, Habermas is concerned primarily with the concepts of 'theory' and 'practice', and how the two can be reconciled. He also demonstrates a philosophical debt to Immanuel Kant, especially in the areas of **ethics** and reason.

Habermas's most monumental work consists of the two volumes of *The Theory of Communicative Action*. In this work, his main argument is that a philosophy of language is the best way to resolve the discourse of **modernity** and complete the enlightenment project.

The Philosophical Discourse of Modernity represents arguably his most controversial work. According to Habermas, Hegel set in motion the discourse of modernity by undermining Kantian philosophy. However, Friedrich **Nietzsche** causes the main rupture to the philosophy of modernity through his opposition to subject-centred reason and the Enlightenment project. Nietzsche represents the entry into post-modernity, which Habermas sees as a reaction against modernism. From Nietzsche, two strands of anti-modernity arise: on the one hand, the destruction of **metaphysics** through Martin **Heidegger** and Jacques **Derrida** and, on the other hand, the will to **power** through Georges **Bataille** and Michel **Foucault**. Habermas offers his theory of communicative action, both as an alternative to such anti-reason and as the way out of a philosophy of consciousness. [JS]

See also Chapters 3 and 10.

Further reading

Habermas, Jürgen (1978) *Knowledge and Human Interests*, trans. Jeremy J. Shapiro, London: Heinemann.

Habermas, Jürgen (1987) *The Philosophical Discourse of Modernity*, trans. Frederick Lawrence, Cambridge, MA: MIT Press.

HALL, STUART (1932–) Jamaican-born cultural critic who has played a central role in the development of cultural studies in Britain. Hall's biography is indicative of his importance to cultural studies: he was the founding editor of the *New Left Review*; co-founder and then director of Birmingham University's Centre for Contemporary Cultural Studies (1967–79); and Professor of Sociology at the Open University until his retirement in 1997.

Along with other black British cultural critics such as Paul **Gilroy**, Hall's work is centrally concerned with questions of race, ethnicity and identity. His much-anthologized essay 'New Ethnicities' (1988) has been particularly influential in conceptualizing postcolonial and ethnic identities. Hall notices a shift from debate about how blacks should be represented to an increasingly complicated politics of representation. Questioning old binaries of black and white, and models of 'essential' racial identity, Hall articulates a complex and diverse concept of ethnicity which recognizes that such identities are always informed by the divisions of class, gender and sexuality. This theorization of identity has been influential because it argues for a politically engaged notion of ethnicity, which mobilizes rather than suppresses diversity. Hall deployed his theory against the right-wing politics of Margaret Thatcher, the Conservative Prime Minister who was at the height of her power in the 1980s. Acknowledging the diversity of black experiences and subject positions, he challenged Thatcher's use of a static conception of Englishness to stabilize the state.

Hall's work has been central to the formation of cultural studies as a politically engaged discipline with an inclusive approach to cultural expression. By successfully combining political activism with a critical engagement with **Marxism**, postmodernism and postcolonial theory, Hall has helped to shape understanding of the politics of culture. [RF]

See also Chapter 11.

Further reading

Morley, David and Kuan-Hsing, Chen (eds) (1996) *Stuart Hall: Critical Dialogues in Cultural Studies*, London: Routledge.

HARAWAY, DONNA (1944–) Feminist philosopher and theoretician of the sciences. Her best-known work is her highly influential essay 'A Manifesto for Cyborgs' (1985) in which she concludes that new technology can be used to interrogate and dismantle the conventional binarisms of Western **ideology**, such as self and other, mind and body, or culture and nature. She creates the concept of the '**cyborg**' (a sophisticated hybrid that resists the distinction between organism and machine) to illustrate this potential, and argues that advances in medicine and technology have made cyborgs of us all; in other words, that our 'biology' is constantly being altered by various interventions. Haraway sees this dissolution of dualisms as enabling a new kind of feminist project, and famously concludes her essay by stating that she would 'rather be a cyborg than a goddess' (1985: 81). Her emphasis on the uses of science and technology is also important, as feminism has traditionally adopted an anti-science standpoint. Her later book *Modest Witness@ Second_Millennium: Femaleman Meets OncoMouse* continues to explore the complex interrelations between feminism and science.

Haraway's iconoclastic and playful style can at times be off-putting, but it importantly reflects both her eclecticism and her radical insistence upon the blurring of boundaries. She continues to have an abiding influence across diverse academic disciplines. [GC]

See also Chapters 8, 9 and 10.

Further reading

Haraway, Donna (1985) 'A Manifesto for Cyborgs: Science, Technology, and Socialist Feminism in the 1980s', *Socialist Review* 80 (1985): 65–108.

Haraway, Donna (2004) *The Haraway Reader*, London and New York: Routledge.

HEGEMONY A political concept that explains the oppression-based relationships between the dominant and compliant classes of Western capitalist democracies. Whilst Karl **Marx** and Georg **Lukács** have also written extensively about hegemonic states, it is the Italian Marxist Antonio **Gramsci** whose name is synonymous with the term.

Unlike many theories of **power**, hegemony

does not advocate a 'top-down' dictatorial model of rule. Within hegemonic relations, the dominant class or classes favour encouragement over coercion. Rather than autocratic rule, hegemony functions through consensus, in spite of the inherent oppression and/or intergroup exploitation. Hegemonic societies are characterized by an absence of revolution and social up-risings, their sense of equilibrium brought about by the subaltern group's *acceptance* of the dominant ideals. This does not, however, rule out the potential for conflict and protestation by the subordinate classes. Agreeing to 'empty compromises', the ruling class(es) accommodate the demands of the ruled and suppress potential unrest. Crucially, those sectors of society that are challenged and changed by such inter-actions are never key strategic ones such as those that maintain the status quo.

The concept of hegemony also features extensively within Louis **Althusser**'s writing on the **Ideological State Apparatus**, those social bodies that can only function through society's acceptance. These are in stark contrast to the Repressive State Apparatus such as the army and the penal system that often encounter, and are based upon, aggression and resistance.

More recently Ernesto Laclau and Chantal Mouffe's *Hegemony and Socialist Strategy: Towards a Radical Democratic Politics* provides a comprehensive critique of the term. Investigating its **genealogy**, they argue that in its current and accepted guise, hegemony is – to borrow from Michel **Foucault** – 'the archaeology of silence'. For Laclau and Mouffe, hege-mony is not so much a localized space of 'unthought' but of a reductive closed paradigm. [PSW]

See also Chapter 3.

Further reading

Hoare, Quinton and Nowell Smith, Geoffrey (eds) (1971) *Selections from the Prison Notebooks of Antonio Gramsci*, trans.

Quinton Hoare and Geoffrey Nowell Smith, London: Lawrence and Wishart.

Laclau, Ernesto and Mouffe, Chantal (1987) *Hegemony and Socialist Strategy: Towards a Radical Democratic Politics*, London: Verso.

HEIDEGGER, MARTIN (1889–1976) Ger-man philosopher who developed the discipline of **phenomenology** as advanced by Edmund Husserl. Heidegger served as Professor of Philosophy at the University of Freiburg during the last years of the Weimar Republic and the period of the Third Reich. He has been regarded as a controversial figure, mainly due to the fact that at one time he was a Nazi sympathizer. However, his influence on twentieth-century philosophy has been immense, especially his work on human existence entitled *Being and Time*.

Being and Time is arguably Heidegger's single most important work. A hugely complex project, it essentially represents an attempt at the destruction of Western **metaphysics** through a re-evaluation of questions concerning human existence. Heidegger's main argument is that the tradition of Western metaphysical philoso-phy has consistently ignored the question of Being (understood in its most general form) in favour of the analysis of the particular attributes of individual kinds of being. Heidegger goes on to investigate the meaning of Being, which he describes as the fundamental ontological question, through an analysis of the concept of Dasein (being there), which he claims represents a particular type of being (i.e. humans): the being that is able to question its own existence. In other words, Heidegger uses the individual concept of being (Dasein) to arrive at an overall understanding of the concept of Being in general. Heidegger then develops these ideas further by situating them within a temporal framework (thus dealing with the time aspect of *Being and Time*). According to Heidegger, time is constitutive for the condition of beings, and indeed Being, as it forms the horizon of all experience for beings rather than existing as a separate thing within which beings could be situated. *Being and Time* was never completed, but the arguments developed there continued to occupy Heidegger throughout his career.

Heidegger's thought has exerted a significant influence on much contemporary philosophy and theory. In particular, the work of Jacques **Derrida** can be seen to be closely related to that of Heidegger, especially regarding the radical re-evaluation of metaphysical philosophy. In addition, he has influenced the writing of a number of other theorists, including Michel **Foucault**, Jacques **Lacan** and Jean-François **Lyotard**. [JS]

Further reading

Clark, Timothy (2002) *Heidegger*, London: Routledge.

Heidegger, Martin (1990) *Being and Time*, trans. John Macquarrie and Edward Robinson, Oxford: Blackwell.

Heidegger, Martin (2000) *Introduction to Metaphysics*, trans. Gregory Freid and Richard Polt, London and New Haven, CT: Yale Nota Bene.

HERMENEUTICS The study of understanding, which takes its name from the Greek god Hermes, the deliverer and interpreter of messages. Although traditionally reserved for the interpretation of biblical texts, 'modern' hermeneutics embodies two distinct branches, the interpretation of textual artefacts, and cultural events.

Evolving in the early nineteenth century, it is widely held that modern hermeneutics began with the work of Friedrich Schleiermacher who, in his 1838 *Hermeneutik und Kritik*, sought through textual analyses to establish 'what the **author** meant'. As the study of hermeneutics has developed, however, the presence and intention of the author has become less significant.

Modern hermeneutics is now applicable to a myriad of texts, and irrespective of whether written, performed or photographic, all texts undergoing hermeneutic analysis are processed in the same manner, with the analyst alternating between general and specific evaluations. Having initially studied the text, the analyst forms a general hypothesis of its meaning. This initial evaluation is then tempered with a closer rereading of the text based on what is now 'known'. Subsequent rereadings and alternations between the general and the specific, the 'familiar' and the 'unfamiliar', are repeated until the disparate factions merge and a tentative interpretation can be formed.

In addition to the pioneering work of Schleiermacher, theorists such as Paul **Ricoeur** and Hans-Georg **Gadamer** have provided valuable insight into the field of hermeneutics. In 1960 Gadamer published *Truth and Method*, regarded by many as philosophical hermeneutics' most significant advance since Martin **Heidegger**'s *Being and Time*. A central tenet of *Truth and Method* is Gadamer's contention that 'truth' can be revealed through scientific investigation. Acknowledging a major limitation of hermeneutic analysis, Gadamer announces that 'every translation is clearer and flatter than its original'; any understanding has to be appreciated as an act of interpretation that excludes certain textual components whilst 'spotlighting' others.

In *The Conflict of Interpretations: Essays in Hermeneutics*, Ricoeur provides a more holistic interpretation than that offered by traditional approaches to hermeneutics. Addressing the impact of hermeneutics' cultural heritage Ricoeur discusses how differences in analysts' backgrounds will influence their 'readings': analysts from diverse cultures will inevitably interpret the same text or component differently.

As Ricoeur explains, 'every reading takes place in a culture which imposes its own framework of interpretation'. [PSW]

Further reading
Gadamer, Hans-Georg (1993) *Truth and Method*, trans. Joel Weinsheimer and Donald G. Marshall, London: Sheed and Ward.
Ricoeur, Paul (1974) *The Conflict of Interpretations: Essays in Hermeneutics*, ed. Don Ihde, Evanston, IL: Northwestern University Press.

HOGGART, RICHARD (1918–) Literary and cultural critic who was the first director of the University of Birmingham's Centre for Contemporary Cultural Studies from 1963 until 1968, when he was succeeded by Stuart **Hall**.

Hoggart grew up in a working-class home in northern England during the interwar period, and his main critical preoccupation has been the quality of the cultural life of the English working class. His pioneering study *The Uses of Literacy* (1957) broadened the notion of what could legitimately be studied by considering the post-war 'mass culture' of 'publications and entertainments' (popular songs, films and magazines). Hoggart felt that these were inferior to the 'working-class culture' that they were displacing.

Hoggart has been criticized as an elitist and 'cultural Luddite', but he (along with his contemporaries, E. P. **Thompson** and Raymond **Williams**) played a major role in establishing cultural studies as an academic discipline, and he has actively campaigned to maintain and improve the quality of the culture consumed by the English working class. [CRC]

Further reading
Hoggart, Richard (1957) *The Uses of Literacy: Aspects of Working-Class Life with Special Reference to Publications and Entertainments*, London: Chatto and Windus.

HOOKS, BELL (1955–) Cultural critic who broadly sympathizes with the feminist and black rights movements, while interrogating the former's **ethnocentricity** and the latter's **patriarchal** tendencies. In her first text, *Ain't I a Woman* (1981), she writes about black women's marginalization from the feminist mainstream, while stopping short of endorsing the creation of a separate black feminist movement. Since then, she has published prolifically on subjects as diverse as art and film criticism, pedagogy, popular culture and human geography. Born Gloria Watkins, she writes under her grandmother's name as a reminder of the silencing of generations of black women. She uses all lower-case letters for her name to denote a suspicion of the **egotism** of writing, and self-reflexively analyses the incongruities of her position as a working-class black academic, for example in *Breaking Bread*. She also rejects many of the conventions of academic writing, often choosing to write for popular magazines, using anecdotes or the dialogue format. [CC]
See also Chapters 8, 9 and 11.

Further reading
hooks, bell (1981) *Ain't I a Woman: Black Women and Feminism*, London: Pluto.
hooks, bell (1990) *Yearning: Race, Gender and Cultural Politics*, Boston, MA: South End Press.
hooks, bell and Cornel West (1991) *Breaking Bread: Insurgent Black Intellectual Life*, Boston, MA: South End Press.

HORKHEIMER, MAX (1895–1973) German cultural theorist and philosopher who helped establish the Institute of Social Research, or **Frankfurt School**. He became the director in 1931, overseeing its exile to America under the Nazi threat and its return to Germany in 1947.

Horkheimer's essay on 'Traditional and Critical Theory' (1937) articulated the ambitions of the Frankfurt School, describing the necessity of integrating philosophy into the field of social science. In partnership with Theodor **Adorno**, he produced the *Dialectic of Enlightenment* (1947), which argued that destruction had been born out of modern rationality. He continued this theme in *Eclipse of Reason* (1967), arguing that objective ideals, for example democracy, had been co-opted by subjective functionality, i.e. social norms or needs. He urges a return to a higher state of rationality where pure reason can be used to diagnose and solve the problems of society.

In his later life, Horkheimer became more pessimistic about the prospects for political renewal as commercialism gradually eroded cultural integrity. His commitment to the liberation of the socially repressed through both philosophy and praxis remains vital to cultural theory today. [RW]

See also Chapter 3.

Further reading

Stirk, Peter M. R. (1982) *Max Horkheimer: A New Interpretation*, New York: Harvester Wheatsheaf.

HYPERREALITY Term used by the philosopher Jean **Baudrillard** to describe the postmodern situation. Baudrillard argues that contemporary culture is increasingly in thrall to electronic images from television, video and computing. These images are becoming more legitimate than the real. For example, now that we can do our banking, shopping and even socializing on-line without leaving our houses, Baudrillard suggests that the boundary between reality and its model is being blurred.

Drawing on the ideas of **Saussure** and **Marx**, Baudrillard suggests that in this consumer society commodities should not be analysed for their use-value, as Marx would have it, but treated as **signs**. In the postmodern age, he argues that signs irrevocably float away from their **referent**. As such, hyperreality is the term used to describe a state of being whereby reality dissolves and reproductions and **simulations** stand in for the real. For example, in the essay 'Simulacra and Simulations', Baudrillard discusses Jorge Luis Borges's famous story in which cartographers draw up a map so detailed that it is an exact, full-scale representation of the land. He adduces from Borges's story the notion that in the postmodern age the simulacrum has more potency than the real: 'Henceforth, it is the map that precedes the territory . . . it is the map that engenders the territory' (Baudrillard 1983: 2).

Another example that Baudrillard gives of the simulacrum preceding the referent is Disneyland. Disneyland presents itself as an exuberantly imaginary world, distinct from the 'real' world outside its gates. Yet Baudrillard argues that the hyperreal excesses of Disneyland mask the fact that America itself is almost as artificial and unreal, and that the 'reality principle' has imploded. [CC]

See also Chapter 10.

Further reading

Poster, Mark (ed.) (2001) *Jean Baudrillard: Selected Writings*, Stanford, CA: Stanford University Press.

HYPERTEXT Hypertext is a computing term used to denote a sense of the relationships between nodes of texts connected electronically in **cyberspace**. The internet, for instance, links texts with other texts, diagrams and visual images in a non-hierarchical, unconsecutive fashion. In common usage, hypertext is an abbreviation for hypertext mark-up language, or HTML, the language used to create documents on the world wide web.

The critic George P. Landow argues that electronic hypertext has much in common with recent poststructuralist theory. For example, the nature of electronic linking makes it difficult to discern where one text ends and another begins. Similarly, theorists such as **Barthes**, **Foucault** and **Derrida** stress the interconnectedness of all written works, frequently using the imagery of networks, nodes and webs.

Furthermore, hypertext complicates the notion of writer and reader, because the internet user plays a more active role than is possible for readers of printed media. The nature of hypertext alters our methods of reading. If one has a particular interest in a certain topic, it is often possible to click on a highlighted link and move to a new domain, making digression and disjointedness an inevitable feature of the medium. Hypertext also allows the reader to add her own links or comments, so that it is often seen as an open-ended, collaborative medium. Such features bring electronic hypertext close to Derrida's and Barthes' theoretical challenges to common preconceptions about **authors**, readers and texts. [CC]

See also Chapters 2 and 10.

Further reading

Landow, George P. (1992) *Hypertext: The Convergence of Contemporary Critical Theory and Technology*, Baltimore, MD: Johns Hopkins University Press.

Landow, George P. (ed.) (1994) *Hyper/Text/Theory*, Baltimore, MD: Johns Hopkins University Press.

I

Id A term that designates one of the three conflicting internal agencies of the mind outlined by **Freud**, the others being **ego** and **superego**. This tripartite division is consolidated quite late in Freud's work (*The Ego and the Id*, 1923), and can be seen as reworking his first 'topography' of the mind, the binary divide conscious/**unconscious**.

Freud originally used the term unconscious to distinguish a part of the mind distinct from any conscious control. Seen by many as the most significant aspect of psychoanalysis, over many years Freud went on to develop a whole theory around the unconscious: how it was created out of primary repression, how its contents represented the **drives** and how it was enslaved to the pleasure principle.

The term id (via **Nietzsche** from the German *das Es*, meaning 'the it') was introduced by Freud in order to temper the distinction between the conscious and the unconscious. Rather, the id and ego interact through the process of sublimation, the ego harnessing the drives for non-sexual aims. [DD]

See also Chapter 6.

Further reading

Freud, Sigmund (1991c) 'The Ego and the Id', in *The Essentials of Psycho-Analysis*, trans. James Strachey, London: Penguin.

IDEOLOGICAL STATE APPARATUS (ISA) This concept is central to the French **Marxist** critic Louis **Althusser**'s theory of ideology. ISAs are the institutions that generate the value systems which serve to perpetuate the injustices that lie at the core of capitalist societies. Examples include literature and art, trade unions, religion, electoral democracy (the choice of political parties and the voting rights we have), the family and advertising. The values that the many different ISAs produce are varied, and they sometimes even contradict each other. They are, however, united in their task of preserving dominant power structures in their society. By far the most important ISA, according to Althusser, is the education system. In his view, the idea that schools and universities are neutral non-political spaces is a myth. They are the places where each one of us is trained to learn, reproduce, and live in accordance with the mode of production that structures our society. Each level of education prepares a section of the population to participate in specific roles with regard to the capitalist mode of production. [AW]

See also Chapter 3.

IDEOLOGY A central concept in critical theory, which is most commonly used in one of three ways. The first takes 'ideology' to be a set of conscious or **unconscious** beliefs held by a particular group of people. The second holds that these beliefs are incorrect, and that this fact can objectively be proven. This theory, which Friedrich **Engels** called 'false consciousness', is the basis of the **Marxist/Freudian** take on religion. The third uses the term to denote the process whereby people come to hold their beliefs: the most influential theories of this are articulated by Antonio **Gramsci** and Louis **Althusser**.

The term 'ideology' was coined in the

late eighteenth century by the French philosopher Destut de Tracy, to denote a 'philosophy of mind' or 'science of ideas'. Soon afterwards, the French Emperor Napoleon Bonaparte was the first to use the word in a pejorative sense, employing the now familiar conservative debating tactic of contrasting an opponent's allegedly dogmatic thought with his own common sense pragmatism.

The groups most concerned with ideology have been those interested in why societies are organized as they are, and in how they may be changed. One of the most important conceptions of ideology is that advanced by the nineteenth-century German political philosopher Karl **Marx**. Marx's central contention regarding ideology is that 'The ideas of the ruling class are in every epoch the ruling ideas: i.e., the class which is the ruling material force of society is at the same time its ruling intellectual force' (Marx and Engels 1977: 176). For Marx, society's economic 'base', the means of production and distribution, is the primary determinant of its social and ideological 'superstructure', its art, religion, etc., and hence its ideological beliefs.

Soviet thinking about ideology was rooted in the attempt to translate Marxist theory into revolutionary practice. A crude application of the **base/superstructure** model, known variously as mechanical materialism, determinism or economism, considers the base to be not the primary but the sole determinant of the superstructure. This reading of Marx reduces the complex changing, and sometimes contradictory, ideas of a 40-year career to a sterile, static orthodoxy, but this did not prevent it from becoming dominant in official Communist Party interpretations of his work in the early twentieth century. Subsequent theorists, including Georg **Lukács**, Antonio Gramsci, Louis Althusser and Raymond **Williams**, have refined the base/superstructure formulation, suggesting that the superstructure possesses a 'relative autonomy' and can bring about changes in the base.

The Italian Communist politician and theorist Antonio Gramsci formulated a 'culturalist' Marxism, in which the consent of citizens is secured by the cultural exercise of '**hegemony**', which works by subliminal persuasion rather than coercion.

Gramsci's theory influenced the French structuralist Louis Althusser's formulation of the **Ideological State Apparatus** and the Repressive State Apparatus. For Althusser, who also draws upon the psychoanalytic theories of Jacques **Lacan**, ideology '**interpellates**' (hails) individual citizens 'as **subjects**'. Althusser goes further, arguing that ideology is 'eternal' and 'individuals are always-already subjects'. This has led to the accusation that Althusser has simply replaced the orthodox economic determinism with a heretical, and no less sinister, cultural determinism.

The theory of ideology advanced by Althusser, and adopted and adapted by subsequent theoreticians, including his student Michel **Foucault**, has been criticized by humanists because it furthers the psychoanalytic challenge to the idea of the unitary self, and by Marxists who consider it unduly pessimistic in its view of the potentiality of workers and other oppressed groups to recognize and change their situation. Though it has proved controversial, Althusserianism has been embraced as potentially emancipatory by 'post-Marxist' theorists of gender and race such as Judith **Butler** and Stuart **Hall**, who are keen to demonstrate that characteristics ascribed to certain groups are not essential but ideological 'social constructs' and thus either have no basis in reality, or are at least changeable. As such, the theory of ideology remains a focus of debates about existing social structures, and the prospects for social transformation. [CRC]

See also Chapter 3.

Further reading

Eagleton, Terry (1991) *Ideology: An Introduction*, London: Verso.

Hawkes, David (1996) *Ideology*, London: Routledge.

IMAGINARY A concept developed by the French psychoanalyst Jacques **Lacan**. It forms, along with the concepts of the **symbolic** and the **real**, one part of a triadic structure that interacts and overlaps. The category of the imaginary is associated with Lacan's **mirror stage**, in which the infant recognizes itself as the image it sees reflected back to it in a mirror. The concept of the imaginary is concerned with the **subject**'s captivation by the image, the way in which the primal components of subjective identity are constituted in the relay between spectator and image. This focus upon the image is vital for the constitution of the subject in that it permits the delineation of the boundaries between the self and the **other**, and it sets up, in Lacan's words 'a relation between the organism and its reality' (Lacan 1977: 4). What is constituted in the imaginary relation between the spectator and the image is the enclosed space of the **ego**, the inner world, and what lies beyond the ego's boundaries, the outside world, the *not-I*, the other. In order to accomplish this, the gaze of the spectator is focused upon a petrified image, a freeze-frame, from which is reflected back to it the coordinates of bodily unity. However, this process of mutual reconfirmation between spectator and image is dependent upon the split between the two, between the inner and the outer, being acknowledged and then repressed. This is because what the subject derives from the imaginary is the conviction that the self is unitary, but the act of imaginary identification, 'that is me', already implies a constitutive split, that the self is divided between gaze and image and that part of its identity is out there, beyond the enclosure of the ego. The act of imaginary identification can only succeed by means of a detour through the **symbolic order**, since it is from the symbolic that the illusory cohesion of the body image is reflected back into the imaginary. The maintenance of imaginary identity requires the subject to behave as if the unitary identity of the ego is unproblematic, that it is not the result of a primary division. This pretence is always ongoing since an awareness of the ego's dispersal cannot be fully banished from the subject's composition. [HJ]

See also Chapter 6.

Further reading

Bowie, Malcolm (1991) *Lacan*, London: Fontana.

Lacan, Jacques (1977) *Écrits: A Selection*, trans. Alan Sheridan, London: Routledge.

INTERPELLATION A key element of the French Marxist Louis **Althusser**'s theory of ideology. The word derives from the French verb *appeller*, which means, 'to name'. It is the process by which individuals internalize the cultural values, or ideologies, which are essential to the maintenance of the capitalist system. Althusser explains that **ideology** calls on us to accept unquestioningly certain elements of our culture as fixed, natural and disinterested, when they are actually contingent, learned and crucial to preserving existing power structures. It does this by interpellating us as free, autonomous, choosing **subjects**. So, for example, thousands of advertisements address us every day as consumers with unlimited free choice; when there is an election the various political parties invite us to see ourselves as powerful actors in the democratic process. If we accept these positions we have consented to our interpellation as subjects of the ideologies of freedom, consumerism and democracy. These are not necessarily false positions, but the choice between consumer products or between political parties is limited. Our acceptance of ideological subject positions implicates us in the preservation of society and politics as it stands, instead of inviting us to imagine a non-consumerist world with a more genuinely representative and participatory democratic system. [AW]

See also Chapter 3.

INTERTEXTUALITY A term employed by poststructuralist critics. To say that a text's meaning is 'intertextual' is to claim that it derives its meanings from its relationships with other texts, for example through overt or covert allusions and references. Meaning is not, therefore, something which inheres in that text and only that text; it is relational. Similarly, no text is seen as autonomous; instead, every text is made up of many other texts.

Derived in part from **Saussure**'s theory of language as a system of differences, the notion of intertextuality implies that a text does not contain stable and definitive meanings, but instead produces meanings through its relations with other texts and through the contexts into which it is put. As the text is constantly entering into new relations and contexts, it is always producing new meanings beyond those that might have been intended by its **author**.

More recently, internet narratives, with their use of **hypertext**, have been cited to demonstrate the interweaving and interconnectedness of texts, i.e. their fundamental intertextuality. [KM]

See also Chapters 2, 4 and 7.

Further reading

Allen, Graham (2000) *Intertextuality*, London: Routledge.

Barthes, Roland (1977) *Image, Music, Text*, trans. Stephen Heath, London: Fontana.

IRIGARAY, LUCE (1932–) Philosopher, psychoanalyst and linguist, whose criticism of **patriarchal** production of meanings and **subjectivity** has been among the most influential in French post-war feminist writings. Although her works have at times been dismissed by Anglo-American theorists, whether because of what they perceive as her 'essentialist' position on sexual **difference** or because of her poetic, even cryptic, writing style, the significance of her intervention in patriarchal **discourses** across a wide range of disciplines started to receive more recognition in the 1990s.

Irigaray became widely known to Anglo-American critics with *Speculum of the Other Woman* (1974; trans. 1985) and *This Sex Which Is Not One* (1977; trans. 1985), where she criticizes **phallocentrism** in Western philosophical discourse, especially in psychoanalysis. Instead of the **Lacanian** psychoanalysis which postulates a male body as the **imaginary** ideal upon which the bodily **ego** is constructed, and which therefore can only represent 'woman' as a lack/hole, Irigaray calls for the 'speculum' which accounts for women's sexual difference and enables feminine subjectivity. She maintains that phallocentrism itself is founded on the repression of the feminine/maternal, and that, in this sexually indifferent, or 'hom(m)osexual' system, there can be only one sex, which is the masculine sex. Since women already exist within the system, the only way to recover the exploited feminine position is to mimic the assigned position within the system and bring forth the feminine 'excess'. Irigaray herself took up the mimetic style in her writing, appropriating and infiltrating the philosophical or psychoanalytic discourses and criticizing them from within.

While her 'mimetic' style may seem to have affinity with deconstruction, Irigaray's 'mimicry' in fact aims at reconstructing the feminine subjectivity rather than merely deconstructing the **phallogocentric** system. This emphasis on feminine subjectivity, along with the trope of 'caressing two lips' that she uses to describe the feminine economy, as opposed to the masculine economy of 'one', has sometimes resulted in the accusation of biological essentialism. Critics are divided, however, as to what extent her writing can be read as mimetic strategy and to what extent it is 'essentialist'. [AS]

See also Chapters 6, 8 and 9.

Further reading

Irigaray, Luce (1985a) *This Sex Which is Not One*, trans. Catherine Porter, Ithaca, NY: Cornell University Press.

Irigaray, Luce (1985b) *Speculum of the Other Woman*, trans. Gillian C. Gill, Ithaca, NY: Cornell University Press.

ISER, WOLFGANG (1926–) With Hans Robert **Jauss** and Karl-Heinz Stierle, Iser is one of the founding figures of reader-response criticism, the first major movement which systematically elevated the reader and the act of reading over traditional criticism with its emphasis on **authorial** intention. Iser's main concern lies in the delineation of those acts by which the reader synthesizes the literary text into an aesthetic totality. According to Iser, the meaning of a text is never given as such, but only provides basic elements such as the repertoire (cultural norms) and textual perspectives which the reader accumulates in the reading process and eventually synthesizes into a meaningful whole. He calls this process 'reciprocal spotlighting'. Iser's theory is mainly **phenomenological** in so far as it postulates a transcendental reading **subject** in the form of a wandering viewpoint. Iser's interest lies consequently not in how a specific empirical reader synthesizes the various textual elements into a meaningful totality. Rather, he is interested in the universal and thus empty structure of the reading experience as such. This is why Iser also calls his theory a 'theory of affect' ('*Wirkung*') whereas Jauss's theory is called 'reception-aesthetics' since it is concerned with empirical readers and their embeddedness in a specific cultural horizon. In his later work, Iser becomes more anthropological, exploring the mechanisms by which a text enables the reader to discern his or her anthropological make-up. [RS]

See also Chapter 2.

Further reading

Holub, Robert C. (1984) *Reception Theory: A Critical Introduction*, London: Methuen.

Iser, Wolfgang (1978) *The Act of Reading: A Theory of Aesthetic Response*, London: Routledge and Kegan Paul.

J

JAKOBSON, ROMAN (1896–1982) Co-founder of both the Moscow Linguistic Circle (1915) and the Prague Linguistic Circle (1926), Jakobson was a key figure in **Russian formalism** and a major influence on French structuralism, in particular Claude **Lévi-Strauss**, later in the century.

In his phonological studies, Jakobson examined the relationship between sound and meaning; in his study of poetry, he showed how the effects produced depend on the relationships between **signifiers** which have become divorced from their **signifieds** and on the self-consciousness of poetic language. His theory of parallelism in poetry focuses on how words are combined in ways which evoke and create similarities or connections between them. He applied his analysis of metonymy (where one sign is associated with another: for example, 'the crown' with 'monarchy') and metaphor (where one sign is substituted for another: 'pig' for 'greedy man') to a study of aphasia, arguing that it involves a failure of one of these two processes of word selection and combination.

In the course of a wide-ranging scholarly career, Jakobson also found time to write on Russian and Czech folktales, mythology and film. [KM]

See also Chapters 1, 2 and 4.

Further reading

Bradford, Richard (1994) *Roman Jakobson: Life, Literature, Art*, London: Routledge.

Jakobson, Roman (1987) *Language in Literature*, ed. Krystyna Pomorska and Stephen Rudy, Cambridge, MA: Belknap Press of Harvard University Press.

JAMESON, FREDRIC (1934–) American-born **Marxist** theoretician of culture, language and literature, who has sought to trace the shifting relationships between cultural forms and the historical situations in which they are produced and consumed, and so to illuminate the peculiar trajectory from the modern to the postmodern and beyond.

Thus, in *Marxism and Form* (1972a) he argues that form embodies **ideological** messages and so has more revolutionary potential than content, and in *The Prison-House of Language* (1972) he takes issue with what he judges to be the anti-historical formalism of structuralism and **Russian formalism**, insisting that literary and cultural works cannot be abstracted from their historical and economic circumstances. He builds on this in *The Political Unconscious* (1981), with a Marxist analysis of the form of certain nineteenth-century novels (by Balzac, Gissing and Conrad) which opens with the memorable slogan: 'Always historicize!'

In the 1980s and 1990s, Jameson turned his attention to contemporary culture, and in the hugely influential *Postmodernism, or, the Cultural Logic of Late Capitalism* (1991), he writes eloquently about architecture, film and video and their relation to the global market, in a bid to elucidate what he sees as the gradual merging of the cultural and the economic (or aesthetics and politics, respectively) in the twentieth century.

Throughout his work, then, major preoccupations with literary and cultural form, history and the relationship of the aesthetic and the political run alongside a continuing belief in the utility of utopian thinking. [KM]

See also Chapters 3 and 10.

Further reading

Jameson, Fredric (1991) *Postmodernism, or, the Cultural Logic of Late Capitalism*, London: Verso.

Jameson, Fredric (2002a) *The Political Unconscious: Narrative as a Socially Symbolic Act*, London: Routledge.

Roberts, Adam (2000) *Fredric Jameson*, London: Routledge.

JAUSS, HANS ROBERT (1921–97) Critic whose work is inextricably linked with that of Wolfgang **Iser** and other members of the Konstance School reception aesthetics. Jauss's main concern lies in how literary texts have been received at different times or epochs. His approach consequently incorporates a mode of historical thought: that is, an awareness that a text does not exist as an independent or a-temporal entity but requires realization in a specific historical context. Since a text does not exist outside history, it can be thought of as always historically situated. Jauss himself argues that a text is situated within a horizon of expectations which is constituted by a specific readership. A readership is defined by such factors as education, class and age. Jauss's notion of horizon of expectations corresponds closely to Stanley **Fish**'s concept of interpretive communities. What both theorists share is the view that texts have no universal status per se, but receive a quasi-universal status once various interpretive communities or readerships with different horizons of expectations have upheld a text's importance or significance. If a text is repeatedly passed on from community to community over a longer period of time, it constitutes part of what we call tradition. According to Jauss, universality is nothing but veiled or unacknowledged tradition. Jauss differs from or supplements Iser's work in so far as he introduces a historical mode of thought. Whilst Iser is interested in the general structure of acts of reading, Jauss shows how a text is realized by a particular readership. Jauss's work anticipates aspects of deconstruction by showing that a text does not exist outside the text of history (**Derrida**'s famous 'There is no outside text') and of new historicism by focusing on horizons of expectations. [RS]

See also Chapter 2.

Further reading

Jauss, Hans Robert (1982) *Toward and Aesthetic of Reception*, trans. Timothy Bahti, Brighton: Harvester Press.

Jauss, Hans Robert (1989) *Question and Answer: Forms of Dialogic Understanding*, trans. Michael Hays, Minneapolis, MN: University of Minnesota Press.

JOUISSANCE French term derived from the verb *jouir*, which means to enjoy or to take pleasure, and also to have the right to something. In contrast to a similar term, *plaisir*, it denotes an extreme form of pleasure: ecstatic or orgasmic bliss that transcends or even shatters one's everyday experience of the world. The term is most frequently employed by psychoanalytic theorists, and is most influentially defined by Jacques **Lacan**, for whom it denotes the ecstatic moment of opening to the **Other** that disrupts the illusion of being in control of oneself: it is, he claims, 'what serves no purpose' (Lacan 1998: 3) in that it breaks open **imaginary** identity and social convention. The term is also crucial to the work of feminist theorists such as Julia **Kristeva** and Luce **Irigaray** who deploy it as a means to disturb the rules of **patriarchal** discourse. It is related to literature by Roland **Barthes**, whose *The Pleasure of the Text* explores the way in which *jouissance* is produced at those moments in reading where literal meaning collapses to give rise to bliss. [SM]

See also Chapters 6, 8 and 9.

Further reading

Barthes, Roland (1975) *The Pleasure of the Text*, trans. Richard Miller, Oxford: Blackwell.

Irigaray, Luce (1985b) *Speculum of the Other Woman*, trans. Gillian C. Gill, Ithaca, NY: Cornell University Press.

Lacan, Jacques (1998) *On Feminine Sexuality: The Limits of Love and Knowledge. Book XX: Encore 1972–1973*, New York and London: Norton.

JUNG, CARL GUSTAV (1875–1961) Swiss-born psychologist, who in his early career was a follower of Sigmund **Freud**, and contributed to the formation of psycho-analysis. Later he came to disagree with many of Freud's formulations, in particular Freud's theory of libido, splitting from him to form his own movement, which he dubbed *analytical psychology*.

The central tenet of Jung's technique, which he shared with Freud, was the interpretation of dreams. His departure from Freud took the form of his postulation of a 'collective unconscious', rendered distinct from Freud's '**unconscious**'. According to Jung, the collective unconscious is shared by everyone and is the space in which the cultural experiences and memories of the human race are retained. These distilled memories Jung called *archetypes*. It is the inherited images of the archetypes that comprise the collective unconscious and allow it to generate **mythological** material that shapes our sense of who we are. The archetypes represent primal wisdom and arise from the collective unconscious to the *personal unconscious* in the form of dreams and myths which, properly interpreted, allow the dreamer or myth reader to understand the myriad crises affecting their lives, and resolve them.

Within the personal unconscious there are four archetypes: the first is the '**ego**', which represents our conscious personality. The second is the 'shadow': the dark or negative side of our personality that we consciously seek to repress, and as such can bring light to our unconscious desires. The third archetype is the 'anima' (feminine) or 'animus' (masculine), which represent the attributes of our personality belonging to the opposite sex and can guide emotional decisions. The fourth and seminal archetype is the 'self'. This embodies the unification of the other three archetypes and acts as a guide to the conscious mind.

Thus the self forms the unification of the psyche, its full realization and, therefore, its ultimate goal. In this sense both dreams and mythological material form the model for this process, called by Jung *individuation*. The ultimate goal of life is the realization of the self and the function of psychoanalysis, he argues, is to aid and facilitate that process. [MB]

See also Chapter 6.

Further reading

Jung, Carl Gustav (1974) *Synchronicity: An Acausal Connecting Principle*, trans. R. F. C. Hull, Princeton, NJ: Princeton University Press.

Jung, Carl Gustav (1978) *Man and his Symbols*, London: Picador.

Jung, Carl Gustav (2002) *The Undiscovered Self*, trans. R. F. C. Hull, London: Routledge.

K

KERMODE, FRANK (1919–) Author and editor of over 40 books, Frank Kermode is an extremely versatile British critic and writer, whose work has played a significant role in shaping modern literature courses worldwide. His early work demonstrates his interest in the literary **canon** and includes books and essays on, among others, Spenser (1965), Donne (1957), Milton (1960), and, most notably, William Shakespeare about whom Kermode has written throughout his career. This interest in the literary canon and on literary value is the subject of much of Kermode's work, including *History and Value* (1988) and his recent book *Pleasure and Change: The Aesthetics of Canon* (2004a).

Kermode's influence on literary theory should not be underestimated: his later work is more overtly theoretical and includes *The Sense of an Ending* (1967), a lively account of narrative ending, *The Genesis of Secrecy* (1979), a work of poststructuralist narrative theory examining the Gospels of Matthew, Mark, Luke and John, and his wide-ranging study *The Art of Telling* (1983). In his role as Lord Northcliffe Professor at University College London, Kermode chaired a series of graduate seminars that brought the work of key European critical theorists to Britain and, as series editor of the popular Fontana Modern Masters series, he has continued to bring this work to the attention of generations of scholars. However, Kermode continues to argue for the value of literary criticism alongside the ever increasing interest in theory. [PW]

Further reading

Gorak, Jan (1987) *Critic of Crisis: A Study of Frank Kermode*, Columbia, SC: University of Missouri Press.

Kermode, Frank (2000) *The Sense of an Ending: Studies in the Theory of Fiction with a New Epilogue*, Oxford: Oxford University Press.

Kermode, Frank (2004b) *Pieces of My Mind: Writings 1958–2002*, London: Penguin.

KLEIN, MELANIE (1882–1960) Austrian psychoanalyst who, together with Sigmund **Freud**, was one of the founders of psychoanalysis. Whereas in Freud's work the **Oedipal** and post-Oedipal sphere is given theoretical priority, Klein concentrated on the pre-Oedipal relationship between infant and mother and, differently from Freud, gave the mother a more dominant role in the construction of identity. After she moved to London in 1926 Klein's object-relations theory became one of the major strands of modern psychoanalysis. The Kleinian School was established after the Second World War and developed into the major institutional and theoretical framework for a psychoanalysis that was in particular dedicated to the understanding of early infantile anxieties and their impact on how children and adults relate to other people and the world. From a theoretical perspective Klein's most important contribution to psychoanalysis was her redefinition of the Freudian Oedipal complex, where she shifts the focus away from sexual desire onto emotional and intellectual development, and from the paternal to the maternal figure as crucial for the construction of identity. Klein's refiguration of the mother had particular impact on the critical work of Julia **Kristeva**. [AM]

See also Chapter 6.

Further reading

Kristeva, Julia (2001) *Melanie Klein*, trans. Ross Guberman, New York: Columbia University Press.

Likierman, Meira (2001) *Melanie Klein: Her Work in Context*, London: Continuum.

Mitchell, Juliet (ed.) (1991) *The Selected Melanie Klein*, Harmondsworth: Penguin.

KLEIN, NAOMI (1970–) Canadian journalist best known for her writing about global capitalism and anti-corporate activism. Her first book, the bestseller *No Logo* (2000), was published two months after the infamous 'Battle of Seattle' in November 1999, when mass protests disrupted a meeting of the World Trade Organization.

No Logo focuses on the advertising strategies of multinational corporations and the tactics adopted by activists who oppose them. One activist strategy is 'culture jamming', whereby a company's logo or slogan is modified so that the brand remains recognizable but the message is subverted. The company's malpractice is not treated as an isolated anomalous case, but as a symptom of wider disease, a 'large-scale political metaphor'. Thus a brand like McDonald's comes to exemplify mass production ('McDonaldization') and low-paid work ('McJob'). Klein calls this technique of taking the symbolic capital that accrues to the brand and turning it back against the company the 'brand boomerang'.

Klein's work draws together the cultural, political and economic implications of **globalization** and is a guide to the operations of, and the opposition to, multinational corporations. [CRC]

See also Chapter 10.

Further reading

Klein, Naomi (2000) *No Logo: Taking Aim at the Brand Bullies*, London: Flamingo.

KOJÈVE, ALEXANDRE (1902–68) Philosopher who introduced the work of G. W. F. Hegel into contemporary French thought. Kojève's readings of Hegel are strongly influenced by Martin **Heidegger**'s existential phenomenology and Karl **Marx**'s materialist critiques of capitalism, and the interrelation of these three thinkers in his work produced the existential **materialism** that remains important for much contemporary French theory. In a series of influential seminars in the 1930s (which were later collected and published as *Introduction to the Reading of Hegel*, 1969), Kojève produced a reading of Hegel that has profoundly influenced a range of philosophers and theorists including Jean-Paul Sartre, Jacques **Lacan**, Georges **Bataille**, Louis **Althusser**, and Maurice **Merleau-Ponty**. More recently Kojève's legacy has been the subject of a disagreement between Francis **Fukuyama**, who drew heavily on his analyses of Hegel to discuss contemporary society in *The End of History and the Last Man* (1992), and Jacques **Derrida**, who challenges both Fukuyama's reading of Kojève and his apology for free-market capitalism in *Specters of Marx* (1994). [SM]

See also Chapter 3.

Further reading

Kojève, Alexandre (1969) *Introduction to the Reading of Hegel*, New York: Basic Books.

KRISTEVA, JULIA (1941–) Linguist, cultural theorist and psychoanalyst, whose main concern is the relation of the system of **signs** to what precedes and exceeds the system. Although she has resisted being called a feminist, her theories, especially those concerning the **semiotic** and the **abject**, have had a vital influence on a great deal of feminist and cultural theory. Essays from two of her earlier books, *Sémeiótiké* (1969) and *Polylogue* (1977) have been collected in *Desire in Language* (1980), and there is a selection of translations of her writings, *The Kristeva Reader* (1986).

As a student of Roland **Barthes**, Kristeva started to publish articles on linguistics, and soon established herself as one of the leading literary critics and semiologists in late 1960s Paris. In her first book, *Sémeiótiké*, she focused on how meaning is made possible in a text, rather than on what a particular text means, and argues that a text must consist of citations and traces from multiple other texts in order to have any meaning at all. This concept of **intertextuality**, which she derives from Mikhail **Bakhtin**, perceives a textual space as polyvocal, that is, as containing multiple voices that cannot be reduced to a single communicable meaning.

In *Revolution in Poetic Language* (1974; trans. 1984), Kristeva argues that language, the system of meaning itself, cannot function without what is usually seen as its 'outside'. According to Kristeva, all linguistic activity, or more generally signification, takes place as a dialogical interaction between two aspects of language: the **symbolic** and the semiotic. The former is similar to Jacques **Lacan**'s concept of the symbolic. It is a dimension of what is usually regarded as 'language', of the grammatical system and social order. It depends on articulation and separation, especially between the **subject** and the object. The semiotic is the discharge in language of the pre-**Oedipal** bodily **drives** and instinctive energies repressed by the symbolic, and is associated with such non-linguistic and corporeal signifying practices as the rhythms or tones of voices, bodily movements or infant babble. Since the pre-Oedipal drives are not only repressed by,

and excluded from, the symbolic, but are essential for the speaking subject to exist, the semiotic is also associated with the '**chora**', the womb or receptacle that underlies signification and subjectivity and, hence, with the maternal body. Kristeva argues that the semiotic always flows into the symbolic to some extent, implying that the subject, which contains the two contradictory forces of the symbolic and the semiotic, is never static but always in the process of disintegration and reconfiguration. The semiotic, however, is activated in the most creative manner in poetic language. By disrupting the normative system of signification based on communicability, and bringing forth the usually unintelligible semiotic energy, poetry cannot only create new and possibly subversive meanings, but can also encourage the reconfiguration of subjectivity.

This power of the semiotic, however, is feared and loathed as a threat to the subject, rather than celebrated for its radical possibilities. As Kristeva further expands in her more psychoanalytic work, *Powers of Horror* (1980; trans. 1982), it is the realm of the abject, or what the subject has to repress and expel in order to establish a clear border between its proper self and the object. The abject was originally a part of what then became the subject through this operation of abjection, and the subject hates and despises it, precisely because it still desires it and depends on it to some extent, but can no longer possess it. Since it allows us to analyse how our sense of 'identity' is constructed through excluding and abhorring something that is part of ourselves, and how, in turn, what is detested or derided might be essential to us, the notion of abjection has been particularly influential with feminist and cultural theorists in examining the relation between the feminine and the masculine, homosexuality and heterosexuality, blackness and whiteness, etc. This line of thought continues in Kristeva's later, more overtly political work, *Strangers to Ourselves* (1989; trans. 1994). It shows her continued interest in how a seemingly independent and self-contained system, whether it is the symbolic, the subject, or communal 'identity', is in fact inseparable from, or even dependent upon, its **other**. [AS]

See also Chapters 6, 8 and 9.

Further reading

Kristeva, Julia (1982) *Powers of Horror: An Essay on Abjection*, trans. Leon S. Roudiez, New York: Columbia University Press.

Kristeva, Julia (1986) *The Kristeva Reader*, trans. Toril Moi, Oxford: Blackwell.

L

LACAN, JACQUES (1901–81) French psychoanalyst whose influence extends beyond the confines of clinical practice to the study of literature, politics and **ideology**. Lacan wrote no books in the standard sense; the majority of works published under his name are transcriptions of seminars that he delivered between 1948 and 1980. His most influential work, in terms of an English-speaking audience, is contained in *Écrits: A Selection* (1977), especially the opening essay 'The mirror stage as formative of the function of the I as revealed in psychoanalytic experience'.

Lacan regarded his work as a return to the tradition of psychoanalysis begun by Sigmund **Freud** which had been betrayed by his North American acolytes. Despite his claimed allegiance to the message of Freud, Lacan produced two key innovations in the theory of human **subjectivity**. The first of these is concerned with the moment at which the infant comes to identify itself with the human form, the **mirror stage**, in which a child recognizes itself as the image that it sees in a mirror. The key aspect of this moment lies in Lacan's insistence that the child misrecognizes itself in the unified, coordinated mirror image, and that bodily and psychical unity are dependent upon a fundamental error of perspective. He develops this idea into an account of how human subjectivity involves the maintenance of the illusory consolations of the mirror stage. The mirror stage essay influenced the conception of ideology produced by the **Marxist** philosopher Louis **Althusser**, whose essay 'Ideology and **Ideological State Apparatuses**' develops the idea that

subjectivity is bestowed upon the individual through an outside agency, to encompass the notion that capitalist society provides the individual with reflective confirmation in a similar way to Lacan's mirror stage.

Lacan's second major contribution to psychoanalysis was his adoption of aspects of Ferdinand de **Saussure**'s linguistic theory. In his essay 'The agency of the letter in the unconscious or reason since Freud', he states that 'no signification can be sustained other than by reference to another signification' (1977: 150). In a way this is analogous to the theory of identity developed in the mirror stage in that Lacan endorses the Saussurean idea that meaning is produced only through a system of differences: it is not self-contained or self-identical. Lacan adapted two terms of Saussure's celebrated division of the verbal sign, the **signifier** and the **signified**, to form an algorithm that asserts the primacy of the signifier. In doing this he disrupts any simple idea of a parallel theoretical and practical weight between the signifier or material sign, and the signified or mental concept conventionally associated with it. Lacan's algorithm rewrites the relationship between the signifier and signified as S/s, by which he infers that meaning is a product of the signifier, not of any necessary relationship of equivalence between signifier and signified. A large part of Lacan's project is then devoted to producing an explanation of how, given that there is no automatic correlation between the signifier and the signified, the human subject manages to produce a relatively stable order of signification in which meaning can be lived as if it inheres in an automatic parallel between the two orders of the sign. In this way psychoanalysis can produce an account of the way in which meaning and identity can be socially constructed and validated and also, given that it is the study of the breakdown of meaning and identity, the way in which this precarious process can go wrong and produce other alternative meanings. This aspect of Lacanian psychoanalysis addresses questions that have been central to post-war French thinkers, most notably Jacques **Derrida**, who, along with Michel **Foucault**, attended Lacan's seminars. Although Derrida's work can be quite different from Lacan's, and their relationship was often hostile, they can be read as two distinct but interrelated approaches to the question of language and meaning. [HJ]

See also Chapter 6.

Further reading

Bowie, Malcolm (1991) *Lacan*, London: Fontana.

Lacan, Jacques (1977) *Écrits: A Selection*, trans. Alan Sheridan, London: Routledge.

Žižek, Slavoj (1992) *Looking Awry: An Introduction to Jacques Lacan through Popular Culture*, Cambridge, MA: October.

LANGUE **AND** *PAROLE* *Langue* and *parole* are two terms introduced to critical theory within Ferdinand de **Saussure**'s synchronic approach to **semiotic** analysis. Departing from the traditional diachronic, or historical, analysis of language structures, Saussure's model separates language into passive and active elements, the *langue* and *parole*.

Deriving from the French *la langue* meaning tongue, *langue* refers to a language in its entirety, at any one point in time, and includes the rules and conventions of its use – rules which pre-exist individual users. It is this determining element of *langue*'s characteristic that marks its *active* nature.

In contrast, *parole*, translated from the French *la parole*, meaning speech or word, refers to individual utterances of written or spoken language that *passively* adhere to the rules of the *langue*. Whilst Saussurean investigation focuses upon the *langue* of societal communication, any understanding of it is inevitably enhanced by analyses of *parole*. For example, analysis into English *parole* would reveal that whilst it is appropriate to pronounce 'the ball is red' announcing that 'the red is ball' contravenes the rules of the *langue* and is subsequently nonsensical.

Ultimately, the distinction between *langue* and *parole* is a distinction between code and message, structure and performance. To be understood, the latter must observe the dictates of the former. [PSW]

See also Chapter 1.

LEAVIS, FRANK RAYMOND (1895–1978) Probably the most influential and controversial British literary critic of the twentieth century, Leavis occupied a curious oppositional place within Cambridge University's English Faculty, heading a significant but marginal group, which established the journal *Scrutiny*. Published quarterly between 1932 and 1953, *Scrutiny* disseminated Leavis's ideas to a generation of teachers and students.

Leavis is the most prominent representative of a 'common sense' approach to literature that relates literary works to the lives and minds of their **authors**, placing a particular emphasis on the text itself. Actively opposed to the idea of abstract literary theory, Leavis preferred to make specific critical judgements, and the prime concern of his work was with assigning literary value. For Leavis, this was closely related to morality, and he identified great writers as those who 'not only change the possibilities of the art for practitioners and readers, but . . . are significant in terms of that human awareness they promote; awareness of the possibilities of life' (1966: 10).

Leavis wrote numerous important books on poetry and fiction, and considered 'great' literature a potential antidote to the 'standardization and levelling-down' of modern culture (Leavis and Thompson 1933: 3). The implicit elitism of Leavis's position was resisted by 'left-Leavisite' critics such as the young Raymond **Williams**. Later, when the liberal humanist view of literature was called into question by poststructuralist thinkers, 'Leavisite' came to be used as a pejorative term. Recently, however, a number of critics have begun to return to his texts to make a case for his continuing importance to critical thought, especially with regard to ethical criticism. [CRC]

See also Chapter 2.

Further reading

Day, Gary (1996) *Re-Reading Leavis: 'Culture' and Literary Criticism*, Basingstoke: Macmillan.

Leavis, Frank Raymond (1966) *The Great Tradition*, London: Peregrine Books.

Leavis, Frank Raymond and Thompson, Denys (1933) *Culture and Environment: The Training of Critical Awareness*, London: Chatto and Windus.

LEVINAS, EMMANUEL (1905–95) Lithuanian Jewish philosopher and one of the key figures in contemporary ethical philosophy. Levinas's **ethics** is not prescriptive in the sense that it tells us how we should lead our lives. Rather, his is a transcendental ethics in so far as it is interested in how ethics happens, or, more precisely, in the type of experience that would be characterized as ethical. Calling Levinas's ethics transcendental means that he is interested in the conditions which make ethical behaviour possible. Transcendental must always be distinguished from transcendent which refers to a metaphysical beyond, such as God. By focusing on this specific ethical experience, Levinas shows his allegiance to **phenomenology**. According to the early Levinas, the ethical experience takes place in the face of the **other** in which the other transcends (goes beyond) the image that I behold of him or her. In the classical phenomenological sense, it is thus not correct to speak of an experience, since experience always implies the possibility of translating the other into an object of thought. In Levinas, the other radically interrupts and remains outside the realm of objectification. In fact, the other inverts the process of intentionality (the process of intending the other as identifiable other), placing the subject in the object position and also, as Levinas says, under accusation. The encounter between subject and other does not lead to a dialogue but, first of all, to an asymmetrical constellation in which the other speaks to the subject from a height. Initially there is thus no reciprocity but a priority accorded to the other. In this encounter, the I becomes truly self-reflexive in so far as it is put into question and asked to legitimize its own existence. Although Levinas does not say it like this, the anarchical encounter with the other – anarchical because there are no rules which would stipulate how I ought to engage either with him or her or with myself – provides the possibility of re-evaluating and reinventing existing moral laws. The ethical encounter with the other is consequently the transcendental (underlying, constituting) condition for morality and, ultimately, justice. [RS]

See also Chapter 7.

Further reading

Davis, Colin (1996) *Levinas: An Introduction*, Cambridge: Polity Press.

Eaglestone, Robert (1997) *Ethical Criticism: Reading After Levinas*, Edinburgh: Edinburgh University Press.

Levinas, Emmanuel (1996) *Basic Philosophical Writings*, ed. Adriaan Peperzak, Simon Critchley and Robert Bernasconi, Bloomington, IN: Indiana University Press.

LÉVI-STRAUSS, CLAUDE (1908–) One of the most prominent exponents of structuralism, his work in the field of anthropology continued the project begun by Ferdinand de **Saussure** on the structural principles of language and took the analysis implied there to the study of culture as a whole. In one of his most prominent works, *Structural Anthropology* (1963) Lévi-Strauss redefines the study of anthropology as the study of structural relationships and argues for an understanding of 'man' and society as effects of the logic of the systems that sustain them. Focusing on analysis of customs, institutions and accepted patterns of behaviour, Lévi-Strauss moved Saussure's study of language into a realm where a general theory of communication could be seen to inform all cultural practices as well as the structural relationships through which they were made to circulate. During the course of his career at the Collège de France, Lévi-Strauss published a number of studies on the basis of his framework for anthropology, which have now become instituted in the **canon** of anthropological study. Of these, *Myth and Meaning* (1978), *The Savage Mind* (1962), *The Elementary Structure of Kinship* (1949) and *The Raw and the Cooked* (1962) are perhaps the most widely read. [KMc]

See also Chapters 1 and 4.

Further reading

Leach, Edmund (1974) *Levi-Strauss*, London: Fontana.

Lévi-Strauss, (1963) *Structural Anthropology*, trans. Claire Jacobson and Brooker Grundfast Schoepf, New York: Basic Books.

LOGOCENTRISM A term emerging from the deconstructive philosophy of Jacques **Derrida**, it is derived from the Greek *logos*, meaning 'word' (but also sometimes 'thought' or 'reason').

Derrida attacks what he identifies as the logocentrism of Western philosophy: its search for a foundation to all knowledge in a logic or reason or truth which is self-evident and self-confirming. In particular he criticizes the emphasis on presence within Western philosophy: for example, the belief in self-presence as the essence of being and the foundation of knowledge; the argued transparency or presence to mind of a meaning, intention or idea; and the alleged immediacy of the voice. This last example of logocentric thinking, according to Derrida, results in phonocentrism: the privileging of speech over writing, which is seen as secondary, merely the representation of speech and thought. In *Of Grammatology* (1997) and elsewhere, Derrida tackles this phonocentrism, opposing to it his own 'graphocentrism' and desire for a 'science of writing' which figures writing as originating rather than merely representing meaning, as primary rather than secondary. This 'primary writing' is not, however, present and transparent to itself in the way that speech has traditionally been figured as being, but is a product of **difference** and the **trace**.

Derrida also sets out to reveal the dependence of presence upon its opposite, absence, in this way demonstrating that there is no such thing as pure presence or an absolute origin or foundation. So anything which is brought forward as an example of pure presence or meaning-in-itself can be revealed to be a product or effect of something else, or to owe its meaning to its relation with some other (absent) word or thing.

Feminist critics such as Hélène **Cixous** have put their own slant upon this Derridean idea of logocentrism by attacking what they regard as the **phallogocentrism** of Western culture – so they are interpreting the focus on reason, logic and presence which Derrida has identified as a peculiarly masculinist obsession and one designed to perpetuate **patriarchal** dominance. [KM]

See also Chapter 7.

Further reading

Cixous, Hélène and Catherine Clément (1986) *The Newly Born Woman*, trans. Betsy Wing, Minneapolis, MN: University of Minnesota Press.

Derrida, Jacques (1997) *Of Grammatology*, trans. Gayatri Chakravorty Spivak, Baltimore, MD: Johns Hopkins University Press.

LUKÁCS, GEORG (1885–1971) Hungarian philosopher and aesthetician, best known for his development of **Marxist** literary and cultural theory. An advocate of the **realist** novel, Lukács' theories are most clearly set out in *The Historical Novel* (1937) and *History and Class Consciousness* (1923)

Throughout the 1930s, Lukács participated in a series of debates about the politics of aesthetics with other Marxist thinkers such as Theodor **Adorno**, Walter **Benjamin**, and Bertolt Brecht (collected as *Aesthetics and Politics,* 1980). Lukács supported the realist position, questioning the political value of the obscure and fragmentary forms of expressionism and high **modernism**, which he regarded as symptoms of 'reification', the alienation that comes with living under the capitalism. Realist literature, on the other hand, provides a 'totality', a total world-view, which gives an insight into the historical forces that contribute to the shaping of that world – a vision denied the reader by the obscuring structure of modernism.

It is this account of the development of realism as a genre in which the 'total world-view' is presented that Lukács develops in *The Historical Novel*, in which he argues that the realist novels of the nineteenth century operate as literary illustrations of the ideology of European bourgeois as they overturned the feudal aristocratic order and emerged as the new ruling class.

Lukács' theories regarding realism and reification continue to be influential in contemporary critical theory. His influence is clear in both the work of the German defender of modernity Jürgen **Habermas** and American postmodern critic Fredric **Jameson**. [TES]

See also Chapter 3.

Further reading

Lukács, Georg (1974) *The Theory of the Novel*, trans. Anna Bostock, Cambridge, MA: MIT Press.

Lukács, Georg (1983) *The Historical Novel*, trans. Hannah Mitchell and Stanley Mitchell, Lincoln, NE: University of Nebraska Press.

LYOTARD, JEAN-FRANÇOIS (1925–98) French political philosopher and cultural critic who is best known as one of the key proponents of postmodernism. As a young and radical **Marxist**, Lyotard became involved in the struggle for independence in the French colony of Algeria while working there as a teacher during the 1950s. His experiences here and during the student uprisings of May 1968 led him to turn his back on traditional politics and launch a series of critiques of the ideas of his former comrades. These culminated in the publication of *Libidinal Economy* (1974), which violently synthesizes the ideas of Marx and **Freud** to explore ways in which theories that attempt to provide universal catch-all accounts of the world necessarily fail to grasp the complexities of particular situations and can serve to undermine the potential for resistance or transformation. This analysis of the problems of universality is modified and extended in his best-known book, *The Postmodern Condition: A Report on Knowledge* (1979; trans. 1984), in which he defines the postmodern as an 'incredulity toward **metanarratives**' (Lyotard 1984: xxiv), and argues that the totalizing structures that underpinned **modernity** no longer provide a basis for critique or action in the contemporary postmodern world. Instead, interventions must be local and provisional, and can no longer justify themselves on the basis of universal theories.

In his later postmodern work, Lyotard turns to the philosophy of Immanuel Kant, and particularly his theory of the **sublime**, to continue to challenge those structures that pretend to present universal positions. According to Lyotard, the sublime presents 'the fact that the unpresentable exists' (Lyotard 1984: 78). Or, in other words, it indicates that there are things that are impossible to present in established languages, voices that have been silenced, or ideas that cannot be formulated.

The political potential of this postmodern sublime is explored in one of his most important books, *The Differend: Phrases in Dispute*, which was first published in French in 1983. Here, Lyotard develops the idea that experience is constructed through a range of competing **genres** of **discourse** that organize knowledge and identity in relation to particular ends. He argues that these genres permit certain types of phrasing but prohibit others, thereby erecting value systems that always have the potential to exclude or silence particular groups or interests. What he calls a **differend** occurs when a genre of discourse prevents the possibility of testifying to an idea or experience, and the role of the thinker, he argues, is to expose those moments where ideas or people are silenced and to develop new genres where they can appear.

Lyotard's most recent writings continue to work through these problems, focusing on the potentialities of postmodernism, the impact of art on culture and the problems of contemporary capitalism and technological development. [SM]

See also Chapter 10.

Further reading

Lyotard, Jean-François (1984) *The Postmodern Condition: A Report on Knowledge*, trans. Geoff Bennington and Brian Massumi, Manchester: Manchester University Press.

Lyotard, Jean-François (1988) *The Differend: Phrases in Dispute*, trans. Georges Van Den Abbeele, Manchester: Manchester University Press.

Malpas, Simon (2003) *Jean-François Lyotard*, London: Routledge.

M

MACHEREY, PIERRE (1938–) French **Marxist** literary theorist and philosopher. Macherey's major work of 1966 was translated into English in 1978 as *A Theory of Literary Production*. He is also the author of *The Object of Literature* (1990) and studies of Hegel and Spinoza.

A Theory of Literary Production explores the relationship between literature and **ideology**. It is primarily concerned with the process of literary construction and production. Macherey argues that traditional critical discourses, which attempt either to render the text explicit or locate its 'truth', are inadequate. He proposes a new way of reading, one which draws attention to the contradictions, gaps, absences and silences which constitute the text. The unspoken – what Macherey calls the '**unconscious**' of the text (which is not, crucially, the same as the **author**'s unconscious) – is central to his theory. For Macherey, 'What is important in the work is what it does not say.'

Macherey's work has proved to be a major contribution to the development of critical theory. The notion that the 'speech of a book comes from a certain silence' offered a radical new perspective on the complex relationship between texts, ideology and the act of reading. [SP and CHC]

See also Chapter 3.

Further reading

Macherey, Pierre (1978) *A Theory of Literary Production*, trans. Geoffrey Wall, London: Routledge.

MARCUSE, HERBERT (1898–1979) German social theorist known for his **Freudian-** **Marxist** analysis of capitalist society. After working with philosopher Martin **Heidegger**, in 1933 he began working at the **Frankfurt School**, which relocated to America during the Second World War. Unlike other members, he remained there and came to prominence in the 1960s.

Marcuse considered Marxist orthodoxy static and unable to accommodate the needs of the individual. This prompted him, in *Eros and Civilisation* (1955), to apply Freudian psychoanalysis to Marxist political philosophy. Marcuse's desire to emancipate individuals from the homogeneous capitalist system led to his adoption by 1960s radicals. In *One Dimensional Man* (1964) Marcuse continued this approach, discussing the possibility of reconciling rationality with spontaneity. He suggested that the revolutionary potential of the proletariat has been nullified by their integration into a cohesive social system, and argued that only marginalized groups, for example African-Americans, can affect the system, as they cannot be 'deflected' by that system.

Despite his political passion, Marcuse was pessimistic about the potential of actual social renewal. However, his work remains central to considerations of the **subject**'s role in oppressive societies. [RW]

See also Chapter 3.

Further reading

Kellner, Douglas (1984) *Herbert Marcuse and the Crisis of Marxism*, Berkeley, CA: University of California Press.

MARX, KARL (1818–83) German philosopher and political theorist whose work explored politics, economics and class. As a political activist involved in many of the communist movements of his time, Marx was exiled from a number of European countries, ending up in Britain where he was able to produce a substantial body of extremely influential work ranging from the complex economic theories of *Capital* (1867–94) to the revolutionary and accessible pamphlet *The Communist Manifesto* (1848), co-written with Friedrich **Engels**. Marx's **materialist** philosophy sets out from the premise that 'it is not the consciousness of men that determines their being, but, on the contrary, their social being that determines consciousness' (2000: 425). In other words, the fundamental principle of his work is that human identities, ideas and aspirations are produced by the material economic and social conditions in which they exist. On this basis, his writings investigate the processes by which capitalism produces social conditions in which one class, the bourgeoisie, dominates and exploits another, the proletariat, and explore the means by which such exploitation can be eliminated. [SM]

See also Chapter 3.

Further reading

Marx, Karl (2000) *Selected Writings*, 2nd edition, ed. David McLellan, Oxford: Oxford University Press.

Marx, Karl and Engels, Friedrich (1967) *The Communist Manifesto*, Harmondsworth: Penguin.

MATERIALISM   Denotes the belief that the principal element of all things is matter, or the physical. In this it is opposed to idealism, which accords primacy to ideas, or the spiritual.

The most important modern materialist thinker is Karl **Marx**. Marx's application of materialist philosophy to the study of human history is called 'historical materialism' (Marx's collaborator Friedrich **Engels** preferred the term '**dialectical** material-

ism'). The central contention of historical materialism is that economic activity, society's '**base**', is the primary factor in determining other cultural activity, the 'superstructure'.

In one interpretation of materialist philosophy, known variously as determinism, economism, and 'vulgar' or mechanical materialism, economic activity is not just the primary but the sole determining factor. Though this reductive reading of Marx became dominant in the early twentieth-century Communist Party, subsequent theorists have attempted to refine the base/superstructure formulation.

Cultural materialism, developed by Welsh critic Raymond **Williams**, sees cultural phenomena such as literary works as inseparable from, but not determined by, the contexts in which they are produced and consumed. This is the most influential current of materialist thought in contemporary cultural studies. [CRC]

See also Chapter 3.

Further reading

Williams, Raymond (1977) *Marxism and Literature*, Oxford: Oxford University Press.

MCLUHAN, HERBERT MARSHALL (1911–80) Pioneer of mass-media criticism who coined the terms 'global village' and 'the medium is the message'.

His first book, *The Mechanical Bride: Folklore of Industrial Man* demonstrates his concern to 'enlighten the prey' of the mass media against complacency. Published in 1951, some six years before Roland **Barthes**' *Mythologies*, *The Mechanical Bride* consists of 59 short analyses of everyday printed media. Like Barthes, McLuhan critiques the image's use of **myth** to strengthen the dominant **ideology** and its prevention of independent thought.

In *The Medium is the Massage* (1967), McLuhan's focus shifts slightly to demonstrate how the media shape and influence society. Using analogous illustration, he argues that the railway, not the freight it carries, has the greater impact upon civilization. Hence, it is not the content of the media that *massages* society so much as the media per se.

The Global Village: Transformations in World Life and Media in the Twenty-First Century (1989) is regarded by many as McLuhan's most important contribution to criticism. Acknowledging the impact of worldwide communications and the planet's shrinkage to a 'global village', McLuhan details how 'global robotism' is creating increasingly homogenized societies. Whilst slightly overreaching in the extent of its claims, this area of McLuhan's work is still of crucial significance within contemporary critical theory and provides a sound starting-point for further studies. As technologies such as the internet grow in popularity and influence, one can appreciate McLuhan's foresight in identifying the modern global media with their erosion of cultural and geographical borders as influential 'shapers' of society. [PSW]

See also Chapter 10.

Further reading

McLuhan, Herbert Marshall and Powers, Bruce R. (eds) (1989) *The Global Village: Transformations in World Life and Media in the Twenty-First Century*, Oxford: Oxford University Press.

MERLEAU-PONTY, MAURICE (1908–61) Along with Jean-Paul Sartre, the foremost French exponent of **phenomenology**, and one of those most responsible for introducing it into France. Merleau-Ponty's work explores the question of what it means to be embodied. Refusing the common philosophical distinction between the immaterial soul and the materiality of the physical body, he argues that consciousness is not something that simply goes on in our minds, but is experienced in and through our bodies, their interactions with our thoughts and with the world: 'Bodily experience forces us to acknowledge an imposition of meaning which is not the work of a universal constituting consciousness ... My body is that meaningful core' (Merleau-Ponty 2004: 124). For Merleau-Ponty, the exploration of 'lived' bodily perceptions must be the starting place for thought, and this in turn calls for a reconception of what is meant by thought itself. The influence of Merleau-Ponty's work can be traced in theorists as diverse as Michel **Foucault**, Jacques **Derrida** and Jacques **Lacan**. [SM]

Further reading

Merleau-Ponty, Maurice (1962) *Phenomenology of Perception*, trans. Colin Smith, London: Routledge.

Merleau-Ponty, Maurice (2004) *Basic Writings*, ed. Thomas Baldwin, London: Routledge.

METALANGUAGE A concept that has been present in Western thought since the pre-Socratics, but was of particular concern to structuralism and the work of, amongst others, Roman **Jakobson**. In linguistics it is used to describe the way in which one language talks about another language (the object-language). For example, the object-language may be a literary text and the metalanguage a commentary on it. Within the domain of critical theory the term was popularized in 1974 in the film journal *Screen* by Colin MacCabe. His *Realism and the Cinema* begins by describing the way in which the nineteenth-century classical-**realist** novel organizes its **discourse** with regards to the metalanguage and 'truth'.

The classical-realist novel presents the reader with a hierarchy of discourses. For instance, characters speak and their speech is presented to the reader within inverted commas:

'I will serve you selflessly'

This speech is then commented upon by a narrative prose:

'I will serve you selflessly' said Nathanial, in order to ingratiate himself with Simone's inheritance.

However, this narrative prose (meta-language) tends towards, as MacCabe puts it, the 'unwritten'. It simply presents the 'truth' about what has been spoken. However, a critical reader will see this hierarchy in the novel as a ruse, the metalanguage an instance of **ideology**. The point for MacCabe is that in realist cinema this ruse is much harder to detect, as the meta-language is the camera shots and the editing, which ideally attempt to be invisible.

The psychoanalysis of Jacques **Lacan** and the deconstruction of Jacques **Derrida**, however, deny there can ever be a meta-language. Lacan says that a **signifier** simply leads on to another signifier, endlessly deferring meaning, while Derrida argues that there can be nothing outside the text. [DD]

See also Chapters 4 and 10.

Further reading

Derrida, Jacques (1997) *Of Grammatology*, trans. Gayatri Chakravorty Spivak, Baltimore, MD: Johns Hopkins University Press.

Lacan, Jacques (1989) *Écrits: A Selection*, trans. Alan Sheridan, London: Routledge.

MacCabe, Colin (1985) 'Realism and the Cinema: Notes on some Brechtian Thesis', in *Theoretical Essays*, Manchester: Manchester University Press.

METANARRATIVE This term is used in two distinct ways. In narratology it was coined by Gérard **Genette** in his highly influential *Narrative Discourse* to refer to embedded narratives, i.e. to stories within stories. These embedded narratives often form the main part of the text but are framed by another story (known as a frame narrative). Well-known examples of the use of meta-narrative as a structuring device include Geoffrey Chaucer's *The Canterbury Tales* where each tale is a metanarrative within the frame narrative of the pilgrims' journey

to Canterbury; Henry James' *The Turn of the Screw* where acquaintances are gathered together for Christmas and are told the story that becomes the longer metanarrative; Joseph Conrad's *Heart of Darkness* where the narrator Marlow and his fellow sailors are reciting tales to pass the time and Marlow recounts the story of his search for Kurtz which again forms a much longer narrative.

'Metanarrative' is used in a different way by the French critic Jean-François **Lyotard** in *The Postmodern Condition*. He characterizes postmodernism as 'an incredulity towards metanarratives' (Lyotard 1984: xxiv), by which he means that it challenges and interrogates the dominant 'stories' (or totalizing **discourses**) that are used to uphold Western **modernity**. Such 'stories' are those that seek to provide a 'total' or overarching explanation for the way things are, and include Christianity, liberal humanism and **Marxism**. Lyotard argues that these metanarratives are deceptive in that they restrict heterogeneity, and that postmodern criticism should actively refuse the homogenization they impose upon language and identity. [GC]

See also Chapters 4 and 10.

Further reading

Genette, Gérard (1980) *Narrative Discourse*, trans. Jane E. Lewin, Oxford: Blackwell.

Lyotard, Jean-François (1984) *The Postmodern Condition: A Report on Knowledge*, trans. Geoff Bennington and Brian Massumi, Manchester: Manchester University Press.

METAPHYSICS A branch of philosophical enquiry which is primarily concerned with first principles, in particular those concerning the question of existence. Metaphysics represents a search for foundations and origins within philosophy. It centres on the question of 'what is' and seeks to discover an encompassing solution to the problem of the nature of existence. In this sense it has much in common with the notion of ontology, a philosophical system that is also concerned with existence (Being) and what exists (beings).

Metaphysics therefore claims that reality has its own independence, separate from our consciousness. In other words, everything that is to be found in nature already has a pre-given existence. Metaphysical philosophy attempts to explain all that is to be found in nature within one broad theory of reality.

Metaphysical questions have been crucial aspects of philosophy since the time of Aristotle. However, the twentieth century has witnessed sustained attacks on the principles of metaphysics. The philosophy of Martin **Heidegger** attempted the so-called 'destruction' of metaphysics, whilst the rise of poststructuralism and postmodernism resulted in scepticism concerning totalizing philosophies of origins and foundations. The strategies of Jacques **Derrida**, for example, have attempted a radical undermining of metaphysical principles in order to question such notions of origins and foundations. [JS]

See also Chapter 7.

Further reading

Kim, Jaegwon and Sosa, Ernest (eds) (1996) *A Companion to Metaphysics*, Oxford: Blackwell.

Van Inwagen, Peter and Zimmerman, Dean W. (eds) (1998) *Metaphysics: The Big Questions*, Oxford: Blackwell.

MILLER, J. HILLIS (1928–) American literary theorist, originally influenced by the Geneva School and then closely associated with the Yale School of deconstruction. His main works include, *Theory Now and Then*, *Ariadne's Thread* and *Topographies*.

Miller's work has been significantly influenced by European philosophy and literature. In particular, his writing has focused on exploring how deconstructive strategies can be seen at work within literary texts. According to Miller, deconstruction is not simply a method that one applies to a text, but is rather always already inherent within the text. The task of the literary critic is therefore to identify the deconstructive movements already at work and to analyse how they contribute to an understanding of the ways in which the text literally deconstructs itself. Miller regards this as nothing more or less than simply 'good reading'. To this end, he has much in common with Paul **De Man**, who was also closely involved with the Yale School.

Arguably Miller's main contribution to literary theory has been his sustained attempt to move theory towards an amalgamation of Anglo-American and European philosophy. In particular, the work of the Yale School has been instrumental in developing a method that draws upon the work of Jacques **Derrida** and utilizes it for literary studies. [JS]

See also Chapter 7.

Further reading

Miller, J. Hillis (1990) *Theory Now and Then*, Hemel Hempstead: Harvester Wheatsheaf.

Miller, J. Hillis (1994) *Topographies*, Palo Alto, CA: Stanford University Press.

MILLETT, KATE (1943–) Millett's *Sexual Politics* (1969) became a key text of second-wave feminism and made a significant contribution to the development of both feminist criticism and feminist literary theory. Millett defines politics as the means by which certain groups exert **power** and control over others and argues that 'sexual politics' are strengthened and reproduced by the workings of **patriarchy**. She presents a critique of how patriarchy works to 'naturalize' the power imbalance between women and men by its insistence upon biological **difference** and identifies marriage and the family structure as a key way in which these 'differences' are reinforced. Millett promotes the idea of a 'sexual revolution' that will overturn patriarchy and its means of replication, and, on this basis, is particularly critical of **Freud**'s role in the reinforcement of biological determinism: the idea that gender identity, as well as identities of race and sexuality, is defined by the biological rather than cultural differences.

As a literary critic, Millett is also concerned with the textual reinforcement of patriarchal **discourse**, and much of her discussion is devoted to literary analysis. She insists upon a way of reading that rejects the authority of the (male) **author** in the creation of meaning and allows the reader agency to resist and challenge the patriarchal assumptions of the text. This idea of resisting the text has become significant in feminist literary theory, but Millett has been criticized for her lack of reference to earlier feminists and her focus upon male authors. Despite accusations of oversimplification and reductionism (particularly in her analysis of Freud) *Sexual Politics* is still considered a ground-breaking text and Millett a significant critic.

Millett's ensuing work is eclectic and includes *The Prostitution Papers* (1973), a series of interviews with prostitutes, and *The Loony Bin Trip* (1990), the story of her own breakdown and institutionalization. [GC]

See also Chapters 8 and 9.

Further reading

Millett, Kate (1979) *Sexual Politics*, London: Virago.

Moi, Toril (1985) *Sexual/Textual Politics: Feminist Literary Theory*, London: Routledge.

MIMESIS A concept originally developed by Aristotle within the context of theatrical tragedy, mimesis is essentially concerned with how art imitates **reality**. Such imitation involves the display or presentation of action rather than the imaginative concept of action, which is termed diegesis. In other words, to imitate an action and present it as real is mimetic, whereas the imagination of an action is diegetic.

According to Aristotle, mimesis involves the representation of reality, in particular with regards to human emotions rather than human intellect. Aristotle was particularly concerned with how the concept of mimesis functions in tragedy and sought to show how drama was an imitation of reality.

Mimesis is the subject of a comprehensive study by Erich Auerbach, which is primarily concerned with how reality is imitated in Western literature. Despite being 50 years old, this work remains one of the most important studies written on mimesis. [JS]

See also Chapters 1, 2 and 4.

Further reading

Auerbach, Erich (1953) *Mimesis: The Representation of Reality in Western Literature*, Princeton, NJ: Princeton University Press.

Gebauer, Gunter and Wulf, Christoph (1995) *Mimesis: Culture, Art, Society*, trans. Don Reneau, Berkeley, CA: University of California Press.

MINH-HA, TRINH T. (1953–) Theorist, writer, composer and film-maker who has made important contributions to feminist and postcolonial theory by challenging the definition of overarching categories, such as woman, artist and Third World. Her writing on postcolonial theory and gender includes *Woman, Native, Other* (1989), *When the Moon Waxes Red* (1991) and *Framer Framed* (1992).

Minh-ha's work is important because it theorizes what became known in the 1980s as 'double colonization': the idea that women in formerly colonized societies were subjugated by both imperial and **patriarchal ideologies**. Minh-ha grapples with the difficulties of such a position, complicating both feminist and post-colonial perspectives in the process.

In *Woman, Native, Other*, she draws on the feminist Audre Lorde's work to raise questions about the effectiveness of using the masters' tools to dismantle his house. Minh-ha refuses to be defined or circumscribed by the essentialisms of race, gender and ethnicity, seeing these positions as consolidating the master's definition of the world. Politically strategic as they may at first appear, such terms limit, even police, the borders of individual identity. One way in which Minh-ha attempts to escape categorization is through linguistic and generic experimentation. Viewing expressions of authenticity as a political trap, she unsettles such ideas by resisting closure and insisting that identity is always complex and multiple. [RF]

See also Chapter 11.

Further reading

Minh-ha, Trinh T. (1989) *Woman, Native, Other: Postcoloniality and Feminism*, Bloomington, IN: Indiana University Press.
Minh-ha, Trinh T. (1991) *When the Moon Waxes Red*, London: Routledge.

MIRROR STAGE Concept associated with the French psychoanalyst Jacques **Lacan**, which provides an account of the **imaginary** component of **subjectivity**. It is concerned with the beginning of subjectivity, the moment at which the child first misrecognizes itself as the image in the mirror, and the subsequent way in which this misrecognition is negotiated. The child, typically between the ages of 9 and 12 months 'still sunk in his motor incapacity and nursling dependence' (Lacan 1977: 2), is lured into an identification with a unified bodily image. It is at this moment that the child, previously an uncoordinated assemblage of limbs and organs, is compelled to conceive itself as a unified being. However, the primal unity that the mirror stage theory elucidates is the product of a split

between the viewer and the reflected image. The foundational moment of human subjectivity is, for Lacan, a precarious negotiation of this necessary division between spectator and image. The identification with the image is what provides the subject with the minimal coordinates of a unified identity, but this unity is founded upon a primary division of which, crucially, the subject is aware. Consequently, the moment at which the mirror stage bestows a concept of the self as a unified and autonomous subject, it also threatens to undercut this achievement via the uncomfortable awareness that such autonomy is illusory: that it is premised upon an act of identification with something external to the core of the self, namely the image. Lacan's theory of the mirror stage has been influential, in that the continual renegotiation of the boundaries of the subject and the **unconscious** symptoms of the division between spectator and image can provide an account of the problematic and unstable nature of identity that has applications in fields as diverse as political theory and the study of literature and art. [HJ]

See also Chapter 6.

Further reading

Lacan, Jacques (1977) *Écrits: A Selection*, trans. Alan Sheridan, London: Routledge.

MODERN / MODERNISM / MODERNITY
Modern (from the Latin *modus* meaning 'just now') refers to the new, the recent and the up-to-date. For critical theory, the modern is often linked either to modernism or modernity.

The term 'modernism' tends to be used to refer to those artistic and cultural movements that began in the late nineteenth century and sought to break with traditional modes of artistic production, experimenting with new forms and genres in order both to challenge its audience and to better explore the increasingly technologically framed experience of life. So, for example, literary writers such as Charles Baudelaire, T. S. Eliot and Virginia Woolf, artistic movements such as cubism and surrealism, and architects including Le Corbusier and Frank Lloyd Wright, have all been identified as modernists because of the ways in which they rejected traditional models of writing, painting or designing and sought to develop new theories and practices for the twentieth century.

If modernism tends to be seen as an artistic or cultural phenomenon, modernity is more concerned with science, philosophy and social organization. It also tends to encompass a much longer period. Different critics have located the origins of modernity in a range of periods, including the fifteenth century, the English Renaissance, the **Enlightenment**, the end of the eighteenth century, or even as early as the fourth century. Whichever one of these alternatives is chosen, modernity is almost always identified as a break from a pre-modern form of society based on **mythological** or metaphysical sets of beliefs, and an entry into history as change and transformation become central aspects of day-to-day experience. As Fredric **Jameson** argues, though, 'Modernity is not a concept but rather a narrative category' (2002b: 94). In other words, it is a means by which a society or culture links together the events, people and ideas from its past so as to conceive of itself as breaking from that past and progressing towards a more rational and just future. For postmodern theorists such as Jean-François **Lyotard** modernity is thus the epoch of the **grand narrative** that is coming to be challenged by the postmodern, whereas defenders of modernity like Jürgen **Habermas** see it as an 'unfinished project' that should be sustained. [SM]

See also Chapters 3, 5 and 10.

Further reading

Habermas, Jürgen (1987) *The Philosophical Discourse of Modernity: Twelve Lectures*, trans. Frederick Lawrence, London: Polity Press.

Jameson, Fredric (2002b) *A Singular Modernity: Essay on the Ontology of the Present*, London: Verso.

MYTH According to Roland **Barthes**, myth is both a type of speech and a semiological system. Its **genealogy** replaced with a façade of unmediated origin, mythical discourse is firmly situated within the realms of **ideology**. For Barthes everything man-made or articulated through **discourse** can become mythical. In *Mythologies* (first published 1957) he illustrates the value in 'demystifying' the seemingly innocuous **signs** that often pass unnoticed, where the 'ideological is read as the factual'. He argues that through their amalgamation into cultural events as diverse as advertising and wrestling, ideological values are extensively peddled within and accepted by society. Myth's **power** derives from its ability to escape extensive interrogation *because* of its familiarity. [PSW]

Further reading

Barthes, Roland (1993) *Mythologies*, trans. Annette Lavers, London: Vintage.

N

NEGATIVE DIALECTICS A method of critical analysis developed by German theoretician Theodor W. **Adorno** in order to decode the expanding world of multinational capitalism. Along with his colleague Max **Horkheimer**, Adorno produced a critique of reason in *The Dialectic of Enlightenment* (first published 1947), drawing both on their experience of German fascism and American commodity capitalism. The mode of thought seen in embryonic form in this book is further developed in Adorno's posthumously published *Negative Dialectics* (1970).

Adorno attempted to bridge the gap between aesthetics and deterministic **Marxist** thinking by harnessing the work of the influential cultural theorist Walter **Benjamin**, after working with him at the **Frankfurt School**. Drawing on Karl **Marx**'s **materialist** adaptation of Hegel's **dialectic**, Adorno sought to develop dialectical analysis for the demands of the unregulated growth of global capitalism. Essentially his method works backwards through the dialectical process of synthesis, attempting to unearth the contradiction at the core of dialectical production. He set out to detail the tools and methodologies necessary for interrogating the authoritarian ideologies that had been crucial not only for instigating conflict but for resisting cultural change (for example, nationalist rejections of anything alien or other). These tools included the 'dialectics of disassembly', a demystifying procedure that traces the patterns of history behind superficial cultural phenomena, and the concept of non-identity, the shadow of what identity excludes in its formative process. Adorno used these strategies to critique the capitalist exchange values that artificially organize and configure identity.

Adorno's technique remains central to the practice of modern philosophy and cultural theory. His work opened the way for analyses of **globalization**, neoliberalization and consumerization, and brings to bear a heavy influence on the work of contemporary critics of capitalism such as Fredric **Jameson** and Pierre **Bourdieu**. [RW]

See also Chapter 3.

Further reading

Buck-Morss, Susan (1977) *The Origin of Negative Dialectics: Theodor W. Adorno, Walter Benjamin and the Frankfurt Institute*, New York: Harvester.

NEW CRITICISM Anglo-American school of literary criticism which held sway from the 1930s until well into the 1950s, although its influence extends beyond this period.

A type of formalist criticism, New Criticism focused predominantly upon 'the text itself', seeing it as a kind of organic unity and, importantly, as a public object, whose meaning was in principle determinable. With their articles on 'The Intentional Fallacy' (1946) and 'The Affective Fallacy' (1949), W. K. Wimsatt and Monroe Beardsley disputed the critical relevance of attention to either the **authorial** intention motivating a work or the emotional responses of readers. Similarly, the New Critics held that the historical context in which a work was created was significant only in giving clues to particularities of linguistic usage in that work; in general, their doctrine is one of semantic autonomy – the suggestion being that the proper task of the literary critic is to attend to the text, not to matters of history, psychology, autobiography or philology. Thus, New Criticism did much to set the parameters of the relatively new discipline of English literary studies.

The New Critical method of close reading, which owed something to I. A. **Richards**' 'practical criticism', quickly became established pedagogical practice in American and British universities, and was only really challenged by the emergence of structuralism in the late 1950s. The New Critics tended to concentrate on poetry, particularly lyric poetry, seeing the poem as, in Wimsatt's phrase, a 'verbal icon' and attending to the presence of ambiguity, irony and paradox: moments where tensions and oppositions were resolved for the coherence of the 'whole'.

In recent years, links have been traced between this influential literary critical school and subsequent theories such as deconstruction. [KM]

See also Chapter 5.

Further reading

Brooks, Cleanth (1968) *The Well Wrought Urn: Studies in the Structure of Poetry*, London: Dobson.

Lentricchia, Frank (1980) *After the New Criticism*, Chicago, IL: University of Chicago Press.

Wimsatt, William Kurtz (1970) *The Verbal Icon: Studies in the Meaning of Poetry*, London: Methuen.

NGŪGĪ WA THIONG'O (1938–) Kenyan novelist, playwright and critic best known for his intervention in the debate about the use of English in postcolonial African literature. His novels include *Weep Not, Child* (1964), *The River Between* (1965), *A Grain of Wheat* (1967), *Petals of Blood* (1977) and *Matigari* (1989). He is also the author of several critical works, including *Decolonising the Mind* (1986), which explains his decision to abandon writing in English in favour of his mother tongue, Gīyūkū.

Ngūgī is centrally concerned with the cultural effects of colonization. Arguing that imperialism is still the root cause of many problems in Africa, he challenges the 'mental colonization' achieved through colonial and neo-colonial education. Claiming that the denigration of African languages is detrimental to African culture and individual self-worth, Ngūgī sees choice of language as central to a people's self-definition. This underlies both his decision to write in Gīyūkū and his commitment to community-based theatre projects. An active campaigner for the African language, Ngūgī was imprisoned by the Kenyan government without trial in 1977 after successfully staging his Gīyūkū play *Ngaahika Ndeenda* (*I Will Marry When I Want* (1980)). He has lived in exile since the publication of his prison memoirs *Detained: A Prison Diary* (1981). [RF]

See also Chapter 11.

Further reading

Cook, David and Okenimkpe, Michael (1983) *Ngūgī wa Thiong'o: An Exploration of His Writings*, Oxford: Heinemann.

Ngūgī wa Thiong'o (1986) *Decolonising the Mind: The Politics of Language in African Literature*, Portsmouth, NH: Heinemann.

NIETZSCHE, FRIEDRICH (1844–1900) German philosopher widely acknowledged as a forerunner of existentialism and poststructuralism. Influenced by the philosopher Arthur Schopenhauer (1788–1860), Nietzsche sought to recuperate individual existence and condemned traditional, oppressive structures.

Nietzsche is perhaps most famous for his trenchant critique of the Judaeo-Christian tradition. He contended that religious practice was part of a 'slave morality' instituted by the weak. This culminated in his famous proclamation that 'God is dead.' Countering the dogmatic accept-ance of pity and sympathy espoused by pious society, he argued that the **power** instinct or 'will to power' is necessary for humans to liberate themselves from the mundane. This results in the *Übermensch*, or Superman, who eschews promises of immortality, embracing independence in order to be responsible for his own morality. He embodies the 'will to power', harnessing his creative energy by relishing organic, vital existence. He would create a 'master morality' where individuals reject oppression in favour of autonomy.

His legacy is notable in the works of late twentieth-century theorists concerned with socio-cultural systems that inhibit the formation of identity, such as Gilles **Deleuze**, Michel **Foucault** and Jacques **Derrida**. The notion of moral relativity central to postmodernism is also indebted to Nietzsche's disregard for accepted organizing principles such as religion, culture and sexuality. [RW]

Further reading

Kaufmann, Walter Arnold (1975) *Nietzsche: Philosopher, Psychologist, Antichrist*, Princeton, NJ: Princeton University Press.

Nietzsche, Friedrich (1977) *The Portable Nietzsche*, trans. Walter Kaufmann, New York: Penguin.

Spinks, Lee (2003) *Friedrich Nietzsche*, New York: Routledge.

NOMADOLOGY This term does not concern actual nomads but the approach to philo-sophy of French poststructuralist thinkers Gilles **Deleuze** and Félix **Guattari**. In *A Thousand Plateaus* (1980; trans. 1987), Deleuze and Guattari use the concept of nomadology to historicize and critique the idea of the state, which they suggest constitutes a static, hierarchical way of thinking that pervades the whole Western tradition. In opposition to the state, nomadology defines a way of thinking that, rather than rooting itself down in defence of one place or perspective, attempts to remain mobile and open to **alterity** and **difference** (see **rhizome**). In this sense it extends German philosopher Friedrich **Nietzsche**'s 'perspectivist' critique of philo-sophy, which argues that meaning and value are dependent on point of view rather than any pre-existing universal order. However, nomadology is by no means an 'anything goes' relativism and is deeply opposed to subjective models of philo-sophical thinking. The concept and differ-ence, rather than the **subject**, orientate nomadic thought, which concerns an impersonal, inhuman world of desire and force. As a radical style of doing philo-sophy, nomadology involves constructing new concepts that multiply difference and variation in thought, rather than searching for one way of thinking that totalizes phenomena or unifies the subject. [DH]

Further reading

Deleuze, Gilles and Guattari, Félix (1988) '1227: Treatise on Nomadology – The War Machine', in *A Thousand Plateaus: Capitalism and Schizophrenia*, trans. Brian Massumi, London: Athlone Press.

O

OEDIPUS COMPLEX A controversial theory advanced by Sigmund **Freud**, for whom the ancient Greek myth of Oedipus held unacknowledged truths about the family unit. In the story, not knowing his real parents, Oedipus kills his father and marries his mother. Horrified when he discovers the truth, he blinds himself.

Freud's *The Interpretation of Dreams* (1900) claimed that the myth confirmed an insight he had gained in his work with children: that a little boy's first sexual wish is directed at his mother, and his first murderous wish is aimed at his father as rival. This 'Oedipus complex' is (usually) resolved because the boy fears as well as hates his father, whom he invests with the power of castration. He internalizes his father's authority which becomes his **superego** or conscience (Oedipus punishes *himself*), represses his original wishes and finds other sexual objects. Pushed into the **unconscious**, the repressed wishes return to disrupt conscious existence in the form of slips of the tongue, double meanings and symptoms. They are also released in dreams, which Freud calls the 'royal road' to the unconscious.

Initially Freud thought that girls desire their fathers and hate their mothers. He later reconsidered: the female infant also finds her first sexual object in her mother, later transferring affection to her father. Freud has attracted feminist criticism for his argument that women are already 'castrated' and therefore never acquire a full superego.

Freud's theory describes civilization beginning when an illegitimate urge is subjected to the rule of law. For Freud's reinterpreter Jacques **Lacan**, this takes the form of internalizing a language, and the name of the Father as symbol of Law, by a **subject** whose **desire** nonetheless persists in the unconscious. We may not want our mothers all our lives, but we never stop wanting something that language cannot give. The Oedipus complex thus generates an account of subjectivity as a site of perpetual conflict between desire and law. [RLS]

See also Chapter 6.

ORIENTALISM This term refers to the ways in which the West has represented, or rather misrepresented, the East throughout history. In his ground-breaking work, *Orientalism* (1978), Edward W. **Said** describes Orientalism as the construction of a 'system of knowledge' about the East by and *for* the West. This knowledge was compiled by a range of European travellers, explorers, colonialists, archivists, writers and novelists over centuries. For major theorists working in the field, Orientalism rests on the idea that, in the process of misrepresentation, the West has fundamentally constructed the East in order to define itself.

European culture plays a significant role in this process. Just as the history of English literature, for example, has always been bound up in defining the concept of nationhood, in representing what it means to be British or rather English, so for commentators such as Said it has defined the Orient (and the rest of the world). In the nineteenth-century English novel, in particular, the East is frequently described as a distinctly different, irrational and '**other**' space to England. The Orient is portrayed as a place of mystery, enchantment, adventure and colour, but also one of sex, sensuality and some danger for Europeans. As Said puts it, 'the Orient was almost a European invention, and had been since antiquity a place of romance, exotic beings, haunting memories and landscapes, remarkable experiences'. He goes on to argue that the West identified itself as the complete antithesis of these representations. The resulting conflict between a familiar, rational Europe, and a strange, irrational Orient is crucial to the development of Western notions about its identity. Said maintains that Orientalism is 'a collective notion identifying "us" Europeans as against all "those" non-Europeans'. It is this tension, he concludes, that underpins the continued sense of opposition between East and West throughout the modern world.

Since Said's intervention, critical theory has increasingly questioned Western assumptions about the East. Orientalism is now also explored as a crucial but complex feature of the relationship between Western culture and imperialism. It has become a key concept in literary, cultural and postcolonial studies. [SP and CHC]

See also Chapter 11

Further reading

Said, Edward W. (2003) *Orientalism: Western Conceptions of the Orient*, London: Penguin.

OTHER A term used widely within critical theory, predominantely in disciplines such as psychoanalysis and postcolonial theory. However, the term also emerges from traditions of philosophy, such as **Levinas**'s **ethical** theory. It must therefore be apparent that 'other' as concept will have a wide variety of applications. Although this is the case, it can be said that the 'other' – either as a human being or an inanimate object – exists in relationship to a **subject** from which it differs.

The theoretical framework that surrounds the use of the term in psychoanalysis is perhaps the most extensive and cohesive in mapping out this specific relationship, though it could be said to have had origins in Alexandre **Kojève**'s work as much as in that of Sigmund **Freud**. Jacques **Lacan** centres this discussion around '*objet petit a*', where the '*a*' is a quasi-algebraic sign indicating '*autre*' (other). This '*objet petit a*' is a concept developed from Freud, and his term 'object', where 'object' is defined as the aim of a subject's **drive**. For instance, the object of the sexual drive in a certain human being at a certain time may be an actor or an actress on the front cover of a glossy magazine, or a part of that body, such as the breast or the torso. Alternatively, the aim of a subject's drive at a particular time may be for an object that is not human: a new house, a new car, a new dress or a new DVD.

In this way '*objet petit a*', in Lacan, emerges from the 'other'. However the term 'other' is in turn divided in meaning, becoming 'other' and 'Other' (the '*Autre*' or '*grand-Autre*'). Lacan makes this distinction in order to indicate a radical differentiation in the relationship of the subject between these two modalities. The small 'other' is used to represent the mapping of the subject's own **desire** onto something or someone else. For example, that boy must be in love with me because I am in love with him. In this way it can be seen that the small 'other' indicates that which is not really 'other'. Indeed, Lacan's privileged example is the **mirror image**, where not only identification occurs, but also alienation, due to the decentring effect of contemplating the otherness of the image of me.

In contrast, the big 'Other' is used to indicate the law, society, religion and other people. Or rather, the law, society, religion and other people encountered symbolically through their effects on me, the subject. In this way, 'I', or 'me' (my identity), is possible only through the symbolic order. If I am born in France of French parents I will tend to grow up French, speaking French. Thus 'I' am not really 'me' at all. My identity is an internalized version of the **symbolic order**, the big 'Other'. It was this line of thought that Louis **Althusser** developed in conjunction with **ideology** (from Karl **Marx**) when he outlined law, society and religion as **Ideological State Apparatuses** and the concept of **interpellation** as the way in which their effects are internalized.

In **postcolonial theory** the term 'other' is more straightforward, but, perhaps because of this, much more politically immediate. It refers, in essence, to the 'other' as produced by discursive practices. This idea of discursive practices structuring the relationship with the other is developed from the work of Michel **Foucault** by Gayatri **Spivak**, Edward **Said** and Trinh T. **Minh-ha** who use the term to capture the way in which the 'truth' about the East (in all its multifarious facets) is produced by the West. [DD]

See also Chapter 11.

Further reading

Lacan, Jacques (1989) *Écrits: A Selection*, trans. Alan Sheridan, London: Routledge.

Said, Edward (2003) *Orientalism: Western Conceptions of the Orient*, London: Penguin.

Spivak, Gayatri Chakravorty (1988a) 'Can the Subaltern Speak?', in Cary Nelson and Lawrence Grossberg (eds), *Marxism and the Interpretation of Culture*, Basingstoke: Macmillan Education.

P

PANOPTICISM A term formed from 'pan' and 'optic' ('all-seeing'), used by Michel **Foucault** in *Discipline and Punish.*

Foucault derives the concept of panopticism from a diagram drawn up by the British philosopher Jeremy Bentham in 1791. Bentham's Panopticon was a model prison in which supervisors could observe prisoners in their individual cells without being seen themselves. According to Foucault, this system was effective because prisoners never knew whether or not they were being watched: 'he is seen, but he does not see . . . what matters is that he knows himself to be observed'. Foucault goes on to argue that this constant sense of surveillance and visibility is what characterizes the development of disciplinary societies *in toto*. In such a society, 'the automatic functioning of **power**' is guaranteed because individuals police themselves and each other.

For Foucault, the notion of individualism in Western society is in fact a direct effect of panopticism. The individual is constructed by having internalized the disciplinary power of penitentiary and/or medicinal discourses, with their numerous methods of segregation and social exclusion. This is why, as Foucault concludes, modern institutions such as hospitals, schools and factories all resemble prisons. [SP and CHC]

Further reading

Foucault, Michel (1977a) *Discipline and Punish: The Birth of the Prison*, trans. Alan Sheridan, London: Penguin.

PATRIARCHY A term used – especially but not exclusively in feminist theory – to analyse male dominance as a conventional or institutionalized form. Literally the 'rule of the father', patriarchy historically describes systems in which the male has absolute legal and economic control over the family. The patriarch is the male head of a tribe, religion or church hierarchy.

Friedrich **Engels** argued that the rise of the nuclear family was the basis for the 'world historic defeat of the female sex' (1972: 120). Patriarchy was established as a system, defeating the 'mother right' and controlling women's sexuality in order to establish paternity and protect private property. Although the anthropology on which this argument is based is largely discredited, Engels' historicization of an apparently natural system set the scene for later feminist criticism.

In the 1970s, the **power** of patriarchy was located in the exchange of women (specifically, their reproductive capacity) as commodities in the form of brides or slaves. This search for origins had a utopian aim: if patriarchy has a beginning, it must also have an end. Patriarchy was theorized as the most pervasive cultural ideology. Despite its entrenchment, patriarchy varies in detail from place to place and throughout history. Male supremacy was denaturalized and shown to be the effect of social conditioning that positions children as 'masculine' and 'feminine'. Positive qualities are then attributed to the former. This conditioning (also disseminated through force, class, biology, economy and education) is primarily reproduced by patriarchy's chief institution – the family – and subsequently produces disproportionate numbers of men in positions of power.

Patriarchy both defines women and simultaneously oppresses them. Recent work has sought to show how patriarchy also constructs masculinities: by identifying a woman's place it also defines a man's. Although still employed in feminist criticism, 'patriarchy' has been supplemented by other terms which attempt to account for the perpetuation of male **hegemony**, including **phallocentrism** and **phallogocentrism**. [JP]

See also Chapters 8 and 9.

Further reading

Belsey, Catherine and Moore, Jane (1989) *The Feminist Reader: Essays in Gender and the Politics of Literary Criticism*, London: Macmillan Education.

Engels, Friedrich (1972) *The Origin of the Family, Private Property and the State: In the Light of the Researches of Lewis H. Morgan*, London: Lawrence and Wishart.

PERFORMANCE / PERFORMATIVITY The principle of performativity is used, if not always explicitly, by such thinkers as Jacques **Derrida**, Judith **Butler**, J. Hillis **Miller** and Michel **Foucault**. In one of its most important aspects, the principle of performativity has come to replace traditional notions of identity. Who, or what, one is is no longer based on the notion of an existing core identity, something in each of us which remains the same throughout all our changes in life, nor on teleological becoming in which one develops one's natural predisposition into a fully fledged character. Overall, what the principle of performance reveals is the absence of any natural order that would constitute the ground for one's identity. In a more complicated argument, it can be shown that any proclaimed natural order hides its own performative dimension and thus the fact that it is constructed. Here the space opens for **ideological** criticism and, accordingly, contemporary theory suggests that identity is based on enactment, i.e. on the

performative construction of one's identity by following culturally derived patterns of behaviour. Derrida and Miller emphasize the importance of language as a means of constructing identity. Miller's concept of 'prosopopeia' (personification) in particular underlines the performative dimension of language. Here, we do not exist as *meaningful* beings apart from our enactment in language. Foucault and Butler, on the other hand, are more interested in how identity is generated within culture, or, more precisely, in the discursive formations which are constitutive of identity. According to Butler, for example, we are constantly forced to re-enact and reconfirm our heterosexuality. [RS]

See also Chapters 8 and 9.

Further reading

Butler, Judith (1990) *Gender Trouble*, London: Routledge.

Miller, J. Hillis (1990) *Tropes, Parables, Performatives: Essays on Twentieth-Century Literature*, London: Harvester Wheatsheaf.

PHALLOCENTRISM A value system centred on the **phallus**, perceived as both a representation of male power and the source of it. Some psychoanalytic explanations of sexual and social development, for example, have been critiqued as phallocentric.

French feminist Luce **Irigaray** asserts that psychoanalysis conceptualizes female sexuality from a masculine viewpoint and thus reproduces the norms of **patriarchy** in a phallus-centred **discourse**. She argues that psychoanalysis claims the phallus as the origin and standard of truth and therefore privileges it as an agent and emblem of patriarchy. For Hélène **Cixous**, phallocentrism is equated with the ways in which patriarchy's binary logic structures language. The phallus represents the positive term as masculine and desirable: it is aligned with virility, authority, activity and power. The positive term is privileged over the negative, feminine, term, constructing an unequal hierarchy. Woman is thereby defined, in opposition to man, as lack – she is what man is not – by means of this primary **signifier**. This type of critique interrogates language, history and writing as phallocentric systems. [JP]

See also Chapters 6, 8 and 9.

Further reading

Cixous, Hélène and Catherine Clément (1986) *The Newly Born Woman*, trans. Betsy Wing, Minneapolis, MN: University of Minnesota Press.

Irigaray, Luce (1985a) *This Sex Which is Not One*, trans. Catherine Porter, Ithaca, NY: Cornell University Press.

PHALLOGOCENTRISM A combination of the terms **phallocentrism** and **logocentrism**, which is used to critique psychoanalysis as a **phallus**-centred **discourse** that locates truth in speech. For French philosopher Jacques **Derrida,** who coined the term to critique **Freud** and, especially, **Lacan**, psychoanalysis positions the phallus as the origin of both sexual difference and the use of language. Derrida argues that by giving the phallus such a central role, psycho-analytical explanations of sexual and social development continue to reproduce patri-archal norms. Furthermore, as a 'talking cure', psychoanalysis grants speech privi-leged access to the truth of a patient's internal consciousness while simul-taneously determining what that truth is.

Critics of Derrida's attack on psycho-analysis argue that he confuses the phallus with the penis, asserting that the phallus is a **signifier** of **desire** that no-one possesses. Some feminist criticism uses this symbolic reconceptualization of the phallus as a point of departure for a radical reappraisal of the cultural construction of gender and sexuality. Other critics have used 'phallogo-centrism' to theorize more generally the ways in which phallocentric discourse is made to seem natural in order to perpetu-ate patriarchy. [JP]

See also Chapter 7.

Further reading

Derrida, Jacques (1987) *The Postcard: From Socrates to Freud and Beyond*, trans. Alan Bass, Chicago: University of Chicago Press.

PHALLUS Theorized by the French psychoanalyst Jacques **Lacan**, who observes its function as a privileged **signifier** in culture. Phallus does not simply signify the penis, but is associated with the impossible fantasies of mastery, comple-tion and autonomy which haunt all speak-ing **subjects**, whose entry into language has cut them off from their organic existence. Since naming a thing distances it, 'the subject designates his being only by barring everything he signifies'; 'man cannot [rationally] aim at being whole' (Lacan 1977: 288, 287). Yet everybody (male and female) desires the phallus (though in different ways). No-one can have it, but men often mistake their organ for it. Lacan's innuendo-laden account illustrates how easily such confusion occurs, and is encouraged by traditional ideals of masculinity and femininity which involve, respectively, *having* the phallus and *being* the phallus (as object of **desire**) for another. Though Lacan emphasizes that these are subject positions in culture, not biologically given roles, he has been accused of **phallocentrism**. However, the Lacanian phallus signifies its own absence, the lack within human subjectivity that Lacan regards as central, and whose effect is desire. [RLS]

See also Chapter 6.

Further reading

Easthope, Antony (1999) *The Unconscious*, London: Routledge.

Lacan, Jacques (1977) 'The Signification of the Phallus', in *Écrits: A Selection*, trans. Alan Sheridan, London: Routledge.

PHENOMENOLOGY The study of struc-tures of experience as they appear to consciousness. Such experience is directed towards something in what is termed its 'intentionality'. Although we cannot ascertain whether something really exists or not, phenomenology claims that we can understand something from the point of view of our own experience of it. Such reasoning suggests that anything external to consciousness should be disregarded in what is termed the 'phenomenological reduction'.

The German philosopher Edmund Husserl is widely regarded as the originator of phenomenology as a philosophical discipline and he was followed by Martin **Heidegger**, who produced the hugely influential text, *Being and Time*. In France, phenomenology was developed by Jean-Paul Sartre and Maurice **Merleau-Ponty** who, like Heidegger, advanced an existentialist phenomenology which concerned itself more with questions of *existence* rather than *experience*.

In terms of literary theory, phenomenological criticism brackets off all aspects of a text that are external to it. In other words, such concepts as **authorial** intent, biography and audience are completely superfluous to a phenomenological reading of the text. What really matters is the actual content of the text and the manifestation of experience within it. [JS]

Further reading

Macann, Christopher E. (1993) *Four Phenomenological Philosophers: Husserl, Heidegger, Sartre, Merleau-Ponty*, London: Routledge.

PHONEME (Greek *phone* = sound) The term given to the differential units of resonance within human speech. Exact in their nature, phonemes do not relate to any and all sounds vocalized by humans. Specifically, a phoneme is the smallest recognized sound formation of any *langue* or *parole*, a linguistic building block.

Whilst phonemes articulate letters (graphemes), there is not necessarily a direct correlation between the numbers of each. The English language uses 26 graphemes within its alphabet, yet has a total of 45 phonemes. The difference between these two figures is due to the differing pronunciation of certain single letters or collections of letters within its articulation. The formation /ough/, for example, creates five different phonemes when occurring in bough, cough, ought, thorough, and through.

With the exception of /a/ and /I/, phonemes in themselves lack meaning and only become effective communication when formulated into a recognized word or **signifier**. Not until they are combined in this way, in accordance with the rules of the language system, can phonemes achieve signification and lose their individual status of incoherent sounds. [PSW]

See also Chapter 1.

POSTHUMANISM The theosophist, H. P. Blavatsky discussed the '*post-Human*' as long ago as 1888. Since approximately the early 1990s, however, the term has become increasingly commonplace in a wide range of disciplines, including cultural criticism, literary studies, geography, science studies, gender studies, theology and media studies.

Posthumanism calls into question the traditional humanist, or anthropocentric, way of understanding who we are. According to humanism, the figure of 'Man' (a term with which feminists have, quite understandably, taken issue) naturally stands at the centre of things, where 'he' is absolutely distinct from – and superior to – animals and machines, where 'he' is the origin of meaning and the sovereign subject of history, and where 'he' shares with all other human beings a universal essence. Deep down, for humanists, we are all the same.

Posthumanists realize that humanism is no longer, and perhaps never was, a convincing account. While posthumanism owes many debts to antihumanist thinkers such as Michel **Foucault**, Jacques **Lacan** and Louis **Althusser**, it tends to differ from antihumanism in one principal respect: while the antihumanists actively set out to overturn the **hegemony** of anthropocentrism, posthumanists begin with the recognition that 'Man' is (always) already a falling or fallen figure. What this means is that posthumanism often tends to take humanism's waning or disappearance as something of a given.

Often taking their cue from Donna **Haraway**'s theory of the **cyborg** (1985), many accounts of posthumanism have focused upon the ways in which recent developments in science and technology have unsettled anthropocentric assumptions. In the work of N. Katherine Hayles (1999), Chris Hables Gray (2001), and Elaine L. Graham (2002), for instance, advances made in fields such as cybernetics and **cyberspace**, artificial intelligence (AI), genetics, and medicine bring us to a point at which the **metanarrative** of humanism begins to falter. In a world where computers can think faster and have better memories than we do, where the Genome Project has cracked and made malleable the 'code' of life (revealing, in the process, that humans share 98 per cent of their genes with apes), where a remarkably sophisticated array of artificial limbs and organs proliferate, and where experts in AI believe that it will soon be possible to achieve immortality by transferring oneself into a computer, 'Man' finds 'his' traditional position of privilege and purity radically called into question.

Posthumanism should not, however, simply be equated with the recent rise of technoculture, for other critics have discussed the concept in terms of architecture, education, the uncertain relationship between humans and animals, fetishism and extraterrestrials. Neither should it be assumed that all studies of posthumanist culture actually embrace the phenomena that they describe. Francis **Fukuyama**'s *Our Posthuman Future* (2002), for instance, proposes an urgent revival of the faded principles of anthropocentrism. But if there is no critical consensus concerning the question of posthumanism, there is at least a shared and growing recognition that humanism now (and perhaps always) finds itself in a state of profound crisis. 'Man' is not all that 'he' claims to be. [NB]

See also Chapter 10.

Further reading

Badmington, Neil (ed.) (2000) *Posthumanism*, Basingstoke and New York: Palgrave.

Haraway, Donna (1985) 'A Manifesto for Cyborgs: Science, Technology, and Socialist Feminism in the 1980s', *Socialist Review* 80 (1985): 65–108.

Hayles, N. Katherine (1999) *How We Became Posthuman: Virtual Bodies in Cybernetics, Literature, and Informatics*, Chicago, IL and London: University of Chicago Press.

POWER   In the most general terms, power can be understood as the ability to effect change. Typically, this is thought to be achieved through the domination or control exerted by one individual, or group, over another in a power relationship. In this traditional understanding of the term, power is conceived as the end result of a difference in status between the two parties. The sovereign, or king, for example, is understood to be of a different status to his subjects and is therefore in possession of power over them. This asymmetrical and one-directional model of power was traditionally understood to be replicated in all social relations, so that the landlord has power over the tenant, the parent over the child, and so on, each possessing power in a manner similar to the sovereign. As a static model, this traditional conception of power proves inadequate to explain the means by which **subjects** gain status (and hence power) in the first place, or the tendency for power to shift, often through resistance.

Within critical theory, the work of Michel **Foucault** provides the most thoroughgoing analysis of power. For Foucault, power is not conceived as residing in a single source, as the possession of the king, but is rather diffused throughout the social structure and is exercised within and through it. All social relations are relations of power, but, in this instance, power is a causal factor for social asymmetry, rather than its peripheral end result. In his historical analysis of the development of modern institutions such as the asylum or the prison, Foucault demonstrates the mechanisms of power which operate by means of the constitution of the modern autonomous subject.

The shift from sovereign to state control in the last 200 years has not, Foucault argues, brought about the liberation of individuals from relations of power. Instead, we have seen a transferral from a sovereign power located at a remote distance from individuals to one of state power in which the individual is constantly subject to discursive mechanisms of regulation and control. These mechanisms take the form of modern classificatory knowledge regimes such as medicine or psychiatry, which work, at a discursive and institutional level, to identify and regulate the movement of subjects, taking effect even at the level of the body through the techniques of 'bio-power'. This process is exacerbated by the tendency of modern subjects to regulate themselves, collaborating in their own subjection. Foucault's best-known metaphor for the process by which individual subjects internalize the mechanisms of social control is Jeremy Bentham's Panopticon (see **panopticism**). A nineteenth-century architectural design for prisons, Bentham's Panopticon works on the principle that individuals, isolated from one another, and open to the gaze of an unseen central power, need only perceive that they are under surveillance for them to regulate their own behaviour in the service of social control. The self-awareness and apparent autonomy of the modern subject is thus conceived, by Foucault, as the outcome of new levels of visibility and surveillance engendered by the explosion of discourse around the newly autonomous subject at the end of the eighteenth century. New regimes of knowledge thus resulted in the formulation of ever more powerful techniques for social control. Thus, in *Discipline and Punish* Foucault shows that the new disciplinary regimes of the nineteenth century which sought to reform prisoners rather than punish acts were just as repressive as earlier systems. The complex structure of medical and juridical observation required to assess the reformation of the individual soul exemplifies Foucault's observation that 'the soul becomes the prison of the body' as the power of modern governments is internalized by its subjects.

While Foucault ably demonstrates the networks of power relationships which operate within modern society, and the complex interface between power and knowledge, in his earlier writings he still conceived of power as both controlling and prohibitive, operating through the exclusion, for example, of unsanctioned behaviour. In the *History of Sexuality*, Foucault sought to revise this, conceiving of power instead as strategically dispersed throughout all social relations, located only in temporary shifting effects, and he included in his analysis what he termed micro-power or 'power from below', and the tendency for power to include resistance. In this aspect of Foucault's work it may be possible to trace the influence of **Nietzsche** who, in searching for the causes for human action, claimed that a 'will to power' operated as a continuously dissembling field of effects, motivating behaviour. Foucault's own influence has been diffuse, provoking new examinations of micro-power and resistance, particularly, for example, in gender studies, while feminism had already noted the distinction between power and authority which makes such analysis possible. [AT]

See also Chapters 3, 4, 5, 8, 9 and 11.

Further reading

Foucault, Michel (1977a) *Discipline and Punish: The Birth of the Prison*, trans. Alan Sheridan, London: Penguin.

Foucault, Michel (1980) *Power/Knowledge: Selected Interviews and Other Writings, 1972–1977*, ed. Colin Gordon, New York: Pantheon.

Foucault, Michel (1984) *The History of Sexuality, vol. 1: An Introduction*, trans. Robert Hurley, London: Penguin.

PROPP, VLADIMIR (1895–1970) Russian scholar of folktales best known for his work on narrative structure. His major work on Russian folktales is *Morphology of the Folktale* (1928), which identifies recurring narrative motifs in the tales.

Propp's work is not concerned with the content or social significance of traditional folktales, but rather with their form or 'morphology'. Basing his analysis upon detailed study of 100 folktales, Propp concludes that despite their apparent diversity these tales depend upon the same underlying structures. They are constructed by selecting items from a repertoire of 31 'functions' or actions which serve to advance the tale's plot, such as 'the villain is defeated' and 'the hero receives a magic token'. Although Propp regards character as subordinate to action, he also identifies seven 'actors' or roles that appear repeatedly. The tales achieve both originality and familiarity because each one uses a different combination of elements and 'functions' are not automatically assigned to the same 'actors'.

Propp's method of analysis shows that beneath the diversity of the tales there is a relatively simple underlying structure. His work alerts us to formal features of which the unsuspecting reader may be unaware. Propp's emphasis on form and structure was influential in the development of narratology, which offers a systematic framework for the analysis of narrative. [RF]

See also Chapters 1, 2 and 4.

Further reading

Propp, Vladimir (1958) *Morphology of the Folktale*, trans. Laurence Scott, Austin, TX and London: University of Texas Press.

R

REAL A theoretical concept associated primarily with the work of Jacques **Lacan**. The real should be sharply distinguished from reality, which for Lacan is a product of language. Lacan famously stated that 'It is the world of words that creates the world of things' (Lacan 1977: 65), by which he means that what is experienced as reality, the **symbolic order** in which the **subject** exists, is constituted by words and signs. The real designates that which falls outside the sway of symbolization and signification, and therefore cannot be assimilated into the symbolic order. The foundational gesture of language is to cut into the real and posit a moment at which a word stands in for something, creating a symbolic reality. However, the word does not touch the real or represent it, except in the sense that it represents nothingness, which, from the perspective of human symbolic reality, is what the undifferentiated mass of the real actually is. An encounter with the real is **traumatic** precisely because it represents an encounter with the thing itself and a breaking down of symbolic reality, rather than the thing as chaperoned by symbolic thing-presentation. [HJ]

See also Chapter 6.

REALISM The artistic endeavour to represent accurately the real world through the medium of literature, film or painting. It was primarily in the nineteenth-century novel, in France and Britain, that realism was first developed as a generic style. Realist texts value truth and authenticity and are typically concerned with accurately depicting the individual's experience in relation to their social conditions. This is particularly the case in the British tradition, where social realism sought to give accounts of the actual differences in living conditions between the social classes. Detailed descriptions of both character and society thus often override considerations of plot and style in realist texts. Despite such specific generic roots, the term realism is typically used today to describe any text which purports unproblematically to reflect the real world. Thus most mainstream fiction and cinema can be described as realist texts. Their reality effect relies, however, on complex rules of composition to which the reader has grown accustomed. In fiction, for example, classic realist narrative depends upon a linear plotline which proceeds towards closure, and upon an omniscient narrator who does not draw the reader's attention to the act of narration or the text's own processes of construction. Further, in order to achieve veracity, realist texts inevitably present the reader with a world-view which corresponds to their own **subject** position, perpetuating, rather than simply reflecting, cultural meanings and norms. As Catherine Belsey states, 'realism is plausible not because it reflects the world, but because it is constructed out of what is (discursively) familiar' (Belsey 2002a: 44). For this reason, Jean-François **Lyotard** argues that realism consolidates both artistic and social conformity. In order to challenge such conformity and effect social change, the cultural avant-garde must experiment with the rules of realism. The experimentations of modernism and postmodernism include examples of such a challenge. [AT]

See also Chapter 4.

Further reading

Belsey, Catherine (2002a) *Critical Practice*, London: Routledge.

RECEPTION THEORY A form of reader-response criticism that is associated with the Konstance School of *Receptionkritik* and the work of Hans Robert **Jauss** and Wolfgang **Iser**. Reception theory is concerned with both the aesthetic and the historical aspects of reading, i.e. the ways in which readers use texts for pleasure, and how readings alter and shift through history. Iser distinguishes these two strands by claiming that 'A theory of response has its roots in the text; a theory of reception arises from a history of readers' judgements' (Iser 1978: x). However, whether concerned with textual affect or historical reaction, reception theory reflects a wider movement in literary studies that rejects the ascendancy and dominance of **New Criticism**. This movement is broadly labelled reader-response theory and, rather confusingly, the term reception theory is often used in this more general sense to refer to the many different strands of analysis that focus on the reader as active participant in the creation of meaning. Despite their diversity of approach, all reader-response theorists share a resistance to the textual determinism of New Criticism and, in particular, to Wimsatt and Beardsley's 'affective fallacy' in which they argue that textual meaning must be divorced from the effect of the text upon the reader. Thus, all reader-response critics are concerned with the ways in which a text is received, but the ways in which they theorize this reception vary greatly (see Tompkins 1980), and many are also aligned with other schools of interpretation (such as Jonathan Culler who explores the relations of both structuralism and deconstruction to reception theory). [GC]

See also Chapter 4.

Further reading

Fish, Stanley (1980) *Is there a Text in This Class? The Authority of Interpretive Communities*, Cambridge, MA: Harvard University Press.

Freund, Elizabeth (1987) *The Return of the Reader: Reader-Response Criticism*, London: Methuen.

Tompkins, Jane P. (ed.) (1980) *Reader-Response Criticism: From Formalism to Post-Structuralism*, Baltimore, MD and London: Johns Hopkins University Press.

REFERENT A concept employed to designate an object in the world. The term came to prominence through the **semiotics** of Swiss linguist Ferdinand de **Saussure**. Saussure divides a **sign** into **signifier** (sound or image) and **signified** (mental concept). The sign and the referent, it is important to realize, are not (as in Charles Sanders Peirce and his deployment of the concepts) the same thing. The referent is the extra-linguistic material object to which the sign points. In Saussure's work, the referent is the least important part of the equation, or really not part of the equation at all. It remains 'bracketed off', outside the domain of the pure structure of signification. [DD]

See also Chapters 1, 2 and 4.

RHIZOME In origin a botanical term classifying the growth and organization of tuber plants, the rhizome entered critical thought in French poststructuralist philosophers Gilles **Deleuze** and Félix **Guattari**'s *A Thousand Plateaus* (1980). They develop a 'rhizomatic' model of organization in terms of material, non-hierarchical relations and apply it not just to organic but also to cultural, biological, and geological phenomena. A rhizome grows in multiple directions without following any predetermined plan or reaching a predestined ideal end. The importance of this concept for critical theory is that it provides an alternative to the Western philosophical tradition of thinking in terms of unities, fixed **subjects** and transcendent essences. Thus the meaning of the term 'rhizome' is given as part of a critique of the long theoretical domination of tree-like models of thinking in which central unities subordinate real plurality and **difference**. Subsequent critics have often used the term loosely to describe everything from grassroots political movements to the internet, seeing a rhizome as an inherently libertarian, anarchic resistance against oppressive, totalitarian structures. However, for Deleuze and Guattari rhizomatic and tree-like types of organization are constantly shifting. They are inseparable processes, rather than empirical or political entities to be described or judged. [DH]

Further reading
Deleuze, Gilles and Guattari, Félix (1988) 'Introduction: Rhizome', in *A Thousand Plateaus: Capitalism and Schizophrenia*, trans. Brian Massumi, London: Athlone Press.

RICHARDS, IVOR ARMSTRONG (1893–1979) As first student and then lecturer at Cambridge University, I. A. Richards was instrumental in the development of the Cambridge English degree, and in works like *The Principles of Literary Criticism* (1924) and *Practical Criticism* (1929) he helped to define the parameters and methodology of this 'new' discipline.

Building on his earlier study of semantics and communication, *The Meaning of Meaning* (1923, with C. K. Ogden), *Principles* sets out to describe literary criticism as a branch of psychology and therefore as properly 'scientific', rather than subjective and emotional.

For the writing of *Practical Criticism*, he gave his students copies of poems with the **author**'s name, the title and the publication date removed and asked them to comment on them freely (and anonymously). Out of the diverse critical readings that resulted, he hoped to draw general lessons – about the nature of poetry, the function of criticism, and good and bad critical methods – and so to move from **subjective** opinion to objective knowledge. His close-reading approach was enormously influential – in particular upon the American **New Criticism** – and both F. R. **Leavis** and William **Empson** studied under him. [KM]
See also Chapter 5.

Further reading
Richards, Ivor Armstrong (2001a) *Practical Criticism*, London: Routledge.
Richards, Ivor Armstrong (2001b) *Principles of Literary Criticism*, London: Routledge.
Russo, John Paul (1989) *I. A. Richards: His Life and Work*, London: Routledge.

RICOEUR, PAUL (1913–2005) French philosopher who has written extensively on a wide range of subjects that includes not only philosophy (his early work focused on **phenomenology**) but also religion, ethics, history, literature, politics, psychoanalysis and linguistics. He is perhaps best known for his phenomenological **hermeneutics**.

It was with the publication of *The Symbolism of Evil* in 1960 (trans. 1970) that Ricoeur's work began to combine existential phenomenology with hermeneutic interpretation, thereby establishing the methodology of his later work. Ricoeur refines his notion of the text, the appropriate subject of hermeneutics, to include **discourse** as a whole. His hermeneutics thus regards the world as textual, in as much as human existence is expressed, and read, through discourse. By placing an emphasis on the connection between discourse and human action, Ricoeur suggests that it is through the act of reading texts, of doing hermeneutics, that human beings can arrive at self-understanding. An example of this approach is found in Ricoeur's three-volume *Time and Narrative* in which he argues that 'time becomes human time to the extent that it is organized after the manner of a narrative' (Ricoeur 1984: 3). In other words, it is through, and during, the interpretation of time as narrative, the hermeneutic act itself, that we reach a phenomenological understanding of the human experience of time. [PW]

See also Chapter 2.

Further reading

Ricoeur, Paul (1977) *The Rule of Metaphor: Multi-Disciplinary Studies of the Creation of Meaning in Language*, trans. Robert Czerny with Kathleen McLaughlin and John Costello, Toronto and Buffalo: University of Toronto Press.

Simms, Karl (2003) *Paul Ricoeur*, London: Routledge.

RORTY, RICHARD (1931–) American philosopher who originally trained in the area of analytic philosophy before developing a neo-pragmatism which has much in common with aspects of continental philosophy. Neo-pragmatism is anti-foundationalist, a concern shared with continental poststructuralist theory. Like its continental counterpart, neo-pragmatism also emphasizes the importance of linguistic analysis. Rorty's major works include *Philosophy and the Mirror of Nature*, *Consequences of Pragmatism* and *Contingency, Irony and Solidarity*.

Rorty argues against the founding principles of traditional Western philosophy that are concerned with totalizing concepts such as truth and origins. In this sense his work can be seen to converge with postmodern thought in its rejection of totalities and **grand narratives**. According to Rorty, the function of pragmatism is to dispense with philosophical issues such as the search for an absolute truth and instead to pursue aims that are more immediately beneficial and interesting, such as the betterment of the human condition.

In his rejection of totality, Rorty goes on to claim that we should look at issues from a variety of standpoints rather than forming unifying, monolithic theories. His later work argues that philosophy as a discipline is in fact now almost redundant and of less use than the likes of literary, social and political theory. In this sense, Rorty has much in common with certain poststructuralist theorists, such as Jacques **Derrida**, who argue that there are no clear lines of distinction between philosophy and literature and that in fact philosophy actually becomes a form of literature in itself. [JS]

See also Chapter 10.

Further reading

Rorty, Richard (1980) *Philosophy and the Mirror of Nature*, Oxford: Blackwell.

Rorty, Richard (1989) *Contingency, Irony, Solidarity*, Cambridge: Cambridge University Press.

RUSSIAN FORMALISM A movement that emerged from the desire for an independent and coherent discipline of literary studies amidst the propagandist art of post-revolutionary Russia. The chief concern of Russian formalism was not with what literature is about, nor why or how a particular text appeared, but with what constitutes literature: its aim was to identify 'literariness'. Russian formalism developed in two schools, the OPOYAZ group (1916), 'The Society for the Study of Poetic Language', and the Moscow Linguistic Circle (1915). Russian formalism's main proponents included Victor **Shklovsky**, Boris Eichenbaum, Boris Tomashevsky, Yuri Tynyanov and, later, Roman **Jakobson**.

The focus of Russian formalism is on form, style and technique as opposed to, and to the exclusion of, questions of content, be they concerned with social, political or philosophical aspects of a text. The text need not point to anything outside itself, and, crucially, this means a shift of critical attention from the author of a text to its form. A fundamental tenet of Russian formalist thinking is *Ostranenie*, which has been variously translated as 'defamiliarization', or 'making strange'. This idea is most clearly outlined in Shklovsky's essay 'Art as Technique': 'The technique of art is to make objects "unfamiliar", to make forms difficult, to increase the difficulty and length of perception because the process of perception is an aesthetic end in itself and must be prolonged' (Lemon and Reis 1965: 12). Defamiliarization reacts against what the Russian formalists called habituation, the process by which the **referent** (object) is replaced by its **sign** (word): 'Habitualization devours works, clothes, furniture, one's wife, and the fear of war' (Lemon and Reis 1965: 12). 'Literariness' was thus defined as the reversal of this pragmatic use of language, in that it draws attention to the process (form) of language itself. Russian formalism has been applied to both poetry, which has yielded fertile ground, and prose, which demanded further refinement of the techniques. This led to the distinction between *fabula* (story) and *sjuzet* (plot), with the focus of formalist criticism being on the latter.

In the late 1920s Russian formalism fell prey to Stalinist orthodoxy. However, its concerns were developed by the Prague Linguistic Circle (1926–39) whose members notably included Jakobson. Russian formalist theory has also played a significant role in preparing the field for the development of modern literary theory, and was highly influential in the rise of structuralism and the work of the **Bakhtin** circle. Its use of linguistic methodology marks it as a clear predecessor to the fields of narratology and poetics. [PW]

See also Chapter 2.

Further reading

Erlich, Victor (1981) *Russian Formalism: History – Doctrine*, New Haven, CT and London: Yale University Press.

Lemon, Lee T. and Reis, Marion J. (eds) (1965) *Russian Formalist Criticism: Four Essays*, Lincoln, NE: University of Nebraska Press.

S

SAID, EDWARD WILLIAM (1935–2003) Palestinian American academic, literary critic and writer born in Jerusalem. Said's lifelong sympathy with the Palestinian cause is reflected in works including *The Question of Palestine* (1979), *Covering Islam* (1981), *After the Last Sky* (1986) and *Blaming the Victims* (1988). He was a prominent member of the Palestinian National Council, the parliament-in-exile, for 14 years until he quietly stepped down in 1991. After emigrating to the United States, he was Professor of English and Comparative Literature at Columbia University. He lived in New York until his death in 2003.

Said's most influential and widely read work is ***Orientalism*** (first published 1978). This explores the way in which Orientalists, those Westerners that compiled 'knowledge' of the Orient, have perceived and defined the East throughout history. Said criticizes a range of Western social, religious and cultural representations of the East. A central claim, for example, is that 'Islam *has* been fundamentally misrepresented in the West'. Crucially, though, the conflict this gave rise to between East and West has had serious implications for the development of the modern world. Over the centuries, as Said argues, Western society came to view itself as the harbinger of rationalism and civilization, a society which, in particular, defined itself against its own construction of an 'irrational', 'uncivilized' and therefore 'inferior' East. In doing so, the West also **mythologized** the East as a place of fantasy, mystery, exoticism and eroticism, a land inhabited by sinister men and sensuous women.

According to Said, the West effectively constructed an image of the East *by* and *for* the West, in order that the West could thereby attain knowledge of itself. Ultimately, as Said concludes, **Orientalism** is a 'Western style for dominating, restructuring, and having authority over the Orient'. Said's theories were largely informed by Michel **Foucault**'s studies of the relationship between knowledge and power.

More ambitious in terms of scope and ideas is *Culture and Imperialism* (1993). This book explores empire and the expansion of European culture throughout the world. Said is particularly concerned with the British and French empires of the nineteenth and twentieth centuries, the histories of which reveal, as Said puts it, something 'systematic about imperial culture'. In a series of illuminating studies, Said provides an account of the ways in which Western culture is implicated in the European imperial project, a process which amounts to 'a general effort to rule distant lands and peoples'. Western culture is, in other words, bound up in Europe's domination of the world. It acts both to export Western ideas and languages to other countries and represent these countries back home. As Said says, 'stories are at the heart of what explorers and novelists say about strange regions of the world'. He then offers a number of insights into 'Europe's special ways of representing the Caribbean Islands . . . and the Far East', as well as important works of English literature such as Charles Dickens's *Great Expectations* (1861) and Joseph Conrad's *Heart of Darkness* (1902). In these he describes the encounter between the protagonists of these novels and the 'shadowy presence' of Australia and Africa as crucial to understanding both the novels and the nature of imperialism. Furthermore, Said maintains that it is only by acknowledging the imperial process of which these novels are part, as well as the way they are shaped by imperialism, that we can 'truly enhance ... our reading and understanding of them'. To underline this point, he draws upon the famous example of Daniel Defoe's *Robinson Crusoe* (1719). This story is, of course, about a shipwrecked Englishman who effectively colonizes a desert island. On what is subsequently described throughout as 'his' island, Crusoe then encounters a black 'cannibal' figure, Friday, whom he quickly enslaves and 'civilizes' by teaching him English. As such a précis suggests, *Robinson Crusoe* is significant for two reasons: it is widely regarded as the first English novel and as an allegory of empire. In short, the timing and status of Defoe's novel underpins Said's arguments about the relationship between culture and imperialism. For Said and subsequent commentators working in the field, it is no historical accident that the rise of the English novel and the emergence of the British empire coincided; each gave rise to and legitimated the other.

As both writer and activist, Said was an outspoken advocate of political rights and a stern critic of American foreign policy in the Middle East throughout his life. His two major studies are now regarded as founding texts in postcolonial theory. [SP and CHC]

See also Chapter 11.

Further reading

Ashcroft, Bill and Ahluwalia, Pal (2000) *Edward Said*, London: Routledge.

Said, Edward (1993) *Culture and Imperialism*, London: Chatto and Windus.

Said, Edward (2003) *Orientalism: Western Conceptions of the Orient*, London: Penguin.

SAUSSURE, FERDINAND DE (1857–1913) One of the founders of modern linguistics, Saussure established the structural study of language (**semiology**), emphasizing the arbitrary relationship of the linguistic **sign** to that which it refers to in the world: the **referent**. Saussure's most influential work is the *Course in General Linguistics* (first published 1916), published posthumously, which played a significant part in the development of structuralism.

In his lifetime, Saussure published comparatively little. His foremost work, the *Course*, was transcribed by his students from a series of lectures he offered from 1907 to 1911 in general linguistics while professor at the University of Geneva. In the *Course* Saussure calls for the scientific study of language as opposed to the work in historical linguistics that had been done in the nineteenth century. Philology (historical or diachronic linguistics) traced the origin and development of European languages from a presumed common language stock, first an Indo-European language and then an earlier proto-Indo-European language. Saussure, however, proposed privileging synchronic linguistics (studying the state of language at a given moment) against diachronic linguistics (the study of languages across time) as well as privileging what he named *langue* (the rules of a language) over *parole* (the speech of an individual human being).

In concentrating on the synchronic *langue*, Saussure opposed the object-in-the-world (the referent) to the sign, bracketing the former in order to concentrate upon the latter. He also created a further theoretical division within the sign itself: the **signifier** (the acoustic or written image) and the **signified** (the mental concept). For Saussure, as with the sign–referent correlation, the relationship between signifier and signified is also arbitrary: no sound equals inherently a mental concept. The sound or written word m-u-l-e is an ejaculation of phonemes that comprise a signifier which has been ascribed the cultural mental image (signified) of the offspring of a donkey and a horse. In the same way, the sign 'mule' has an arbitrary connection to a stubborn furry quadruped in a field (the referent). If this quadruped were to be cut in half, there would not be the letters m-u-l-e written through it as in a stick of seaside rock. Accordingly, then, meanings are not specified by the relationship between signifiers and signifieds, nor by the relationship between signs and referents, but, rather, meanings occur through **difference**: 'mule' has meaning only because it is not, for example, 'donkey', nor is it 'horse'. *Langue* is this system of difference.

The significance of Saussure's work should not be underestimated. Saussure's radical reworking of philological linguistics (arguably engendered by the research of Charles Sanders Peirce) went on to generate many of the disciplines within critical theory, and perhaps could even be said to have laid the groundwork for the emergence of the domain of critical theory itself. It fed into the work of the early **Russian formalists** who applied structural linguistics to literature, particularly in the work of Roman **Jakobson**, Vladimir **Propp** and Claude **Lévi-Strauss**. It underpinned the work of Roland **Barthes**, who reworked the concept of **ideology** through his conception of **myth** in order to observe the sign in operation within society. Jacques **Lacan** organized his 'return to **Freud**' and Julia **Kristeva** her 'semanalysis' through the structuralism of Saussure, allowing theoretical psychoanalysis to explore the void between the subject and language. The work of Karl **Marx** was re-evaluated by Pierre **Macherey**, Louis **Althusser** and Herbert **Marcuse** who explored ideology through the maxim that every sign is ideological. It goes without saying that poststructuralism similarly owes a debt to Saussure, particularly the work of Jacques **Derrida** who develops Saussure's concept of difference into the neologism of **differance**. [DD]

See also Chapters 1, 2, 4 and 5.

Further reading

Culler, Jonathan (1976) *Saussure*, London: Fontana.

Saussure, Ferdinand de (1974) *Course in General Linguistics*, trans. Wade Baskin, London: Fontana.

SCHIZOANALYSIS Coined in French poststructuralist philosophers Gilles **Deleuze** and Félix **Guattari**'s *Anti-Oedipus* (first published 1972), this term distinguishes their analysis of the **unconscious** from that of psychoanalysis. They argue that psychoanalysis treats the unconscious as a dangerous disruption to the *unity* of an ideal **subject** (psyche) and to the capitalist society by which this kind of subject is constituted. Continuing a long tradition of Western thinking about the subject and **desire**, psychoanalytic interpretation constructs the **Oedipus complex** to give the unconscious a single, **mythical** meaning. In the process, desire becomes a private melodrama, played without any social or political significance. It thus no longer threatens the subject or society. Extending French psychoanalyst Jacques **Lacan**'s analysis of desire as a constitutive lack, schizoanalysis rejects this domesticating interpretation of the unconscious. Deleuze and Guattari make the splittings or 'schizzes' that constitute unconscious production the object of their analysis. Desire is understood as a process in which unconscious differences simply *produce* rather than meaning anything. Where psychoanalytic interpretation tries to *reassure* a fixed, unified subject with a metaphysical ontology, schizoanalysis attempts to continue the process of desiring-production. Rather than *interpreting*, it constructs a **rhizomatic** unconscious which further undercuts the subject's supposed rationality and unity. [DH]

See also Chapter 6.

SEDGWICK, EVE KOSOFSKY (1950–) American theorist best known for her work on queer theory, which sets out to challenge established definitions of male and female sexuality, incorporating a study of gay and lesbian sexualities, as well as transgendered subjects, cross-dressing and transsexuality.

Sedgwick's key ideas regarding the relationship between literature, gender and sexuality are set out in *Between Men: English Literature and Male Homosocial Desire* (1985). Influenced by Michel **Foucault**'s work on sexuality, Sedgwick examines the relationship between 'homosociality' – bonds formed between people of the same sex – and homosexuality – sexual desire between people of the same sex. Sedgwick argues that whilst the two positions are distinct, they exist on a 'continuum'. For men, the 'continuum' can be interrupted by homophobia – the fear of homosexuality – that is typical of capitalist cultures. Women, however, are less likely to experience this disruption. Exploring English literature between 1750 and 1850, Sedgwick discusses the formation of a male homosociality formed out of rivalry for a woman, whose presence in the text will avert any potential hint of homoeroticism, or homosexual desire.

Whilst some critics have voiced concerns that queer theory leads to an apolitical study of gender that elides individual identity positions, such as lesbianism, Sedgwick's foundational work, which reassesses the ways in which gender and sexuality inscribe and define identities, has restructured our awareness of the relationship between literary practices and sexuality. [TES]

See also Chapter 9.

Further reading

Sedgwick, Eve Kosofsky (1985) *Between Men: English Literature and Male Homosocial Desire*, New York: Columbia University Press.

Sedgwick, Eve Kosofsky (1990) *The Epistemology of the Closet*, New York: Penguin.

Sedgwick, Eve Kosofsky (1997) *Novel Gazing: Queer Readings in Fiction*, Durham, NC: Duke University Press.

SEMIOLOGY / SEMIOTICS Terms given to the study of signs and **sign** systems. Etymologically derived from the Greek *semeion* meaning sign, it was Charles Sanders Peirce who formulated semiology's first comprehensive model. For Peirce, an individual can only make sense of their thoughts and experiences through the interpretation of signs. Whilst anything can be a sign, signification is dependent upon meaning 'something to someone', which means that nothing is a sign until it becomes interpreted as such. Presenting a triadic model of the semiotic, Peirce separates its components into the representamen, the interpretant, and the object, the three terms being correlative with the form of the sign, its mental image, and that to which it refers. Peirce also divides the potential structure of signs into symbolic, iconic and indexical where the relationship between representamen and object is either arbitrary, representative or causal.

In a series of lectures that became the basis for his *Course in General Linguistics*, Ferdinand de **Saussure** develops Peirce's initial hypotheses. Departing from the earlier triadic formulation of semiosis, Saussure presents a dyadic model structured around the **signifier** and the **signified**, the sign's form, and its concept.

Common within both theorists' approach to semiology is a shared belief in the ontologically arbitrary nature of language, a phenomenon demonstrated by the fact that, for example, the terms 'tree', 'arbre', and 'Baum', all signify the same **referent**.

Semiology's pivotal position within critical theory is demonstrated by its centrality to language and thought. It is the basis from which all other interpretations stem.

Language does not passively reflect our reality and experiences but is actively involved in their construction. Semiotics helps us to interpret and make sense of our environs, and without it our lives would consist entirely of meaningless babble. [PSW]

See also Chapters 1, 2 and 4.

Further reading

Peirce, Charles Sanders (1998) *The Essential Writings*, ed. Edward C. Moore, Amherst, NY: Prometheus Books.

Saussure, Ferdinand de (1974) *Course in General Linguistics*, trans. Wade Baskin. London: Fontana.

SHKLOVSKY, VICTOR BORISOVICH (1893–1984)   Russian novelist, scriptwriter and critic. Victor Shklovsky, along with Osip Brik, Leo Yakubinsky and Evgenii Polivanov, was one of the founding members of the OPOYAZ (the Society for the Study of Poetic Language) in 1916, and a key figure in the development of **Russian formalism**.

Shklovsky's significance to critical theory comes in his contribution to formalist studies which can be seen in his early work on the Russian futurists, who considered language to be the true material of their works (rather than the world itself), in *The Resurrection of the Word* (1914). Shklovsky considered literary works as constructed objects and worked on establishing theories of plot development, both in terms of individual texts and of **genres**, and on notions of literariness. Shklovsky's most significant single essay is the widely anthologized 'Art as Technique' (1917) in which he introduces the idea of *ostranenie* or 'estrangement'. According to Shklovsky's argument, literary language defamiliarizes the ways in which objects are perceived, as opposed to 'everyday language' which does the opposite, foregrounding the artifice of the text itself. Shklovsky's key essays are anthologized in *Theory of Prose* (1990). [PW]

See also Chapter 2.

Further reading

Shklovsky, Victor (1990) *Theory of Prose*, trans. Benjamin Sher, Normal, IL: Dalkey Archive Press.

SIGN / SIGNIFIER / SIGNIFIED   Concepts defined by the Swiss linguist Ferdinand de **Saussure**. According to Saussure, language is a system of signs. The sign is defined as the complete linguistic unit. It is the combination of a sound image, the *signifier*, and an idea or concept which that sound denotes, the *signified*.

The central point of Saussure's theory is that the relationship between signifier and signified is arbitrary; it is neither natural nor inevitable. A sign, for Saussure, is not the simple result of the combination of an object and a name for it. There is no logical connection, for example, between the acoustic image or written signifier 'banana', and the concept of the yellow fruit being described. Similarly, there is no intrinsic or obvious reason why the signifier 'duck', and not the signifier 'cat', should designate the species of bird. In other words, there is nothing duck-like about the word 'duck'. Equally, there is no necessary or natural reason why the letters 'q', 'c' and 'k' should denote the sound [ke]. The relationship between letters and their sounds, asserts Saussure, is also arbitrary, a matter of social convention. Indeed the only requirement, in order to ensure effective communication, is that the sign for 'c', for example, is not confused in spoken or written language with other signs such as 'p', 't' or 'd'. Language, for Saussure, is in this respect a system of differences, where signs can exist only in negative opposition to other signs. As he explains further, signs can only be identified by contrast with other similar signs, because their 'most precise characteristic is in being what the others are not'.

Despite its arbitrary nature, language

remains governed by certain rules and principles, according to Saussure. As he puts it himself, 'the arbitrary nature of the sign explains . . . why the social fact alone can create a linguistic system'. This is enough for Saussure to prove that language is not a natural or logical process, but a highly constructed medium, a set of conventions designed by and for the community. One such social convention is traffic lights. Traffic lights are a set of signifiers or a 'language' which the community agrees upon and understands in order to prevent chaos on the roads. However, the colours red, amber and green do not intrinsically mean 'stop', 'get ready' and 'go'. There is nothing inherently 'dangerous' about the colour red, nothing obvious about 'amber' which says 'get into a state of preparedness', and nothing inevitably or naturally 'go-like' about green. This is merely a system of conventions between signifier and signified drawn up by society.

Language cannot, as Saussure maintains, be reduced to a list of names attached to a series of objects. In fact the very existence of different languages proves the highly unnatural relationship between signifier and signified. Saussure explains it this way: 'if words stood for pre-existing concepts, they would all have exact equivalents in meaning from one language to the next; but this is not true'. This point is best illustrated by two examples, one being the seemingly paradoxical case of onomatopoeia. Onomatopoeic signifiers such as 'moo' or 'quack quack' seem to imitate the concepts they refer to, in this case the noises that cows or ducks make. But they are still, as Saussure maintains, only 'approximate and more or less conventional imitations of certain sounds'. As with all language, onomatopoeic signs have been chosen arbitrarily. How, otherwise, does one explain the fact that unlike their English equivalents, French cows and ducks go 'meuh' and 'coin coin' respectively? Second, despite the apparent spontaneity

or naturalness of certain human sounds or exclamations, these still do not imply any natural bond between signifier and signified. In English, for example, the common interjection 'ouch!' is pronounced in French as 'aïe!' Our responses, as this suggests, are conditioned by societal conventions. For Saussure, all of our ideas and concepts are in fact constructed by language, and not vice versa. He concludes that language is a system which pre-exists the individual and creates our responses to a world in which 'nothing is distinct before the appearance of language'. [SP and CHC]

See also Chapters 1, 2 and 4.

SIMULATION A concept most associated with Jean **Baudrillard**, who argues that the postmodern age is characterized by a proliferation of simulations. The increasingly global reach of mass media and advertising, and the development of information and communication technologies that work in 'real time', has caused our society to be dominated by reproductions and images.

Baudrillard argues that history has advanced through three stages: first, the counterfeit era, from the invention of the printing press to the industrial revolution, in which signs were intended either as reflections or 'perversions' of reality; second, the era of production, from the industrial revolution onwards, in which signs masked 'the *absence* of a basic reality' (Baudrillard 2001: 173); and finally the current era, in which signs bear no relation to reality. In this postmodern world of simulation, where the sign no longer corresponds to the real, reality 'implodes', generating what Baudrillard terms **hyperreality**.

While many commentators have found in this thesis cause for concern, Baudrillard celebrates simulation. In a notorious essay, 'The Year 2000 Will Not Take Place', he argues that the age of simulation signals the end of history, which also means the end of **Marx**'s idea of alienation. Marx argues that under capitalism workers experience a sense of extreme separation from each other, the products of their labour, and even from themselves. Marxists have looked askance at Baudrillard's easy assumption that alienation will only come to an end along with history itself, rather than by any material change. In common with **Fukuyama**, Baudrillard is criticized for nihilism and vagueness in his 'end of history' thesis. Yet his description of simulation is seen as perspicacious by many working in the fields of cybernetics, virtual reality and hyperspace. [CC]

See also Chapter 10.

Further reading

Baudrillard, Jean (1987) 'The Year 2000 will Not Take Place', in Elizabeth Grosz (ed.), *Futur*Fall: Excursions into Post-modernity*, Sydney: Power Institute Publications.

Baudrillard, Jean (2001) *Jean Baudrillard: Selected Writings*, ed. Mark Poster, Stanford, CA: Stanford University Press.

SONTAG, SUSAN (1933–2004) American critical theorist whose work addresses subjects as diverse as the **metalanguage** of disease and the restrictive nature of critique. In *Illness as Metaphor* (1983) and *AIDS and its Metaphors* (1989) Sontag argues that the **discourses** surrounding conditions such as cancer and AIDS are often more distressing and harmful than the ailment's physical symptoms. *Against Interpretation and Other Essays* (1994) demonstrates her belief that the **mimesis** of critique stifles through its prevention of creativity. It is, however, Sontag's collection of essays *On Photography* (first published 1971) that represents her most insightful contribution to critical theory and academic thinking.

On Photography presents a diverse analysis of the medium's historical development alongside a critical evaluation of its status both as an art form and as a means of social control. Undoubtedly inspired by **Foucault**'s writing on 'the birth of the prison', Sontag discusses the **ethics** of the camera and reveals the covert **panopticism** of photography's discourse. Analysing terms such as 'loading', 'aiming' and 'shooting', she argues that, since its inception, photography has been widely utilized within the policing of society. Whether used in colonial or domestic spaces, the camera has at its disposal the ability to create and then capture its **subject** in a celluloid prison. For Sontag, the **power** of photography derives from its ability to present itself as 'true' and unmediated whilst hiding the human intervention that 'frames' the subject.

In addition to her academic writing, Sontag was a novelist, playwright and filmmaker. [PSW]

Further reading

Sontag, Susan (1983) *A Susan Sontag Reader*, Harmondsworth: Penguin.

Sontag, Susan (1991) *Illness as Metaphor and AIDS and its Metaphors*, London: Penguin.

Sontag, Susan (2002) *On Photography*, London: Penguin.

SPEECH ACT THEORY A theory that considers the linguistic utterance as a kind of action and has its founding statement in J. L. **Austin**'s *How to Do Things with Words* (1962).

Speech act theory analyses the different acts performed when language is used, regarding the whole process as systematic and rule-governed. Austin classifies the different acts involved in speaking as locutionary (the act of saying something), illocutionary (what you do *in* saying something, e.g. remind, assert), and perlocutionary (what further actions you may accomplish *by* saying something, e.g. by asserting, I may persuade you of the truth of a statement). In making an utterance, a speaker generally performs two or even all three of these actions.

As well as receiving much attention from philosophers of language, speech act theory has also been applied to literature by critics such as J. Hillis **Miller** and Mary-Louise Pratt. [KM]

Further reading

Austin, John Langshaw (1962) *How to Do Things with Words*, Oxford: Oxford University Press.

Miller, J. Hillis (2001) *Speech Acts in Literature*, Stanford, CA: Stanford University Press.

Pratt, Mary-Louise (1977) *Toward a Speech Act Theory of Literary Discourse*, London: Indiana University Press.

SPIVAK, GAYATRI CHAKRAVORTY (1942–) Born in India, Gayatri Spivak's work has been highly influential to critical theory in general and postcolonial theory in particular. She first came to prominence through her translation of Jacques **Derrida**'s seminal work, *Of Grammatology*, which also included an extensive explication of this text and the strategy of **deconstruction**. Since then, her main works have included *In Other Worlds*, *A Critique of Post-Colonial Reason* and *Death of a Discipline*.

Spivak's work has to a large degree been concerned with advancing deconstructive theory into the areas of postcolonial studies, feminism and **Marxism**. Following on from Derrida's attempt to collapse binary oppositions, Spivak's work focuses on the idea of 'margins' and how the idea of the 'outside' can unsettle hegemonic discourse.

In addition, Spivak has been instrumental in developing subaltern studies. Subalterns are those who are absolutely repressed or marginalized but, significantly, for Spivak this can only be understood in the postcolonial sense, and much of her work in this area has been to emphasize how the term subaltern cannot

be applied to any disenfranchised group in general.

Spivak's recent work has been concerned with rethinking and radicalizing the concept of postcolonialism, a concept that appears in danger of being institutionalized and therefore less effective as a strategy of emancipation. [JS]

See also Chapters 7, 8 and 9.

Further reading

Spivak, Gayatri Chakravorty (1988b) *In Other Worlds: Essays in Cultural Politics*, London: Methuen.

Spivak, Gayatri Chakravorty (1996) *The Spivak Reader*, ed. Donna Landry and Gerald MacLean, London: Routledge.

SUBJECT A term used in both psychoanalytic and cultural theory that refers to the rational, active mind of the human individual. It is defined in opposition to the object – that which is other than consciousness. This notion relates to the formulation of the seventeenth-century philosopher René Descartes, 'I think, therefore I am', where objects can only be understood in relation to subjective knowledge. Throughout the twentieth century this formulation has undergone re-evaluation with the condition or conceptualization of the subject a heated area of analysis and debate.

The political philosophy derived from the work of Karl **Marx** contended that the subject is constituted through material conditions. Various European Marxists later refined this economic determinism. Antonio **Gramsci** formulated a notion of **hegemony** where the subject was enmeshed in a cultural network, which persuaded it to act in a certain way. The work of the **Frankfurt School** explored how the **culture industry** had resulted in a standardization of individual identity.

Another alternative to economic determinism was to medicalize the formation of individual subjectivity. At the beginning of the twentieth century Sigmund **Freud** had developed psychoanalysis as a way of recuperating a coherent sense of self from the pressures of modern existence. For him the civilizing process and culture had arisen in response to the dangerous drives of the **unconscious** or **id**, which threatened to erupt at any moment. Through careful analysis of unconscious expression such as dreams and jokes he endeavoured to detail a clinical method for maintaining the individual psyche.

Many practising psychoanalysts adopted this notion, but Jacques **Lacan** developed the way Freudian ideas were implemented. In Lacanian psychoanalysis, the subject's perception of the world is made up of three layers: the **symbolic**, the **imaginary** and the **real**. The real exists completely outside the reach of language and representation, which is the symbolic realm; the imaginary is the fantasy zone where the subject and the world are presented as undifferentiated. For Lacan the subject is barred or obstructed from surfacing by the **ego**, which operates as an imaginary platform for the speaker and an alternate site of identification. Lacan sought to revive the subject by isolating its specific desires, representations and significations through systematic clinical practice.

Crucially for cultural theory, Lacanian psychoanalysis problematized the notion of an essential subject, decentring the self as a locus for political contestation. For Marxist Louis **Althusser** the subject is coordinated by manufactured social structures operating through **ideology**. Following Lacan, individuals are '**interpellated**', or have their identities configured, primarily through **Ideological State Apparatuses** which induce an 'imaginary' perception of everyday existence. Through this mechanism people's sense of identity can be manipulated and controlled.

This notion of identity had particular implications for marginalized subcultures that objected to the dominant cultural configuration. The French cultural theorist Michel **Foucault**, himself tutored by Althusser, explored how apparently objective structures in society censure certain groups which they categorize as deviant. He outlined how identity was constructed through the dominant **discourse**, and how **power** induced an internalization of its conventions though surveillance and punishment. Subsequent theorists of race, sexuality, gender and class have drawn on his ideas to emphasize repressive social structures that arbitrarily exclude one group or another.

Alongside this theoretical re-evaluation, poststructuralists such as the French deconstructionist Jacques **Derrida** question the very basis of identity. For Derrida the subject is only constructed though **différance**. Any signifier or series of signification – for example, a text or identity – must continually defer its meaning because the **sign** is itself made up of signifiers. This results in the infinite play of possibilities and the ability to switch, or slip, through different identities.

Derrida's notion that everything is relational and unfixed became crucial to the development of postmodernism. With no stable values or identities, culture was seen as endlessly fluid and able to be shaped according to individual lifestyles and desires. However, this was fiercely criticized by many analysts including Fredric **Jameson**, who viewed it as the ultimate expression of multinational capitalism, amorphous and impossible to combat. This argument has shaped the resistance to the economic form of postmodernism, **globalization**, with a focus on cultural specificity in an international context rather than corporate homogenization. [RW]

See also Chapter 6.

SUBLIME Along with the beautiful, the sublime is one of the key categories of aesthetics. While an experience of beauty tends to work in terms of a perceived harmony between the subject and the object, a sublime experience entails a mixture of exhilaration and terror through the sense that one might be overwhelmed or even annihilated by the magnitude or power of what is experienced. In classical aesthetics, the stress generally falls upon the **subject**'s ability to resolve and be ennobled by such an experience, whereas for more recent theorists its interest lies in the ways in which sublimity is able to shatter the everyday flow of experience and reconfigure identity. This latter idea of the sublime is a cornerstone of postmodern theory, and is crucial to the work of thinkers such as Jean-François **Lyotard**. [SM]

See also Chapter 10.

Further reading

Lyotard, Jean-François (1992) *The Postmodern Explained to Children: Correspondence 1982–1985*, trans. Don Barry, Bernadette Maher, Julian Pefanis, Virginia Spate and Morgan Thomas, London: Turnaround.

SUPEREGO The superego is a **Freudian** concept that refers to the first and most important identification with a world beyond the confines of the **ego**. For Freud the object of this identification is a father figure, a position of **symbolic** authority that represents the foundational prohibition of access to the maternal body. The superego is produced by the identification with the position of symbolic authority, a process in which the act of identification with something outside the ego ('I am like that') involves a part of the ego becoming detached. This process of detachment produces the paradoxical agency of the superego, a process in which the portion of the ego that has become detached is now set against the narcissism of the ego because it represents both a limitation ('you cannot have that') and a position from which the conduct and value of the ego can be judged. The superego mediates between the defensive inwardness of the ego and the social world beyond it by setting limits to its otherwise boundless drive for self-gratification. As an agency of prohibition it is what permits the provisional social co-existence of a multiplicity of egos and it is associated with the law, custom, tradition and moral codes. [HJ]

See also Chapter 6.

Further reading

Freud, Sigmund (1991) 'The Ego and the Id', in *The Essentials of Psycho-Analysis*, trans. James Strachey, London: Penguin.

SUPPLEMENT In ordinary language, a supplement is something added to an already complete whole. The possibility of something being added, however, reveals a lack in the original it is meant to complete. A supplement therefore has the potential to supplant the very thing which it is meant to restore to its proper, original state. Dietary supplements, for example, which are usually taken to compensate for dietary inadequacies, can become a substitute for healthy eating. French philosopher Jacques **Derrida** extends the contradictory logic of the word 'supplement' in order to interrogate the conventional Western idea that speech, as the original form of language, is merely represented by writing. Derrida argues that the structure of writing is not secondary to, but inextricable from, that of speech itself. This challenges the supposed 'originality' of speech in relation to writing. More importantly, it upsets the idea of a natural relationship between speech and truth. Sharing the structure of speech, writing can nevertheless signify without the presence of its **author**. It thus threatens the idea that language's meaning has its origin in the speaking **subject**. [JP]

See also Chapters 4 and 7.

SYMBOLIC ORDER A concept associated with the psychoanalytic theory of Jacques **Lacan**. In contrast to the **imaginary**, which is premised upon the **subject**'s fascination with a fixed image that it takes to be confirmation of its unitary identity, the symbolic order contains images and **signs**, or **signifiers**, whose signified meaning is not fixed or automatically given. The Lacanian conception of the symbolic order emphasizes that words stand in for the absence of things themselves, so that the verbal sign does not mimic a pre-given reality but carves reality into conceptual shape for human subjects. In order to produce a consistent symbolic reality, such as the linguistic, cultural and conventional norms that underpin social groupings, the symbolic order is regularly punctuated in such a way as to produce a unity of signification. In this way certain key signifiers, for example 'freedom', can be associated with a specific signified meaning, such as

in the discourse of Western liberal democracy where it stands for human rights and the primacy of commerce. There is no automatic or natural equivalence between the two; different societies at various stages of history have operated with other signified meanings of 'freedom', and even within one discursive community the production of signified meaning is the basis for social and political engagement. In short, the symbolic order is the world of language and culture in which subjects exist. [HJ]

See also Chapter 6.

Further reading

Bowie, Malcolm (1991) *Lacan*, London: Fontana.

Lacan, Jacques (1977) *Écrits: A Selection*, trans. Alan Sheridan, London: Routledge.

T

TERRITORIALIZATION / DETERRITORIALIZ-
ATION / RETERRITORIALIZATION Coined
by French poststructuralist thinkers Gilles
Deleuze and Félix **Guattari**, these terms
describe a concept of material change
often used in postmodern and postcolonial
theory. In *A Thousand Plateaus* (first published 1980), Deleuze and Guattari argue
that the physical, biological and cultural
world is made up of layered regulatory
systems or 'strata'. Preserving unity and
uniformity, these strata work within the
fixed elements and limits that they also
constitute and maintain. While experience
presents constant variation, these differences are always cancelled out by the strata.
Changes to individual elements cannot
transform the whole system. However, the
variable potentials and qualities of matter
itself constantly overflow the strata, forming a **body without organs** that gives rise to
new systems and structures. And since they
do not depend upon but *constitute* the fixed
units they order, the strata also have a
virtual existence 'alongside' the actual
matter they affect. Deleuze and Guattari
therefore characterize stratified systems as
'territorialized', embodied instances of an
abstract function. This abstract or virtual
function differs from Plato's unchanging,
intangible Idea, however, as it is precisely
because strata are 'territorialized' that they
are also subject to processes of *de*territorialization, where **differences** escape
from territorialized functions, and *re*territorialization, where new systems are
formed or, conversely, an old one is re-
embodied in a different situation. Rather
than a Platonic denial of change and difference, Deleuze and Guattari offer a novel
way of thinking its concrete reality. [DH]

THOMPSON, EDWARD PALMER (1924–1993)
Left-wing historian and political activist
who, alongside the critics Raymond
Williams and Richard **Hoggart**, played
an important role in the foundation of
'cultural studies' as an academic discipline.

Thompson's *The Making of the English
Working Class* (first published 1963) was a
pioneering work of social history which
aimed to rescue the ordinary lives of working people from 'the enormous conde-
scension of posterity' (1968: 13), and to
demonstrate that the development of class-
consciousness is 'an active process, which
owes as much to agency as to conditioning'
(1968: 9).

Thompson's belief in the autonomy of
the individual was reflected in his politics.
Amongst the first 'New Left' intellectuals,
Thompson quit the Communist Party and
established *New Reasoner*, a journal of
'socialist humanism' that was later
subsumed into *New Left Review*. Soon
afterwards, its editorial agenda moved
towards continental theorists such as Louis
Althusser, prompting Thompson, in 'The
Poverty of Theory' (1978), to declare
'unrelenting intellectual war' (1978: 381)
against Althusserian theory, which, he felt,
presented citizens as 'utterly passive'
(1978: 366) victims of **ideology**. [CRC]
See also Chapters 3 and 5.

Further reading
Thompson, Edward Palmer (1968) *The
Making of the English Working* Class,
Harmondsworth: Penguin.
Thompson, Edward Palmer (1978) *The
Poverty of Theory and Other Essays*,
London: Merlin Press.

TODOROV, TZVETAN (1939–) Theorist best known for his work on French structuralism and his scientific study of narrative, an approach that has come to be known as narratology. His most recent critical assessments, such as *The Fragility of Goodness: Why Bulgaria's Jews Survived the Holocaust* (2001) and *Hopes and Memory: Lessons from the Twentieth Century* (2003), have been carried out in the critical field of Holocaust studies.

Todorov clarifies his narratological methodology in *Poetics of Prose* (1971; trans. 1977). Influenced by the work of Ferdinand de **Saussure** and Roland **Barthes** in linguistics, and Vladimir **Propp**'s study of folklore, Todorov reinvigorated interest in earlier **Russian formalists** such as Boris Eichenbaum and Victor **Shklovsky**, and is specifically associated with the production of a scientific study, or 'grammar', of narrative. Todorov names his study of literature a 'poetics', referring to Aristotle's definition of poetics as the study of human-made rather than natural artefacts. Todorov's grammar of narrative charts similarities in plot between stories. According to this schema, each tale begins in a state of 'equilibrium', with all as it should be, then moves to the disruption of that state, or 'disequilibrium', and evidence that the disturbance has been recognized. Then attempts are made to sort out the consequences of the disturbance, concluding with a transformed 'equilibrium', that is different from the equilibrium of the beginning. Todorov points out that narratives do not need to be linear to follow this 'broad schema', but that the pattern is apparent in all tales, regardless of subject matter.

Todorov's theories have been appropriated by more recent criticism in cultural studies, such as **Marxism**, feminism, postmodernism and new historicism, and his narratological paradigm, widely acknowledged as formative, remains highly influential, constituting a significant field in critical theory more generally. [TES]

See also Chapters 1 and 2.

Further reading

Culler, Jonathan (1975) *Structuralist Poetics: Structuralism, Linguistics and the Study of Literature*, London: Routledge and Kegan Paul.

Todorov, Tzvetan (1977) *The Poetics of Prose*, trans. Richard Howard, Oxford: Blackwell.

Todorov, Tzvetan (1990) *Genres in Discourse*, translated Catherine Porter, New York: Cambridge University Press.

TRACE That component of language which differentiates between **signs** and makes meaning possible. Coined by the French philosopher Jacques **Derrida**, the trace encompasses everything that a **sign** is not and through the marking of its **difference** creates structured meanings. To comprehend any given sign, one must first acknowledge all that it is not and then erase it. That which is erased is the trace, and without it language as a system of differences could not function.

For Derrida, the trace represents the absolute origin of sense. He then clarifies this notion and concludes that because every trace is always the trace of another, there can be no such origin. Similarly, as each **signifier** only ever signifies in relation to others, the search for any absolute meaning is an endless and fruitless one.

Although referred to in the affirmative, the trace is actually a lack, the presence of an absence or the absence of presence, the antithesis of the sign. Because of the arbitrary make-up of language, of signifiers having no natural connection with their **signified**, the functioning of the trace is crucial. Without the trace, signs would be indiscernible, their opposition impossible, and language systems ineffectual. [PSW]

See also Chapter 7.

Further reading

Derrida, Jacques (1997) *Of Grammatology*, trans. Gayatri Chakravorty Spivak, Baltimore, MD: Johns Hopkins University Press.

TRAUMA THEORY A theory developed from the work of Sigmund **Freud** and his predecessors, notably Pierre Janet. Freud drew an analogy between the breaking of the skin (physical trauma) and the breaking of the psyche's 'protective shield' (psychological trauma). The psychologically traumatized person was flooded by unprocessed affect or emotion and might be shocked into a condition of numbness. More generally, the effect of trauma was the inability to integrate affect and representation: one felt overwhelmingly what one could not represent with a sufficient degree of critical control or recall, and one might be able to represent numbly or with aloofness what one could not feel. The most controversial aspect of Freud's theory was the notion that trauma pointed to the role of delayed temporality (*Nachträglichkeit*) whereby an early traumatizing event or the fantasy thereof (such as sexual abuse or 'seduction') was repressed or dissociated only to be reactivated after a period of 'latency' by a later, perhaps trivial, event that triggered, through repetition, the onset of post-traumatic symptoms.

The First World War involved battle conditions that subjected significant numbers of soldiers to 'shell shock' or trauma. More recently, the study of the Holocaust has been instrumental in the crystallization of the subfield of trauma theory in various areas of inquiry: literary theory, narrative, medicine, neurophysiology, philosophy, psychology, and intellectual and cultural history. A focus of exploration has been the link between trauma and extreme events such as child abuse, rape, the Holocaust, atrocities in colonial or postcolonial territories, or the bombing of Hiroshima and Nagasaki, among other events, especially those of genocidal proportions.

Post-traumatic symptoms include various forms of intrusive behaviour that do not seem appropriate or called for in a given context: startle reactions, nightmares, anxiety attacks, and other types of compulsive behaviour. The person in the throes of a post-traumatic symptom feels as if he or she were reliving the past, and the future is blocked. Freud terms such compulsive reliving of a past experience 'acting out', and he contrasts it with 'working through', which enables remembering the past in its distinction from the present, thereby allowing a measure of critical control over behaviour and an opening to possible futures. Forms of working through include mourning, which attempts to exorcise or lay to rest the haunting presences of the past that continue to have unsettling and **uncanny** effects in the present. Yet there are many complex combinations of acting out and working through, and the severely traumatized person is subject to remission and may never definitively transcend the tendency to relive or act out the past. The problem of whether and how it might be possible to work through post-traumatic symptoms remains an issue in trauma theory, and a related question is what types of activity might effectively assist in the process (psychotherapy, socio-political action, writing and other signifying practices such as ritual, song and dance).

A phenomenon that concerned analysts after Freud was the inter- or transgenerational transmission of trauma whereby one who did not personally live through a traumatic event might nonetheless manifest post-traumatic symptoms. Inter-generational transmission of trauma may especially affect intimates of survivors, but it may also arise in those who live with fraught legacies (the Holocaust, slavery, colonialism, child abuse) or even those who are moved to identify with victims for various reasons. The latter process becomes dubious when a person who did not live through the trauma claims he or she is indeed an actual survivor, the case, for example, with Binjamin Wilkomirski, author of the false memoir *Fragments: Memories of a Wartime Childhood* (1995;

trans. 1996), in which the author-narrator claims to be a Holocaust survivor. In the recent past, the discussion of 'false memory' has been especially heated in cases involving accusations of abuse with respect to parents or other authority figures.

The phenomenon of reliving, through identification, what others have lived, as well as that of the inter-generational transmission of trauma, has been a topic in literature and art. For example, the ghost in Toni Morrison's acclaimed novel, *Beloved* (1987), might be interpreted as a hallucinatory post-traumatic symptom that is experienced even by those who are not former slaves but who participate in a context marked by the legacies of slavery. The ghost is ambivalent – both a haunting negative force and something 'beloved' that is a bond between the living and the dead. It is worked through or laid to rest through a complex process that may never reach closure, including a mourning chant of a collectivity of African-American women toward the end of the novel. In Henri Raczymow's novel, *Writing the Book of Esther* (1985; trans. 1995), the protagonist Esther relives the experience of an aunt who died in Auschwitz, even going to the extreme of shaving her head, wearing prison garb, starving and finally gassing herself.

A further significant phenomenon, sometimes enacted by trauma theorists themselves, is the sacralization or rendering **sublime** of trauma. In addition, events such as the Holocaust or the bombing of Hiroshima and Nagasaki may become founding or foundational traumas for a collectivity and sacralized as centres of a civic religion with its ceremonies and memorials (including the ritualized viewing of a film such as Claude Lanzmann's *Shoah* as well as the figuration of Lanzmann himself as a kind of secular saint or prophet). In the history of Christianity, the crucifixion of Christ might be seen as a founding trauma commemorated in the mass, indeed a trauma that has an inter-

generational dimension in the 'imitation' of Christ, which may even lead to stigmata as somatic, mimetically induced symptoms of trauma in those who have not been crucified. The tendency to sacralize or 'sublimate' trauma marks both groups and individuals, and (as indicated in Morrison's *Beloved*) those who have been traumatized may even experience certain 'symptoms', or haunting presences such as recurrent nightmares, not as mere pathologies but as tributes or memorials binding them to dead intimates.

The tendency to sacralize or render trauma sublime may be most open to question when it is performed by commentators or theorists with respect to the suffering of others, as in Giorgio **Agamben**'s rhetorical flights in discussing the most **abject** of camp victims (the *Muselmänner*) or even in Slavoj **Žižek**'s notion of the 'ethic' of psychoanalysis as requiring 'fidelity' to the sublimely traumatic **Lacanian** 'real'. One important point such cases bring out is that trauma theory itself is not a unified field but one which is repeatedly in crisis, in that there is debate on crucial issues of definition, understanding, analysis and justifiable response. [DL]

See also Chapter 6.

Further reading

Caruth, Cathy (1996) *Unclaimed Experience: Trauma, Narrative and History*, Baltimore, MD: John Hopkins University Press.

Eisenstein, Paul (2003) *Traumatic Encounters: Holocaust Representation and the Hegelian Subject*, Albany, NY: State University of New York Press.

LaCapra, Dominick (2000) *Writing History, Writing Trauma*, Baltimore, MD: Johns Hopkins University Press.

Leys, Ruth (2000) *Trauma: A Genealogy*, Chicago, IL: University of Chicago Press.

Rothberg, Michael (2000) *Traumatic Realism: The Demands of Holocaust Representation*, Minneapolis, MN: University of Minnesota Press.

U

UNCANNY An experience of the unexpected in life or art which has the effect of rendering the familiar strange or the strange familiar. It also denotes a particular disconcerting effect of eerie fear which brings to mind something so long familiar that it has become taken for granted or forgotten. Sigmund **Freud** suggests that this can be read as a symptom of an early repression. The uncanny is a sign that something once familiar from a community or an individual's childhood or 'prehistory' has now returned from a state of repression. It is manifested as a feeling of being at odds with oneself. Psychoanalysis reads the uncanny symptom in order to diagnose a patient's neurosis. Similarly, by being attentive to uncanny effects in conventional narratives – for example, the intrusion of odd coincidences, repetition, *déjà vu* and automatism – literary and cultural critics can examine how texts are constructed to give an effect of **realism** or truth. The uncanny thus unsettles conventional forms and definitions. [JP]

See also Chapter 6.

Further reading

Freud, Sigmund (1985) 'The "Uncanny"', in *Art and Literature: Jensen's 'Gradiva', Leonardo da Vinci and Other Works*, trans. James Strachey, Harmondsworth: Penguin.
Royle, Nicholas (2003b) *The Uncanny*, Manchester: Manchester University Press.

UNCONSCIOUS The idea of the unconscious is most closely associated with Sigmund **Freud**, although it was given an influential reinterpretation in the work of Jacques **Lacan**. Freud developed his theory of the unconscious as a way of explaining how human speech and actions are distorted and influenced by the actions of a domain of the psyche that is radically discontinuous with the **subject**'s conscious self-image, the **ego**. The unconscious component of the subject's psyche is individual and pre-social; it is the domain where the biological **drives** are initially lodged, not yet domesticated within language and culture, but registered as mental impressions. Freud also developed the idea of the unconscious as a place in which experiences and recollections that were unpalatable to the ego were repressed. One of Freud's clearest accounts of this is given in his 1915 essay, 'The Unconscious'.

While the unconscious was, for Freud, remote from the primarily linguistic and symbolic functions of the conscious ego, this did not mean that it had no influence on the ego. Whether as the repository of the primal drives or repressed memories, the unconscious can, and frequently does, disturb the operation of the ego. This was evident to Freud not only through the analysis of dreams, a process in which the conscious censorship of the ego is partially suspended, but also in the speech of the subject, such as the notorious 'Freudian slip' in which the unconscious desire of the subject is held to be revealed.

Lacan produced a theory of the unconscious that drew heavily on structural linguistics. He posited the idea that the unconscious was divided between **signifiers** and **signifieds** in a way analogous to language. In one of his most famous pronouncements Lacan stated that 'the unconscious is structured like a language'

(Lacan 1994: 20), by which he means that a dream, for example, can be studied in terms of the signifier or manifest recollected content, and a signified or latent meaning which the process of analysis can decode. While Freud's initial conception of the unconscious called for a study of the way in which this mute domain influences conscious speech, Lacan allowed the unconscious to be studied as a place in which meaning can be generated in its own right. [HJ]

See also Chapter 6.

Further reading

Easthope, Antony (1999) *The Unconscious*, London: Routledge.

Freud, Sigmund (1991) 'The Unconscious', in (1991b) *On Metapsychology: The Theory of Psychoanalysis, Beyond the Pleasure Principle, The Ego and the Id, and Other Works*, London: Penguin.

VIRILIO, PAUL (1932–) French cultural theorist best known for his work on the organization of military space, the logic of acceleration and futurology. His works include *Speed and Politics*, *The Vision Machine*, *The Art of the Motor* and *Open Sky*.

Virilio's early theoretical work was concerned essentially with military space and was developed through an analysis of German bunkers from the Second World War along the Atlantic coast of France. He argued that the construction of urban space has been dictated by military considerations and, therefore, that war is a crucial determinant of cultural development. Throughout his early work, Virilio also took a major interest in architectural theory, especially in terms of what he calls 'the oblique function' which disrupts a notion of architecture centred on vertical and horizontal constructs.

From this Virilio develops his theory of 'dromology', or the logic of speed, to explore the condition of contemporary culture. According to Virilio, modern society is characterized by the need for ever increasing acceleration (for travel, communications, etc.). However, he argues that this increase in speed in society does not necessarily imply an increase in progress.

Virilio's recent work has focused on issues surrounding the internet, genetics and the war on terrorism. Despite seeming to share similar interests to Jean **Baudrillard**, Virilio remains anti-postmodern and regards his own work as being more closely linked to themes concerned with a continuing modernity. [JS]

See also Chapter 10.

Further reading

Virilio, Paul (1995) *The Art of the Motor*, trans. Julie Rose, Minneapolis, MN: University of Minnesota Press.

Virilio, Paul (2002) *Ground Zero*, trans. Chris Turner, London: Verso.

WEST, CORNEL (1953–) As a leading African-American academic philosopher, public intellectual and social critic, Cornel West deliberately equates his own work with that of earlier American public thinkers/activists such as Ralph Waldo Emerson, Walt Whitman, W. E. B. **Du Bois** and Martin Luther King Jr. As a philosopher, West writes in the Socratic mode of inquiry and open scepticism; his work openly displays a huge range of influences including **Marxist** materialism, Christian ethics, and American pragmatism. West's writing can seem self-contradictory and inconclusive at times, but that is the point; for example, in *The Future of the Race* (1996) West writes of Du Bois's 'intellectual defects' but also of his 'broad shoulders', upon whom West and others stand. A key element of West's work is a determination to connect African-American culture with other cultures, most specifically Russian and (often controversially) Jewish culture. In his most powerful essays, West evokes the force of Hegelian **Enlightenment** thinking, **Nietzschean** post-Enlightenment thinking, the absurdism of Kafka and Beckett *and* straightforward political activism: for the reader, this can often be exhilarating and an impetus to new ways of thinking about a problem/idea. West has written over 20 books, and his most important essays have been collected in *The Cornel West Reader* (1999). Some significant essays are 'Race and Modernity', 'Black Strivings in a Twilight Civilization', 'Race and Social Theory' and 'The Dilemma of the Black Intellectual'. [KH]

See also Chapter 11.

Further reading

Cruse, Harold (2005) *The Crisis of the Negro Intellectual*, London: Granta.

Gates, Henry Louis Jr, and West, Cornel (1997) *The Future of the Race*, London: Vintage.

West, Cornel (1994) *Race Matters*, London: Vintage.

WHITE, HAYDEN V. (1928–) American historian whose work has been highly influential for contemporary historiography. White's best-known contribution to historical theory is the notion of 'metahistory', a term borrowed from Northrop **Frye**'s major work of literary criticism *Anatomy of Criticism* (1957). The literary lineage of the term is apt as White argues that rather than being somehow natural, verifiable and objective, historical narratives are themselves governed by the same mechanism as their self-avowed literary counterparts. In other words, historical narratives are created, or rather **authored**, objects that attempt to conceal their fictional status through their own **mimetic** practices. White argues that there is no single 'correct' view of historical 'reality', and that by recognizing the possibility of shifting methodological approaches

> we should no longer naively expect that statements about a given epoch or complex of events in the past 'correspond' to some pre-existent body of 'raw facts'. For we should recognize that what constitutes the facts themselves is the problem that the historian . . . has tried to solve in the choice of metaphor by which he orders his world, past, present and future.
>
> (White 1978: 47)

Consequently, there is no position from which the question of historical legitimacy can be resolved, and therefore historical texts should be subjected to the sorts of critical analysis that are used by critics of literature. [PW]

See also Chapters 5 and 10.

Further reading

White, Hayden (1973) *Metahistory: The Historical Imagination in Nineteenth-Century Europe*, Baltimore, MD: Johns Hopkins University Press.

White, Hayden (1978) *Tropics of Discourse: Essays in Cultural Criticism*, Baltimore, MD: Johns Hopkins University Press.

WILLIAMS, RAYMOND HENRY (1921–88) Welsh literary critic who, along with the English critic Richard **Hoggart** and historian E. P. **Thompson**, played an important role in the establishment of 'cultural studies' as an academic discipline.

Considered a pioneer in this field, Williams broadened the notion of what could legitimately be studied by including films, television and advertising, as well as 'literary' texts as objects of critical analysis, while also locating them historically and politically. Where early work such as the influential *Culture and Society 1780–1850* (1958) is representative of 'left-Leavisism', which attempted to harness the critical methodology of F. R. **Leavis** to a 'socialist humanism', Williams would later engage more overtly with **Marxist** theory. This is most evident in the essays collected in *Marxism and Literature* (1977), which articulate a theory of **cultural materialism**. This theory, which has been a major influence on subsequent generations of Marxist critics, is Williams' most important legacy. [CRC]

See also Chapter 5.

Further reading

Williams, Raymond (1958) *Culture and Society 1780–1950*, London: Chatto and Windus.

Williams, Raymond (1976) *Keywords: A Vocabulary of Culture and Society*, London: Fontana.

Williams, Raymond (1977) *Marxism and Literature*, Oxford: Oxford University Press.

Z

ŽIŽEK, SLAVOJ (1949–) Slovenian philosopher and cultural theorist, whose main works include *Looking Awry: An Introduction to Jacques Lacan through Popular Culture*, *Tarrying with the Negative* and *The Sublime Object of Ideology*.

Žižek's work is primarily concerned with the psychoanalytic theories of Jacques **Lacan**, an influence that has remained significant within his thought to the present day. In particular, Žižek uses Lacanian psychoanalysis in order to investigate elements of popular culture, especially cinema. This approach has proved particularly useful to those who are normally put off by the sheer density and complexity of Lacan's arguments. Žižek's use of popular culture has therefore provided a way into an extremely complex branch of critical theory that might otherwise have remained closed off to a large number of readers.

This use of theory in order to explain and explore aspects of contemporary and popular culture is also developed by Žižek in the areas of philosophy and political economy. In *Tarrying with the Negative*, Žižek analyses how the philosophy of Hegel and Kant can be used to elucidate current issues within society, whereas in *The Sublime Object of Ideology* he investigates questions of ideology and control through a complex mix of **Marxism**, Lacanian psychoanalysis and popular culture.

Žižek's latest work demonstrates a wide variety of concerns. He has written prolifically on topical areas such as totalitarianism, September 11th and the war in Iraq. His most recent work has centred on a re-evaluation of the understanding of Lenin through a careful analysis of his revolutionary writings. His approach to these topics has developed out of the Lacanian-style thinking that was prevalent in his earlier work. [JS]

See also Chapters 3 and 6.

Further reading
Žižek, Slavoj (1989) *The Sublime Object of Ideology*, London: Verso.

Žižek, Slavoj (1991) *Looking Awry: An Introduction to Lacan through Popular Culture*, Cambridge, MA: MIT Press.

Žižek, Slavoj (1993) *Tarrying with the Negative: Kant, Hegel and the Critique of Ideology*, Durham, NC: Duke University Press.

Žižek, Slavoj (1999) *The Žižek Reader*, ed. Elizabeth Wright and Edmund Wright, Oxford: Blackwell.

Žižek, Slavoj (2002) *Welcome to the Desert of the Real!: Five Essays on September 11th and Related Dates*, London: Verso.

BIBLIOGRAPHY

Abelove, Henry, Barale, Michèle Aina and Halperin, David (eds) (1993) *The Lesbian and Gay Studies Reader*, London: Routledge.

Adorno, Theodor W. (1978) 'On the Fetish-Character in Music and the Regression of Listening', in Andrew Arato and Eike Gebhardt (eds), *The Essential Frankfurt School Reader*, New York: Urizen Books.

Adorno, Theodor W. (1983) *Prisms*, Cambridge, MA: MIT Press.

Adorno, Theodor W. (2001) *The Culture Industry: Selected Essays on Mass Culture*, ed. J. M. Bernstein, New York: Routledge.

Adorno, Theodor W. and Horkheimer, Max (1992) *Dialectic of Enlightenment*, trans. John Cumming, London: Verso.

Adorno, Theodor W., Benjamin, Walter, Bloch, Ernst, Brecht, Bertolt and Lukács, Georg (1980) *Aesthetics and Politics: The Key Texts of the Classic Debate within German Marxism*, London: Verso.

Agamben, Giorgio (1998) *Homo Sacer: Sovereign Power and Bare Life*, trans. Daniel Heller-Roazen, Stanford, CA: Stanford University Press.

Agamben, Giorgio (1999) *The Man Without Content*, trans. Georgia Albert, Stanford, CA: Stanford University Press.

Allen, Graham (1994) *Harold Bloom: Poetics of Conflict*, New York: Harvester Wheatsheaf.

Allen, Graham (2000) *Intertextuality*, London: Routledge.

Althusser, Louis (1996) *For Marx*, trans. Ben Brewster, London: Verso.

Althusser, Louis (2001) *Lenin and Philosophy and Other Essays*, trans. Ben Brewster, New York: Monthly Review Press.

Anzaldúa, Gloria (1987) *Borderlands/La Frontera: The New Mestiza*, San Francisco, CA: Aunt Lute Books.

Appiah, Kwame Anthony (1990) 'Racisms', in *Anatomy of Racism*, ed. David Theo Goldberg, Minneapolis, MN: University of Minnesota Press.

Appiah, Kwame Anthony (1992) *In My Father's House: Africa in the Philosophy of Culture*, New York: Oxford University Press.

Arato, Andrew and Gebhardt, Eike (eds) (1978) *The Essential Frankfurt School Reader*, New York: Urizen Books.

Arendt, Hannah (1999) *The Origins of Totalitarianism*, Orlando, FL: Harcourt Brace.

Aristotle (1996) *Poetics*, trans. Malcolm Heath, Harmondsworth: Penguin.

Ashcroft, Bill and Ahluwalia, Pal (2000) *Edward Said*, London: Routledge.

Ashcroft, Bill, Griffith, Gareth and Tiffin, Helen (1989) *The Empire Writes Back: Theory and Practice in Post-Colonial Literatures*, London: Routledge.

Atkins, Barry (2003) *More than a Game: The Computer Game as Fictional Form*, Manchester: Manchester University Press.

Auerbach, Erich (1953) *Mimesis: The Representation of Reality in Western Literature*, Princeton, NJ: Princeton University Press.

Austen, Jane (2003) *Northanger Abbey*, London: Penguin.

Austin, John Langshaw (1962a) *How to Do Things with Words*, Oxford: Oxford University Press.

Austin, John Langshaw (1962b) *Sense and Sensibilia*, Oxford: Oxford University Press.

Bachelard, Gaston (1968) *The Philosophy of No: A Philosophy of the New Scientific Mind*, trans. G. C. Waterston, New York: Orion Press.

Bachelard, Gaston (1971) *On Poetic Imagination and Reverie: Selections from the Works of Gaston Bachelard*, trans. Colette Gaudin, Indianapolis, IN: Bobbs Merrill.

Badiou, Alain (2001) *Ethics: An Essay on the Understanding of Evil*, trans. Peter Hallward, London: Verso.

Badiou, Alain (2004) *Infinite Thought: Truth and the Return of Philosophy*, trans. Oliver Feltham and Justin Clemens, London: Continuum.

Badmington, Neil (ed.) (2000) *Posthumanism*, Basingstoke and New York: Palgrave.

Bakhtin, Mikhail (1981) *The Dialogic Imagination: Four Essays*, ed. Michael Holquist, trans. Caryl Emerson and Michael Holquist, Austin, TX: University of Texas Press.

Bakhtin, Mikhail (1984) *Rabelais and his World*, trans. Hélène Iswolsky, Bloomington, IN: Indiana University Press.

Bakshi, Ralph (dir.) (1978) *The Lord of the Rings*, New York: Warner Bros.

Bal, Mieke (1985) *Narratology: Introduction to the Theory of Narrative*, trans. Christine van Boheemen, Toronto: University of Toronto Press.

Barthes, Roland (1975) *The Pleasure of the Text*, trans. Richard Miller, Oxford: Blackwell.

Barthes, Roland (1977a) *Image, Music, Text*, trans. Stephen Heath, London: Fontana.

Barthes, Roland (1977b) *Roland Barthes by Roland Barthes*, trans. Richard Howard, New York: Hill and Wang.

Barthes, Roland (1990a) *A Lover's Discourse: Fragments*, trans. Richard Howard, London: Penguin.

Barthes, Roland (1990b) *S/Z*, trans. Richard Miller, Oxford: Blackwell.

Barthes, Roland (1993) *Mythologies*, trans. Annette Lavers, London: Vintage.

Bataille, Georges (1990) *Literature and Evil*, trans. Alastair Hamilton, London: Marion Boyars Publishers.

Bataille, Georges (1991) *Eroticism*, trans. Mary Dalwood, San Francisco, CA: City Lights.

Baudrillard, Jean (1983) *Simulations*, trans. Paul Foss, Paul Patton and Philip Beitchman, New York: Semiotext(e).

Baudrillard, Jean (1987) 'The Year 2000 will Not Take Place', in Elizabeth Grosz (ed.), *Futur*Fall: Excursions into Postmodernity*, Sydney: Power Institute Publications.

Baudrillard, Jean (1994) *Simulacra and Simulation*, trans Sheila Glaser, Ann Arbor, MI: University of Michigan Press.

Baudrillard, Jean (1995) *The Gulf War Did Not Take Place*, trans. Paul Patton, Bloomington, IN: Indiana University Press.

Baudrillard, Jean (2001) *Jean Baudrillard: Selected Writings*, ed. Mark Poster, Stanford, CA: Stanford University Press.

Baudrillard, Jean (2002) *The Spirit of Terrorism*, trans. Chris Turner, London: Verso.

Bauman, Zygmunt (1998) *Globalization: The Human Consequences*, Cambridge: Polity Press.

Beauvoir, Simone de (1988) *The Second Sex*, trans. H. M. Parshley, London: Picador.

Belsey, Catherine (1985) *The Subject of Tragedy: Identity and Difference in Renaissance Drama*, London: Methuen.

Belsey, Catherine (1994) *Desire: Love Stories in Western Culture*, Oxford: Blackwell.

Belsey, Catherine (2002a) *Critical Practice*, London: Routledge.

Belsey, Catherine (2002b) *Poststructuralism: A Very Short Introduction*, Oxford: Oxford University Press.

Belsey, Catherine (2005) *Culture and the Real: Theorizing Cultural Criticism*, London: Routledge.

Belsey, Catherine and Moore, Jane (1989) *The Feminist Reader: Essays in Gender and the Politics of Literary Criticism*, London: Macmillan Education.

Benhabib, Seyla (1992) *Situating the Self: Gender, Community, and Postmodernism in Contemporary Ethics*, New York: Routledge.

Benjamin, Walter (1999) *Illuminations*, trans. Harry Zohn, London: Pimlico.

Benjamin, Walter (2000) *Selected Writings*, vol. 2: *1927–1934*, ed. Michael W. Jennings, Howard Eiland and Gary Smith, Cambridge, MA: Harvard University Press, pp. 507–30.

Bennett, David (1998) *Multicultural States: Rethinking Difference and Identity*, London: Routledge.

Bennington, Geoffrey (1999) *Jacques Derrida*, Chicago, IL: University of Chicago Press.

Benveniste, Emile (1971) *Problems in General Linguistics*, trans. Mary E. Meek, Miami, FL: University of Miami Press.

Bertens, Hans (1986) 'The Postmodern *Weltanschauung* and its Relation to Modernism: An Introductory Survey', in Douwe Fokkema and Hans Bertens (eds), *Approaching Postmodernism*, Amsterdam and Philadelphia: John Benjamins.

Bertens, Hans (1995) *The Idea of the Postmodern: A History*, London: Routledge.

Bhabha, Homi K. (1994) *The Location of Culture*, London: Routledge.

Blanchot, Maurice (1981) *The Gaze of Orpheus and other Literary Essays*, ed. P. Adams Sitney, trans. Lydia Davis, Barrytown, NY: Station Hill Press.

Blanchot, Maurice (1982) *The Space of Literature*, trans. Ann Smock, Lincoln, NE: University of Nebraska Press.

Blanchot, Maurice (1993) *The Infinite Conversation*, trans. Susan Hanson, Minneapolis, MN: University of Minnesota Press.

Blanchot, Maurice (1995) *The Blanchot Reader*, ed. Michael Holland, Oxford: Blackwell.

Bloom, Harold (1995) *The Western Canon: The Books and Schools of the Ages*, New York: Harcourt Brace.

Bloom, Harold (1997) *The Anxiety of Influence: A Theory of Poetry*, New York: Oxford University Press.

Booth, Wayne C. (1961) *The Rhetoric of Fiction*, Chicago, IL: University of Chicago Press.

Bordwell, David (1985) *Narration in the Fiction Film*, Madison, WI: University of Wisconsin Press.

Boswell, John (1980) *Christianity, Social Tolerance, and Homosexuality: Gay People in Western Europe from the Beginning of the Christian Era to the Fourteenth Century*, Chicago, IL and London: University of Chicago Press.

Bottomore, Tom (2002) *The Frankfurt School and its Critics*, London: Routledge.

Bourdieu, Pierre (1984) *Distinction: A Social Critique of the Judgement of Taste*, trans. Richard Nice, London: Routledge.

Bourdieu, Pierre (1993) *The Field of Cultural Production: Essays on Art and Literature*, ed. Randal Johnson, Cambridge: Polity Press.

Bowie, Malcolm (1991) *Lacan*, London: Fontana.

Bradford, Richard (1994) *Roman Jakobson: Life, Literature, Art*, London: Routledge.

Brambilla, Marco, dir. (1993) *Demolition Man*, New York: Warner Bros.

Breuer, Josef and Freud, Sigmund (1991) *Studies on Hysteria*, trans. James A. Strachey, Harmondsworth: Penguin.

Bristow, Joseph (1997) *Sexuality*, London: Routledge.

Brontë, Emily (1985) *Wuthering Heights*, Harmondsworth: Penguin.

Brooks, Cleanth (1968) *The Well Wrought Urn: Studies in the Structure of Poetry*, London: Dobson.

Brooks, Peter (1984) *Reading for the Plot: Design and Intention in Narrative*, Cambridge, MA: Harvard University Press.

Buck-Morss, Susan (1977) *The Origin of Negative Dialectics: Theodor W. Adorno, Walter Benjamin and the Frankfurt Institute*, New York: Harvester.

Burke, Kenneth (1989) *On Symbols and Society*, ed. Joseph R. Gusfield, Chicago, IL: University of Chicago Press.

Burke, Sean (1998) *The Death and Return of the Author*, Edinburgh: Edinburgh University Press.

Butler, Judith (1990) *Gender Trouble: Feminism and the Subversion of Identity*, London: Routledge.

Butler, Judith (1993a) *Bodies that Matter: On the Discursive Limits of Sex*, London: Routledge.

Butler, Judith (1993b) 'Imitation and Gender Insubordination', in Henry Abelove, Michèle Aina Barale and David Halperin (eds), *The Lesbian and Gay Studies Reader*, London: Routledge.

Butler, Judith (1997) *Excitable Speech: A Politics of the Performative*, New York: Routledge.

Butler, Judith, Laclau, Ernesto and Žižek, Slavoj (2000) *Contingency, Hegemony, Universality*, London: Verso.

Butler, Rex (2005) *Slavoj Žižek: Live Theory*, London: Continuum.

Caeser, Michael (1999) *Umberto Eco: Philosophy, Semiotics and the Work of Fiction*, Cambridge: Polity Press.

Caputo, John D. (1984) 'Husserl, Heidegger and the Question of "Hermeneutic" Phenomenology', *Husserl Studies* 1: 157–78.

Caruth, Cathy (1996) *Unclaimed Experience: Trauma, Narrative and History*, Baltimore, MD: Johns Hopkins University Press.

Certeau, Michel de (1984) *The Practice of Everyday Life*, trans. Steven Rendall, Berkeley, CA: University of California Press.

Certeau, Michel de (1988) *The Practice of Everyday Life*, vol. 2: *Living and Cooking*, trans. Timothy J. Tomasik, Minneapolis, MN: University of Minnesota Press.

Certeau, Michel de (2000) *The Certeau Reader*, ed. Graham Ward, Oxford: Blackwell.

Cervantes Saavedra, Miguel de (2003) *Don Quixote*, trans. John Rutherford, London: Penguin.

Chasin, Alexandra (2000) *Selling Out: The Gay and Lesbian Movement Goes to Market*, Basingstoke and New York: Palgrave.

Chatman, Seymour (1980) *Story and Discourse: Narrative Structure in Fiction and Film*, Ithaca, NY: Cornell University Press.

Cixous, Hélène (1981) 'The Laugh of the Medusa', trans. Keith Cohen and Paula Cohen, in Elaine Marks and Isabel de Courtivron (eds), *New French Feminisms: An Anthology*, New York: Harvester Wheatsheaf.

Cixous, Hélène (1986) 'Sorties: Out and Out: Attacks/ Ways Out/ Forays', in Hélène

Cixous and Catherine Clément, *The Newly Born Woman*, trans. Betsy Wing, Minneapolis, MN: University of Minnesota Press.

Cobley, Paul (2001) *Narrative*, London: Routledge.

Colebrook, Claire (1997) *New Literary Histories: New Historicism and Contemporary Criticism*, Manchester: Manchester University Press.

Conrad, Joseph (1983) *Heart of Darkness*, Harmondsworth: Penguin.

Cook, David and Okenimkpe, Michael (1983) *Ngũgĩ wa Thiong'o: An Exploration of his Writings*, Oxford: Heinemann.

Coupe, Laurence (ed.) (2000) *The Green Studies Reader*, London: Routledge.

Coupe, Laurence (2005) *Kenneth Burke on Myth: An Introduction*, New York: Routledge.

Creed, Barbara (1987) 'From Here to Modernity: Feminism and Postmodernism', *Screen* 28.2: 47–67.

Critchley, Simon (1992) *The Ethics of Deconstruction: Derrida and Levinas*, Oxford: Blackwell.

Cruse, Harold (2005) *The Crisis of the Negro Intellectual*, London: Granta.

Culler, Jonathan (1975) *Structuralist Poetics: Structuralism, Linguistics and the Study of Literature*, London: Routledge and Kegan Paul.

Culler, Jonathan (1976) *Saussure*, London: Fontana Modern Masters.

Culler, Jonathan (1983) *On Deconstruction*, London: Routledge.

Daly, Glyn (1994) 'Post-metaphysical Culture and Politics: Richard Rorty and Laclau and Mouffe', *Economy and Society*, 23(2): 173–200.

Daly, Glyn (1999) 'Ideology and its Paradoxes: Dimensions of Fantasy and Enjoyment', *Journal of Political Ideologies*, 4(2): 219–38.

Daly, Glyn (2005) 'Žižek', in Terrell Carver and James Martin (eds), *Advances in Continental Political Thought*, Hampshire: Palgrave.

Davis, Colin (1996) *Levinas: An Introduction*, Cambridge: Polity Press.

Day, Gary (1996) *Re-Reading Leavis: 'Culture' and Literary Criticism*, Basingstoke: Macmillan.

Debord, Guy (1995) *The Society of the Spectacle*, trans. Donald Nicholson-Smith, New York: Zone Books.

Deleuze, Gilles (1983) *Nietzsche and Philosophy*, trans. Hugh Tomlinson, New York: Columbia University Press.

Deleuze, Gilles (1985) 'Nomad Thought', in David B. Allison (ed.), *The New Nietzsche: Contemporary Styles of Interpretation*, London and Cambridge, MA: MIT Press.

Deleuze, Gilles (1994) *Difference and Repetition*, trans. Paul Patton, London: Athlone.

Deleuze, Gilles and Guattari, Félix (1984) *Anti-Oedipus: Capitalism and Schizophrenia*, trans. Robert Hurley, Mark Seem and Helen R. Lane, London: Athlone Press.

Deleuze, Gilles and Guattari, Félix (1988) *A Thousand Plateaus: Capitalism and Schizophrenia*, trans. Brian Massumi, London: Athlone Press.

De Man, Paul (1982) *Allegories of Reading*, London: Yale University Press.

De Man, Paul (1983) *Blindness and Insight*, 2nd edition, London: Routledge.

De Man, Paul (1984) *The Rhetoric of Romanticism*, New York: Columbia University Press.

D'Emilio, John (1993) 'Capitalism and Gay Identity', in Henry Abelove, Michèle Aina Barale and David Halperin (eds), *The Lesbian and Gay Studies Reader*, London: Routledge.

Dentith, Simon (1995) *Bakhtinian Thought: An Introductory Reader*, London: Routledge.

Derrida, Jacques (1967) 'La théâtre de la cruauté et la clôture de la représentation', in *L'écriture et la différence*, Paris: Éditions de Seuil.

Derrida, Jacques (1973) 'Differance', in *'Speech and Phenomena' and Other Essays on Husserl's Theory of Signs*, trans. David B. Allison, Evanston, IL: Northwestern University Press.

Derrida, Jacques (1978) *Writing and Difference*, trans. Alan Bass, London: Routledge.

Derrida, Jacques (1980) *La carte postale de Socrate à Freud et au delà*, Paris: Galilée.

Derrida, Jacques (1982) *Margins of Philosophy*, trans. Alan Bass, London: Prentice Hall.

Derrida, Jacques (1983) 'Le langue et le discours de la méthode', in *Recherches sur la philosophie et le langage*, no. 3: 35–51.

Derrida, Jacques (1987) *The Post Card: From Socrates to Freud and Beyond*, trans. Alan Bass, Chicago, IL: University of Chicago Press.

Derrida, Jacques (1988) *Limited Inc*, Evanston, IL: Northwestern University Press.

Derrida, Jacques (1993a) *Aporias*, trans. Thomas Dutoit, Stanford, CA: Stanford University Press.

Derrida, Jacques (1993b) *Dissemination*, trans. B. Johnson, London: Althone.

Derrida, Jacques (1993c) *Pregnancies*, Paris: Brandes.

Derrida, Jacques (1994) *Specters of Marx: The State of the Debt, the Work of Mourning, and the New International*, trans. Peggy Kamuf, London: Routledge.

Derrida, Jacques (1997) *Of Grammatology*, trans. Gayatri Chakravorty Spivak, Baltimore, MD: Johns Hopkins University Press.

Derrida, Jacques (1998) *Monolingualism of the Other; or, The Prosthesis of Origin*, Stanford, CA: Stanford University Press.

Derrida, Jacques (2003) *Voyous*, Paris: Galilée.

Derrida, Jacques and Thévin, Paule (1986) *Antonin Artaud: Dessins et portraits*, Paris: Gallimard.

Docherty, Thomas (1996) *Alterities: Criticism, History, Representation*, Oxford: Clarendon Press.

Dollimore, Jonathan (1991) *Sexual Dissidence: Augustine to Wilde, Freud to Foucault*, Oxford: Clarendon Press.

Dollimore, Jonathan and Sinfield, Alan (eds) (1985) *Political Shakespeare: New Essays in Cultural Materialism*, Manchester: Manchester University Press.

Du Bois, W. E. B. (1995) *Dark Princess*, Jackson, MI: University Press of Mississippi.

Du Bois, W. E. B. (2001) *The Negro*, University Park, PA: University of Pennsylvania State Press.

Eaglestone, Robert (1997) *Ethical Criticism: Reading After Levinas*, Edinburgh: Edinburgh University Press.

Eagleton, Terry (1991) *Ideology: An Introduction*, London: Verso.

Eagleton, Terry (1996) *The Illusion of Postmodernism*, Oxford: Blackwell.

Easthope, Antony (1999) *The Unconscious*, London: Routledge.

Eco, Umberto (1976) *A Theory of Semiotics*, Bloomington, IN: Indiana University Press.

Eco, Umberto (1979) *The Role of the Reader: Explorations in the Semiotics of Texts*, Bloomington, IN: Indiana University Press.

Eco, Umberto (1983, 1992) *The Name of the Rose*, trans. William Weaver, London: Vintage.

Eco, Umberto (1989) *The Open Work*, trans. Anna Cancogni, Cambridge, MA: Harvard University Press.

Eisenstein, Paul (2003) *Traumatic Encounters: Holocaust Representation and the Hegelian Subject,* Albany, NY: State University of New York Press.

Elias, Amy J. (2001) *Sublime Desire: History and Post-1960s Fiction,* Baltimore, MD: Johns Hopkins University Press.

Elster, Jon (1986) *Karl Marx: A Reader,* Cambridge: Cambridge University Press.

Empson, William (1995a) *Seven Types of Ambiguity,* London: Penguin.

Empson, William (1995b) *Some Versions of Pastoral,* London: Penguin.

Empson, William (1995c) *The Structure of Complex Words,* London: Penguin.

Engels, Friedrich (1972) *The Origin of the Family, Private Property and the State: In the Light of the Researches of Lewis H. Morgan,* London: Lawrence and Wishart.

Engels, Friedrich (1987) *The Condition of the Working Classes in England in 1844,* London: Penguin

Engels, Friedrich and Marx, Karl (1939) *The German Ideology,* trans. B. Fowles, New York: International Publishers.

Engels, Friedrich and Marx, Karl (1985) *The Communist Manifesto,* London: Penguin.

Erlich, Victor (1981) *Russian Formalism: History – Doctrine,* New Haven, CT and London: Yale University Press.

Ermarth, Elizabeth D. (1992) *Sequel to History: Postmodernism and the Crisis of Representational Time,* Princeton, NJ: Princeton University Press.

Eze, Emmanuel Chukwudi (1997) *Race and the Enlightenment: A Reader,* Oxford: Blackwell.

Fanon, Frantz (1986) *Black Skin, White Masks,* trans. Charles Lam Markmann, London: Pluto Press.

Fanon, Frantz (2001) *The Wretched of the Earth,* trans. Constance Farrington, London: Penguin.

Feldstein, Richard, Fink, Bruce and Jaanus, Maire (eds) (1995) *Reading Seminar 11, Lacan's Four Fundamental Concepts of Psychoanalysis,* Albany, NY: State University of New York.

Ferguson, R., Gever, M., Minh-ha, Trinh T. and West, Cornel (eds) (1990) *Out There: Marginalization and Contemporary Cultures,* New York: New Museum of Contemporary Art; Cambridge, MA: MIT Press.

Fetterley, Judith (1978) *The Resisting Reader: A Feminist Approach to American Fiction,* Bloomington, IN and London: Indiana University Press.

Fielding, Henry (1999) *Joseph Andrews and Shamela,* Oxford: Oxford University Press.

Findlen, Barbara (ed.) (1995) *Listen Up: Voices from the Next Feminist Generation,* Seattle, WA: Seal Press.

Fink, Bruce (1995) *The Lacanian Subject,* Princeton, NJ: Princeton University Press.

Fish, Stanley (1967) *Surprised by Sin: The Reader in Paradise Lost,* London: Macmillan.

Fish, Stanley (1980) *Is there a Text in This Class?: The Authority of Interpretive Communities,* Cambridge, MA: Harvard University Press.

Fish, Stanley (1989) *Doing What Comes Naturally,* Oxford: Clarendon Press.

Fish, Stanley (2001) *How Milton Works,* Cambridge, MA: Harvard University Press.

Foster, Hal (ed.) (1983) *The Anti-Aesthetic: Essays on Postmodern Culture,* Port Townsend, WA: Bay Press.

Foucault, Michel (1967) *Madness and Civilisation: A History of Insanity in the Age of Reason,* London: Tavistock.

Foucault, Michel (1977a) *Discipline and Punish: The Birth of the Prison,* trans. Alan Sheridan, London: Penguin.

Foucault, Michel (1977b) *Language, Counter-Memory, Practice*, trans. Donald F. Bouchard and Sherry Simon, ed. Donald F. Bouchard, Ithaca, NY: Cornell University Press.

Foucault, Michel (1980) *Power/Knowledge: Selected Interviews and Other Writings, 1972–1977*, ed. Colin Gordon, New York: Pantheon.

Foucault, Michel (1984) *The History of Sexuality*, vol. 1: *An Introduction,* trans. Robert Hurley, London: Penguin.

Foucault, Michel (1991) *The Foucault Reader: An Introduction to Foucault's Thought*, ed. Paul Rabinow, Harmondsworth: Penguin.

Foucault, Michel (2002) *The Archaeology of Knowledge*, trans. A. M. Sheridan Smith. London: Routledge.

Freedman, Aviva and Medway, Peter (eds) (1994) *Genre and the New Rhetoric*, London: Taylor & Francis.

Freud, Sigmund (1961) *The Complete Psychological Works of Sigmund Freud*, trans. and ed. James Strachey, London: Hogarth Press.

Freud, Sigmund (1976) *Jokes and their Relation to the Unconscious*, trans. James A. Strachey, Harmondsworth: Penguin.

Freud, Sigmund (1985) 'The "Uncanny"', in *Art and Literature: Jensen's 'Gradiva', Leonardo da Vinci and Other Works*, trans. James Strachey, Harmondsworth: Penguin.

Freud, Sigmund (1991a) *Introductory Lectures on Psychoanalysis*, trans. James A. Strachey, Harmondsworth: Penguin.

Freud, Sigmund (1991b) *On Metapsychology: The Theory of Psychoanalysis, Beyond the Pleasure Principle, the Ego and the Id, and Other Works*, London: Penguin.

Freud, Sigmund (1991c) *The Essentials of Psycho-Analysis*, trans James A. Strachey, London: Penguin.

Freud, Sigmund (1991d) *The Interpretation of Dreams*, trans. James A. Strachey, Harmondsworth: Penguin.

Freund, Elizabeth (1987) *The Return of the Reader: Reader-Response Criticism*, London: Methuen.

Frye, Northrop (1957) *Anatomy of Criticism*, Princeton, NJ: Princeton University Press.

Frye, Northrop (1976) *The Secular Scripture: A Study of the Structure of Romance*, London: Harvard University Press.

Frye, Northrop (1978) *Northrop Frye on Culture and Literature: A Collection of Review Essays*, ed. Robert Denham, Chicago, IL: Chicago University Press.

Frye, Northrop (1982) *The Great Code: The Bible and Literature*, London: Routledge and Kegan Paul.

Frye, Northrop (1990) *Anatomy of Criticism: Four Essays*, Oxford: Princeton University Press.

Fukuyama, Francis (1992) *The End of History and the Last Man*, London: Penguin.

Fukuyama, Francis (2002) *Our Posthuman Future: Consequences of the Biotechnology Revolution*, London: Profile.

Gadamer, Hans-Georg (1993) *Truth and Method*, trans. Joel Weinsheimer and Donald G. Marshall, London: Sheed and Ward.

Gallagher, Catherine and Greenblatt, Stephen (2000) *Practicing New Historicism*, Chicago, IL and London: University of Chicago Press.

Garber, Linda (2001) *Identity Poetics: Race, Class, and the Lesbian-Feminist Roots of Queer Theory*, New York: Columbia University Press.

Garrard, Greg (2004) *Ecocriticism*, London: Routledge.

Gasché, Rodolphe (1988) *The Tain of the Mirror*, Cambridge, MA: Harvard University Press.

Gates, Henry Louis Jr (ed.) (1984) *Black Literature and Literary Theory*, New York: Routledge.

Gates, Henry Louis Jr (ed.) (1986) *'Race,' Writing, and Difference*, Chicago, IL: University of Chicago Press.

Gates, Henry Louis Jr (1988) *The Signifying Monkey: A Theory of Afro-American Literary Criticism*, New York: Oxford University Press.

Gates, Henry Louis Jr and West, Cornel (1997) *The Future of the Race*, London: Vintage.

Gebauer, Gunter and Wulf, Christoph (1995) *Mimesis: Culture, Art, Society*, trans. Don Reneau, Berkeley, CA: University of California Press.

Geertz, Clifford (1993) *The Interpretation of Cultures*, London: Fontana.

Genette, Gérard (1980) *Narrative Discourse*, trans. Jane E. Lewin, Oxford: Blackwell.

Genette, Gérard (1982) *Figures of Literary Discourse*, trans. A Sheridan, New York: Columbia University Press.

Genette, Gérard (1997) *Paratexts: Thresholds of Interpretation*, trans. Jane E. Lewin, Cambridge: Cambridge University Press.

Gibson, Andrew (1999) *Postmodernity, Ethics and the Novel: From Leavis to Levinas*, London: Routledge.

Gikandi, Simon (2001) 'Globalization and the Claims of Postcoloniality', *South Atlantic Quarterly* 100.3: 627–58.

Gilbert, Sandra M. and Gubar, Susan (1979) *The Madwoman in the Attic*, New Haven, CT and London: Yale University Press.

Gilbert, Sandra M. and Gubar, Susan (1985) *The Norton Anthology of Literature by Women: The Traditions in English*, New York and London: W. W. Norton.

Gilbert, Sandra M. and Gubar, Susan (1988) *No Man's Land*, vol. 1: *The War of the Words*, New Haven, CT and London: Yale University Press.

Gilbert, Sandra M. and Gubar, Susan (1989) *No Man's Land*, vol. 2: *Sexchanges*, New Haven, CT and London: Yale University Press.

Gilbert, Sandra M. and Gubar, Susan (1994) *No Man's Land*, vol. 3: *Letters from the Front*, New Haven, CT and London: Yale University Press.

Gilligan, Carol (1982) *In a Different Voice*, Cambridge, MA: Harvard University Press.

Gilroy, Paul (1993) *The Black Atlantic: Modernity and Double Consciousness*, London: Verso.

Gilroy, Paul (2004) *Between Camps: Nations, Cultures, and the Allure of Race*, London: Routledge.

Glotfelty, Cheryll and Fromm, Harold (eds) (1996) *The Ecocriticism Reader: Landmarks in Literary Ecology*, Athens, GA: University of Georgia Press.

Glover, David and Kaplan, Cora (2000) *Genders*, London: Routledge.

Gorak, Jan (1987) *Critic of Crisis: A Study of Frank Kermode*, Columbia, MO: University of Missouri Press.

Gorz, Andre (1983) *Farewell to the Working Class*, London: Pluto.

Graff, Gerald (1987) *Professing Literature: An Institutional History*, Chicago, IL: University of Chicago Press.

Graham, Elaine L. (2002) *Representations of the Post/Human: Monsters, Aliens and Others in Popular Culture*, Manchester: Manchester University Press.

Grahn, Judy (1984) *Another Mother Tongue: Gay Words, Gay Worlds*, Boston, MA: Beacon Press.

Grahn, Judy (1985) *The Highest Apple: Sappho and the Lesbian Poetic Tradition*, San Francisco, CA: Spinsters, Ink.

Gramsci, Antonio (1988) *A Gramsci Reader: Selected Writings 1916–1935*, ed. D. Forgacs, London: Lawrence and Wishart.

Gramsci, Antonio (2003) *Selections from the Prison Notebooks*, London: Lawrence and Wishart.

Gray, Chris Hables (2001) *Cyborg Citizen: Politics in the Posthuman Age*, London: Routledge.

Gray, Chris Hables, Figueroa-Sarriera, Heidi J. and Mentor, Steven (eds) (1995) *The Cyborg Handbook*, London: Routledge.

Grayling, Anthony C. (ed.) (1997) *Philosophy: A Guide Through the Subject*, Oxford: Oxford University Press.

Greenblatt, Stephen (1980) *Renaissance Self-Fashioning: From More to Shakespeare*, Chicago, IL: University of Chicago Press.

Greenblatt, Stephen (1985) 'Invisible Bullets: Renaissance Authority and its Subversion, *Henry IV* and *Henry V*', in J. Dollimore and A. Sinfield (eds), *Political Shakespeare: New Essays in Cultural Materialism*, Manchester: Manchester University Press.

Greenblatt, Stephen (1989) 'Towards a Poetics of Culture', in H. Aram Veeser (ed.), *The New Historicism*, New York and London: Routledge.

Greimas, Algirdas Julien (1987) *On Meaning: Selected Writings in Semiotic Theory*, trans. Paul Perron and Frank Collins, Minneapolis, MN: University of Minnesota Press.

Guattari, Félix (1996) *The Guattari Reader*, ed. Gary Genosko, Oxford: Blackwell.

Haase, Ullrich and Large, William (2001) *Maurice Blanchot*, London: Routledge.

Habermas, Jürgen (1978) *Knowledge and Human Interests*, trans. Jeremy J. Shapiro, London: Heinemann.

Habermas, Jürgen (1983) 'Modernity – an Incomplete Project', in Hal Foster (ed.), *The Anti-Aesthetic: Essays on Postmodern Culture,* Port Townsend, WA: Bay Press.

Habermas, Jürgen (1987) *The Philosophical Discourse of Modernity*, trans. Frederick Lawrence, Cambridge, MA: MIT Press.

Halberstam, Judith (1998) *Female Masculinity*, Durham, NC and London: Duke University Press.

Hall, Donald E. (2003) *Queer Theories*, Basingstoke: Palgrave.

Hamilton, Paul (1996) *Historicism*, London: Routledge.

Haraway, Donna (1985) 'A Manifesto for Cyborgs: Science, Technology, and Socialist Feminism in the 1980s', *Socialist Review* 80: 65–108.

Haraway, Donna (1991) *Simians, Cyborgs and Women: The Reinvention of Nature*, New York: Routledge.

Haraway, Donna (1997) *Modest Witness@Second_Millennium: Femaleman Meets OncoMouse*, London: Routledge.

Haraway, Donna (2004) *The Haraway Reader*, London and New York: Routledge.

Hassan, Ihab (1987) *The Postmodern Turn,* Columbus, OH: Ohio State University Press.

Hawkes, David (1996) *Ideology*, London: Routledge.

Hayles, N. Katherine (1999) *How We Became Posthuman: Virtual Bodies in Cybernetics, Literature, and Informatics*, Chicago, IL and London: University of Chicago Press.

Hebdige, Dick (1991) *Hiding in the Light: Of Images and Things*, London: Routledge.

Heble, Ajay (1996) 'New Contexts of Canadian Criticism: Democracy, Counterpoint, Responsibility', in Ajay Heble, Donna Palmateer Pennee and J. R. (Tim) Struthers (eds), *New Contexts of Canadian Criticism*, Peterborough, ON: Broadview Press.

Hegel, G. W. F. (1991) *The Philosophy of History*, trans. J. Sibree, Amhert, NY: Prometheus Books.

Heidegger, Martin (1972) *On the Way to Language*, trans. P. D. Hertz, New York: Harper and Row.

Heidegger, Martin (1990) *Being and Time*, trans. John Macquarrie and Edward Robinson, Oxford: Blackwell.

Hekman, Susan (1990) *Gender and Knowledge*, Cambridge: Polity Press.

Held, David and McGrew, Anthony (eds) (2000) *The Global Transformations Reader: An Introduction to the Global Debate*, Cambridge: Polity Press.

Hoare, Quinton and Nowell Smith, Geoffrey (eds) (1971) *Selections from the Prison Notebooks of Antonio Gramsci*, trans. Quinton Hoare and Geoffrey Nowell Smith, London: Lawrence and Wishart.

Hoggart, Richard (1957) *The Uses of Literacy: Aspects of Working-Class Life with Special Reference to Publications and Entertainments*, London: Chatto and Windus.

Holquist, Michael (2002) *Dialogism: Bakhtin and his World*, London: Routledge.

Holub, Robert C. (1984) *Reception Theory: A Critical Introduction*, London: Methuen.

Homer, Sean (1998) *Fredric Jameson: Marxism, Hermeneutics, Postmodernism*, London: Routledge.

hooks, bell (1981) *Ain't I a Woman: Black Women and Feminism*, London: Pluto.

hooks, bell (1984) *Feminist Theory: From Margin to Center*, Boston, MA: South End Press.

hooks, bell (1989) *Talking Back: Thinking Feminist, Thinking Black*, Boston, MA: South End Press.

hooks, bell (1990) *Yearning: Race, Gender and Cultural Politics*, Boston, MA: South End Press.

hooks, bell and Cornel West (1991) *Breaking Bread: Insurgent Black Intellectual Life*, Boston, MA: South End Press.

Horkheimer, Max (1998) *Critical Theory*, London: Continuum.

Huddart, David (2005) *Homi Bhabha*, London: Routledge.

Huntington, Samuel P. (1998) *The Clash of Civilizations and the Remaking of World Order*, London: Touchstone.

Hutcheon, Linda (1987) 'Beginning to Theorize Postmodernism', *Textual Practice* 1.1: 10–31.

Hutcheon, Linda (1988) *A Poetics of Postmodernism: History, Theory, Fiction*, London: Routledge.

Huyssen, Andreas (1986) *After the Great Divide: Modernism, Mass Culture, Post-modernism*, Bloomington, IN: Indiana University Press.

Irigaray, Luce (1985a) *This Sex Which is Not One*, trans. Catherine Porter, Ithaca, NY: Cornell University Press.

Irigaray, Luce (1985b) *Speculum of the Other Woman*, trans. Gillian C. Gill, Ithaca, NY: Cornell University Press.

Iser, Wolfgang (1978) *The Act of Reading: A Theory of Aesthetic Response*, London: Routledge and Kegan Paul.

Jackson, Peter (2001) *The Lord of the Rings: The Fellowship of the Ring*, New York: New Line Cinema.

Jackson, Peter (2002) *The Lord of the Rings: The Two Towers*, New York: New Line Cinema.

Jackson, Peter (2003) *The Lord of the Rings: The Return of the King*, New York: New Line Cinema.

Jagose, Annamarie (1996) *Queer Theory: An Introduction*, New York: New York University Press.

Jakobson, Roman (1987) *Language in Literature*, ed. Krystyna Pomorska and Stephen Rudy, Cambridge, MA: Belknap Press of Harvard University Press.

Jameson, Fredric (1972a) *Marxism and Form: Twentieth-Century Dialectical Theories of Literature*, Princeton, NJ: Princeton University Press.

Jameson, Fredric (1972b) *The Prison-House of Language: A Critical Account of Structuralism and Russian Formalism*, Princeton, NJ: Princeton University Press.

Jameson, Fredric (1981) *The Political Unconscious: Narrative as a Socially Symbolic Act*, Ithaca, NY: Cornell University Press.

Jameson, Fredric (1984) 'Postmodernism, or the Cultural Logic of Late Capitalism', *New Left Review* 146: 53–92.

Jameson, Fredric (1990) *Late Marxism: Adorno, Or, the Persistence of the Dialectic*, New York: Verso.

Jameson, Fredric (1992) *Postmodernism, or, the Cultural Logic of Late Capitalism*, London: Verso.

Jameson, Fredric (2002a) *The Political Unconscious: Narrative as a Socially Symbolic Act*, London: Routledge.

Jameson, Fredric (2002b) *A Singular Modernity: Essay on the Ontology of the Present*, London: Verso.

Jauss, Hans Robert (1982) *Toward and Aesthetic of Reception*, trans. Timothy Bahti, Brighton: Harvester Press.

Jauss, Hans Robert (1989) *Question and Answer: Forms of Dialogic Understanding*, trans. Michael Hays, Minneapolis, MN: University of Minnesota Press.

Jay, Martin (1973) *The Dialectical Imagination: A History of the Frankfurt School and the Institute of Social Research, 1923–1950*, London: Heinemann.

Jencks, Charles (1986) *What Is Post-Modernism?*, London: Academy Editions.

Jung, Carl Gustav (1974) *Synchronicity: An Acausal Connecting Principle*, trans. R. F. C. Hull, Princeton, NJ: Princeton University Press.

Jung, Carl Gustav (1978) *Man and his Symbols*, Picador, London.

Jung, Carl Gustav (2002) *The Undiscovered Self*, trans. R. F. C. Hull, London: Routledge.

Kaufmann, Walter Arnold (1975) *Nietzsche: Philosopher, Psychologist, Antichrist*, Princeton, NJ: Princeton University Press.

Kellner, Douglas (1984) *Herbert Marcuse and the Crisis of Marxism*, Berkeley, CA: University of California Press.

Kellner, Douglas (1989) *Critical Theory, Marxism, and Modernity*, Cambridge: Polity Press.

Kermode, Frank (1979) *The Genesis of Secrecy: On the Interpretation of Narrative*, Cambridge, MA: Harvard University Press.

Kermode, Frank (1983) *The Art of Telling: Essays on Fiction*, Cambridge, MA: Harvard University Press.

Kermode, Frank (1988) *History and Value*, Oxford: Clarendon Press.

Kermode, Frank (2000) *The Sense of an Ending: Studies in the Theory of Fiction with a New Epilogue*, Oxford: Oxford University Press.

Kermode, Frank (2004a) *Pleasure and Change: The Aesthetics of Canon*, Oxford: Oxford University Press.

Kermode, Frank (2004b) *Pieces of My Mind: Writings 1958–2002*, London: Penguin.

Kerouac, Jack (1991) *On the Road*, London: Penguin.

Kim, Jaegwon and Sosa, Ernest (eds) (1996) *A Companion to Metaphysics*, Oxford: Blackwell.

Kirkup, Gill, Janes, Linda, Woodward, Kathryn and Hovenden, Fiona (eds) (2000) *The Gendered Cyborg: A Reader*, London: Routledge.

Klein, Naomi (2000) *No Logo: Taking Aim at the Brand Bullies*, London: Flamingo.

Kojève, Alexandre (1969) *Introduction to the Reading of Hegel*, New York: Basic Books.

Kristeva, Julia (1982) *Powers of Horror: An Essay on Abjection*, trans. Leon S. Roudiez, New York: Columbia University Press.

Kristeva, Julia (1984) *Revolution in Poetic Language*, trans. Margaret Waller, New York: Columbia University Press.

Kristeva, Julia (1986) *The Kristeva Reader*, trans. Toril Moi, Oxford: Blackwell.

Kristeva, Julia (2001) *Melanie Klein*, trans. Ross Guberman, New York: Columbia University Press.

Lacan, Jacques (1977) *Écrits: A Selection*, trans. Alan Sheridan, London: Routledge.

Lacan, Jacques (1992) *Seminar 7: The Ethics of Psychoanalysis*, ed. Jacques-Alain Miller, trans. Dennis Porter, London: Tavistock/Routledge.

Lacan, Jacques (1994) *Seminar 11: The Four Fundamental Concepts of Psychoanalysis*, ed. Jacques-Alain Miller, trans. Alan Sheridan, London: Penguin.

Lacan, Jacques (1998) *On Feminine Sexuality: The Limits of Love and Knowledge. Book XX: Encore 1972–1973*, New York and London: Norton.

LaCapra, Dominick (2000) *Writing History, Writing Trauma*, Baltimore, MD: Johns Hopkins University Press.

Laclau, Ernesto (1990) *New Reflections on the Revolution of our Time*, London: Verso.

Laclau, Ernesto (1996) 'The Death and Resurrection of the Theory of Ideology', *Journal of Political Ideologies* 1.3: 201–20.

Laclau, Ernesto and Mouffe, Chantal (1987) *Hegemony and Socialist Strategy: Towards a Radical Democratic Politics*, London: Verso.

Laclau, Ernesto and Žižek, Slavoj (2000) *Contingency, Hegemony, Universality: Contemporary Dialogues on the Left*, London: Verso.

Landow, George P. (1992) *Hypertext: The Convergence of Contemporary Critical Theory and Technology*, Baltimore, MD: Johns Hopkins University Press.

Landow, George P. (ed.) (1994) *Hyper/Text/Theory*, Baltimore, MD: Johns Hopkins University Press.

Landow, George P. (1997) *Hypertext 2.0: The Convergence of Contemporary Critical Theory and Technology*, Baltimore, MD and London: Johns Hopkins University Press.

Lane, Richard J. (2000) *Jean Baudrillard*, London: Routledge.

Lawrence, David Herbert (1990) *Studies in Classic American Literature*, London: Penguin.

Leach, Edmund (1974) *Lévi-Strauss*, London: Fontana.

Leader, Darian and Groves, Judy (1995) *Introducing Lacan*, Cambridge: Icon.

Leavis, Frank Raymond (1966) *The Great Tradition*, London: Peregrine Books.

Leavis, Frank Raymond and Thompson, Denys (1933) *Culture and Environment: The Training of Critical Awareness,* London: Chatto and Windus.

Lefort, Claude (1989), *Democracy and Political Theory*, Minneapolis, MN: University of Minnesota Press.

Lemon, Lee T. and Reis, Marion J. (eds) (1965) *Russian Formalist Criticism: Four Essays*, Lincoln, NE: University of Nebraska Press.

Lentricchia, Frank (1980) *After the New Criticism*, Chicago, IL: University of Chicago Press.

Levinas, Emmanuel (1996) *Basic Philosophical Writings*, ed. Adriaan Peperzak, Simon Critchley and Robert Bernasconi, Bloomington, IN: Indiana University Press.

Lévi-Strauss, Claude (1963) *Structural Anthropology*, trans. Claire Jacobson and Brooker Grundfast Schoepf, New York: Basic Books.

Lévi-Strauss, Claude (1966) *The Savage Mind*, London: Weidenfeld and Nicolson.

Leys, Ruth (2000) *Trauma: A Genealogy*, Chicago, IL: University of Chicago Press.

Lichtheim, George (1974) *Marxism: An Historical and Critical Study*, London: Routledge.

Likierman, Meira (2001) *Melanie Klein: Her Work in Context*, London: Continuum.

Lodge, David (1992) *The Art of Fiction: Illustrated from Classic and Modern Texts*, London: Penguin.

Loomba, Ania (1998) *Colonialism/Postcolonialism*, London: Routledge.

Lorde, Audre (1984) *Sister Outsider*, Trumansburg, NY: Crossing Press.

Lukács, Georg (1974) *The Theory of the Novel*, trans. Anna Bostock, Cambridge, MA: MIT Press.

Lukács, Georg (1980) *Essays on Realism*, trans. Rodney Livingstone, London: Lawrence and Wishart.

Lukács, Georg (1983) *The Historical Novel*, trans. Hannah Mitchell and Stanley Mitchell, Lincoln, NE: University of Nebraska Press.

Lyotard, Jean-François (1984) *The Postmodern Condition: A Report on Knowledge*, trans. Geoff Bennington and Brian Massumi, Manchester: Manchester University Press.

Lyotard, Jean-François (1991a) *The Differend: Phrases in Dispute*, trans. G. V. D. Abbeele, Minneapolis, MN: University of Minnesota Press.

Lyotard, Jean-François (1991b) *The Inhuman: Reflections on Time*, trans. Geoffrey Bennington and Rachel Bowlby, Stanford, CA: Stanford University Press.

Lyotard, Jean-François (1992) *The Postmodern Explained to Children: Correspondence 1982–1985*, trans. Don Barry, Bernadette Maher, Julian Pefanis, Virginia Spate and Morgan Thomas, London: Turnaround.

McAllester Jones, Mary (1991) *Gaston Bachelard: Subversive Humanist*, Madison, WI: University of Wisconsin Press.

Macann, Christopher E. (1993) *Four Phenomenological Philosophers: Husserl, Heidegger, Sartre, Merleau-Ponty*, London: Routledge.

Macaulay, Thomas Babington (1995) 'Minute on Indian Education', in Bill Ashcroft, Gareth Griffiths and Helen Tiffin (eds), *The Postcolonial Studies Reader*, London: Routledge.

MacCabe, Colin (1985) 'Realism and the Cinema: Notes on some Brechtian Thesis', in *Theoretical Essays*, Manchester: Manchester University Press.

McEwan, Ian (1997) *The Cement Garden*, London: Vintage.

McGann, Jerome J. (1985) *The Romantic Ideology: A Critical Investigation*, Chicago, IL and London: University of Chicago Press.

Macherey, Pierre (1978) *A Theory of Literary Production*, trans. Geoffrey Wall, London: Routledge.

MacKillop, Ian (1995) *F. R. Leavis: A Life in Criticism*, London: Penguin.

MacKinnon, Catharine A. (1977) *Feminism Unmodified*, Cambridge, MA: Harvard University Press.

McLuhan, Herbert Marshall and Powers, Bruce R. (eds) (1989) *The Global Village: Transformations in World Life and Media in the Twenty-First Century*, Oxford: Oxford University Press.

McQuillan, Martin, (ed.) (2000) *The Narrative Reader*, London: Routledge.

Malpas, Simon (2003) *Jean-François Lyotard,* London: Routledge.

Marcuse, Herbert (2002) *One Dimensional Man*, London: Routledge.

Marks, Elaine and Courtivron, Isabel de (eds) (1981) *New French Feminisms: An Anthology*, New York: Harvester Wheatsheaf.

Marshall, Brenda K. (1992) *Teaching the Postmodern: Fiction and Theory*, New York: Routledge.

Marx, Karl (2000) *Selected Writings*, 2nd edition, ed. David McLellan, Oxford: Oxford University Press.

Marx, Karl and Engels, Friedrich (1959) *On Colonialism*, Moscow: Progress Publishers.

Marx, Karl and Engels, Friedrich (1967) *The Communist Manifesto*, Harmondsworth: Penguin.

Marx, Karl and Engels, Friedrich (1977) *Selected Works*, vol. 1, Moscow: Progress Publishers.

Merleau-Ponty, Maurice (1962) *Phenomenology of Perception*, trans. Colin Smith, London: Routledge.

Merleau-Ponty, Maurice (2004) *Basic Writings*, ed. Thomas Baldwin, London: Routledge.

Miller, J. Hillis (1990) *Tropes, Parables, Performatives: Essays on Twentieth-Century Literature*, London: Harvester Wheatsheaf.

Miller, J. Hillis (2001) *Speech Acts in Literature*, Stanford, CA: Stanford University Press.

Millett, Kate (1979) *Sexual Politics*, London: Virago.

Minh-ha, Trinh T. (1989) *Woman, Native, Other: Postcoloniality and Feminism*, Bloomington, IN: Indiana University Press.

Minh-ha, Trinh T. (1991) *When the Moon Waxes Red*, London: Routledge.

Mitchell, Juliet (ed.) (1991) *The Selected Melanie Klein*, Harmondsworth: Penguin.

Mitchell, W. J. T. (ed.) (1981) *On Narrative*, Chicago, IL: University of Chicago Press.

Moi, Toril (1985) *Sexual/Textual Politics: Feminist Literary Theory*, London: Routledge.

Morley, David and Kuan-Hsing, Chen (eds) (1996) *Stuart Hall: Critical Dialogues in Cultural Studies*, London: Routledge.

Morton, Donald (1996) *The Material Queer: A LesBiGay Cultural Studies Reader*, Boulder, CO: Westview Press.

Mulhern, Francis (1979) *The Moment of 'Scrutiny'*, London: Verso.

Muñoz, José Estaban (1999) *Disidentifications: Queens of Color and the Performance of Politics*, Minneapolis, MN: University of Minnesota Press.

Murray, Janet (1997) *Hamlet on the Holodeck: The Future of Narrative in Cyberspace*, Cambridge MA: MIT Press.

Naas, Michael (2002) *Taking on the Tradition: Jacques Derrida and the Legacies of Deconstruction*, Stanford, CA: Stanford University Press.

Namaste, Viviane K. (2000) *Invisible Lives: The Erasure of Transsexual and Transgendered People*, Chicago, IL and London: University of Chicago Press.

Nelson, Cary and Grossberg, Lawrence (eds) (1988) *Marxism and the Interpretation of Culture*, Basingstoke: Macmillan Education.

Ngũgĩ wa Thiong'o (1986) *Decolonising the Mind: The Politics of Language in African Literature*, Portsmouth, NH: Heinemann.

Nietzsche, Friedrich (1977) *The Portable Nietzsche*, trans. Walter Kaufmann, New York: Penguin.

Nietzsche, Friedrich (1994) *On the Genealogy of Morality*, ed. Keith Ansell-Pearson, trans. Carol Diethe, Cambridge: Cambridge University Press.

Nobus, Dany (ed.) (1999) *Key Concepts of Lacanian Psychoanalysis*, New York: Other Press.

Norris, Christopher (1978) *William Empson and the Philosophy of Literary Criticism*, London: Athlone Press.

Norris, Christopher (1987) *Derrida*, London: Fontana.

Norris, Christopher (1988) *Paul De Man: Deconstruction and the Critique of Aesthetic Ideology,* London: Routledge.

Palahniuk, Chuck (1997) *Fight Club*, London: Vintage.

Payne, Michael and Schad, John (eds) (2004) *Life.After.Theory: Interviews with Jacques Derrida, Sir Frank Kermode, Toril Moi and Christopher Norris*, London: Continuum.

Peirce, Charles Sanders (1998) *The Essential Writings*, ed. Edward C. Moore, Amherst, NY: Prometheus Books.

Petersen, Kirstin Holst and Rutherford, Anna (1986a) *A Double Colonization: Colonial and Post-Colonial Women's Writing*, Oxford: Dangaroo Press.

Petersen, Kirstin Holst and Rutherford, Anna (1986b) 'Foreword', in *A Double Colonization: Colonial and Post-Colonial Women's Writing*, Oxford: Dangaroo Press.

Plato (2003) *Republic*, trans. Desmond Lee, intro. Rachana Kamtekar, Harmondsworth: Penguin.

Portoghesi, Paolo (1983) *Postmodern Architecture of Postindustrial Society,* New York: Rizzoli.

Pratt, Mary-Louise (1977) *Toward a Speech Act Theory of Literary Discourse*, London: Indiana University Press.

Prince, Gerald (2004) *A Dictionary of Narratology*, Nebraska: University of Nebraska Press.

Propp, Vladimir (1958) *Morphology of the Folktale*, trans. Laurence Scott, Austin, TX and London: University of Texas Press.

Rancière, Jacques (1999) *Disagreement: Politics and Philosophy*, Minneapolis, MN: University of Minnesota Press.

Readings, Bill (1991) *Introducing Lyotard: Art and Politics*, London: Routledge.

Rees, John (1998) *The Algebra of Revolution: The Dialectic and the Classical Marxist Tradition*, London: Routledge.

Reid-Pharr, Robert F. (2001) *Black Gay Man: Essays*, New York: New York University Press.

Rice, Alan (2002) *Radical Narratives of the Black Atlantic*, New York and London: Continuum.

Richards, Ivor Armstrong (2001a) *Practical Criticism*, London: Routledge.

Richards, Ivor Armstrong (2001b) *Principles of Literary Criticism*, London: Routledge.

Ricoeur, Paul (1974) *The Conflict of Interpretations: Essays in Hermeneutics*, ed. Don Ihde, Evanston, IL: Northwestern University Press.

Ricoeur, Paul (1977) *The Rule of Metaphor: Multi-Disciplinary Studies of the Creation of Meaning in Language*, trans. Robert Czerny with Kathleen McLaughlin and John Costello, Toronto and Buffalo: University of Toronto Press.

Ricoeur, Paul (1984) *Time and Narrative,* vol. 1, trans. Kathleen McLaughlin and David Pellauer, Chicago, IL and London: University of Chicago Press.

Rimmon-Kenan, Shlomith (1983) *Narrative Fiction: Contemporary Poetics*, London: Routledge.

Rivkin, J. and Ryan, M. (eds) (1998) *Literary Theory: An Anthology*, Oxford: Blackwell.

Roberts, Adam (2000) *Fredric Jameson*, London: Routledge.

Rorty, Richard (1980) *Philosophy and the Mirror of Nature*, Oxford: Blackwell.

Rorty, Richard (1982) *Consequences of Pragmatism: Essays: 1972–1980*, Minneapolis, MN: University of Minnesota Press.

Rorty, Richard (1989) *Contingency, Irony, Solidarity*, Cambridge: Cambridge University Press.

Rorty, Richard (1991) *Objectivity, Relativism, and Truth: Philosophical Papers*, vol. 1, Cambridge: Cambridge University Press.

Rorty, Richard (1998) *Truth and Progress*, Cambridge: Cambridge University Press.

Rothberg, Michael (2000) *Traumatic Realism: The Demands of Holocaust Representation*, Minneapolis, MN: University of Minnesota Press.

Royle, Nicholas (1995) *After Derrida*, Manchester: Manchester University Press.

Royle, Nicholas (2003a) *Jacques Derrida*, London: Routledge.

Royle, Nicholas (2003b) *The Uncanny*, Manchester: Manchester University Press.

Rubin, Gayle (1993) 'Thinking Sex: Notes for a Radical Theory of the Politics of Sexuality', in Henry Abelove, Michèle Aina Barale and David Halperin (eds) *The Lesbian and Gay Studies Reader*, London: Routledge.

Rushdie, Salman (1990) *Haroun and the Sea of Stories*, London: Granta Books.

Russell, Charles (1985) *Poets, Prophets and Revolutionaries: The Literary Avant-Garde from Rimbaud Through Postmodernism*, New York and Oxford: Oxford University Press.

Russo, John Paul (1989) *I. A. Richards: His Life and Work*, London: Routledge.

Sadoff, Diane F. and Kucich, John (2000) *Victorian Afterlife: Postmodern Culture Rewrites the Nineteenth Century*, Minneapolis, MN: University of Minnesota Press.

Said, Edward (1993) *Culture and Imperialism*, London: Chatto and Windus.

Said, Edward (2003) *Orientalism: Western Conceptions of the Orient*, London: Penguin.

Saussure, Ferdinand de (1974) *Course in General Linguistics*, trans. Wade Baskin, London: Fontana.

Schleifer, Ronald (1987) *A. J. Greimas and the Nature of Meaning: Linguistics, Semiotics and Discourse Theory*, Lincoln, NE: University of Nebraska Press.

Schmidt, James (ed.) (1996) *What is Enlightenment?: Eighteenth-Century Answers and Twentieth-Century Questions*, Berkeley, CA: University of California Press.

Sedgwick, Eve Kosofsky (1985) *Between Men: English Literature and Male Homosocial Desire*, New York: Columbia University Press.

Sedgwick, Eve Kosofsky (1990) *The Epistemology of the Closet*, New York: Penguin.

Sedgwick, Eve Kosofsky (1993) *Tendencies*, Durham, NC and London: Duke University Press.

Sedgwick, Eve Kosofsky (1997) *Novel Gazing: Queer Readings in Fiction*, Durham, NC: Duke University Press.

Shklovsky, Victor (1990) *Theory of Prose*, trans. Benjamin Sher, Normal, IL: Dalkey Archive Press.

Sibley, Brian (1981) *Lord of the Rings*, London: BBC Audio.

Simms, Karl (2003) *Paul Ricoeur*, London: Routledge.

Sinfield, Alan (1992) *Faultlines: Cultural Materialism and the Politics of Dissident Reading*, Oxford: Oxford University Press.

Slemon, Stephen (1989) 'Modernism's Last Post', *Ariel* 20.4: 3–17.

Smith, Anna Deavere (1991) *Fires in the Mirror: Crown Heights, Brooklyn and other Identities*, New York: Anchor Books.

Sontag, Susan (1983) *A Susan Sontag Reader*, Harmondsworth: Penguin.

Sontag, Susan (1991) *Illness as Metaphor and AIDS and its Metaphors*, London: Penguin.

Sontag, Susan (2002) *On Photography*, London: Penguin.

Spelman, Elizabeth (1988) *Inessential Woman*, Boston, MA: Beacon Press.

Spinks, Lee (2003) *Friedrich Nietzsche*, New York: Routledge.

Spivak, Gayatri Chakravorty (1988a) 'Can the Subaltern Speak?', in Cary Nelson and Lawrence Grossberg (eds), *Marxism and the Interpretation of Culture*, Basingstoke: Macmillan Education.

Spivak, Gayatri Chakravorty (1988b) *In Other Worlds: Essays in Cultural Politics*, London: Routledge.

Spivak, Gayatri Chakravorty (1996) *The Spivak Reader*, ed. Donna Landry and Gerald MacLean, London: Routledge.

Spivak, Gayatri Chakravorty (1999) *A Critique of Post-Colonial Reason: Towards a History of the Vanishing Present*, Cambridge, MA: Harvard University Press.

Spivak, Gayatri Chakravorty (2003) *Death of a Discipline*, New York: University of Columbia Press.

Sterne, Laurence (1949) *The Life and Opinions of Tristram Shandy, Gentleman*, London: Macdonald.

Stirk, Peter M. R. (1982) *Max Horkheimer: A New Interpretation*, New York: Harvester Wheatsheaf.

Sumner, William Graham (1906) *Folkways: A Study of the Sociological Importance of Usages, Manners, Customs, Mores, and Morals*, Boston, MA: Ginn.

Sundquist, Eric J. (1993) *To Wake the Nations: Race in the Making of American Literature*, Cambridge, MA: Harvard University Press.

Swales, John M. (1990) *Genre Analysis*, Cambridge: Cambridge University Press.

Thompson, Edward Palmer (1968) *The Making of the English Working Class*, Harmondsworth: Penguin.

Thompson, Edward Palmer (1978) *The Poverty of Theory and Other Essays*, London: Merlin Press.

Tillyard, E. M. W. (1943) *The Elizabethan World Picture*, London: Chatto and Windus.

Todorov, Tzvetan (1977) *The Poetics of Prose*, trans. Richard Howard, Oxford: Blackwell.

Todorov, Tzvetan (1990) *Genres in Discourse*, trans. Catherine Porter, New York: Cambridge University Press.

Tolkien, John Ronald Reuel (1995) *Lord of the Rings*, London: HarperCollins.

Tompkins, Jane P. (ed.) (1980) *Reader-Response Criticism: From Formalism to Post-Structuralism*, Baltimore, MD and London: Johns Hopkins University Press.

Toulmin, Stephen (1990) *Cosmopolis: The Hidden Agenda of Modernity*, New York: Free Press.

Trachtenberg, Stanley (1985a) 'Introduction', in Stanley Trachtenberg (ed.), *The Postmodern Moment: A Handbook of Contemporary Innovation in the Arts*, Westport, CT: Greenwood Press.

Trachtenberg, Stanley (ed.) (1985b) *The Postmodern Moment: A Handbook of Contemporary Innovation in the Arts*, Westport, CT: Greenwood Press.

Van Inwagen, Peter and Zimmerman, Dean W. (eds) (1998) *Metaphysics: The Big Questions*, Oxford: Blackwell.

Veeser, H. Aram (ed.) (1989) *The New Historicism*, London: Routledge.

Virilio, Paul (1995) *The Art of the Motor*, trans. Julie Rose, Minneapolis, MN: University of Minnesota Press.

Virilio, Paul (1997) *Open Sky*, trans. Julie Rose, London: Verso.

Virilio, Paul (2002) *Ground Zero*, trans. Chris Turner, London: Verso..

Viswanathan, Gauri (1989) *Masks of Conquest: Literary Study and British Rule in India*, New York: Columbia University Press.

Vizenor, Gerald (1989) *Narrative Chance: Postmodern Discourse on Native American Indian Literatures*, Albuquerque, NM: University of New Mexico Press.

Walvin, James (2000) *Making the Black Atlantic*, New York and London: Continuum.

Warner, Michael (ed.) (1993) *Fear of a Queer Planet: Queer Politics and Social Theory*, ed. Michael Warner, Minneapolis, MN: University of Minnesota Press.

Waugh, Patricia (1984) *Metafiction: The Theory and Practice of Self-Conscious Fiction*, London: Routledge.

West, Cornel (1990) 'The New Cultural Politics of Difference', in R. Ferguson, M. Gever, Trinh T. Minh-ha and Cornel West (eds), *Out There: Marginalization and Contemporary Cultures*, New York: New Museum of Contemporary Art; Cambridge, MA: MIT Press.

West, Cornel (1994) *Race Matters*, London: Vintage.

West, Cornel (1999) *The Cornel West Reader*, New York: Basic Civitas Books.

West, Cornel (2004) *Democracy Matters: Winning the Fight Against Imperialism*, London: Penguin.

White, Hayden (1973) *Metahistory: The Historical Imagination in Nineteenth-Century Europe*, Baltimore, MD: Johns Hopkins University Press.

White, Hayden (1978) *Tropics of Discourse: Essays in Cultural Criticism*, Baltimore, MD: Johns Hopkins University Press.

Wiggershaus, Rolf (1995) *The Frankfurt School: Its History, Theory and Political Significance*, trans. Michael Robertson, London: Polity Press.

Williams, Patricia and Chrisman, Linda (eds) (1994) *Colonial Discourse and Postcolonial Theory: A Reader*, New York: Columbia University Press.

Williams, Raymond (1958) *Culture and Society 1780–1950*, London: Chatto and Windus.

Williams, Raymond (1976) *Keywords: A Vocabulary of Culture and Society*, London: Fontana.

Williams, Raymond (1977) *Marxism and Literature*, Oxford: Oxford University Press.

Williams, Raymond (1980) *Problems in Materialism and Culture*, London: Verso.

Wimsatt, William Kurtz (1970) *The Verbal Icon: Studies in the Meaning of Poetry*, London: Methuen.

Wollheim, Richard (1971) *Freud*, London: Fontana.

Wood, David (1991) *The Deconstruction of Time*, Atlantic Highlands, NJ: Humanities University Press.

Wright, Elizabeth (1984) *Psychoanalytic Criticism*, London: Methuen.

Wright, Elizabeth (ed.) (1992) *Feminism and Psychoanalysis: A Critical Dictionary*, Oxford: Blackwell.

Zamir, Shamoon (1995) *Dark Voices: W.E.B. Du Bois and American Thought, 1888–1903*, Chicago, IL: University of Chicago Press.

Zinn, Maxine Baca (2000) *Gender through the Prism of Difference*, New York: Allyn and Bacon.

Žižek, Slavoj (1989) *The Sublime Object of Ideology*, London: Verso.

Žižek, Slavoj (1992) *Looking Awry: An Introduction to Jacques Lacan through Popular Culture*, Cambridge, MA: October.

Žižek, Slavoj (1993) *Tarrying with the Negative: Kant, Hegel and the Critique of Ideology*, Durham, NC: Duke University Press.

Žižek, Slavoj (1999) *The Žižek Reader*, ed. Elizabeth Wright and Edmund Wright, Oxford: Blackwell.

Žižek, Slavoj (2002) *Welcome to the Desert of the Real!: Five Essays on September 11th and Related Dates*, London: Verso.

Žižek, Slavoj and Daly, Glyn (2004) *Conversations with Žižek*, Cambridge: Polity Press.

INDEX

References in *italics* indicate a substantial discussion. Entries in **bold italics** refer to the 'Names and terms' section.

The Routledge Companion to
Feminism and Postfeminism

Edited by Sarah Gamble

Approachable for general readers as well as for students in women's studies and related courses at all levels, this invaluable guide follows the unique *Companion* format in combining over a dozen in-depth background chapters with more than 400 A–Z dictionary entries. The background chapters are written by major figures in the field of feminist studies, and include thorough coverage of the history of Feminism, as well as extensive discussions of topics such as:

- Postfeminism
- Men in Feminism
- Feminism and New Technologies
- Feminism and Philosophy.

Dictionary entries cover the major individuals (Aphra Behn, Simone de Beauvoir, Princess Diana, Robert Bly) and issues (Afro-American feminism, cosmetic surgery, the 'new man', reproductive technologies) essential to an understanding both of Feminism's roots and of the trends that are shaping its future.

ISBN: 0–415–24309–2 (hbk)
ISBN: 0–415–24310–6 (pbk)

Available at all good bookshops
For ordering and further information please visit
www.routledge.com

The Routledge Companion to Postmodernism (2nd edn)

Edited by Stuart Sim

What does 'postmodernism' mean? Why is it so important? Now in its second edition, *The Routledge Companion to Postmodernism* combines a series of in-depth background chapters with a body of A–Z entries to create an authoritative, yet readable guide to the complex world of postmodernism. Following full-length articles on postmodernism and philosophy, politics, feminism, religion, post-colonialism, lifestyles, television, and other postmodern essentials, readers will find a wide range of alphabetically-organized entries on the people, terms and theories connected with postmodernism, including:

- Peter Ackroyd
- Jean Baudrillard
- Chaos Theory
- Desire

- Michel Foucault
- Frankfurt School
- Poststructuralism
- Retro

Students interested in any aspect of postmodernist thought will find this an indispensable resource.

ISBN: 0–415–33358–X (hbk)
ISBN: 0–415–33359–8 (pbk)

Available at all good bookshops

For ordering and further information please visit

www.routledge.com